Conservative Revolutionaries

Conservative Revolutionaries

Transformation and Tradition in the Religious and Political Thought
of Charles Chauncy and Jonathan Mayhew

John S. Oakes

FOREWORD BY
David D. Hall

◆PICKWICK *Publications* · Eugene, Oregon

CONSERVATIVE REVOLUTIONARIES
Transformation and Tradition in the Religious and Political Thought of Charles Chauncy and Jonathan Mayhew

Copyright © 2016 John S. Oakes. All rights reserved. Except for brief quotations in critical publications or reviews, no part of this book may be reproduced in any manner without prior written permission from the publisher. Write: Permissions, Wipf and Stock Publishers, 199 W. 8th Ave., Suite 3, Eugene, OR 97401.

Pickwick Publications
An Imprint of Wipf and Stock Publishers
199 W. 8th Ave., Suite 3
Eugene, OR 97401

www.wipfandstock.com

PAPERBACK ISBN: 978-1-62564-854-9
HARDCOVER ISBN: 978-1-4982-8755-5
EBOOK ISBN: 978-1-5326-0217-7

Cataloguing-in-Publication data:

Names: Oakes, John S. | Hall, David D., foreword.

Title: Conservative revolutionaries : transformation and tradition in the religious and political thought of Charles Chauncy and Jonathan Mayhew / John S. Oakes.

Description: Eugene, OR : Pickwick Publications, 2016 | Includes bibliographical references and index(es).

Identifiers: ISBN 978-1-62564-854-9 (paperback) | ISBN 978-1-4982-8755-5 (hardcover) | ISBN 978-1-5326-0217-7 (ebook)

Subjects: LCSH: Chauncy, Charles, 1705–1787. | Mayhew, Jonathan, 1720–1766. | Christian sociology—Massachusetts—History of doctrines—18th century.

Classification: BT738 .O25 2016 (print) | BT738 .O25 (ebook)

Manufactured in the U.S.A.   10/17/16

For my family, who have given so much to make it possible for me to pursue my research, and especially, with love and gratitude,

for Kirsten, Nathalie, and Stephanie

"Now is the Time, when we are particularly called to stand up for the good old Way, and bear faithful Testimony against every Thing, that may tend to cast a Blemish on true primitive Christianity."

CHARLES CHAUNCY (1743)

"Having, earlier still learnt from the holy scriptures, that wise, brave and vertuous men were always friends to liberty . . . that the Son of God came down from heaven, to make us 'free indeed'; and that 'where the Spirit of the Lord is, there is liberty'; this made me conclude, that freedom was a great blessing."

JONATHAN MAYHEW (1766)

Contents

List of Illustrations | viii
Foreword by David D. Hall | ix
Acknowledgments | xiii
Introduction | 1

Part 1—Transformation and Tradition

1. Earlier Lives | 15
2. Reshaping the Calvinist Heritage: The Shift to Arminianism | 38
3. Challenging the Boundaries of Orthodoxy: Unitarianism and Universalism | 72
4. Maintaining Tradition: Consistent Puritan Themes | 110

Part 2—Conservative Revolutionaries

5. Engaging the Public Square: Ministers in Politics | 145
6. Fighting the Cause: Languages of Liberty | 185
7. Resolving the Big Issue: Submission or Revolution | 210
8. Mayhew, Chauncy, and Revolutionary Change | 238

Bibliography | 257
Index | 287

Illustrations

Charles Chauncy (1705–1787), by MacKay | 14
  Reproduced by permission of Harvard Art Museums/Fogg Museum, Harvard University Portrait Collection, H5 (Photo: Imaging Department © President and Fellows of Harvard College)

Jonathan Mayhew (1720–1766), by John Greenwood | 144
  Published courtesy of the Congregational Library, Boston, Massachusetts

Foreword

MODERATION HAS AN ENDURING presence in Christianity, and no more so than in early modern Europe and early America. Seventeenth-century England had its "moderate" Puritans and its moderate Calvinists as well. In early New England, the practice of creating "gathered" churches frightened many moderates in England, yet any crisis was eventually mitigated by the fact that the congregationalism of the colonists was an oxymoron, a parochial congregationalism—that is, a single church per town, with every adult required to attend Sunday services and encouraged to have their children catechized. A mere year or two after the pieces of this system were falling into place, its implications for infant baptism were already been queried by lay people who wanted that sacrament for their children. At a moment of stress and strain, the great majority of the ministers and most lay people fashioned a classic compromise, opening up the sacrament to many more children but preserving a stricter set of rules for access to Holy Communion. Weighing the alternatives of exclusion and inclusion, a minister who favored this compromise defended it as "a middle way" between extremes. At this moment as at so many others, a middle way has appealed to churches, ministers, lay people, and theologians as a more satisfactory way of navigating church and world than the alternatives of severity and exclusion.[1]

The Enlightenment in America was a prime example of moderation at work, as, in its own way, was the run-up to 1776 and beyond. Far from being an enemy of Scripture or of the church, the many colonial Americans who endorsed "reason" and the orderly workings of nature as these had been uncovered in the course of the "scientific revolution" (a much-questioned term), found ways of reconciling the natural and the supernatural, free will and human sinfulness, the authority of Scripture and the authority of critical inquiry. The "radicals" were few, their presence exaggerated by moderates

---

1. See Lake, *Moderate Puritans*; Browne and Hall, "Family Strategies and Religious Practice." See also Trueman, *John Owen*.

who benefitted from contrasting their own policies with the specter of a de-Christianized society. So we learn from Henry F. May's classic study of *The Enlightenment in America* (1976). Even someone as staunchly orthodox as Jonathan Edwards had his moderate side, as evidenced by his intense dislike of the Holy Spirit-centered "New Lights" of the mid-eighteenth century. Edwards was no social revolutionary but an elite minister who prided himself on his learnedness.[2]

It must be said, however, that Puritan-style moderation was vulnerable in its own day and remains vulnerable in ours. What seems sensible compromise or sympathetic respect for continuity can, to others, become signs of moral failure. The English Puritans who complained about the defects of the Church of England but stayed within it were outflanked by the more daring who acted on the imperative to "come out from them that are unclean." Separatists such as Robert Browne and Henry Barrow accused the moderates of duplicity. If the Church of England was really so in need of reform, how could it be "true" in the sense of obeying what Christ had mandated? To accusations of this kind, which erupted again at the time of the English Revolution (1640-1660) when radicals of several kinds pressed for a complete reworking of church, government, and society, moderates replied that schism was a far greater sin than putting up with imperfections. Or, as was said in response to the fracturing of the Christian community in the 1640s, "The dispute is not now of what is absolutely best if all were new, but of what is perfectly just as things now stand: It is not the Parliaments work to set up an Utopian Common-Wealth, or to force the people to practice abstractions." Similarly, as word reached ministers in eighteenth-century New England of the conflicts that were fracturing Dissent in England, many of them decided that peace was better than war, agreement on a few basics outweighing certain differences.[3]

Should it surprise us that historians of moderation in early America vary so widely in how they assess the substance of that tendency? Hindsight can be unkind to temporizers, as it has been to moderate anti-slavery. The special merit of *Conservative Revolutionaries* is that it restores depth and complexity to a group of moderate-minded clergy in eighteenth-century New England. John Oakes does so in part because he eludes the traps that others can easily fall into, either by seeking the origins of nineteenth-century Unitarianism and therefore emphasizing the more rationalist or anti-Calvinist aspects of what they find, or by seeking the origins of

---

2. As I have argued in Hall, "Editor's Introduction."

3. Quoted in Fixler, *Milton and the Kingdoms of God*, 92n2. Shagan provides a much more critical appraisal of "moderation" in *Rule of Moderation*.

independence, and therefore emphasizing concepts of liberty. Happily, taking these men on their own terms has already happened in some of the scholarship Oakes cites in his opening pages. Yet no one before him has weighed as carefully as he does the situating of texts that their authors may have designed as ambiguous or open-ended, or as a "middle way" between extremes. Take doctrine, for example. Were we to find ourselves in Boston or Cambridge, Massachusetts, at the close of the seventeenth century, we could have listened to Samuel Willard, a minister on the eve of becoming president of Harvard College, lecture each week on that monument to Reformed confesssionalism, the *Westminster Catechism* fashioned by the Westminster Assembly of Divines in the mid-1640s, a catechism widely used in New England in the eighteenth century. "Westminster" (catechism and Confession) remained the official standard of orthodoxy for much of the eighteenth century. But its status did not paralyze theological reflection or innovation, even though—and this is the paradox of moderation—no one mounted a soapbox and denounced the tradition of which he was part. Jonathan Mayhew, one of the key figures in this book, came close to that kind of posture, but as Oakes points out, he too had his ties to the past, as, most tellingly, did the immensely important Charles Chauncy.

Oakes's, then, is a project of recovery and clarification based on manuscript as well as printed sources. Because he refuses to simplify, readers may miss some big bang of a conclusion of the kind that, at this moment, litter the field of American religious history—today's exciting book (to some), but tomorrow relegated to the shelves of a library to make room for the next new thing. The watchword of the historian should be solidity and, of no less importance, listening to your predecessors and building on them in the service of the goal of a better understanding of the past. We are in John Oakes's debt in both respects.

David D. Hall

March 2016
Harvard Divinity School

Acknowledgments

THIS BOOK SPRANG FROM two chapters of my doctoral dissertation at Simon Fraser University (SFU), and, like that earlier work, it would not have been possible without the help of many individuals and institutions, which I gratefully acknowledge.

At Regent College, Vancouver, Don Lewis and John Toews nurtured an interest in religious history that I had previously failed to recognize. Alan Tully's excellent graduate seminar on Colonial and Revolutionary American History at the University of British Columbia (UBC), where I studied in the 1990s, helped me focus on the area that eventually gave rise to my continuing research program. My dissertation supervisors at SFU, especially John Craig, who offered sterling support and wise counsel throughout, patiently and astutely guided that project to completion. Nicholas Guyatt and Michael Prokopow made strategic contributions along the way.

Three and a half years after graduating with my PhD, an unexpected appointment to spend 2012 as a Visiting Fellow at Yale Divinity School opened up a marvelous opportunity, under the expert supervision of Kenneth Minkema and Harry Stout, to immerse myself more thoroughly in the sources and to reorient the writing plans arising from my dissertation.

This study of the religious and political thought of Charles Chauncy and Jonathan Mayhew represents the second of a resulting three-part series of works. The first was my recently published article on Massachusetts minister John Wise (1652–1725) for the September 2015 issue of *The New England Quarterly*. The third, already in progress, will be a biography of the dissertation's fourth subject, Andrew Eliot (1718–1778)—a fascinating, but largely unsung, contemporary of Chauncy and Mayhew in the Boston ministry.

David Hall, my faculty host at Harvard Divinity School (HDS), where I had the privilege of spending more than a year as a Postdoctoral Fellow in 2013–14, has been of great assistance in my recent academic work. His example of scrupulous scholarship, encyclopedic knowledge, and authorial excellence has been an inspiration to me, as to many other scholars. I am honored that he has agreed to write this book's foreword.

Others at HDS, including David Hempton and David Holland, have also contributed significantly to my thinking, and I have benefitted from participation in the North American Religions Colloquium at HDS and the Historians of American Religion Colloquium at Boston University. In addition to others already named, Chris Beneke of Bentley University took the time and trouble to read earlier chapter drafts. Last but not least, I have profited from the editorial expertise of my friend from Oxford days, Jane Havell, and the photographic skills of Phil Shepherd.

I am financially indebted to all the institutions which have generously helped fund my studies over the years, including the donors of a St. John's Scholarship, an R. Howard Webster Foundation Fellowship, and an Izaac Walton Killam Memorial Predoctoral Fellowship at UBC. I was the grateful recipient of a Social Sciences and Humanities Research Council of Canada Doctoral Fellowship. During my time at SFU, I was awarded two University Graduate Fellowships and a President's PhD Research Stipend. Most recently, I enjoyed the support of two Sabbatical Grants from the Anglican Church of Canada and funding from the W. G. Murrin Fund extended through the Diocese of New Westminster.

No scholar can work effectively without the extensive assistance and resources of libraries and librarians. Especially helpful in the research and writing of this book were those of UBC, SFU, Yale, Harvard, Boston, and Toronto Universities, the Massachusetts Historical Society, and Boston Public Library. I am grateful to the Howard Gotlieb Archival Research Center at Boston University for permission to quote from the Mark and Llora Bortman and Foxcroft and Mayhew Family Papers.

No fewer than eight churches in the Anglican Dioceses of New Westminster, Massachusetts, and Toronto have graciously supported my studies since the 1990s, including, in chronological order: St. Matthias, Oakridge; St. Anne, Steveston; St. John (Shaughnessy); St. Cuthbert, North Delta; St. Mark, Ocean Park; All Saints', Belmont; and my current parish, St. Mary, Richmond Hill. Most generous of all were the people of Holy Trinity, Vancouver, where I served from 2002 to 2012, who sacrificially made possible extended periods of study and sabbatical leave. But those to whom this work is dedicated offered the most crucial support for my academic endeavors and ambitions.

Any errors or omissions that remain are, of course, entirely my own. *Soli Deo gloria!*

John S. Oakes

March 2016
Richmond Hill, Ontario

Introduction

WHEN CHARLES CHAUNCY (1705-1787) wrote to his friend and fellow-minister Ezra Stiles on May 23, 1768, his main purpose was to enclose a brief and largely encomiastic memoir of his great-grandfather. This renowned English Puritan, also Charles Chauncy, had fled persecution to settle in New England in 1638, and had gone on to achieve prominence as the second President of Harvard College from 1654 until his death. Keenly aware of his status as the eldest son of the eldest son of the eldest son of his namesake, the minister of Boston's prestigious First Church informed Stiles that some forty years previously he had taken "considerable pains" to exercise a right of primogeniture and to locate the papers of his illustrious ancestor. Chauncy's efforts had been frustrated when he discovered from one of the president's grand-nephews that his great-grandfather's literary remains had met a tragic end. Because none of his sons had reached the age of maturity, the senior Chauncy's widow had reportedly remained in possession of his papers and she had subsequently married a pie-maker. "Behold now the fate of all the good President's writings of every kind!" his great-grandson told Stiles. "They were put to the bottom of the pies, and in this way brought to utter destruction."[1]

But the news of that loss did not lead Chauncy to formulate plans for the preservation of his own personal archives. On the contrary:

---

1. Chauncy, "Life of the Rev. President Chauncy," 179. Stiles, who was eventually to become President of Yale, was then pastor of the Second Congregationalist Church in Newport, Rhode Island. For a detailed biography, see Morgan, *Gentle Puritan*. Except for occasional stylistic modernizations, including the capitalization of book titles, which has been standardized, primary sources are cited almost entirely unedited. Because of the sheer quantity of Chauncy's and Mayhew's writings over a fifty-four-year period, their publication dates are often cited. Biographical references are given only for a limited number of prominent figures. Readers are otherwise referred to Weis, *Colonial Clergy*; SHG; ANB Online; ODNB Online.

> I was greatly moved to hear this account of them [his great-grandfather's papers]; and it has rivetted in my mind a determination to order all my papers, upon my decease, to be burnt, excepting such as I might mention by name for deliverance from the catastrophe; though I have not as yet excepted any, nor do I know I shall.

Judging from what remains of Chauncy's prodigious output, he was apparently true to this rather mysterious commitment. Except for a limited number of scattered papers, scholars have been left to grapple with more than fifty published works and what they have made of this collection has varied widely. Although his publications were much fewer and his unpublished papers more extensive, the same could be said of Chauncy's colleague at Boston's West Church, Jonathan Mayhew (1720-1766). J. Patrick Mullins (2005) has bemoaned Mayhew's "unwarranted obscurity" and academic "neglect . . . in general." Yet Chauncy and Mayhew have consistently, if sporadically, attracted scholarly attention and John Corrigan (1987) has helpfully outlined three major "schools of interpretation" of their life and work.[2]

The first interpretative paradigm has largely concentrated on one or both of the pastors' political writings, arguing that "certain sermons" were "major contributions toward the formation of the rhetoric of the American Revolution." The second, first advanced by Alan Heimert (1966), has mainly seen Chauncy and Mayhew as social reactionaries, who were ultimately "more interested in preserving the status quo than in fomenting rebellion." The third has primarily focused on their theological ideas, generally viewing the eighteenth-century ministers as "leaders in the move toward 'rational religion' in America." Corrigan's three "schools" can also usefully be supplemented, and to some extent qualified, by a fourth, which is really a combination of the first and third. Thus many scholars have stressed both Chauncy's and Mayhew's political activism and religious heterodoxy,

---

2. Chauncy, "Life of the Rev. President Chauncy," 179; Mullins, "Father of Liberty," 3, 4; Corrigan, *Hidden Balance*, x, 126; Akers, *Called unto Liberty*; Griffin, *Old Brick*; Lippy, *Seasonable Revolutionary*. Corrigan cited, in chronological order, among contributors to his first "school of interpretation": Thornton, *Pulpit of the American Revolution*; Moore, *Patriot Preachers*; Van Tyne, "Influence of the Clergy"; Baldwin, *New England Clergy*; Savelle, *Seeds of Liberty*; Bailyn, *Ideological Origins*; "Religion and Revolution." In addition to Heimert, *Religion and the American Mind*, Corrigan cited Miller, "Religion, Finance, and Democracy"; Wright, *Unitarianism in America* and Jones, *Shattered Synthesis* as representative of his second "school of interpretation" of Chauncy and Mayhew. Among representatives of the third, he listed: Bradford, *Memoir*; Allen and Eddy, *History of the Unitarians*; Cooke, *Unitarianism In America*; Haroutunian, *Piety Versus Moralism*; Morais, *Deism*; Akers, *Called unto Liberty*; Griffin, *Old Brick*. For a much more detailed account of the relevant historiography as of 2008, see Oakes, "Conservative Revolutionaries," 115-26, 221-34.

including a few who have highlighted the ministers' inherent social, even sociopolitical traditionalism.³

Most of the scholarship on Chauncy and Mayhew has been in the form of academic articles or summaries in larger works. Despite their obvious importance, they have been the subjects of just three modern biographies, all of which focused on familiar themes in developing traditional narrative accounts of their lives. Charles Akers's overall portrayal of Mayhew in *Called unto Liberty* (1964) was that of a thorough-going subversive. While continuing to emphasize his theological heterodoxy and political Whiggery, the two major biographers of Chauncy, Edward Griffin (1980) and Charles Lippy (1981), also sought to foreground more conventional motivations, if not content, in his works. Only Corrigan addressed the two Boston pastors concurrently in a significant monograph, which adopted a somewhat broader perspective.⁴

In doctrinal terms, Akers characterized Mayhew as one who "brazenly proclaimed his abandonment of Puritan theology in favor of a 'pure and undefiled' version of Christianity" and a rational "gospel of the Enlightenment."

---

3. In addition to Akers, *Called unto Liberty*, recent scholars to offer interpretations of Mayhew as both theological innovator and political militant have included, in chronological order: Stout, *New England Soul*, 240–44, 262–63, 268; Clark, *Language of Liberty*, 336, 366–68; Noll, *America's God*, 79–80, 138–40; Byrd, *Sacred Scripture*, 29–30, 123–26, 140–41. As well as by Griffin, *Old Brick* and Lippy, *Seasonable Revolutionary*, which Corrigan, *Hidden Balance*, x, 126–27, misleadingly categorized primarily in theological terms, Chauncy's political activism has been latterly highlighted by Noll, *America's God*, 130–33. Jones, *Shattered Synthesis*, while occasionally noting Mayhew's social traditionalism, e.g., 151, 162–63, as Corrigan, *Hidden Balance*, x, suggested, was primarily concerned with the development of Mayhew's theological heterodoxy, rather than with his sociopolitical ideas. Noll also addressed Chauncy's "theological liberalism," but acknowledged his "self-conscious reliance on British authorities and . . . marriage to the ideal of a stratified, elite-dominated, mercantile Boston" (*America's God*, 138 43, esp. 143). Other significant recent works to focus on Chauncy's and Mayhew's theology include: Gibbs and Gibbs, "Charles Chauncy" and "In Our Nature"; Holifield, *Theology in America*, 131–35. Among studies with a more political focus, especially on Mayhew, are: Beneke, "The Critical Turn"; Mullins, "A Kind of War"; Lubert, "Jonathan Mayhew."

4. Akers, *Called unto Liberty*; Griffin, *Old Brick*; Lippy, *Seasonable Revolutionary*; Corrigan, *Hidden Balance*. In 2017, the University Press of Kansas is scheduled to publish a new work by Mullins, *Father of Liberty: Jonathan Mayhew and the Principles of the American Revolution*. According to the author, this will argue that "through the popularization of Real Whig 'revolution principles' within New England's political culture from 1749 to 1766, Mayhew did more than any other individual to prepare New Englanders intellectually for resistance to British authority. Though little remembered today, he was the most politically influential clergyman of colonial British America and a seminal thinker in the intellectual origins of the American Revolution" (Mullins, "Research"). Because of lack of access to this new work, it has unfortunately not been possible to incorporate or address Mullins's findings here.

He highlighted the anti-Trinitarian views expressed by Mayhew from the mid-1750s. Akers also argued that historians of Unitarianism had been "right in hailing [the Arminian] Mayhew as a pioneer of their movement," although "wrong in confusing his theology with their own." Echoing the judgments of "the Revolutionary generation," Akers characterized Mayhew's political views as equally militant. Mayhew was not only "the boldest and most articulate of those colonial preachers who taught that resistance to tyrannical rulers was a Christian duty as well as a human right." He "remained the first commander of the 'black Regiment' of Congregational preachers who incessantly sounded 'the yell of rebellion in the ears of an ignorant and deluded people.'"[5]

By contrast, Griffin sought to portray Chauncy in more nuanced terms in *Old Brick*. This was "a Representative Man" in eighteenth-century America—a "supernatural rationalist" who occupied "the middle ground" between "[Jonathan] Edwards's evangelicalism and [Benjamin] Franklin's Deism." Because Chauncy "considered himself simply a good Congregationalist, true to his own heritage of dissent and free enquiry," Griffin also highlighted themes of continuity, despite the major changes in his theology that were evident from the 1750s. However innovative the results, Griffin argued, as Chauncy reworked his doctrinal understandings of "the nature of God, the creation and destiny of humans, original sin, salvation, ethics, eschatology, and ecclesiology," the Boston minister was attempting "to reconstruct New England theology by applying to his basic Puritan principles the lessons he had learned from the [Great] Awakening." Griffin found similarly traditional influences at work in some of Chauncy's political views and activities. But he ultimately characterized his subject as a willing and active revolutionary, who became "politically radicalized" in the 1770s and was recognized "by the people of Boston as a pugnacious champion of political liberty." Chauncy endorsed rebellion against British rule, Griffin contended, and he "had a part in most of the important crises that jolted New England from 1771 to 1775."[6]

---

5. Akers, *Called unto Liberty*, 2, 115–22, 227, 232, citing Oliver, *Origin and Progress*, 29. The much older biography of Mayhew by Bradford, *Memoir*, is a rambling chronicle which contains little by way of original analysis or insight, but some otherwise unpublished source materials. Cf. Griffin, "A Biography," on which his published biography was based.

6. Griffin, *Old Brick*, 8, 4, 110, 144, 151. Rossiter also emphasized both Mayhew's and Chauncy's "Christian rationalism" as "sons of latitudinarian Harvard" and key representatives of one side of a split in "the apparent monolith of Puritanism" that took place in the aftermath of the Great Awakening (*Seedtime of the Republic*, 136). But Rossiter's main focus was on the political arena, where he highlighted their role in promoting both Stamp Act and revolutionary resistance. Norman Gibbs was really the first to

According to Lippy in his intellectual biography, Chauncy was both a creative theological innovator and an inherent traditionalist, as well as the "seasonable revolutionary" that his title made clear. This was "first and foremost a traditional Puritan cleric" who was "propelled by a passion for order and a fear of disorder." But Chauncy acted in ways that were "seasonable" by adopting "a line of thinking or a course of action . . . particularly appropriate to a given situation." Even in the comprehensive reformulations of theological doctrine that he released toward the end of his life, Lippy thus discerned an essentially "conservative passion to preserve the essential structures and categories of Puritan religious thought". As he shifted the very "cornerstone . . . from a theocentric anthropology to an anthropocentric theology," Chauncy "had not intended to undercut the heart of orthodox theology, although that was the effect of his works. As far as he was concerned," Lippy contended, "he was . . . preserving what he saw as vital to the New England Way by providing a rational and logical defense of present practice and experience." Similar concerns were apparent politically during the 1760s, when Chauncy's "opposition to the Stamp Act represented an effort to maintain intact the structures of political authority which he believed had been operative prior to its passage." Even during the revolutionary period, Chauncy was not driven by any creative vision of a newly independent nation, but by concerns for "the transmission of those social and political patterns which he perceived as integral to a developing American identity and self-awareness." In that sense, "Chauncy's reluctant, but relentless, advocacy of the patriot cause" from 1774 onwards was based on his pursuit of "what he saw as a lost ideal—the ideal of human liberty."[7]

Corrigan's comparative study of the broad outlines of Mayhew's and Chauncy's Enlightenment worldview was much more general in focus. In

---

question seriously the traditional understanding of Chauncy as a theological innovator, arguing that Chauncy's "faith was evangelical first" and "the eternal gospel, as he understood it, transcended the rational ideology of his day" ("Problem of Revelation," 302). The "Great Awakening" is here understood as the religious revival movement that began among Congregationalists in the 1730s, was catalyzed by the ministry of the British evangelist, George Whitefield in the 1740s, and extended as far as Virginia in subsequent decades. It is assumed, *contra* Butler, "Enthusiasm Described," that this was an identifiable, historically significant religious revival movement. For reliable accounts of key aspects of the Awakening, some older works remain indispensable, including: Gewehr, *Great Awakening*; Goen, *Revivalism and Separatism*; Tracy, *Great Awakening*. On Whitefield, see esp. Stout, *Divine Dramatist*; Lambert, *Pedlar in Divinity*. Among newer studies, see esp. Kidd, *George Whitefield*; Kidd, *Great Awakening*; Noll, *Rise of Evangelicalism*. On the Stamp Act, see esp. chapter 6.

7. Lippy, *Seasonable Revolutionary*, 12, 15, 16, 109, 114, 122, 72, 100, 103–4. See, further, Lippy, "Seasonable Revolutionary"; "Restoring a Lost Ideal"; "Trans-Atlantic Dissent."

Hidden Balance (1987), he sought to show how his two subjects countered "tensions" in religion, government, and society by presenting "an understanding of the cosmos" that was "based on two key principles: wholeness and balance." This was rooted in the conceptions of the "Moderate Enlightenment," of which Chauncy and Mayhew were key figures. Their views could be seen as constituting "one of the very few examples among eighteenth-century American writers of the attempt to integrate ideas in all of these areas into a coherent [Geertzian] ideology, a symbolic map of reality." Even Chauncy's later theological heterodoxy could be understood in terms of his quest for "balance," Corrigan contended. Although "ideas contained in these [later] treatises were a departure from previous Puritan theology," they should be seen "not as amendments to or a revision of Chauncy's theology in the 1740s to 1760s but rather as an integral part of his thinking in those years, as a balance or complement to more conservative arguments in his published work." The First Church minister's theories of government and society were influenced by similar considerations. Thus "'mutual dependency' was the key to [his] vision of government," which "could require deference to superiors, but ... must balance this with respect for the good of society as a whole, and the recognition of individual liberties and property."[8]

Notwithstanding Corrigan's bold attempt at synthesis, differing interpretations of Mayhew and Chauncy in the works of Akers, Griffin, Lippy and other scholars thus continue to raise major questions. The first and most obvious concerns the extent to which either can be identified as truly heterodox in his theology. If both ministers embraced Arminianism, how far did they travel beyond that point? Were they really Arian and/or Unitarian, as some have claimed, or both, and if so, how? Did they personally pioneer the Unitarian universalism that eventually became such an important feature of nineteenth-century Congregationalism, or pave the way for it? Secondly, and quite closely related to the issue of their overall heterodoxy, what were their major influences? How much did their religious views reflect the Enlightenment rationalism and moralism to which they were exposed? Whatever their final positions, did their theology continue to be shaped by more traditionalist factors in their Puritan New England heritage? More specifically, to what extent did Chauncy's avowed universalism of the 1780s, for example, or Mayhew's critical questioning of the doctrine of the Trinity in the 1750s and 1760s represent radical disjunctions from their earlier views? Last but not least, what, if any, were the most significant connections between Mayhew's and Chauncy's theological positions and

8. Corrigan, *Hidden Balance*, 5, 7, 112, 23, 64–65. For helpful reviews, see Akers, Review of *Hidden Balance*; Wilson, Review of *Hidden Balance*. See, further, Corrigan's earlier dissertation, "Religion and the Social Theories."

their politics? Did their revolutionary sentiments and attitudes, such as they were, flow from theological or political willingness to break with the status quo, or from other influences, and how did they connect with their sociopolitical views in general? This is the first work to compare and contrast the thought of Chauncy and Mayhew in sufficient detail to allow a thorough re-examination of such issues.[9]

The value of a comparative study of Chauncy and Mayhew, which focuses on their religious and political thought, goes well beyond the fact that they have often been linked by other scholars, most notably by Corrigan. Although Chauncy was fifteen years older and lived twenty-one years longer than Mayhew, the two Boston ministers were friends and colleagues for more than two decades during a crucial period, from the mid-1740s through the mid-1760s, when New England's established structures faced major challenges in both church and state. Theologically, the fresh currents of more rationalist thought that were eventually to contribute to quite a widespread reorientation away from traditional Congregationalist Calvinism towards universalism and Unitarianism were already raising serious questions and beginning to make serious intellectual inroads among the ministerial elite. Politically, the social disruptions arising from mid-eighteenth-century economic and demographic change, as well as from the centrifugal force of religious revivalism, increasingly threatened existing hierarchies. From the 1760s onward, resulting tensions were considerably aggravated by the renewed efforts of British colonial authorities to assert stronger fiscal and governmental control over the American colonies and by

---

9. More recent scholarship on Chauncy and Mayhew will be reviewed in greater depth, where appropriate, in subsequent chapters. Both ministers have been linked with the major historical debate over the nature of New England Congregationalist political militance and causal connections between religious thought and activism and the origins of the American Revolution. Except briefly in the concluding chapter, that debate will not feature in this study. For a helpful overview of the massive historiography of religion and the American Revolution, see esp. Wood, "Religion and the American Revolution." See, further, and more recently, Oakes, "Conservative Revolutionaries," 2–30. Yenter and Vailati defined an "Arian" Christology, together with related "Socinian" and "Sabellian" positions, in the following terms: "Although they were commonly used as abusive terms for anyone holding non-traditional or anti-trinitarian views, they also have more precise meanings. An Arian holds that the Son (the second person of the Trinity) is divine but not eternal; he was created by God the Father out of nothing before the beginning of the world. A Socinian holds that the Son is merely human and was created at or after the conception of Jesus. A Sabellian holds that the Son is a mode of God" ("Samuel Clarke (Revised)"). "Rationalism" is defined in general terms throughout this study. As in *OED Online*, a "rationalist" is understood as "one who emphasizes the role of reason in knowledge," including theological knowledge. "Moralism" is defined, again following *OED Online*, as a "preoccupation with moral teaching or morality" that can result in "religion . . . reduced to moral practice."

growing colonial attempts, fueled by Whig ideologies of resistance, to resist metropolitan interference. As ministers of two of Boston's more prominent and wealthier churches, whose congregations included influential local leaders, Chauncy and Mayhew found themselves right at the heart of such tumultuous developments. They emerged as leading thinkers and actors in different movements for religious and political change, and although their responses sometimes varied, they engaged very similar issues. They both addressed the theological challenges of Arminianism, for example, which they embraced, and of Unitarian and universalist ideas, over which they differed. They also grappled, over different time-frames, with some of the most crucial political questions of their era—not least, the right of resistance against unjust rulers, the continuing validity of traditional social structures, and the role of New England in protecting a heritage, which they both valued, of Protestant, British constitutional liberties.

This book not only makes sense strategically, therefore. It facilitates direct engagement with important issues in the religious and political history of eighteenth-century colonial and revolutionary America. In addressing them through the thought and lived experience of two such influential Boston ministers, *Conservative Revolutionaries* also engages two other key problems connected with histories of intellectual change, which are germane, although by no means identical. The first arguably has as much to do with an oft-critiqued "Whig" interpretation of history which has fostered and facilitated it, as with its main gravamen, which concerns polarizing and potentially misleading historical labeling. The second relates to the challenge of attempting to account for how and why individuals shift positions on key issues without assuming a "narrative of progress" that impedes proper contextualization of various gradations in their thinking.[10]

In a recent study of reforming and "democratizing" elements in seventeenth-century New England Puritanism, Harvard historian David Hall (2011) helpfully highlighted the general dangers in such a context of

10. On the "'Whig' interpretation of history," see esp. the useful summary critique by Cronon, "Two Cheers." For the original source, see Butterfield, who described it as "the tendency in many historians to write on the side of Protestants and Whigs, to praise revolutions provided they have been successful, to emphasise certain principles of progress in the past and to produce a story which is the ratification if not the glorification of the present" (*Whig Interpretation*, v). As Cronon noted, "Butterfield's chief concern was with oversimplified narratives—he called them 'abridgements'—that achieve drama and apparent moral clarity by interpreting past events in light of present politics. Thanks in part to Butterfield, we now recognize such narratives as teleological, and we rightly suspect them of doing violence to the past by understanding and judging it with reference to anachronistic values in the present, however dear those values may be to our own hearts" ("Two Cheers").

"substituting modern usage" of political terminology for more historically authentic "nuances of meaning and practice." In so doing, Hall credited earlier British scholars for showing particular sensitivity to the issue. A striking example of immediate relevance to this study is Jonathan Clark (2000), who rejected usage of terms like "liberalism, radicalism and conservativism" in a pre-nineteenth century English political setting, because, he argued, they were not used to denote anything approaching their modern meanings until the 1820s or 1830s and were, therefore, anachronisms. In light of the persuasive analysis of Hall, Clark and others, an obvious problem with major scholarship on Chauncy and Mayhew is that usage of such terms has been quite widespread. Moreover, inasmuch as their theological journeys have often been portrayed as progressing out of retrograde and irrational positions into more enlightened and reasonable ones, the frequent use of labels like "conservative" and "liberal" has only served to entrench an unbalanced, teleological, "Whig" history of their religious thought which does little justice to the complexities of its immediate contexts. Similar issues emerge in the political arena, where the frequently applied category "radical," for example, which has often, like "liberal" in theological terms, been counterpoised against a "conservative" labeling of more traditionalist positions, has sometimes led to virtual caricatures of the two ministers as either extremist firebrands or social reactionaries, but little in between.[11]

Despite its deliberately provocative title, *Conservative Revolutionaries* will seek to avoid such simplistic labels and offer a more nuanced account of Chauncy's and Mayhew's intellectual histories, both religious and political. It will do so by highlighting areas of continuity, as well as discontinuity over time. In exploring Mayhew's and Chauncy's theological development in Part 1, it will show how they were pioneers of transformation, while remaining, to a hitherto neglected degree, pillars of tradition. Part 2 will then consider how their political and even revolutionary ideas reflected similar trends and tensions. An important theme throughout will be the much discussed, but not always well understood, topics of how religion interacted with "Enlightenment" and related philosophical influences, including political Whiggery, in eighteenth-century New England. Because it focuses so single-mindedly on the intellectual journeys of two individuals, *Conservative Revolutionaries* will address these subjects *en passant* in the course of the first seven chapters. This work makes no claim to offer definitive "case studies"; nor does it assume any inherent narrative of progress. But it does serve to highlight some of the resulting complexities when two intellectual leaders sought to

11. Hall, *A Reforming People*, 14–16, esp. 16, citing, among key British historians, Condren, *Language of Politics* and Hurstfield, *Freedom, Corruption and Government*; Clark, *English Society*, 6–9, esp. 6.

reconcile the demands of faith and reason, as they understood them, in turbulent times. Some of the wider implications of their conclusions will then be considered in the final chapter.[12]

Four major findings emerge from *Conservative Revolutionaries*. The first is that Chauncy and Mayhew were more traditionalist figures than scholars have often portrayed, even when they have sought to identify ongoing connections with Puritan tradition. There is clear evidence that both subscribed to New England orthodoxy in their earliest years and that Chauncy did so publicly until the mid-1760s. However much their ideas changed over time and however innovative they eventually became, the two ministers also continued to share a dissenting worldview that was marked not only by such traditionalist theological distinctives, but by striking commitments to the defence of Congregationalist polity in face of the perceived threats of Catholicism and expansionist Anglicanism, and to a vision of New England that retained what they saw as the best of their Protestant and British heritage. To some extent, Chauncy and Mayhew were clearly figures of Henry May's "moderate [American] Enlightenment"—increasingly influenced, in their religious and political positions, by recent theological and philosophical trends, including Anglican Latitudinarianism and Whig or "Real Whig" ideology. But they remained grounded in intellectual traditions that they shared with earlier figures. Their understandings of liberty, which were foundationally spiritual in origin, were significant to this weltanschauung. Even the ministers' more revolutionary ideas and inclinations, such as they were, were stimulated and informed by an overarching concern to preserve New England's "Protestant interest," with all that that had traditionally entailed. Although they have often been listed and sometimes hailed together as eighteenth-century New England pioneers of theological change, the second major conclusion is that there were important differences in their thought. Thus while both Chauncy and Mayhew moved from Calvinist to Arminian positions, Mayhew did so much earlier and more decisively. Although both traveled further into the realm of theological heterodoxy, Mayhew went beyond Arminianism to a "subordinationist" Christology that foreshadowed full-blown Unitarianism, while Chauncy's

---

12. *Contra* Clark, who has argued that the "Enlightenment"—a word which dates, in a "reified" descriptive sense, from the mid-nineteenth century—represents a "fiction of a unified project," which "can no longer be used as a reliable and agreed term of historical explanation," its usage is retained here. So is use of "radical" in an apolitical sense. The main reason, again quoting Clark, is that "Enlightenment" still represents a sufficiently helpful "shorthand signifier of an accepted body of authors and ideas" (*English Society*, 9). The term "enlightened" is also sometimes used to describe those influenced by Enlightenment ideas. Those authors and ideas will be identified in more specific contexts, as necessary.

radical universalism betrayed little sign of a parallel departure from orthodox Trinitarianism.[13]

Thirdly, *Conservative Revolutionaries* will conclude that such differences reflected not only the two ministers' individual intellectual journeys at Harvard and elsewhere, but also their contrasting personalities, life circumstances, and professional situations at different Congregationalist churches. Secure in his position as sole pastor of Boston's recently established West Church with its Arminian tradition, the younger, bolder and more combative Mayhew felt willing and able to declare the most heterodox of his views within just eight of the nineteen years of his relatively short-lived ministerial career. By contrast, the older and much more cautious Chauncy spent forty-two of his sixty-two years at First Church, not only in a prestigious position at a prominent congregation that was historically considered the *fons et origo* of New England orthodoxy, but with a senior colleague, whose favor he valued and whose Calvinism he long shared. Chauncy thus faced major personal and professional constraints in expressing the Arminian and universalist positions that he seems to have reached by 1760 and fully defined by 1768 at the latest. Although he declared his moderate Arminianism much earlier, it was not until the mid-1780s, by which time the elderly Chauncy was Boston's longest-serving minister in a revolutionary milieu teeming with new ideas, that he finally felt able to release his four most radical works. Even then, he did so carefully.

Finally, as well as summarizing key arguments, chapter 8 will further explore the possible significance of Chauncy and Mayhew as contributors to New England intellectual and political development during a crucial period of colonial and revolutionary history. Locating the findings of this study within the broader framework of recent historiography of the Enlightenment and its connections with the evangelical movement in particular, the chapter will show how such contextualization strengthens a more authentic understanding of the two Boston ministers as men of their times, whose religious and political thought was shaped by multiple intellectual influences, traditionalist as well as contemporary. Such an approach not only avoids the false dichotomy that has previously distorted some previous scholarship—between their alleged "radicalism" on the one hand and their

---

13. For the "moderate [American] Enlightenment," see May, *Enlightenment in America*, 1–101. The term "Protestant interest" is primarily drawn from Kidd, *Protestant Interest*. Mayhew, *Sermon Preached at Boston*, 29, also used the expression himself. "New England orthodoxy"—or elsewhere, "Calvinist," "Puritan," or "reformed" orthodoxy—is here defined in terms of the key doctrines that were central to the belief-system of Calvinist Congregationalists for more than one hundred years after their first settlement in New England.

"conservativism" on the other—it negates Whiggish historical interpretations of Mayhew and Chauncy as progressive, transitional figures on the inevitable march of progress from the dark ages of American Puritanism to intellectual enlightenment, religious liberalism and political revolution. At the same time, because their thought clearly does raise broader issues about changing ideas of personal and communal autonomy and potential under God in a significant period of change, both theologically and politically, chapter 8 will include some suggestive, but inevitably inconclusive exploration of questions surrounding their wider influence.

PART 1

Transformation and Tradition

— 1 —

Earlier Lives

ON JUNE 2, 1748, Jonathan Mayhew began a series of seven Thursday lectures at West Church. By the time they ended on August 25, they had established him as one of the leading critics of the Calvinist orthodoxy of his day. Just under a year after a controversial ordination on June 17, 1747, Mayhew had already been effectively ostracized by most fellow Boston clergy. According to a letter to his father of October 1, 1747, he could rarely get preaching assistance although "The People of my Parish seem to be well united—none having left us since my ordination. As to the Ministers of the Town, I have no correspondence save with one or two of them." The practical implications were considerable. Not only was Mayhew's workload increased because he could not participate in the usual round of pulpit exchanges, he was excluded from a Boston clergy association and from participation in the town's regular Thursday Lecture. In his 1766 "Memoir of Dr. Jonathan Mayhew," prominent parishioner and Massachusetts official Harrison Gray reported that the Boston clergy generally "treated him with great coolness and indifference for some Time," and that neither the First nor Brattle Street churches subsequently "invited him to preach," despite his strong connections with Chauncy at First. The ever-confident and energetic Mayhew assured his father that "thro' God's Goodness to me, I live very happily and contented" without such collegial support. He compensated for his lack of opportunities elsewhere by starting his own lecture series.[1]

Gray may have somewhat exaggerated the immediate popularity of Mayhew's presentations when he reported that they were "attended by Gentlemen of the first Character in Town and Country: And by the generality of the Clergy of the Town of Boston and of the Neighbouring Towns. His Audience was always crowded." The West Church member's subsequent

---

1. Mayhew to Experience Mayhew, October 1, 1747, *MP* 23; Gray, "Memoir of Dr. Jonathan Mayhew," 33, an edited reprint of *MP* 137, which includes a brief biography of Gray.

judgment that Mayhew's sermons "upon these occasions gave universal satisfaction" was certainly misleading. Mayhew's *Seven Sermons* were soon published in Boston (1749) and an edition was released in London in 1750. They went on to attract such acclaim overseas that they were instrumental, if not decisive, in the decision by the University of Aberdeen to award Mayhew an honorary Doctor of Divinity degree the same year. But the response in more orthodox Bostonian circles was much cooler. Akers noted that "with the exception of Chauncy and [Samuel] Cooper [of Brattle Street Church] and later Andrew Eliot [of New North], the Boston clergy treated him with a cold, stony silence." More populist reaction to Mayhew's ministry was much more forthright. An anonymous letter addressed to "The Rev. Mr. J——n M——w," which was published in the *Boston Evening-Post* of April 17, 1749 under the soubriquet "Philanthropos," entreated him rather disingenuously

> to pursue your Design with Modesty, sound Sense and good Reasoning; the two last I'm convinc'd by the Share I have heard of your Sermons you will not be much at a Loss for, and the first you might attain by a good deal of Self-denial, and a little Attention to the Conduct of your Superiours in like Cases.[2]

What was Mayhew's main offense in his West Church lectures and elsewhere? According to "Philanthropos" and others who were less polemical in their criticisms, he had "lately assum'd the Dictator's Chair, and taken upon you to impeach of Weakness and Impie-[ty] the . . . religious Principles of your Country, and seem to think they stand in great need of Correction and Reformation, and that you are bound by virtue of your Office, and by your superior Abilities qualified to undertake that Province." Mayhew had principally challenged Massachusetts orthodoxy in *Seven Sermons* by openly espousing Arminian teaching. This included an explicit denial of the classic reformed doctrine of the total depravity of humankind, as well as open advocacy of a more cooperative understanding of salvation, which required active human participation, rather than depending solely on sovereign and irresistible divine grace.[3]

2. Gray, "Memoir of Dr. Jonathan Mayhew," 34; Mayhew, *Seven Sermons*; Akers, *Called unto Liberty*, 75; Philanthropos, "To the Reverend Mr. J——n M——w," 1. As Akers has argued, the award of such an honorary degree from a Scottish university generally depended on the recommendations and financial contributions of interested friends—in Mayhew's case, "a circle of [British] Dissenters" who were impressed by *Seven Sermons*, some of whose correspondence on this topic is to be found in *MP* 25-30 (*Called unto Liberty*, 77). On Eliot, see esp. Oakes, "Conservative Revolutionaries," 163–206.

3. "Philanthropos," "To the Reverend Mr. J——n M——w," 1. Marsden, *Jonathan*

The West Church minister was just twenty-six years old when he delivered his controversial Thursday lectures and began to establish his longstanding historical reputation as one of New England's most prominent and outspoken Arminians. But historians have often neglected to point out that he did not always hold such views. Both he and Chauncy have been so strongly identified in progressive theological terms that they have tended to become divorced, even in the most recent scholarship, from the traditionalist doctrines of their earliest years, which continued to shape elements of their thinking long after they had formally renounced the rigors of conventional Calvinism. But there is strong evidence that both were not only nurtured in New England orthodoxy, as might have been expected. Chauncy publicly maintained its major tenets for nearly four decades after his entry into ordained ministry in 1727. It was only in the course of the Great Awakening that the Boston ministers distanced themselves from more "enthusiastic" tendencies to adopt a more rationalist outlook, and it was not until the late 1740s and the publication of Mayhew's controversial lectures that either could be clearly identified with Arminianism.

Mayhew's Early Calvinism

Mayhew's Calvinist heritage has been well documented, although the lack of historical detail about his education is one of the most striking features of his early biography. Born at Chilmark, Martha's Vineyard, on October 8, 1720, he was the seventh child of Experience Mayhew by his second wife, Remember Bourne. Experience was the great-grandson of the early settler Thomas Mayhew, who had ruled the Vineyard as "Lord of the Manor," as well as acting as missionary to the local indigenous population for some forty years. Soon after his father's death in 1689, Experience assumed control of the mission that was to be his life's work for the next sixty-five years. Although lacking any university education, he became a pioneer linguist and translator, as well as a published author and prominent missionary, who enjoyed the support of leading figures in the Boston Congregationalist establishment, through the Company for the Propagation of the Gospel in New England and other connections. In 1726 Experience sent Jonathan's older brother Nathan to school in Cambridge to prepare him for admission

---

Edwards, 138, defined Arminianism in the following general terms: "For Edwards and his ministerial friends, 'Arminianism' usually referred both to the specific anti-Calvinist teachings attributed to Arminius and to broader trends to affirm the ability of humans to contribute to their own salvation." For a more detailed discussion and definition of eighteenth-century New England Arminianism, see chapter 2.

to Harvard. But there is no evidence that Jonathan enjoyed such an educational opportunity there or anywhere else, prior to his arrival at the college at the relatively advanced age of nearly twenty in 1740. All that can be safely assumed is that he had the benefit of his father's instruction and personal library, such as they were. What is known of Experience's theological position is that it was generally orthodox, albeit somewhat idiosyncratically and critically so.[4]

Contra Clinton Rossiter's exaggerated claim that Mayhew Sr. imparted to his son "a profound mistrust of religious and political Calvinism," Experience's writings indicate that his theology was consistent with Puritan tradition until the 1740s, by which time Jonathan was already at Harvard. His late departures from New England orthodoxy were significant, although they centered on a couple of fine points of doctrine, which he addressed in *Grace Defended* (1744), one of the two longest, if not the bestselling, of his six published works. Experience had been asking questions for some time and he had been engaged in an ongoing dispute in 1743–4 with Jonathan Dickinson, the future President of Princeton, over the narrow definition of human liberty in Dickinson's Calvinist treatise, *True Scripture-Doctrine* (1741). But the main purpose of *Grace Defended* was not to overturn reformed theology. It was "to remove some Things out of the Way," which Experience thought might "be dismissed from their Hypothesis, being no Ways necessary in order to the Support of the principle Articles in that [Calvinist] scheme," which he generally upheld.[5]

The major points on which he insisted were "that the Offer of Salvation made to Sinners in the Gospel, does comprise in it an Offer, or conditional Promise, of the Grace given in Regeneration" and that this "conditional

---

4. On Mayhew's family background and early education and upbringing, see Akers, *Called unto Liberty*, 5–21. In addition to his published works, the major manuscript sources are *MP* and Mayhew, *Collection of Sermons*.

5. Rossiter, "Life and Mind," 533; Experience Mayhew, *Grace Defended*, iii; Dickinson, *True Scripture-Doctrine*. See *MP* 17–19 for 1743–44 correspondence relating to disagreements between Experience Mayhew and Dickinson. Experience's other published works included *Discourse Shewing*, which attracted attention because of his account of Indian missions on Martha's Vineyard; *All Mankind*; *Letter to a Gentleman*, a response to a question raised by *Grace Defended*, and *Right to the Lord's Supper*. His most famous work, also related to Indian missions, was *Indian Converts*, reissued in 2008 as *Experience Mayhew's Indian Converts*. While maintaining that Experience Mayhew "formally acknowledged the truth of the federalist view of man's native predicament," Smith also drew attention to Mayhew Sr.'s struggles with the traditional Calvinist doctrine of total depravity, and especially to his opposition to "the idea that the best actions of the unregenerate are sinful" (*Changing Conceptions*, 20–22, esp. 21). See, further, *Experience Mayhew's Indian Converts*, 1–76, esp. 1–16, where Liebman provides some helpful theological and biographical information.

Offer" was just as real as that of "Pardon of Sin, Justification, &c." Experience thus asserted that spiritual regeneration, although still a sovereign gift of grace, effectively followed the exercise of faith with repentance that led to Christian conversion, rather than coming prior to it in order to facilitate it. He was well aware that in expressing that view, as well as his parallel contention that people's inability to come to faith, which resulted from human "Corruption, Ignorance, Temptations," and bad habits, could be overcome by suitable Christian "Instructions, Exhortations, and convincing Arguments," he was differing from "most that are in the calvinian Scheme." But Experience did not see the difference as fundamental. He continued to assert his general allegiance to the *Westminster Shorter Catechism* of 1647 and his agreement with "the Writings of Calvinists," as opposed to "the Principles of those who embrace or incline to the Arminian Hypothesis." Mayhew Sr. also took pains to insist that "for many Years," he himself was "otherwise minded" on the main point of argument in *Grace Defended*, which he only published in his seventies.[6]

This supports the view that while Jonathan Mayhew may have been encouraged by his father's questioning of received orthodoxy, he was not schooled in overtly anti-Calvinist doctrine or sentiment at his home on Martha's Vineyard before he left for Harvard in 1740. The first clear indications of more decisive liberalizing influences emerge from what is known of his time at the college, but they are matched by parallel indications of a profound spiritual awakening during the Great Awakening. Samuel Eliot Morison somewhat minimized the extent of what he termed "Harvard liberalism of the eighteenth century," arguing that "there was just enough notion of academic freedom to give Harvard a name among strict Calvinists." But his concise history of developments during the presidencies of John Leverett (1708–1724) and Edward Holyoke (1737–1769) provides significant evidence of intellectual transformation.[7]

Norman Fiering's analysis of the tutorial influence of Leverett and William Brattle in the late seventeenth century, when they helped shift the emphasis "in nearly every discipline" of Harvard's curriculum away from its "Aristotelian-Scholastic inheritance," adds to Morison's account. Although Leverett may have made "no important changes" to the substance of what was taught as president, Fiering also stressed the less tangible, but no less significant impact on students of the more "catholic" attitudes that he shared with a "moderate group" on the Harvard Corporation and with

---

6. Experience Mayhew, *Grace Defended*, ii–iv, 140, "Advertisement," 140. See, further, 154.

7. Morison, *Three Centuries of Harvard*, 53–100 passim, esp. 83.

other influential figures, including long-serving tutor, Henry Flynt. The Latitudinarianism or "philosophical Anglicanism" of John Tillotson and like-minded Church of England clerics to which such leaders looked for "inspiration" may not have undermined their basic commitment to Calvinist doctrine, Fiering contended, but it left them more open-minded. It also facilitated "new forms of integration of reason and religion." The works of Latitudinarians thus joined those of Isaac Newton and John Locke in moving Harvard in more critically minded, rationally and empirically questioning directions. After Holyoke became president in 1737, the college administration became more systematically proactive, introducing so much modernization, especially in the teaching of the natural sciences and related subjects, according to Morison, that "the undergraduate course at the end of Holyoke's regime had little in common with that of Leverett's day."[8]

The Mayhew family's financial resources were stretched and Experience had to secure government support before Jonathan could begin college in August 1740, shortly after being received into Communion at Chilmark Church. Placed eighth in his class in 1741, he was hardly a model student. Mayhew was fined for a number of disciplinary breaches and "degraded" for drinking just over a year into his Harvard studies. His financial needs remained pressing and his ultimate career plans undecided. In terms of Mayhew's intellectual development, what emerges from the earliest of his unpublished papers is that although he was still immersed in traditional Puritan sources that remained part of the Harvard curriculum of the early 1740s, it was the work of more critical thinkers, including Anglican Latitudinarians, that most interested him. An "Alphabetical List of Books" and a "Book of Extracts," both dating from 1741, show that alongside the writings of theological traditionalists like Cotton Mather, Mayhew possessed volumes by Enlightenment rationalists and natural scientists like the Church of England cleric William Wollaston. Among passages that the young Mayhew chose to write out in his commonplace book, extracts from a translation of Blaise Pascal's *Pensées* and from English clergyman Thomas Burnet's *Sacred Theory of the Earth* feature prominently. There is a suggestive citation from the works of Tillotson, together with other indications of what Akers described as Mayhew's "interest . . . in the popular 'physico-theology' of the day."[9]

---

8. Ibid., 57, 89; Fiering, "First American Enlightenment," 322, 329, 334. Morison described Leverett as "liberal in his attitude toward religion" (*Three Centuries of Harvard*, 54). See, further, Morison, *Harvard College in the Seventeenth Century*, 2:504–65, passim; Fiering, *Moral Philosophy*, 242–54. Cf. Fiering, *Jonathan Edwards's Moral Thought*, 227–33 (on Edwards and Tillotson); Wilson, *Benevolent Deity*, 19. Leverett and Brattle became tutors at Harvard in 1685 and 1696 respectively.

9. On Mayhew's Harvard career and the financial arrangements that were made

Around the same time that Mayhew recorded such influences, however, other sources supply further evidence that the religious revival associated with the Great Awakening was making a similarly profound impression on him as on other Harvard contemporaries. It was soon after Mayhew's arrival that itinerant English evangelist George Whitefield first enraptured the college, preaching to an estimated seven thousand people in Harvard Yard. His brief visit was followed to similar effect by that of the fiery Pennsylvania Presbyterian, Gilbert Tennent. The impact was apparently such that contemporary observers enthusiastically reported a spiritually transformed student body. "The College is a new Creature," wrote Benjamin Colman of Brattle Street Church rather breathlessly to Whitefield in the spring of 1741,

> the Students full of God, and hope to come out Blessings in their Generations, and how to be so now to each other. Many of them are now we think truly born again, and several of them happy Instruments of Conversion to their Fellows. The Voice of Prayer and Praise fills their Chamber; and the Sincerity, Fervency, and Joy, the Seriousness of their Heart sits visibly on their Faces. I was told Yesterday that not Seven of a Hundred remain unaffected.

On June 8, 1741, Colman, who later became more critical of the Awakening, wrote with the news that "the overseers of our Colleges have appointed a Day of Prayer and Humiliation with thanksgiving, for the Effusion of the Spirit of God on the Students who are seriously disposed to attend; and are bright Examples to their Instructors." In his diary a few months earlier, Flynt commented on the general spiritual revival in his students and named Mayhew among a group of thirty who "prayed together, sung Psalms, and read good books." Two of Mayhew's letters to his brother Zechariah from the same period indicate the deep impression that the Great Awakening initially made on him.[10]

---

to provide for it, see Akers, *Called unto Liberty*, 18–29, esp. 29. On his receipt into Chilmark Church, see Homes, "Diary," 165. Mayhew's "Alphabetical List of Books" and "Book of Extracts" are found in *MP* 9 and 10 respectively, citing, among other works, Pascal, *Thoughts on Religion*; Burnet, *Sacred Theory of the Earth*, originally published in 1690 as *Theory of the Earth*, an English version of Burnet, *Telluris Theoria Sacra*; Wollaston, *Religion of Nature*. Fiering listed Wollaston with Tillotson as among those "philosophical Anglican" or Latitudinarian authors necessary for the historian to read "to gain an essential understanding of the major currents of religious and philosophical thought in New England from 1685 to 1735" ("First American Enlightenment," 331). With Benjamin Whichcote, others included two authors whom Mayhew later cited in his published works, Gilbert Burnet and Benjamin Hoadly.

10. Colman, "Extract of a Letter," undated, but clearly from 1741, 197–8, esp. 198; Colman to Whitefield [?], June 8, 1741, 202–3; Akers, *Called unto Liberty*, 30–32, esp. 32, citing Flynt, Diary.

On December 26, 1741, Mayhew described the revival as a powerful spiritual visitation. He also told how his recent delivery from illness had apparently resolved any questions about his future vocational direction. He would now pursue ordained ministry. "But what shall I render to the Lord for all his Benefits?" Mayhew asked. "He would write a Law of Gratitude on my Heart and encline me to devote my Spared Life, yea all the Powers and Faculties of my Soul, to his Service." Exactly three months later, Mayhew sent his brother a four-page account of a seventy-mile trip "to the Eastward," where he was "induced to go by an earnest Desire . . . to see and get a right Understanding of Affairs there with Respect to Religion." His conclusions were overwhelmingly positive. "The Spirit seems to set the Word home in a very extraordinary Manner," he noted, with remarkable effects, both physical and spiritual, on those who had previously paid little attention to religion. He described a deep conviction of sin and its consequences among those affected, especially "young Persons," followed by joyful release, conversion and commitment. "Nor is it strange that they should rejoice with Joy unspeakable and full of Glory," Mayhew commented,

> when they are enabled to see the Sufficiency there is in Christ, and his Willingness to receive them, when they are enabled to set open the everlasting Doors of their Hearts for this King of Glory to enter, and when the Spirit witnesseth with their Spirits that they are the Children of God, when they see themselves rescued from Destruction . . . ; when they have a glimmering Prospect of those Mansions above, and some Prelibations and Foretastes of the Joys of the New Jerusalem.

Mayhew expected his letter to come "like good News from a far country and cold Water to a thirsty Soul" to his younger brother, as he read "of the Conquests and Triumphs of the Redeemer's Grace." He also took the opportunity to make a series of personal exhortations, urging Zechariah to be comforted and encouraged and to look forward to the afterlife. "Surely there are Joys in Religion which neither the Sensual & carnal World, nor the self righteous Pharisee know any Thing of," Mayhew wrote. So he exhorted Zechariah to "beware of Hypocrisy" and to join him in being "over jealous over ourselves & each other with a godly Jealousy."[11]

Although he was far from unusual in doing so, one of the most interesting questions about Mayhew's early years is how he moved from such positive views of the Great Awakening to aggressive criticism not only of its first leader, but eventually of what he came to decry as religious

---

11. Mayhew to Zechariah Mayhew, December 26, 1741 and March 26, 1742, *MP* 14 and 15.

"enthusiasm" generally. Sadly, there is no relevant personal testimony from the crucial five-year period before Mayhew wrote to his father in a very different tone on October 1, 1747. "As to Mr. Whitefield, when he was in Town," he observed very dismissively after a visit to Copp's Hill in Boston to hear Whitefield deliver a farewell sermon,

> there were many Persons that attended his preaching; but chiefly of the meanest sort, excepting those that heard him from a Principle of Curiosity—I heard the last Sermon he preached, which was a very low, confused, puerile, conceited, ill-natur'd, enthusiastick, &c. Performance as ever I heard in my Life.

In seeking to explain such a dramatic change of mind, Akers cited the instrumentality of Mayhew's father and the authorities of Harvard, where he remained in residence for another three years following his graduation in 1744. Initially hopeful that Martha's Vineyard might also benefit from religious revivalism, Experience was so provoked by reading Whitefield's early autobiography of 1740 that he composed his own critical, albeit unpublished, "Letter to a Minister of the Gospel." Meanwhile at Harvard, those who had so warmly welcomed the evangelist in 1740 had grown so cold in their opinions of him just four years later that the whole faculty endorsed a devastatingly critical document published as *The Testimony of the President, Professors, Tutors and Hebrew Instructor of* HARVARD COLLEGE *in Cambridge, against the Reverend Mr. George Whitefield, and his Conduct*. To what extent Mayhew was actually moved by such influences remains unclear. Experience's objections obviously did not hinder his son's early enthusiasm for Whitefield. But it would seem reasonable to assume that Mayhew's change of position on the Great Awakening was affected by the shift in opinion at Harvard and his aversion to the perceived excesses of revivalism only seems to have grown.[12]

For example, in the first of two unpublished sermons on Matthew 3:8–9 on the theme of repentance written in December 1762, Mayhew had strong words for preachers in his "Remembrance" who had denied the converted status of life-long church members lacking testimony of a textbook evangelical conversion process. "The preachers of such doctrine as this," he contended, who included both Whitefield and Tennent, "were the men that kept the whole country in an alarm for many months, if not years together,

---

12. Mayhew to Experience Mayhew, October 1, 1747, *MP* 23; Akers, *Called unto Liberty*, 35–39; Experience Mayhew, "A Letter to a Minister of the Gospel Containing Some Queries on Several Ministers in the Rev'd Mr. George Whitefield's Account of his Own Life, Published in the Year 1740," *MP* 8, critiquing Whitefield, *Brief and General Account*; Holyoke et al., *Testimony*.

coming in a sad succession one after another, like Messengers with evil tidings; which people yet, delighted to hear, even to distraction." But what he found even more disconcerting was that

> many persons of age & experience, and before accounted both good & wise, were the encouragers and upholders of such preachers; and not only taught the common people, by their own example, to run after and almost to adore them; but had strange ambition to ape them in all their follies, their crude & extravagant conceits—wonderful instruction indeed!

Unlike his teachers in the Harvard *Testimony*, whom Akers perhaps too readily identified among "'regular lights' who understood both the power and danger of revivalism," Mayhew was not prepared to "presume to say, that some" of those preachers "did not mean well...; or that they might not, in particular cases, do some real good." His main burden was to stress "the more direct tendency, and the far more common [negative] effects, of such irrational, and anti-scriptural preaching."[13]

Mayhew delivered this verdict at least fifteen years after he had originally changed his mind about the religious revival. In the summer of 1748, when the recently ordained West Church minister gave the *Seven Sermons*, there is clear evidence that his thinking, which now embraced elements of Arminian doctrine, had also changed significantly in other ways. But although his theological journey may have been relatively short in duration, there is no reason to believe that it was any less significant than the progression from Calvinism to Arminianism that was to take many years longer for his friend and colleague, Charles Chauncy.[14]

Chauncy's Defense of Tradition

Chauncy was born fifteen years before Mayhew, on January 1, 1705, and in rather more comfortable circumstances. His father Charles was a Boston merchant and his mother Sarah the daughter of Judge John Walley of the Massachusetts Supreme Court. Despite his father's death when he was just six years old, a significant inheritance in 1712 seems to have enabled the family to continue their previous lifestyle. Chauncy apparently entered the Boston Public Latin School that same year in preparation for Harvard, where he matriculated in 1717. He graduated from college four years later

---

13. Mayhew, "Sermon 1 on Matthew 3:8–9, December 1762," in *Collection of Sermons*, 25–7; Akers, *Called unto Liberty*, 38.

14. Mayhew, *Seven Sermons*.

and spent a further three years in residence, in the course of which he took his AM in 1724. Although Clifford Shipton and Griffin have unearthed various biographical details, little is known of Chauncy's time at Harvard. But a clear personal influence to emerge from his student years was Edward Wigglesworth, who was installed as Hollis Professor of Divinity in 1722. Chauncy would later cite one of Wigglesworth's works, a 1724 defense of Congregationalist polity against the claims of the Anglican John Checkley, in two of his own writings. Wigglesworth also featured prominently among eminent New Englanders whom Chauncy commended to Stiles in 1768, and in very glowing terms.[15]

How much Wigglesworth's independent, but irenic, spirit of mind had already shaped Chauncy's thought by the time he entered ordained ministry in 1727 remains unclear. But despite competition for the prestigious position, his progress from Harvard to assistant minister of Boston's traditonalist First Church under Thomas Foxcroft was relatively smooth. According to the church's records for June 12, 1727, Chauncy was selected to assist Foxcroft by a congregational vote of sixty-four to forty-three over his nearest rival, his acceptance was announced publicly a couple of months later, and he was officially ordained on October 25 of that year. As he steadily established himself at First Church, Chauncy engaged in a four-year period of private study in the 1730s that would eventually lead to his extensive publications on episcopacy. But he remained relatively free from the public controversy that was to be such a feature of his later ministerial career. In 1728 he married the well-connected Elizabeth Hirst, granddaughter of Judge Samuel Sewall, and they began to build a family before her premature

---

15. Griffin, *Old Brick*, 13–23; Wigglesworth, *Sober Remarks*, was a response to Checkley, *Modest Proof*. Chauncy cited it in *Validity of Presbyterian Ordination*, 45–46, 86–87; *Appeal to the Public Answered*, 8, 42–43. Chauncy assessed Wigglesworth as follows: "he was one of my best friends and longest acquaintance[s], and had courage to speak honourably of me in the new-light time, when it was dangerous to do so ... He lived at college some years before there was an opportunity for his being chosen into the Professorship; all which time I had the pleasure of being many times a week in company with him, and since that time I familiarly corresponded with him by speech or writing till he died. He is highly deserving of being remembered with honour, not only on account of his character as a man of learning, piety, usefulness in his day, strength of mind, largeness of understanding, and an extraordinary talent at reasoning with clearness and the most nervous cogency, but on account also of his catholick spirit and conduct, notwithstanding great temptations to the contrary. He was one of the most candid men you ever saw; far removed from bigotry, no ways rigid in his attachment to any scheme, yet steady to his own principles, but at the same time charitable to others, though they widely differed from him. He was, in one word, a truly great and excellent man" ("Sketch of Eminent Men," 160). Older biographical accounts of Chauncy include Ellis, *History of the First Church*, 187–208, passim; Johnson and Malone, *Dictionary*, 2:42–3; *SHG*, 6:439–67; Sprague, *Annals*, 8:8–13.

death in 1737. As early as 1731, Chauncy's sermons were attracting enough attention to warrant publication. Six of them were published in the 1730s, including four fairly traditional funeral homilies, an Artillery Election sermon and a general Sunday sermon advocating the need to partake in Communion. Following a near-fatal stroke in 1737, Foxcroft's incapacitation temporarily left Chauncy as sole minister of First Church. Despite the inevitable burden of such responsibilities, he also found time to court his second wife, Elizabeth Phillips Townsend, whom he married in 1739.[16]

Although he subsequently moved in different directions, there is every reason to believe that when Chauncy was first ordained and Cotton Mather, perhaps the most vigorous contemporary defender of Puritan tradition, gave him the customary "right hand of fellowship," the twenty-two-year-old assistant minister was as orthodox in his Calvinist theology as his senior colleague Foxcroft was to remain throughout his career. There is also evidence from his works that Chauncy maintained that position publicly at least until the publication of *Twelve Sermons* in 1765, although the seven years of intensive private studies that led to his eventual departure from it began as early as 1752. The most compelling way to demonstrate the extent of Chauncy's early orthodoxy is to show how he publicly upheld, for nearly the first forty years of his ordained ministry, the doctrines traditionally associated with "five-point Calvinism." In other words, he more or less explicitly affirmed the key Calvinist tenets defined by the 1618–19 Synod of Dort and championed by the vast majority of New England Congregationalists in the seventeenth and early eighteenth centuries as definitive of reformed orthodoxy: total depravity, unconditional election, limited atonement, irresistible grace and the perseverance of the saints.[17]

---

16. Pierce, "Records," 39:149–50; Griffin, *Old Brick*, 26–35; Chauncy, *Man's Life, Early Piety Recommended*; *Nathanael's Character*; *Character and Overthrow*; *Prayer for Help*; *Only Compulsion Proper*. Chauncy was married three times altogether. Following his second wife's death in 1757, he wed Mary Stoddard in 1760. See Griffin, *Old Brick*, 107–8.

17. Pierce, "Records," 39:152. On Cotton Mather's participation in Chauncy's ordination service, see Griffin, *Old Brick*, 9–10. In the 1740s, Foxcroft publicly defended (also against Chauncy) the Calvinist Great Awakening evangelist George Whitefield, for example, and in two published sermons from the 1750s he upheld the doctrine of "imputed righteousness." See Foxcroft, *Some Seasonable Thoughts*; *An Apology*; *Humilis Confessio*; *Like Precious Faith*. Possible tensions between Chauncy and Foxcroft, especially after the advent of the Great Awakening, on which they took opposing views, have not been explored by historians. On Chauncy's early Calvinism, see, further, Wright, *Unitarianism in America*, 56–57. McNeill provided a helpful definition of "five-point Calvinism," as upheld by the Synod of Dort: "The canons of the synod assert: (1) that election is founded on God's purpose 'before the foundation of the world' [unconditional election]; (2) that the efficacy of Christ's atonement extends to the elect

In his first three published funeral sermons, for example, Chauncy clearly identified human "Tempers" as "perverse & depraved . . . since our Fall from GOD" and human nature as "corrupt." The biblical character of Nathanael, whom he took as an example in a funeral sermon for Judge Nathanael Byfield in 1733, was undoubtedly "a real good man; a true Saint and faithful servant of the most high," but he could not be "perfectly and indefectively" so. In such a sense, "'there is not a just man upon earth, that doth good and sinneth not.'" Some ten years later, in his pivotal Great Awakening sermon, *Enthusiasm Described* (1742), Chauncy did not hesitate to warn his hearers that they were inherently vulnerable to sin, including the enthusiastic excesses of revivalism. As a result of original sin, they were "in a corrupt state" following "the fall," which had "introduc'd great weakness into your reasonable nature." His *Seasonable Thoughts* (1743) likewise offered an extensive analysis of human excess at a time of religious revival, as did many of his later sermons. In *Earthquakes a Token* (1755), delivered the Sunday after Boston's "terrible earthquake" of November 18, 1755, Chauncy was in no doubt about the major precipitating cause. Sin had not only infected humanity in the form of total depravity, as Chauncy consistently warned his hearers in the first thirty years of his public ministry. It had also, he argued throughout his career, affected the earth itself—irretrievably so until its final restoration in the purging flames of the "Day of God's wrath," according to the millennial vision presented in a 1756 Thursday Lecture sermon "Occasioned by the late EARTHQUAKES in Spain and Portugal, as well as New-England."[18]

---

only [limited atonement]; (3) that the Fall has left man in a state of corruption and helplessness: his gleams of natural light are of no value for salvation [total depravity]; (4) that regeneration is an inward renewal of the soul and of the will and is wholly a work of God, 'powerful, delightful, astonishing, mysterious, and ineffable' [irresistible grace], (5) that God so preserves the elect, ever renewing their repentance, patience, humility, gratitude, and good works, that, despite their sins, they do not finally fall away from grace [perseverance of the saints]" (*History and Character*, 265). On eighteenth-century New England understandings of Calvinist doctrine, see chapter 3.

18. Chauncy, *Man's Life Considered*, 14; *Early Piety Recommended*, 4; *Nathanael's Character*, 5, 6, citing Ecclesiastes 7:20; *Enthusiasm Described*, 18; *Seasonable Thoughts*; *Earthquakes a Token*, 15–23; *Earth Delivered*, 13. Among transgressions that had offended God prior to the 1755 earthquake, Chauncy saw some particularly obvious causes for divine indignation: "The sins included in the term, uncleanness, have so offended God, as that he has testified his anger against them by an earthquake . . . We might do well to esteem ourselves warned of God against uncleanness . . . Sabbath-breaking is likewise a sin, God has threatened to testify against by shaking the earth . . . Pride is another sin God has testified his anger against by earthquakes." Also threatening were "unrighteousness," "drunkenness," which was "an awakening consideration . . . to the people of New-England," and, worst of all, "Enmity to Christ" (*Earthquakes a Token*, 16–17, 19–22).

Chauncy left no doubt in his earlier sermons of his convictions that those who died faced a truly eternal reward or punishment in heaven or hell according to their possession or lack of saving faith in Christ. He warned hypocrites in *Nathanael's Character* (1733), for example, that they were "persons whose portion it will be to dwell with devouring fire, to dwell with everlasting burnings:—'Tis against this kind of sinners that our SAVIOUR has said, Wo unto you;—for ye shall receive the greater damnation." In *New Creature Describ'd* (1741), his first major Great Awakening account of Christian conversion, he told those attending the Thursday Lecture of June 4, 1741, in remarkably Edwardsean terms: "There is nothing betwixt you and the place of blackness of darkness, but a poor frail, uncertain life. You hang, as it were, over the bottomless pit, by the slender thread of life; and the moment that snaps asunder, you sink down into perdition." In another Awakening sermon, *Unbridled Tongue* (1741), Chauncy's imagery was equally graphic. In 1755, he warned those reeling from a Boston earthquake that "while we refuse to have this man [Christ] to reign over us, and express our disregard to him by our unbelief and disobedience, we are in danger not only of judgments in this world, but of the damnation of hell." Faced with such a predicament, there was ultimately only one place to turn, Chauncy told those at a lecture on January 22, 1756, and that was to Christ. There were obvious means to pursue, such as repentance. But "the plain truth is, there is no safety, no security for us ... but by making him [God] our friend thro' Jesus Christ." Moreover, even at such a relatively advanced juncture in his theological development, just two years before he tentatively began to express open reservations about Calvinism, Chauncy was careful to qualify such a statement with a clear acknowledgment of the primacy of divine grace in human salvation. Turning to God in Christ must be "as God pleases," he stressed, and "that moral change ... which will render us meet objects of the divine favor" needed to be "introduced in us." It could not be secured by human effort.[19]

The Calvinist doctrines of unconditional election and irresistible grace were consistent features of nearly half of Chancy's published works despite a

---

19. Chauncy, *Nathanael's Character*, 16, citing Isa 33:14 and Matt 23:14; *New Creature Describ'd*, 20; *Unbridled Tongue*; *Earthquakes a Token*, 23; *Earth Delivered*, 24. Cf. Chauncy and Foxcroft, "To the Reader"; Edwards, *Sinners*, e.g., 16. See esp. Chauncy, *Unbridled Tongue*, 8, 12, citing Isa 33:14 and Rev 21:8: "Multitudes will be condemned, at the great and last judgment, for their hypocrisy; for their seeming to be religious, while they had really no religion at all ... But if you are yet unmoved, O turn your thoughts to the bar of the coming judgment, and reflect, seriously reflect, on what will then be the awful doom of all those, who only seem to be religious. They shall be sent away to dwell with devouring fire; yea, they shall dwell in the hottest place of that lake, which burneth with fire and brimstone."

parallel and growing emphasis on human free will that was to become more prominent over time. While consistently calling people to salvation, he was thus equally clear during the first half of his public ministry that "of our selves we can never turn to God, or serve him to his acceptance. The assistances of divine grace are absolutely necessary hereto." Chauncy acknowledged the possibility of saving, "Death-bed Repentance," but only "thro' the Uncovenanted Mercy of GOD." In society generally, "when a people are become generally corrupt and wicked, the powerful interposition of God, and this only, will be effectual, to restrain them from vice, and bring them back to the practice of religion and virtue." Physical compulsion was never appropriate to enforce Christian belief or practice and since God had created people as "rational, free Agents, they can't be religious but with the free Consent of their Wills." But there was no doubt for the Calvinist Chauncy, just as there would ultimately be no question, rather paradoxically, for the Arminian and universalist Chauncy more than forty years later, who held the decisive hand in the process of conversion:

> God himself does not . . . go about to make men religious. He uses Violence with no Man; forces no One, contrary to his Will, to betake himself to a religious Course. Whenever he draws Men to a Life of Holiness, 'tis with the Cords of a Man, and with the Bonds of Love. i.e. in a Way suted to their Character as Men; in a Way adapted to their Make as free Agents. He does not make Use of the Methods of Force, turning Men from Sin to himself, whether they will, or no; but so manages the Affair, as to gain the free and full Consent of their Wills.[20]

In that sense, divine grace, however adapted to human nature, was ultimately irresistible. Moreover, salvation was the direct result of God's unconditional election and predetermination. One of the main reasons why "Joy" could justifiably be termed "the Duty of Survivors" on the death of pious friends and relatives, Chauncy informed those mourning Lucy Waldo in 1741, was that "they are gone to dwell with Patriarchs, Prophets, and Apostles; with their pious departed Friends, and Progenitors; and with all, whom GOD, in all Ages, from the Days of Adam, has been selecting from among Men, and preparing to be Heirs to the future, eternal Inheritance." Grace was thus paramount and the connection between divine "selection" [or election] and human conversion unbreakable, because the latter came not by force of will but by the sovereignty of God. It involved people's eyes being opened "to see the force of the great motives of christianity" and "their

20. Chauncy, *Early Piety Recommended*, 6. Cf. 9, 11; *Man's Life*, 27; *Prayer for Help*, 13; *Only Compulsion*, 10–11.

stubbornness" being "hereby... overcome." A sinful humankind, Chauncy told those at the Boston Thursday Lecture of June 4, 1741, could only be God's abject debtor:

> 'Twas not by your own works of righteousness, but according to his mercy, that GOD has saved you by the washing of regeneration, and the renewing of the Holy Ghost... Look upon the DIVINE SPIRIT, as sovereign in the kingdom of grace; and realise that he may dispense the grace of GOD, as to whom he will; so where he will, and in what way or manner soever he will.

He repeated the theme in other Great Awakening publications. "He that has an immediate access to our Spirits can certainly work upon them," he told the people of First Church on a 1741 day of prayer "to ask of GOD the effusion of his SPIRIT" and, "in a reasonable way," to "influence them both to will and to do of his own good pleasure." God was nothing less than "the author of conversion" in the sense that "the change signified by conversion or the new creature, is the work of GOD."[21]

An overarching emphasis on the ultimate sovereignty of God was to remain a paramount theme for Chauncy. But in his earlier years, he interpreted it within a clearly identifiable, Calvinist theological framework, which involved allegiance not only to the doctrines of total depravity, unconditional election and irresistible grace, but to the centrality of Christ's atonement and to the inevitable perseverance of all true Christians in saving faith for eternity. There is no definitive evidence that Chauncy embraced the doctrine of a limited atonement, whereby Christ died to pay the price only for the sins of the "elect," rather than for those of the whole world. But such a position would have been entirely consistent with the commitments to an orthodox Puritan Christology and to a thoroughly reformed understanding of justification by grace through faith which are unmistakable throughout the works of his first thirty-five years as a published theologian.[22]

---

21. Chauncy, *Joy*, 12; *New Creature Describ'd*, 9, 34, 38–9; *Out-pouring of the Holy-Ghost*, 11, 17, 18. In seeking to define "the Work of god" in 1743, Chauncy again went back to Calvinist basics: "'Tis in one Word, That Work of divine Grace, which is sometimes, called the New-Creation; sometimes the New-Birth; sometimes the Spirit's Renovation; sometimes Conversion, or as 'tis otherwise express'd, a being turned from Darkness to Light, and from the Power of Sin and Satan unto god" (*Seasonable Thoughts*, 5).

22. "Justification by faith" is here understood as by "Protestant theologians," according to a definition of "justification" from the *New English Dictionary* (1901) cited in *OED Online*: "an act of grace in which God accounts human beings righteous, not owing to any merit of their own, but through imputation of Christ's righteousness, as apprehended and received by faith."

In defining the character of a "Godly man" in *Prayer for Help* (1737), Chauncy stressed possession of faith as "an active living principle, suitably exciting and moving the several passions and affections of his mind," confidence in the "faithfulness and veracity" of the Bible, and submission to God's providential sovereignty. But he laid major emphasis on belief in Christ's atonement and on "salvation in none but in Christ." In *Only Compulsion Proper* (1739), Chauncy reminded his hearers how God "has even parted with his own dear and only begotten Son. He spared him not, but delivered him up, to shed his Blood on the Cross; and by this Means has got ready for our Acceptance a Provision of Mercy, equal to the Needs of our Souls." Five years later, at the installation of Thomas Frink as minister, he gave a classic exhortation to justification by faith. "We must be Men in CHRIST, justified in his Righteousness, and sanctified by his SPIRIT," he told members of Plymouth's Third Church, "or nothing will prevent our being doom'd, at the great and last Day, to a Departure from CHRIST among the Workers of Iniquity." "It is on the Account of CHRIST's Righteousness that we are justified and saved," Chauncy later repeated, "and it would be highly injurious to his Merits to suppose otherwise."[23]

If Chauncy's 1756 affirmation that "there is no safety, no security for us . . . as God pleases, but by making him our friend thro' Jesus Christ" was remarkable enough, his doctrinal statements in two sermons of 1744–5 were even more striking from one who has since been placed near the pinnacle of eighteenth-century American theological progressivism. "And he was careful, not only that his Aims and Principles might be good," Chauncy said at the funeral of First Church deacon Cornelius Thayer, "but that he might also place his Dependance right; not on his own Works of Righteousness, but the Merits of the LORD JESUS CHRIST." "The Scripture ever takes notice of three Things with Reference to the Affair of Man's Redemption," Chauncy told Massachusetts ministers assembled in Annual Convention on May 31, 1744:

> The first is the Grace of GOD purposing it. It's particular in its Care to fix our Thoughts on the Good-will and free Mercy of GOD, as the true, original, eternal Source of this Blessing. Next to the Grace of GOD, it gives all due Honour to the Merits of the LORD JESUS CHRIST. 'Tis with a View to him, for his Sake, and on his Account, that the Sinner is spoken of as justified and saved. These great Gospel Favours are granted to him, not for any Works of Righteousness which he has done, but in

---

23. Chauncy, *Prayer for Help*, 2–3; *Only Compulsion*, 19, alluding to Romans 8:32; *Ministers Exhorted*, 6, 21.

> Consideration of the mediatorial Performances and Sufferings of the LORD JESUS CHRIST. This Righteousness of the Redeemer is considered as the Ground and Reason, that on the Account of which he is interested in the Mercy of GOD to eternal Life.

Few might have provided a more cogent summary of the orthodox, Calvinist plan of salvation.[24]

Chauncy's view of Christ's crucifixion entailed an equally reformed understanding of his death as both expiatory sacrifice for human sin and substitutionary propitiation of God's wrath. In his first published sermon, he described "the Terms of Salvation" as "bro't down to our present fallen State," "thro' the LORD JESUS CHRIST, who obey'd the Law, and suffer'd the Penalty of it, for us and in our stead." In an ordination sermon delivered two years after his open advocacy of more Arminian positions, he clearly maintained such a view of the atonement. The "great doctrine of 'remission of sin,'" was "founded," he argued "on the 'propitiation' made . . . by the 'blood of Christ,' when he was nailed to the cross." This, Chauncy contended, was "the grand point aimed at, by the wisdom of God, in the sufferings and death of his son Jesus."[25]

Chauncy also argued that there was no way of losing Christian salvation once it had truly been received. In *Out-pouring of the Holy-Ghost* (1742), he went to some lengths to define faith as a divine gift whereby "we are justified freely of GOD's grace, without the deeds of the law." But he also saw it as a crucial work of the Holy Spirit that by the Spirit's "influence," Christians "are kept from falling, and preserved through faith unto salvation." Seeking to distinguish, in *Seasonable Thoughts* (1743), between genuine works of God and false claims to such, Chauncy reiterated his clear affirmation of the perseverance of the saints:

> The Influence of the SPIRIT does not consist in sudden Impulses and Impressions, in Visions, Revelations, extraordinary Missions, and the like; but in working in Men the Preparations for Faith and Repentance, by humbling them for Sin, and shewing them the Necessity of a SAVIOUR; then by effecting such a Change in them, as shall turn them from the Power of Sin and Satan, and make them new Creatures; and in fine, by carrying on this good Work begun in them, enabling them to grow in Grace, and patiently continue doing well, 'till of the Mercy of GOD, thro' CHRIST, they are crowned with eternal Life.[26]

---

24. Chauncy, *Earth Delivered*, 24; *Cornelius's Character*, 28, citing Romans 3:24; *Ministers Cautioned*, 31–32.

25. Chauncy, *Man's Life*, 6–7; *Sermon Preached May 6, 1767*, 30.

26. Chauncy, *Out-pouring of the Holy-Ghost*, 38, 20–21; *Seasonable Thoughts*, 218.

If Chauncy's early theology can be characterized as anything, therefore, it deserves the label "Calvinist." There is consistent evidence from his first sermons through to those published in the mid-1760s that when he exhorted his readers, as he did in his major Great Awakening treatise of the 1740s, that "now is the Time, when we are particularly called to stand up for the good old Way, and bear faithful Testimony against every Thing, that may tend to cast a Blemish on true primitive Christianity," he had more in mind than the simple defense of traditional, Congregationalist polity that was often associated with such discourse. He was urging commitment to reformed orthodoxy in general and this theological inheritance centered on the primacy of divine grace: "'Tis one of the most obvious truths," Chauncy told his church members in a 1757 discourse that otherwise focused on the need for good works, "that all that we have, and are, we derive from God . . . it must forever be acknowledged, that an admission to blessedness in heaven is a reward of grace, and not of debt."[27]

Yet despite his doctrinal traditionalism, Chauncy also faced, like Mayhew and many others, a significant turning point during the Great Awakening of the early 1740s. Moreover, the public positions that he adopted towards the revival movement not only came to divide him from many fellow Calvinists, they subsequently contributed to his historical portrayal as a heterodox theologian much earlier than he actually was.

Griffin carefully reconstructed the series of events and influences over the two years that followed Whitefield's first arrival in Boston on September 17, 1740, which seem to have led Chauncy from initial silence through critical questioning to outright opposition to the perceived excesses of the Great Awakening. Through his public disagreement, in 1740–1741, with the recommendations of church councils that two of his more open-minded colleagues, Samuel Osborn of Eastham and Samuel Mather of Boston's Second Church, be dismissed from their pulpits for heterodox teaching, Chauncy became personally, if not doctrinally, isolated from the ecclesiastical mainstream. As a minister of one of Boston's leading churches, he was also caught up in the increasingly contentious church politics of the early 1740s in other ways and he was distressed by a growing polarization between those who supported and those who questioned or rejected the Great Awakening. Despite such pressures, Chauncy showed considerable restraint in his initial sermons on revival themes. A chronological analysis

---

27. Chauncy, *Seasonable Thoughts*, 337–38; Chauncy, *Charity*, 8. On Puritan "primitivist" discourse, see esp. Bozemann, *To Live Ancient Lives*. The context of Chauncy's call in *Seasonable Thoughts* to "stand up for the good old Way" and defend "true primitive Christianity" makes it clear that Chauncy had in mind what he called, 339, "good Doctrine" generally, not just traditional polity.

of his works shows how he began, in such publications as *New Creature Describ'd* (1741), *Unbridled Tongue* (1741), *Gifts of the Spirit* (1742) and *Out-pouring of the Holy-Ghost* (1742), by formulating relatively cautious and often indirect critiques of revivalist practice, in which his major focus was on outlining what he saw as sound biblical principles in relevant areas. It was only when provoked by a troubling personal encounter with the extremist itinerant, James Davenport, and when faced with the publication of the most significant pro-Awakening treatise by Jonathan Edwards in 1742, that Chauncy became a major critic of the Great Awakening.[28]

In a letter to Davenport prefaced to the publication of *Enthusiasm Described* (1742), dated July 17, 1742, Chauncy initially described his recent confrontation with the evangelist in rather measured tones. "When you came to my house, some days ago," he wrote, "to enquire into the reason of the hope that was in me, my intention was, to deal plainly and faithfully with you: And I believe, you do not think, I was wanting on that head." But it clearly caused deep offense to Chauncy that Davenport, who had already been denied access to the pulpits of Boston ministers because of his "enthusiasm," should have personally challenged him about his salvation. In the main body of his work, Chauncy then showed no hesitation in detailing not just some of Davenport's key errors, as he saw them, but those of the revival movement in general. Chief among them were lack of spiritual discernment, undue emotionalism, failure to respect traditional boundaries between clerical and lay spheres of ministry, and the general social disorder promoted by some revivalists. The publication of Edwards's first and highly influential defense of the Great Awakening in *Some Thoughts Concerning the Present Revival of Religion in New-England* (1742) elicited a much more thorough and carefully researched exposition on similar topics. Chauncy has sometimes, and arguably unfairly, been seen by scholars as offering a rather pedestrian critique of the Awakening compared to the more compelling apologetics of Edwards. But it was *Seasonable Thoughts* (1743), with its comprehensive five-part analysis and detailed reporting of events, that really established Chauncy's position as the most prominent critic of mid-eighteenth-century American revivalism.[29]

28. Chauncy, *New Creature Describ'd*, *Unbridled Tongue*, *Gifts of the Spirit*, and *Out-pouring of the Holy-Ghost* were originally preached as sermons on June 4, September 10, December 17, 1741, and May 13, 1742 respectively. See Griffin, *Old Brick*, 46–70, passim, esp. 48–50, 58–59, for helpful accounts of the "Osborn affair" and Samuel Mather's dismissal. See, further, Osborn, *Case and Complaint*, 22–23; Stiles, *Extracts from the Itineraries*, 304.

29. Chauncy, *Enthusiasm Described*, i–ii, citing part of 1 Pet 3:15; ii–viii; *Seasonable Thoughts*; Edwards, *Some Thoughts*. Edwards's other major work arising out of the Awakening was *Religious Affections*, which can partly be seen as a response to

Since Chauncy produced no fewer than ten separate works in connection with Great Awakening controversies over a period of just four years, it is not surprising that "this labour . . . ," as he told Stiles more than twenty years later, "in addition to my ministerial work . . . broke my constitution." But there is no evidence that it also signaled a break in Chauncy's commitment to, still less an Arminian attack on, reformed orthodoxy. In that sense, scholars like Perry Miller and Barney Jones, who acknowledged Chauncy's Calvinism at the time of the Awakening, made an important point. Chauncy's controversy with Edwards and other revivalists is better viewed as addressing issues of contention within a broadly shared theological framework than as proof of his departure from it. The First Church minister had no problems with seeking a revival of religion per se or with understanding that in traditional terms. He specifically wrote of the need for spiritual renewal in at least four of his Great Awakening publications and his conventional understanding of the process of conversion was just as evident in *New Creature Describ'd* (1741) as in his work of nine years earlier, *Early Piety Recommended* (1732). If anything, as Miller and Harry Stout have suggested, Chauncy's theological anthropology was more traditionally Puritan than that of Edwards and he saw his major role in *Seasonable Thoughts* (1743) as a defender of Protestant order and orthodoxy against revivalist excesses.[30]

It is clear from the attention that he devoted to them in all his Awakening publications that his major critique of the revival centered on its theological "enthusiasm," which he found fundamentally unbiblical, and on the social and ecclesiastical disorder to which it allegedly gave rise. While still allowing ample scope for the kind of religion of the heart, for which he actively called throughout the Great Awakening, Chauncy, like Mayhew, thus emerged from the early 1740s as a champion of a more rational religion and social order. His leadership as an anti-revivalist controversialist gave

Chauncy's *Seasonable Thoughts*. Edwards's earlier *Faithful Narrative*, first written in a letter of 1736, did much to provoke local and international interest in the evangelical revival movement, but was a more specific account of events at his own church in Northampton, Connecticut.

30. Chauncy, "Sketch of Eminent Men," 162; Gaustad, "Charles Chauncy"; Perry Miller, *Jonathan Edwards*, 177–78, 185–86; Barney Jones, "Charles Chauncy and the Great Awakening," 497–98; Stout, *New England Soul*, 203–7, esp. 206–7; Chauncy, *Seasonable Thoughts*, e.g., iii–xxx, 337–38, 366. In addition to works already cited, Gaustad affirmed the authenticity of the following by Chauncy: *Letter from a Gentleman*; *Ministers Cautioned*; *Ministers Exhorted*; *Letter to the Reverend Mr. George Whitefield*. He rejected, however, the attribution to Chauncy of *Letter to the Reverend Mr. George Whitefield, Publickly Calling*, of which he thought Nathaniel Appleton the more likely author, of *Wonderful Narrative*, and of four other more questionable works. See, further, Lippy, *Seasonable Revolutionary*, 24–27.

him a unique standing in the growing community of "Old Light" traditionalists, on which he was to build for years. It also encouraged later scholars like Heimert, in his revisionist study *Religion and the American Mind* (1966), to position him, with Mayhew, at the heart of a new movement of "Liberalism."[31]

Heimert's main thesis was that "evangelical religion," not a more "rationalist" creed, truly "embodied" and presented a "radical and even democratic challenge to the standing order" in colonial and revolutionary America. In support of this argument, the Harvard scholar offered broad-brush definitions of key theological/intellectual movements, and especially of "Calvinism" or "evangelicalism" versus "Liberalism" or "rationalism," which he posited as competing schools of thought following the Great Awakening. Historians were initially very skeptical, if not outright dismissive of Heimert's categorizations. Yet despite their reservations, his "evangelical/liberal" distinction has since become a fairly common frame of reference for describing New England Congregationalist clergy of the latter half of the eighteenth century. In ways that Heimert might never have imagined, because "evangelicals" generally embraced a more traditionalist theology than "liberals," the former have also come to be identified as "conservatives." In the process, figures like Chauncy and Mayhew, who both featured in Heimert's study as almost archetypal "liberals," have sometimes been disconnected from their Calvinist heritage.[32]

---

31. Heimert, *Religion and the American Mind*. In *Seasonable Thoughts*, Chauncy especially critiqued as disorders associated with the Great Awakening: itinerancy (36ff.), abnormal physical and emotional effects (76ff.), judgmentalism (140ff.), false impressions of religious influences (178ff.), the illegitimate rise of lay exhorters and preachers (226ff.), confusion in worship (239ff.), and what he called a "Spirit of Error" giving rise to various doctrinal excesses (242ff.). Chauncy wrote of the need for religious revival, for example, in *New Creature Describ'd*; *Gifts of the Spirit*; *Out-pouring of the Holy-Ghost*.

32. Heimert argued, for example, that the "evangelical impulse," which embodied "radical and emphatic definitions of liberty and equality," became "the avatar and instrument of a fervent American nationalism." By contrast, "Liberals' "adaptation of traditional covenant theology to social contract theory combined with their advocacy of individualism and "enlightened self-interest" to encourage the protection of the sociopolitical status quo, even when faced with the prerevolutionary challenges of growing British imperialism (*Religion and the American Mind*, 12–14, 16–17, 270). Although Heimert raised significant issues that have since taxed scholars for more nearly fifty years, initial reviews of his work were mixed. Among key assessments, see: Bailyn, "Religion and Revolution"; McLoughlin, "American Revolution"; Mead, "Through and beyond the Lines"; and much more recently, Wood "Religion and the American Revolution." Heimert clearly viewed Chauncy and Mayhew as "Liberal" social reactionaries. He hypothetically suggested, for example, that "for Mayhew to have made a different contribution to the uprising of 1775 it would have been necessary for him to overcome his aversions to violence, revivals, awakenings, and popular enthusiasm."

But as has been seen, especially in the case of Chauncy, whose Calvinism fundamentally shaped his theological outlook for more than fifty years, this is misleading. There is strong evidence that neither Mayhew nor Chauncy began to reject key elements of New England orthodoxy until the late 1740s, when the former made his Arminian positions clear in *Seven Sermons* (1749), and that Chauncy did not openly reveal any questioning of it at all until 1758. The Great Awakening undoubtedly prompted both to reject what they came to see as the excesses of revivalist enthusiasm and to identify with a more rationalist approach to religion. But well beyond the religious revival movement, the decisive decades of major intellectual change for both Boston ministers were to extend from the late 1740s through the 1760s, when their more critical tendencies were finally to find theological expression. Even then, the retiring Chauncy took much longer to express his shift to Arminianism than Mayhew, and he might never have published the full extent of his personal transformation at all, had he not lived into his late seventies and found, in the tumultuous period of the early 1780s, a "seasonable" time to unveil it to his contemporaries.

He also described Chauncy as "the greatest Liberal of all" (*Religion and the American Mind*, 291, 418). On Heimert's influence and subsequent historiography, see also, Goff, "Revivals and Revolution." The "evangelical"/"liberal" or "rationalist" frame of reference was echoed by Stout, for example, who explicitly adopted Heimert's distinction between "rationalist" and "evangelical" preaching styles, even while continuing to stress strong elements of doctrinal continuity among those who adopted them (*New England Soul*, 218–22). Holifield distinguished between "Arminians," "moderate" or "Old Calvinists," and "Edwardsean" revivalists (*Theology in America*, 127–28).

— 2 —

Reshaping the Calvinist Heritage

The Shift to Arminianism

ON MAY 6, 1768, just seventeen days before he sent Ezra Stiles his brief biography of his great-grandfather, Charles Chauncy suggested an eclectic selection of some thirty other New England "worthies," whose memory was fit "to embalm in honour to the country." Having dispatched his duty as chronicler and offered further help in the form of "a good many anecdotes," he also took the liberty of informing Stiles about some of his own publishing plans. In that same year, Chauncy released the first of two volumes designed to counter the arguments of the New Jersey clergyman Thomas Chandler and so to defend the American colonies against the perceived threat of a Church of England bishop. But this was not his topic of immediate concern. Instead, Chauncy focused on at least five other major works, more or less fully completed over the previous three and a half decades, which had never seen the light of day.[1]

Chauncy readily admitted that since the late 1740s, on account of health problems apparently brought on by over-work during the Great Awakening, he had not been able to pursue his studies "with that constancy and long attention" of which he had previously been capable. Even so, after four years'

---

1. Chauncy, "Sketch of Eminent Men," 161. Stiles seems to have been compiling materials for an eventually unpublished work, which Morgan, *Gentle Puritan*, 145–46, identified as *The Ecclesiastical History of New England*. But according to Morgan, despite repeated enquiries about Stiles's progress with the work, "though his papers abound with compilations of data and one rough outline—it can scarcely be called a draft—of the first chapters, nothing more has survived." Chauncy's controversy with Chandler centered on *Appeal to the Public Answered*, written in response to Chandler's *Appeal to the Public*, and *Reply to Dr. Chandler's "Appeal Defended."* However, he had already written an earlier work countering the prospect of a Church of England bishop taking up residence in the colonies: Chauncy, *Letter to a Friend, Containing Remarks*. He had also, in his Harvard Dudleian Lecture of 1762, produced *Validity of Presbyterian Ordination*.

earlier intensive research following the decision by his then brother-in-law to seek Anglican orders, he had not only "materials for a complete view of all that is said by the Fathers of the first two centuries relative to the Episcopal controversy," but seven years' further biblical exploration in the 1750s, especially of the Pauline epistles, had also yielded:

1. "a finished quarto volume" about "a most interesting subject." This was "written with too much freedom to admit of a publication in this country," Chauncy thought, and he wondered whether it would "ever see the light till after my death," although he had been asked by friends to publish it anonymously in England.

2. "materials for an octavo volume," which had been "mostly put together" and included three "dissertations" on the theological question of sin and the interpretation of Adam's Fall. Chauncy stressed that "the whole is written from the scripture account of these matters, and not from any human scheme." But he conceded that the work would be considered unorthodox and was unsure whether he would ever publish it under his own name.

3. "materials for another work," although "as yet in a disjoined heap," which was intended as "a key to the New Testament, more especially the Apostles' writings," and designed "to guard one against mistakes, and lead into a true understanding of the inspired writings."

4. "another piece," which Chauncy felt free to publish openly after it had been fully transcribed, "upon the benevolence of GOD, its nature, illustration, and consistency with evil both natural and moral."[2]

Chauncy's earlier work on the episcopacy question was finally published as *Compleat View of Episcopacy* (1771) just three years after his letter to Stiles. Of the other writing projects, the first is probably to be identified with *Mystery Hid* (1784), the second with *Five Dissertations* (1785), and the fourth with *Benevolence of the Deity* (1784). Yet none of these saw publication until the mid-1780s, when Chauncy himself was around his eightieth year: two of them were first released in London, and *Mystery Hid*, Chauncy's most controversial work because of its very explicit advocacy

2. Chauncy, "Sketch of Eminent Men," 161–62, 163–64. See chapter 4 below; Griffin, *Old Brick*, 29–30, on the marriage in 1730 and Anglican conversion soon afterwards of Chauncy's first wife's sister, Jane Hirst, and the lawyer Addington Davenport. The four-year period of intensive study of the episcopacy question referred to in Chauncy's missive to Stiles can be dated to roughly 1732–36.

of universalism, was printed anonymously. In view of his earlier Calvinism, which not only mirrored that of Foxcroft, the more senior minister for the first forty-two years of Chauncy's ministry, but probably of many First Church members, his caution in sharing his most innovative views clearly had wider implications. But whatever the personal and professional pressures (see chapter 3), it remains striking that Chauncy waited some twenty-five years to declare positions that he apparently had reached by 1760 and had already committed to paper at least sixteen years before they finally saw the light of day. Chauncy's caution may also have reflected the controversy that arose when he and Mayhew, who was much bolder and much quicker to publish his views, began to state the first decisive shift in their theology, to Arminianism, in the late 1740s–60s.[3]

Arminian Pioneers

The term "Arminian" was originally applied to those who quite specifically rejected the Calvinism defined by the Synod of Dort. But as William Youngs has contended, it came to be used much more widely in the eighteenth century "to describe anyone who believed that man's own efforts had an important role in winning his salvation." E. Brooks Holifield suggested that "by the eighteenth century, the label . . . acquired an expanding range of meanings" in England. Notwithstanding more scattergun usage, especially in theological polemic, he extended that analysis to New England:

> The [American] Arminians of the 1750s were more adventurous than the earlier theologians of virtue, more willing to break openly from Calvinism. Tracing a progression from Ebenezer Gay to Jonathan Mayhew to the mature Charles Chauncy shows not only an increasing respect for reason . . . but also a movement from a cautious theology of virtue to an open attack on Calvinist orthodoxy.

But even Holifield, who allowed, for example, that such English Arminians "meant to reject not only predestination but also imputed guilt, imputed righteousness, and original sin," ultimately understated the extent to which more open-minded Congregationalist ministers were willing to engage the full panoply of Calvinism from at least the 1730s onwards.[4]

---

3. Chauncy, *Compleat View of Episcopacy*; *Mystery Hid*; *Five Dissertations*; *Benevolence of the Deity*. There is no evidence that his proposed "key to the New Testament" was ever published. It may well have been destroyed soon after his death.

4. Youngs, *God's Messengers*, 85; Holifield, *Theology in America*, 83, 128–35, esp. 128–29. See, further, on New England Calvinism, Perry Miller, *New England Mind:*

Experience Mayhew's careful criticisms of Calvinist orthodoxy in 1744, although he continued to count himself an adherent, have already been noted. But while public statements of Arminian principles by New England Congregationalists were still relatively rare before the 1740s, he was by no means the first to publish such opinions. Growing evidence of denunciations and even of what Robert Wilson aptly called "heresy trials" of ministers with alleged sympathies are indicative of a rising tide of Arminian sentiment, especially among younger clergy, from the mid-1720s. Conrad Wright argued with some justification that "the growth of the Anglican church in New England was . . . a doctrinal as well as a political threat to the churches of the Standing Order." As early as 1720, with the publication of his *Choice Dialogues*, the King's Chapel layman, John Checkley, issued a widescale refutation of the Calvinist doctrines of predestination, election, and irresistible grace. The general charge of Arminianism resurfaced with a vengeance in the "Great Apostasy" controversy surrounding the defections to the Church of England of Yale Rector Timothy Cutler and a few like-minded friends and colleagues. Following the Yale trustees' decision to "excuse" Cutler from further service in October 1722, they also resolved that all future college faculty and officers should show "the Soundness of their Faith in opposition to Armenian [sic] & prelatical Corruptions or any other of Dangerous Consequence to the Purity & Peace of our Churches." But Congregationalist desertions continued elsewhere and one of the original Yale apostates, Samuel Johnson, unrepentantly published his anti-Calvinist, as well as pro-Episcopalian, views in the 1730s. While rejecting the label of Arminianism, Johnson maintained that Calvinist doctrines of predestination and reprobation found no support in the formularies of the Church of England, which he now upheld.[5]

The Seventeenth Century, 92–97; Holifield, *Theology in America*, 25–55. Miller highlighted the ambiguity of seventeenth-century New England definitions of "Arminianism," which included both "the theology developed in Holland by Arminius and his followers" and "the doctrine of the Laudian [high church, Anglican] party in England" (*New England Mind: The Seventeenth Century*, 367). "Imputed righteousness" is here used as by McGrath, who described Luther's doctrine as that whereby "the alien righteousness of Christ . . . is imputed to [believers]—that is, treated as if it were theirs through faith" (*Reformation Thought*, 126).

5. Wilson, *Benevolent Deity*, 63; Wright, *Unitarianism in America*, 17–18; Checkley, *Choice Dialogues*; "Proceedings of the Trustees, October 17–22, 1722," in Dexter, *Documentary History*, 233; Johnson, *Letter from a Minister*, esp. 16; *Second Letter from a Minister*, esp. 21–22. In his first letter, Johnson bluntly stated that "we have no Business with Arminius, he was a Dutch Presbyterian, and we are none of his Followers." But in his second, Johnson argued that "if we take the Articles, Prayers and Homilies altogether, and candidly interpret one Passage by another, and by the general Tenor of the whole, we shall find nothing in them that can be justly interpreted to express the

In 1726, the dean of New England Puritanism, Cotton Mather, who had personally weighed in on the Yale affair, was confident enough to assert, when introducing a vigorous defense of New England Congregationalist church order, that:

> There is no need of Reporting what is the Faith professed by the churches in New-England; For every one knows, That they perfectly adhere to the CONFESSION OF FAITH, published by the Assembly of Divines at Westminster, and afterwards renewed by the Synod at the Savoy: And received by the Renowned Kirk of Scotland. The Doctrinal Articles of the Church of England, also, are more universally held and preached in the Churches of New-England, than in any Nation; and far more than in our own. I cannot learn, That among all the Pastors of Two Hundred Churches, there is one Arminian: much less an Arian, or a Gentilist.

Yet despite Mather's claims, within just a few years prominent ministers were again lobbying and preaching against perceived threats of Arminian corruption, especially among younger members of the New England clergy. On July 8, 1731, a twenty-seven-year-old Edwards took the opportunity of speaking at the Boston public lecture during Harvard commencement week to deliver a ringing call for Calvinist orthodoxy in *God Glorified in the Work of Redemption*. In introducing this early work, Edwards's senior ministerial colleagues, Thomas Prince and William Cooper of Boston, expressed their "Joy and Thankfulness that the great Head of the Church is pleas'd still to raise up from among the Children of his People, for the Supply of His Churches, those who assert & maintain these Evangelical Principles." They also did not hesitate to warn that "if those which we call the Doctrines of Grace, ever come to be contemn'd or disrelished, vital Piety will proportionably languish and wear away; as these Doctrines always sink in the Esteem of Men, upon the Decay of serious Religion."[6]

Calvinistic Doctrine of absolute Predestination and Reprobation." On other Congregationalist defections to the Church of England, see, for example, Wright, *Unitarianism in America*, 18.

6. Mather, "Introduction," in *Ratio Disciplinae*, 5; Edwards, *God Glorified*, ii. After much prompting, Mather wrote a document expressing "the sentiments of several ministers in Boston" concerning issues raised by the Yale controversy, which was reprinted in *CMHS* 2/2 (1814), 133–36. See Mather's earlier statement of May 10, 1715, in a letter to Dr. J. Edwards: "I would with all possible modesty observe, that for ought I can tell, we have in our New England near 200 churches, wherein the faith and order of the gospel is maintained, with as little a measure of the epidemical corruption as any part of the Christian world can pretend to" (cited in Youngs, *God's Messengers*, 85). On the "Great Apostasy" in general, see esp. Warch, *School of the Prophets*, 100–117; Daggy,

In December 1732, following a promised gift of books by Anglican cleric and philosopher George Berkeley, who was then resident in Rhode Island, Colman of Brattle Street was so concerned about a renewed spread of Arminianism at Yale that he lobbied college authorities, including trustee Eliphalet Adams. "I hope it comes to you without the Clog of any Condition that is inconsistent with or subversive of the known and true Intent of the Honourable Founders of your College," Colman wrote of Berkeley's potential Trojan horse. He also begged leave "to add one Word more concerning the Bruit of the Prevalence of Arminianism" at Yale, noting that it would be "acceptable to some superior Friends" in Boston if Adams "would freely write upon that Head." As it turned out, Colman and like-minded fellow Harvard alumni probably had more cause for concern among recent graduates of their own alma mater. By 1734, John White, minister of First Church, Gloucester, deemed the threat of Arminianism, defined in classical Calvinist terms, to be so serious among the younger generation that it featured prominently in *New-England's Lamentations*, a jeremiad sermon addressed "to the Congregational Churches of Christ in New-England." "It is a MATTER of LAMENTATION," White contended, that:

> some of Our Young Men, and such as are devoted to, and educated for, the Ministry of the Gospel, are under Prejudices against, and fall off from, important Articles of the Faith of these Churches, and cast a favourable Eye upon, embrace, argue for, propagate and preach the ARMINIAN Scheme.

White's subsequent exposition, which was endorsed in a prefatory "Epistle Recommendatory" by such Boston clerical luminaries as Joseph Sewall, Peter Thacher, John Webb, Cooper, Prince, and Foxcroft, labeled Arminianism "another Gospel." Its rebuttal of Arminian views on such central Calvinist doctrines as salvation by grace alone, justification by faith, imputed righteousness, and the perseverance of the saints made it very clear that White had much more than general tendencies towards Christian moralism in his sights.[7]

George Marsden has observed that as late as the mid-1720s, "no Congregationalist pastor would publicly deny [the] Westminster [Confession]

"Education, Church, and State"; Ellis, *New England Mind in Transition*; Stiles, *Literary Diary*, 2:339–40.

7. Colman to Adams, December 2, 1732, in Dexter, *Documentary History*, 298; White, *New England's Lamentations*, 16–24, esp. 16, 17. Perry Miller, *New England Mind: From Colony to Province*, 27–39, passim, still offers the best account of the development of "jeremiad" sermons lamenting the sinful decline of New England. Among more recent work on more general themes, see also Bercovitch, *American Jeremiad*. On the significance of gifts of books in the eighteenth century, see Hall, "Learned Culture."

or take an open stance for Arminianism." But from the 1730s onwards a steady stream of ecclesiastic councils was called to investigate the teachings of allegedly unorthodox, Harvard-educated younger ministers. In December 1735, the church of North Yarmouth, Maine, voted to dismiss Ammi Ruhammah Cutter just five years after his ordination following the calling of two councils in as many years to test claims of his "rank Arminianism." Just six months earlier, the church of Marlborough, Massachusetts, had likewise dispensed with the services of Benjamin Kent, who was two years junior to Cutter at Harvard and had been ordained in October 1733. Whereas only the most general charge against Cutter has remained a matter of historical record, those upheld against Kent were deemed of such public interest that they were published in *At a Council of Ten Churches* (1735).[8]

Just eight years after Mather's blanket disavowal of any trace of Arminianism among the New England clergy, this work is highly revealing of the extent of Kent's heterodoxy. He had been denying charges of Arminianism for years and there had been some resistance to his ordination. But so questionable were Kent's teachings that even his publication of a vigorously anti-Arian and anti-Socinian sermon in 1734 did little to sway the deliberations of a diverse group of ecclesiastical council members, who met in the first week of February 1735. Their unanimous conclusions were that Kent had not only rejected such central doctrines as Christ's "full Satisfaction" for the sins of humanity, the "absolute Election" of those predestined for Christian salvation, and the original sin of infants, he had gone so far as to have "held or vented... unsound and dangerous Opinions, with Respect to the great and important Scripture-Doctrine of the Trinity, and subversive of it." Faced with such open departures from New England orthodoxy, the Marlborough church accepted the council's recommendation that Kent be suspended from the ministry for nearly four months even though he had "acknowledged his sinful Inadvertency, and asked Pardon of God therefor." Apparently at his own request. Kent was dismissed altogether less than a month later, after showing no sign of doctrinal rehabilitation.[9]

Judging from the Calvinist tone of Robert Breck's "Confession of Faith" appended to William Cooper's sermon on his ordination, the same could not be said of the minister of Springfield, Massachusetts, at least on January 26, 1736. But Breck did not reach that point without surviving a barrage of heresy charges and church political maneuverings orchestrated by theological opponents led by the minister of First Church, Windham,

---

8. Marsden, *Jonathan Edwards*, 140; *SHG*, 7:502–9, esp. 503–4; *SHG*, 8:220–30, esp. 220–23; Anon., *Council of Ten Churches*.

9. Anon., *Council of Ten Churches*, 1–2. Kent's sole publication was *Sermon Preached*. See, further, *SHG*, 8:220–30, esp. 220–23.

and future Yale President, Thomas Clap, who objected to Breck's teaching in the Scotland Parish in 1733–34, as well as to his denials of youthful indiscretions at Harvard. The chief points of doctrine to which Clap and others took such exception were Breck's alleged refusal to acknowledge the full divine inspiration of certain passages in the New Testament, his stated view that "the Heathen that liv'd up to the Light of Nature should be Saved, & Christ should be immediately Revealed to them or they should be Saved some other way," and, probably most offensively, his denial of "the Necessity of Christ's Satisfaction to Divine Justice for Sin." Breck's 1736 "Confession" shows no trace of such unorthodox opinions, but as Wilson and Shipton have suggested, it should also be read in the context of his later career. He survived "to live to preach his mild Arminianism another day" and thus, over the course of nearly fifty years at Springfield, to influence generations of "young graduates who read theology under his guidance." Other more free-thinking individuals who found themselves caught in the crosshairs of later attempts to target Arminian heterodoxy in the 1740s were arguably less prudent. A few were certainly less successful in protecting their future in the ministry and events surrounding the ecclesiastical trials and tribulations of Samuel Mather, Osborn, and, later, Lemuel Briant, not only directly involved Chauncy or Mayhew, but they may have helped encourage or confirm their own theological journeys in more Arminian directions.[10]

Osborn had already been minister of Eastham, Massachusetts, for twenty years when he was brought before an ecclesiastical council convened in June 1738 to consider charges of heresy, and subsequently dismissed by his church. According to his unrepentant account of these and later proceedings in 1743, when he was still attempting to clear his name, the four "Articles" on which he was judged and found wanting all centered on key points in continuing controversies over Arminianism, and especially over the place of human "works" in the divine plan of salvation. The council had objected, for example, to Osborn's teaching that "what Christ did and suffer'd, did nothing abate or diminish Men's Obligation to the holy Law of God" and that "Men's Sins are not pardoned unconditionally." Even more scandalously to his arbiters of orthodoxy, Osborn had also taught that "Men can do that upon the doing of which they shall certainly be saved" and that "Men's Obedience is a Cause of their Justification." Despite starting a home church of loyal townspeople, which was eventually outlawed, and almost

10. Breck, "Confession of Faith," in Cooper, *Work of Ministers*; Narrative *of the Proceedings*, 4–6, esp. 4–5; Wilson, *Benevolence of the Deity*, 63–64. Hall offers a full account of the controversy surrounding Breck's settlement at Springfield in "Editor's Introduction," especially 4–17. *SHG*, 8:661–80, provides a helpful overview of Breck's life and ministry. See esp. 675.

herculean efforts to secure a reversal of the initial ecclesiastical judgment against him, or at least some rehabilitation of his ministerial reputation, Osborn was never reinstated by the church that had dismissed him.[11]

However, after strenuous lobbying, he did eventually convince a group of eleven ministers that he had been mistreated. These included the subsequently prominent Arminians Chauncy and Gay, as well as Samuel Mather, who was shortly to suffer his own test of faith. "We can't but apprehend that said Mr. Osborn has had hard Measure," they wrote from Salem on June 9, 1740, "in the Treatment he has receiv'd from the major Part of said Church [of Eastham], and from the Council they called in to advise them." Shipton found their judgment on the four "Articles of Charge," upon which Osborn had been "censur'd for Error," to be clear evidence of Chauncy's Arminian sympathies at an early point in his theological development. But while plainly indicative of greater openness to different views than shown by many others over the course of the Osborn controversy, the ministers' statement was carefully crafted to show that their approval of Osborn depended heavily upon the most generous hermeneutic available to them. "We can't find that said Articles necessarily couch or include in them any dangerous Errors," the eleven ministers stated:

> But that taking them with a christian, candid and charitable Construction . . . they well accord with the Truths laid down in the Gospel, and the Doctrine generally receiv'd by these Churches. And upon the View we have taken of the present Case, the great Importance of such Candor and Charity amongst Christians, in construing each other's Expressions, to us appears in a strong Light: For as without it some of Mr. Osborn's Expressions might appear inaccurate and erroneous; so should any take the Expressions of the abovesaid Council's Result, and of the Brethren's Remonstrance, &c. and put a critical and severe Construction upon them, they would some of them appear, not only as inaccurate, but as couching in them dangerous Errors.[12]

The issues surrounding the dismissal of Chauncy's friend and colleague Samuel Mather from his position as assistant to Joshua Gee at Boston's Second Church were complicated by his lukewarm response to the excitement of the Great Awakening, by personal tensions between Mather and Gee, and by what the church's nineteenth-century historian discreetly

---

11. Osborn, *Case and Complaint*, 5–6; Griffin, *Old Brick*, 48–50.

12. Osborn, *Case and Complaint*, 22–23. *SHG*, 6:439–67, esp. 443, exaggerated Chauncy's "Arminian" sympathies with Osborn. All that can be conclusively adduced from the available evidence is that he was prepared to tolerate his opinions, not that he personally supported them.

described as "suspicions and charges of impropriety of conduct which were current against him." But when an ecclesiastical council, comprising members of Boston's Brattle Street, Old South, New North, New South, and First Churches, including Chauncy, met to consider the complaints of members of Mather's congregation against him in June 1741, it required him to sign a public commitment to specific areas of improvement with a view to ultimate reconciliation with Second Church. There were also quite fundamental doctrinal matters at stake. Mather was not only to "walk before [his] brethren with the humility required in the gospel" and to encourage any good effects of the religious revival, including "the work of conviction and conversion among us." He was to "use all proper means to get [his] mind further enlightened and settled in the important points mentioned by the council" and "to be more frequent and distinct in preaching on the nature, and pressing the necessity, of regeneration by the Spirit of grace." The Second Church assistant was given little opportunity to follow through on those commitments. He was very soon condemned for a second time not only by his congregation, but by a meeting of the reconvened council. With Colman of Brattle Street, Chauncy voted against the majority's recommendation that Mather be dismissed. He also prepared a dissenting judgment for Mather to read to Second Church. But there is no evidence that Chauncy objected to anything other than the unseemly dispatch with which the proceedings against Mather were executed. With the support of loyal Second Church members who joined him to found the new Bennett Street Church, which he pastored until his death in 1785, Mather was able to continue in ministry for another forty-four years. But his treatment set something of a precedent.[13]

By the mid-1740s, as divisions intensified between more traditionalist Calvinists like Edwards, those soon labeled "New Lights," who generally supported the Great Awakening, and more rationalist "Old Lights," who, like Chauncy and Mayhew, came to reject its excesses, conflicts over Arminianism were increasingly complicated by such differences. In the case of the minister of Second Church, Bradford, Massachusetts, William Balch, for example, outspoken criticism of the Awakening seems to have combined with his Arminian statements on the relationship between faith and works to provoke concerted opposition over a period of three years. The strength of the reaction against Balch clearly reflected the boldness of his Arminianism, which he was among the first to express so publicly.

---

13. Robbins, *History of the Second Church*, 120–22; Stiles, *Extracts*, 304. See, further, on Samuel Mather, *SHG*, 7:216–38, esp. 222–25.

Two of Balch's published sermons, first delivered within ten days of each other in Bradford, show the militancy which so enraged his opponents. In *False Confidences Exposed*, preached as a regular Sunday sermon on January 23, 1743, Balch exploited a conventional attack on the sins of self-righteousness and hypocrisy to target disorderly revivalist enthusiasm. Exemplary of its vices, he argued, were those who "trust[ed] in themselves as being righteous and despise[d] others" either "on Account of certain Experiences they have had," or on the basis of "their [spiritual] Gifts and Enlargements," or for "being of such a Party, which they esteem more religious than any other." In an exposition otherwise couched in more general terms, Balch made specific references to the problems of "the present Times," not least the excesses of contemporary revivalism. Whilst offering seemingly orthodox Calvinist affirmations of the need for absolute "Dependance upon" the "Grace of God and the Merits of Christ" for salvation, he also laid the kind of emphasis on the "Place and Necessity" of Christian "Duty" that was to lay him open to the charges of outright Arminianism which followed publication of *The Apostles St. Paul and St. James Reconciled*. In this second sermon, which he first preached at a Bradford Lecture on February 2, 1743 and "soon after in some of the neighbouring churches," Balch went so far in urging the need for good works as a constituent part, rather than persuasive evidence of saving faith that his teaching was vigorously condemned by White of First Church, Gloucester, who later sought to intervene in Bradford's affairs.[14]

White described Balch's blatantly Arminian view that "Jesus Christ never purchased eternal Life, but for those, who have Fruit unto Holiness" as "dangerous" evidence of "an Inclination in Ministers and Churches to forsake the sound Principles of the Reformation; The Principles of the good old Puritans, as well as the Principles of the first Planters of this Wilderness." Provoked by such reactions, including vocal criticism in his own congregation, Balch personally called a church council to address heresy charges against him. In August 1744, this hand-picked body largely vindicated him of doctrinal error and upheld the suspensions of dissenting church members. But White and other opponents were not to be placated. Further complaints within and outside the Bradford church eventually led to a publication war between Balch and his detractors and to a second council, which met in July 1746 and again declined to rule decisively against him.[15]

14. Balch, *False Confidences*, 8, 19, 12, 30, 32; *Apostles*, title page; Balch et al., *Letters*.
15. Balch et al., *Letters*, 11–12; Balch, *Apostles*, 12. Balch's full statement reads: "The Apostle [James] was not insensible, that the Death and Sufferings of Christ, or his Obedience and Righteousness, were the sole meritorious and procuring Cause of the returning Favour of God to a lost and perishing World. But he knew withall, that

Throughout this lengthy process Balch apparently remained secure and undeterred in his opinions. Even when fellow Massachusetts "Old Lights," Samuel Wigglesworth of Hamilton and John Chipman of Beverly, found it necessary to defend the orthodoxy of their cause by producing a forty-four-page critique of *St. Paul and St. James Reconciled* (1743), he replied quite unapologetically in his own *Vindication of Some Points* (1746). As Shipton observed, over a sixty-five-year ministry at Bradford, Balch eventually saw off all his earlier "New Light" opponents. But his principal claim to fame, which has often gone unrecognized, was that he was among the first Congregationalist clergy to air his aberrant views so publicly and defiantly. In that sense, he paved the way for others like Chauncy and Mayhew, who became much better known pioneers of New England Arminianism. Gay, who has often been listed with them, fully revealed his Arminian credentials in the even more public setting of the annual convention of ministers meeting in Boston on May 29, 1746. But he delivered this controversial sermon, *True Spirit of a Gospel-Minister,* three years after Balch's incendiary attempt to reconcile the teachings of the apostles Paul and James on faith and works. Gay also spoke at a time when the Balch controversy was a major preoccupation among New England Congregationalists and yet to be resolved by the Bradford church's second ecclesiastical council.[16]

Gay's Arminianism, like that of Balch, stood in stark contrast to the militant Calvinism of many revivalist preachers and supporters, some of whose errors he also sought to counter in his 1746 sermon. His primary call to the Boston convention was for mutual tolerance and unity among ministers of all stripes, but he had particularly harsh words for undue emotionalism, anti-intellectualism and factionalism. Nor did Gay hesitate to nail his theological colors firmly to the mast. In one particularly noteworthy passage, where he cautioned against "the Abuse of the Doctrines of Grace," he effectively reinterpreted traditional Calvinist teachings on Christian election, redemption, grace, justification, and perseverance, recasting them all in overtly Arminian terms. He thus redefined those doctrines "according to Godliness, and designed to promote universal Holiness." Rather than describing election to salvation as an unconditional result of divine decree, he saw it as a matter of "Means," as well as "End," expressed "thro' Sanctification

---

Faith and Repentance, Faith and Obedience, Faith and Holiness, Piety, Charity, Justice, Temperance, &c. were necessary on our Part, in Order to our being in the Way to Happiness; because Jesus Christ never purchased eternal Life, but for those, who have Fruit unto Holiness." See, further, Bayly et al., *Brief Narrative*; Balch, *Vindication of the Second Church.*

16. Wigglesworth and Chipman, *Remarks*; Balch, *Vindication of Some Points*; *SHG,* 7:296–304, esp. 301–2; Gay, *True Spirit.*

of the [Holy] Spirit unto Obedience." "Redemption from the Curse of the Law" likewise entailed "a special Engagement to keep the Commandments of God," and "Effectual Vocation," or calling, did not merely involve the irresistible "Operations of the divine Spirit," as Calvinists had traditionally taught. It was "unto Holiness" and those "operations" did not exclude "humane Endeavours after Grace" or supersede "all use of our enfeebled Faculties in the Work of it." Even "Justifying Faith," which required "receiving whole Christ, not dividing his Offices," could not be separated from moral virtue. So Christians could not rely on traditional notions of Christ's righteousness being imputed to them; nor could they substitute "his Obedience in the Place of ours." Last but not least, Gay argued, "Perseverance in Grace" could not be a matter of grace alone. It was "to be accomplished," not simply received, and the way to secure it was through "continual Circumspection, and dutiful Diligence, working out our own Salvation with Fear and Trembling."[17]

Together with Balch's two ground-breaking sermons of three years earlier, Gay's 1746 convention sermon was one of the earliest public statements of fully fledged Arminianism by a Congregationalist minister. It gained added weight and provoked greater controversy because of Gay's relative seniority. But it was left to Mayhew's troubled and tragically short-lived Harvard contemporary, Briant of First Church, Braintree, to present the most outspoken critique of Calvinist orthodoxy of the late 1740s. In some ways, Briant's major offense was the sheer brazenness of his views in *Absurdity and Blasphemy of Depretiating Moral Virtue* (1749). As Wilson observed, he did not explicitly reject "the great Reformation principle that men are ultimately justified by grace" and he continued to deny that he did in subsequent defenses of his ideas against the publications of Bridgewater minister, John Porter, and others. But Briant did offer a widescale and often satirical critique of Calvinist doctrine, focusing on the foundational tenets of election and imputed righteousness. He especially decried the belief that "particular Persons are unconditionally chosen to eternal Life hereafter" on the grounds that "when they hear of our being saved by Grace, they conceive of it so as to destroy all moral Agency, and set themselves down with this vain Thought, that nothing on their Part is necessary to Salvation, but if they are designed for it, they shall irresistably be driven into Heaven, whether they will or not."[18]

17. Gay, *True Spirit*, 10.
18. Wilson, *Benevolent Deity*, 147; Briant, *Absurdity and Blasphemy*, 7. Briant's sermon was answered by Porter, *Absurdity and Blasphemy*, to which Briant responded in turn with *Some Friendly Remarks*. Porter and Cotton then issued *Vindication*, a counter-response. Briant subsequently replied to Porter and Cotton in *Some More Friendly*

Briant's primary target was thus what he perceived as lawless antinomianism based on a lack of appreciation for the value of good works. Instead, he argued, "it is the Righteousness of the Saints that renders them amiable in God's Sight, that is the Condition of all his Favours to them, and the sole Rule he will proceed by in judging of them; and dispensing eternal Rewards to them." The facts that Briant delivered this sermon from the pulpit of Boston's West Church just two years after Mayhew's 1747 ordination there, that Mayhew himself became a target in the pamphlet war of the early 1750s which followed, and that Briant subsequently suffered the same kind of heresy trial by ecclesiastical council as Arminians like Kent, Osborn, and Balch some years earlier, only serve to underline the explosive nature of the positions that Briant expounded and with which Mayhew was publicly identified, especially after the publication of his own *Seven Sermons* in 1749.[19]

Arminianism at West Church

Akers overstated his case in contending that "before his thirtieth birthday," Mayhew "had knocked down the creeds of Puritanism and on their ruins had erected a monument to the rational Christian who never neglected his sacred duty to resist both political and ecclesiastical tyrants." But it is clear that by June 1748, when he began to preach the *Seven Sermons* that were to become his first publication the following year, Mayhew had not only moved decisively to embrace Arminianism over orthodox Calvinism, he was prepared to make that transition very public. Where historians have differed significantly is over precisely when Mayhew's theology can first be identified as Arminian and exactly how he came to that position. Among other influences, Akers argued that "Harvard had encouraged him to mine fully the vein of rationalism inherent in Puritanism and to explore widely and freely the ideas of the European scholars who struggled to keep

---

Remarks. Finally, the elderly Calvinist, Samuel Niles, released his own thoughts on Briant's teachings in *A Vindication*.

19. Briant, *Absurdity and Blasphemy*, 20. In 1753, the second of two ecclesiastical councils held to consider charges against Briant which extended into the realm of personal morality, judged it "a Duty incumbent on" him "to endeavor to clear up your moral Character, as to the several scandalous Sins your Wife has charged you with, and to give your dissatisfied Brethren all Christian Satisfaction on these Points" (*Result of a Late Ecclesiastical Council*, 4). But as Shipton noted, a committee appointed by his church subsequently "both cleared him and nailed to the mast the flag of theological liberalism" (*New England Life*, 449–55, esp. 454). Briant soon resigned because of poor health, however, and he died just a year later in his early thirties on October 1, 1754. See, further, Anon, *Report of a Committee*.

Christianity alive in the Age of Reason." Rossiter claimed that between 1744 and 1747, Mayhew "had been moving steadily away from the five points of Calvinism," attributing major significance, with Alden Bradford, to a "liberalizing residence with the celebrated Dr. Ebenezer Gay of Hingham" in addition to his studies at Harvard. Wilson offered a more balanced account of this last relationship, which certainly became influential over time. While recognizing both the "close and enduring" friendship between Mayhew and Gay, to which the latter gave personal testimony in his ordination sermon at West Church, Wilson highlighted the lack of persuasive evidence that Mayhew either stayed with or was formally taught by Gay prior to that occasion. Rossiter further suggested that Mayhew's ordination was hindered by a pre-existing reputation for heterodoxy, but the problems at West Church in 1747 were more seriously complicated by other factors.[20]

The congregation had been founded under the leadership of the Scottish-born William Hooper just ten years earlier to meet the spiritual needs of the growing, upwardly mobile population of West Boston. Hooper was well received by his new parishioners, but less so by other Boston clergy, whom he soon unsettled with evidence of less than orthodox views on such questions as "the doctrines of grace and holiness, as preached in this country." Despite this rather inauspicious start, the first West Church minister seems to have avoided alienating his Congregationalist colleagues completely. But on November 19, 1746, he shocked them with the revelation that he had been called to serve as Rector of the nearby Church of England congregation, Trinity Church. A bereft West Church was left reeling. "Had it been possible," observed Gay at Mayhew's ordination seven months later, "ye would have almost plucked out your own Eyes, rather than have parted with him."[21]

20. Akers, *Called unto Liberty*, 60–61; Rossiter, "Life and Mind," 531–58, esp. 534; Bradford, *Memoir*, 21; Wilson, *Benevolent Deity*, 137–38; Gay, *Alienation of Affections*, 26. Akers, *Called unto Liberty*, 40–41, questioned the extent of Gay's influence, but Wilson argued that "while Alden Bradford's unsupported assertion that Gay was principally responsible for sending Mayhew down the Arminian road is an exaggeration, it should be noted that Gay and Mayhew did share a notably similar interest in certain authors" (*The Benevolent Deity*, 138). See, further, Gray, "Memoir of Dr. Jonathan Mayhew."

21. Akers, *Called unto Liberty*, 44–48; Wilson, *Benevolent Deity*, 138–39; Gay, *Alienation of Affections*, 23. On the relatively high social standing of members of West Church, as of First Church, see Corrigan, *Hidden Balance*, 114–25. In an appendix to a nineteenth-century history of West Church, Lowell included an extract from a February 13, 1740 letter from Hooper to Benjamin Colman, in which he defended himself against the charge, 74, that he had expressed the view, in a recent Thursday Lecture sermon, that "the doctrines of grace and holiness, as preached in this country, serve to lead the people into apprehensions of God as a peevish, vindictive, or revengeful Being" ("Discourse on William Hooper," 74–77, esp. 74).

Although a 1742 sermon, *Apostles Neither Impostors Nor Enthusiasts*, took a decidedly "Old Light" view of the Great Awakening, Hooper's published works from his years at West Church betray no sign of aggressive Arminianism. But the substance of his colleagues' early complaints against him tends to support the view of a nineteenth-century successor at the church, Charles Lowell, who described Hooper as appearing "not to have been a Calvinist." In that sense, West Church was already accustomed to a minister whom Wilson described as "a mild Arminian" when Mayhew arrived. Nor, according to Bradford, did members of the pre-ordination council conduct "a particular inquiry as to the doctrinal creed of Mr. Mayhew." Had they done so, it remains unclear precisely what they would have found, and not only because of the lack of extant evidence from Mayhew himself. The fact that his ordination had to be postponed to June 17 from May 20, 1747, when only two of the invited ministers arrived to conduct it, seems to have reflected West Church's impolitic decision to restrict invitations to just five congregations, including two of Boston's ten Congregationalist churches, rather than a theological boycott of Mayhew of the kind that Rossiter suggested. Both Colman of Brattle Street and Foxcroft of First Church, who were initially invited alongside Experience Mayhew, Gay, and Nathaniel Appleton of Cambridge, to help form the ordination council, were troubled by the congregation's failure to include representatives from the eight other city churches and ultimately demurred. According to the West Church records, on "the [first] Day appointed for the Ordination there were only Two Ch[urche]s that favoured us with their presence . . . the Ch[urc]h at Cambridge, & the Ch[urc]h at Hingham which not being the major part of those that were Invited, the Revd. Pastors thought it advisable not to proceed & advised the Ch[urc]h to apply to other Churches."[22]

Mayhew's ordination was finally completed on the second attempt by representatives from eleven of the fifteen churches invited from outside

22. Hooper, *Apostles Neither Impostors*; Lowell, "Discourse on William Hooper," 64; Wilson, *Benevolent Deity*, 139; Bradford, *Memoir*, 27; Rossiter, "Life and Mind," 531–58, esp. 534; West Church Record Book, 8–10, esp. 9. According to Gray, since Mayhew "voluntarily declared to the Council, his hearty belief of the Doctrines of Grace as revealed in the holy Scriptures the only rule of Faith And his resolution by Gods grace to preach such doctrines and such only as should therein appear to be revealed: And as the Church declared, their being satisfied, with his principles, The Council had no difficulty in ordaining him. They were Gentlemen of too much good sense and understanding, to make any human Creeds whatever the Standard of Orthodoxy" ("Memoir of Dr. Jonathan Mayhew," 32–33). West Church officially recorded that "the Procedure of the Ch[urc]h in accepting a Pastor was carefully examined into, and unanimously approved" (West Church Record Book, 10). For the most reliable secondary account of the circumstances surrounding Mayhew's ordination, see Akers, *Called unto Liberty*, 47–53.

Boston, led by Gay, whose sermon on that occasion has been interpreted by Wilson as a carefully worded but nonetheless clarion call to Mayhew and his new congregation to claim their liberty from Calvinist dogma and elitism and to preach and receive the uncorrupted, inherently reasonable message of authentic Christianity. But although the Hingham pastor clearly spoke out against ecclesiastical factionalism and highlighted, among other things, "the great and indispensable Duty of Ministers, to tell People the Truth," however uncomfortable or inconvenient, his biblical exegesis of Galatians 4:13-16 interpreted "Christian Liberty" within the quite narrow context of Christians' "Freedom from the Servitude of the Mosaic Yoke," and from "the Bondage of the Ceremonial Law." It was left to Mayhew himself, in his series of *Seven Sermons* delivered at Thursday lectures between June and August, 1748, to begin to clarify the contours of the Arminian gospel for which he was to become so famous over the next eighteen years of his ministry.[23]

Mayhew gave the fullest expositions of his major problems with traditional, reformed doctrine in his fourteen sermons *On Hearing the Word* (1755) and in *Two Sermons on Divine Goodness* (1763). But his anti-Calvinism is evident throughout his published career, beginning in the late 1740s. As the titles of the individual sermons make clear, one of Mayhew's central burdens in *Seven Sermons* (1749) was to urge the rational reliability and open accessibility of all truth, including moral truth, and so the human ability, right, and duty to exercise free and informed judgment, especially in matters of religion and morality. Mayhew explicitly denied "the doctrine of a total ignorance, and incapacity to judge of moral and religious truths, brought upon mankind by the apostacy of our First Parents" and he cited apostolic precedent for "freedom of thought." In appealing to one of the key texts which he deployed in that connection throughout his ministerial career, he clearly extended its application from "freedom from the mosaic law" in a strictly Pauline sense to a much broader definition of religious liberty. But this freedom was primarily available so that humankind could freely serve God by obeying Christ's twofold commandment to love God and one's neighbor. Right from the beginning of his most public phase of ministry, Mayhew thus urged the fulfillment of moral duty as the *summum bonum* of true religion and the primary source of human happiness. He defined "the whole tenor of our Lord's preaching" as "moral" and contended that "all the gospel of Jesus Christ hangs on these two commandments, in the same sense that all the law and the prophets did."[24]

23. Wilson, *Benevolence of the Deity,* 140-42; Gay, *Alienation of Affections,* 10, 19. The ministers of two of the eleven churches represented by delegates did not attend "by Reason of their Indisposition of Body" (West Church Record Book, 10).

24. Mayhew, *Seven Sermons,* 38, 53, 55-56, esp. 56, 148, 143; *Divine Goodness*; *On*

Such an optimistic yet moralistic vision of the Christian life would have been problematic enough for traditional Calvinists. For them the bonds of total depravity ultimately constrained and frustrated independent human efforts to know God's truth, still less to live by it, without the prior revelation, regeneration, and reinvigoration of the overwhelming power of divine grace. But Mayhew compounded his offense against orthodox teaching by failing to resist the seemingly logical corollary of his positive affirmations of human potential. Having established the importance of free ethical decision-making and moral virtue, Mayhew devoted the last of his *Seven Sermons* to "The Love of God, the first and great Commandment, &c." He not only concluded that "the main design of the christian institution is evidently to bring men to that moral purity of heart and life, which is comprised in the love of God and of our neighbour," he also rejected what he termed "solifidian [faith-only] doctrines," including the classical reformed understanding of justification by grace through faith [in Christ] alone, as well as the central Calvinist tenet of unconditional election. "Neither the most exact compliance with the positive precepts of the gospel," Mayhew argued, "nor any kind or degree of faith, unaccompanied with a principle of sincere piety and charity; nor, indeed, any thing else, where the love of God and man are wanting, can intitle us to the divine acceptance hereafter; or make us meet to be partakers of the inheritance of the saints in light." Then, just in case his readers mistook this stipulation of good works as a necessary prerequisite for Christian salvation, he left no one in any doubt:

> If we believe in Christ and his gospel, so far it is well: but this does but lay the foundation for our doing that, upon which our salvation finally turns . . . It is practical religion, the love of God, and a life of righteousness and charity, proceeding from faith in Christ and the gospel, that denominates us good men and good Christians . . . —Not the belief of any doctrines, however true, concerning the atonement of Christ—Not a lazy recumbency upon the righteousness of another . . . Not a firm perswasion that we are elected of God . . . Some of the worst men in the world, have as much faith as any in it—attend upon sermons and sacraments as often—rely as confidently—have as warm frames and lively imaginations—and are as fully perswaded of their being chosen to salvation. But what does all this avail, if that faith be without works?[25]

Hearing the Word. The "key text" was Gal 5:1: "Stand fast therefore in the liberty wherewith Christ hath made us free, and be not entangled again with the yoke of bondage." All biblical quotations are from the *King James Version*.

25. Mayhew, *Seven Sermons*, 131, 145–46, citing Col 1:12, 148. See, further, 54.

Confronted with this open rejection of New England orthodoxy, it is not surprising that the often reserved Foxcroft of First Church took the opportunity, in a note attached to Porter's and John Cotton's *Vindication* (1751), to suggest that that the "distinguishing Tenet" of Briant's friend, "Dr. Mayhew," was "that Christ did not preach the Gospel, nor design'd to do it, but his Doctrines and Manner of Preaching were LEGAL." Yet Mayhew was quite unrepentant. In fact, he returned to his understanding of justification six years later in *On Hearing the Word*, where he also stated Arminian positions in other key areas. In a long note on the topic of freedom and necessity appended to Sermon IX, for example, Mayhew re-affirmed his inherently cooperative understanding of divine grace working with human initiative to yield obedience to Christian principles and commandments. He also implicitly denied Calvinist teaching on total depravity.[26]

As defined by Mayhew's contemporary, Dickinson, in 1741, the classical Reformed doctrine of original sin entailed:

1. That the whole World of Mankind are by Nature in a State of Sin and Guilt.

2. That this State of Sin and Guilt, which we are naturally in, is the Fruit of Adam's Apostacy.

3. That we are by Vertue [sic] of this Sin and Guilt justly liable to Death, temporal, spiritual, and eternal.

But Mayhew restated a more optimistic view of human nature. "God does actually afford, or is at least ready to afford, his aid and assistance to men, in such manner and such measure, that they may, thereby, work out their own salvation," he argued. So "if they do not, it is owing to criminal neglect of the power which they have, notwithstanding the supposed depravity, and real imbecility of human nature," which he clearly rejected in classical terms. In an unpublished sermon written as early as March 1749, Mayhew upheld the traditional view that all people were sinners and thus "obnoxious to the wrath and curse of God" pending compliance with "the Terms of the

---

For other generally dismissive comments about Calvinism, see, for example, Mayhew, *Striving to Enter*, 82–87; *On Hearing the Word*, 303n, 403–4. It is significant to note, however, as Howe has argued, that the leading Calvinist of Mayhew's age, Jonathan Edwards, shared the views that "people were capable of knowing the right by means of their natural conscience" and that "there was such a thing as a natural morality, discoverable by human reason." For Edwards, "the problem lay in the will, in the helplessness of the conscience to motivate right action" (*Making the American Self*, 35–36).

26. Porter and Cotton, *Vindication*, 43–46n, esp. 46n, where Foxcroft specifically referenced [and slightly misquoted] Mayhew's *Seven Sermons*, 148–49; Mayhew, *On Hearing the Word*, 294–303n.

Gospel." He also stated that "the only way in which we can be received into favour again" was by virtue of the "gracious method of Salvation," whereby Christ had been "set forth to be a propit[iat]ion for our sins, thro' faith in his Blood." But Mayhew refuted any understanding of original sin as directly inherited from Adam and Eve. It was not his "design," he told the congregation of West Church, "to intimate that the Transgression of our first Parents was not the source of various Calamities to their Offspring," yet he could not accept that "we are strictly and properly speaking transgressors of the Law, and Sinners, antecedent to our own personal Sins; and by Virtue of the Sin of our Progenitors." This was simply "not agreable to truth, Reason or Scripture." For God "would not act as becomes the righteous Governor of the world, in imputing that Sin to us, which we never committed, and then punishing us for it as tho' we had actually committed."[27]

The basic assumption of human freedom of choice was consistently central to Mayhew's theological anthropology. In *Seven Sermons* (1749) he argued that "men are naturally endowed with faculties proper for distinguishing betwixt truth and error, right and wrong," and he extended that argument in *On Hearing the Word* (1755). "There is not the least contradiction or absurdity," Mayhew contended, "in the supposition of a creature's having active power, or being a free agent." In fact, "to deny to this great first Cause [i.e., to God], the power of imparting to his creatures a measure of freedom; or of making a free creature, who can either chuse and act, or not, within a certain sphere, (how narrow and limited soever that sphere may be) is making much too free with him." Mayhew's sense of the need to uphold free will thus weighed heavily in his rejection of the traditional doctrine of total depravity, as did his desire not to limit divine sovereignty by denying God the power to bestow genuine freedom on humankind. Similar considerations applied in his refusal to endorse the Calvinist doctrine of "unconditional election." The traditional position expressed by Dickinson was that "God never design'd Salvation to any Unbeliever: but eternally determin'd to give his own Son a Ransom for the Elect; and to give an Interest in him by Faith, and thereby a Title to eternal Life, unto all those that are chosen to it." But for Mayhew, this not only represented an unduly deterministic view of salvation history, it also made a mockery of the infinite goodness of God,

27. Dickinson, *True Scripture-Doctrine*, 76; Mayhew, *On Hearing the Word*, 298–302; Mayhew, "Sermon on 1 John 3:3–4," March 1749, *Collection of Sermons*, esp. 19–21, 30–31, 24. Calvin defined original sin as "a hereditary depravity and corruption of our nature, diffused into all parts of the soul, which first makes us liable to God's wrath, then also brings forth in us those works which Scripture calls 'works of the flesh' [Gal 5:19]" (*Institutes*, 251).This quotation is taken from Ford Lewis Battles's translation of the 1559 version of *Institutes*. On Mayhew's understanding of original sin see, further, Smith, *Changing Conceptions*, 22–25.

for which he argued so forcefully throughout his career, most notably in *Divine Goodness* (1763). The idea of eternal reprobation, in particular, was anathema:

> What shall we say to the doctrine of God's having reprobated a great proportion of mankind; or, from eternity devoted them in his absolute decree and purpose, to eternal torments, without any respect or regard to any sins of theirs, as the procuring and meritorious cause of their perdition? . . . I will tell you, in a very few words, what I have to say to it at present. And that is, first, That if any persons really hold such a doctrine, neither any man on earth, nor angel in heaven, can reconcile it with the goodness of God. And, secondly, That I have not my self the least inclination to attempt a reconciliation of these doctrines; being perswaded, that they are just as contrary as light and darkness, Christ & Belial.[28]

Although he openly questioned whether "all the heathen will actually be miserable in the world to come," Mayhew was no universalist. But he had strong words for what he called "dark systems of divinity," which had the perceived effect of narrowing the scope of God's saving love and "disturbing truly pious and good christians with doubts and fears." Instead of the insecurities, speculative uncertainties, and dangerous errors of Calvinist orthodoxy, Mayhew preferred a grander, more confident vision of divine grace. Great punishment was indeed to be expected for "those who die impenitently under the gospel." But "God certainly exercises great goodness and mercy towards such sinners in this world," in that "all are invited and perswaded, in the most gracious and pathetic terms, to accept of eternal life, thro' Him [i.e., Jesus Christ] that 'gave himself a ransom for all.'" Mayhew thus wrote of an unlimited rather than a limited atonement, achieved through the saving death of Christ. He did not deny the role and importance of divine grace in his soteriology. But rather than maintaining, with Dickinson, that through his atoning sacrifice on the cross, Christ's "Satisfaction is sufficient for all; but actually applied and effectual to none but the Believer," Mayhew vigorously upheld that all may work out their own salvation.[29]

---

28. Mayhew, *Seven Sermons*, 38; *On Hearing the Word*, 296n; *Divine Goodness*, 66; Dickinson, *True Scripture-Doctrine*, 4. See the statement by the 1618–19 Synod of Dort that "the good pleasure of God is the sole cause of . . . gracious election," whereby God "was pleased out of the common mass of sinners to adopt some certain persons as a peculiar people to himself" (cited in Ferm, *Readings*, 401).

29. Mayhew, *Divine Goodness*, 65, 50, 66–67, citing 1 Tim 2:6; Dickinson, *True Scripture-Doctrine*, 179; *On Hearing the Word*, 300. Mayhew offered a more extensive definition of justification as involving "the remission of sins, the acceptance of our

Mayhew also went beyond a reformed understanding of the atonement as penal substitution in the sense that Christ died in the place of and to pay the price and bear the punishment for the sins of humanity. He nowhere explicitly denied the doctrine espoused by Dickinson and like-minded Calvinists, that "God the Father, as sustaining the Character of Supreme in the Oeconomy of Redemption, demands Satisfaction to offended Justice [as a result of human sin], and has allotted this Way of obtaining it, by Christ's being a Propitiation for us." In fact, he affirmed it on a number of occasions. But Mayhew additionally advanced a more "governmental" interpretation of the atonement. "Infinite goodness itself," he argued, "considered in connection with infinite wisdom, requires that order, and the highest veneration for the majesty of God, his laws and government, should be preserved amongst all his reasonable creatures. Their own good essentially depends on it." For Mayhew, "this important end" was "most effectually attained by the sacrifice of Christ 'by whom we have received the atonement.'" The underlying assumptions here, as the West Church minister made clear in *Christian Sobriety*, a collection of eight sermons published in 1763, as well as in *Divine Goodness* (1755), were that "SINFUL men, as such, need a mediator between God and them; a redeemer and saviour from sin and death," and that Jesus Christ performed that role, thus "supporting the honor of God's violated commandments, and the dignity of his government."[30]

Another important way in which Mayhew departed from Calvinist orthodoxy was in his decidedly Arminian reinterpretation of justification by faith as a work that not only required human cooperation, but could not rest on the imputed righteousness of Christ. "I cannot but just observe here," Mayhew wrote in a footnote to Sermon VI of *On Hearing the Word*

---

persons to the favour and friendship of God, and a title to eternal life in the kingdom of heaven" (*On Hearing the Word*, 206-7). For Mayhew's doctrine of an unlimited atonement, see also *Christian Sobriety*, 66. The Synod of Dort stated that "it was the will of God, that Christ by the blood of the cross ... should effectually redeem ... all those, and those only, who were from eternity chosen to salvation" (cited in Ferm, *Readings*, 402). Soteriology" is here understood as theology of Christian salvation.

30. Dickinson, *True Scripture-Doctrine*, 179; Mayhew, *Divine Goodness*, 64, citing Rom 5:11, 49; *Christian Sobriety*, 90. Mayhew clearly subscribed to a penal substitutionary, as well as a "governmental," doctrine of the atonement. "Christ's atonement," he argued, "or his suffering, the just for the unjust, or in the room, place or stead of sinners, (which I suppose the true, natural import of that expression) was not in order to their being exempted from any disciplinary correction, or medicinal punishment, for their real good; ... but in order to their being exempted from that punishment, to which they might otherwise have been subjected; in order to vindicate the honor of God's law and government; for the support of order, and therein for the good of the universe, which essentially depends thereon" (*Letter of Reproof*, 12). See further James Jones, *Shattered Synthesis*, 152-54.

(1755), "that the scripture teaches no such doctrine as that of God's imputing the perfect righteousness of Christ to sinners for justification." On the contrary, it was a "grand, capital error" to suggest that "the merits of Christ's obedience and sufferings, may be so applied or imputed to sinners, as to be available to their justification and salvation, altho' they are destitute of all personal inherent goodness." Mayhew understood "justification," in a traditional sense, to signify "the remission of the penalty denounced against the violators of God's law." But while "the doctrine of the gospel undoubtedly is, that we are justified by faith," it was, nevertheless, "a great mistake to infer from hence, that we are accepted to the divine favour, and entitled to eternal life, without unfeigned repentance, and new obedience." On the one hand, "they go upon a wrong hypothesis, who suppose that any acts of external obedience are the ground of our justification, or necessary in order thereto"; it was faith, not works, which served that purpose and Mayhew "constantly disclaim[ed] the doctrine of merit." On the other, faith itself involved not only "an hearty belief," but an "inward submission" to the terms of the gospel, and such submission "will, whenever there is opportunity and scope for it, be accompanied with a corresponding obedience of life."[31]

Because it required active repentance and good works, Mayhew's resulting vision of faith in action was more complex and more morally demanding than that of Protestant Reformers like Martin Luther, whose ["solifidian"] "article of a standing, or a falling church" he plainly rejected. But although it was clearly Arminian, it did not involve a Pelagian understanding of salvation by works. Mayhew stated his position with some specificity in *On Hearing the Word* (1755):

> WHATSOEVER is necessary, according to the terms laid down in the gospel, in order to our having a title to eternal life in the kingdom of heaven, is necessary in order to our being justified in this world. But in order to our having such a title, it is necessary, that we repent of our sins and obey the gospel: This is, therefore, necessary in order to our justification.

As James Jones has argued, the West Church minister's understanding of salvation was thus both "conditional," in the sense that it required the

---

31. Mayhew, *On Hearing the Word*, 157n, 107, 175, 171–72, 179–80n, 180. Mayhew strongly argued that "if this quality is essential to a true justifying faith; viz. that it is operative, and productive of good works; and if the faith which has this property, certainly justifies the subject of it; it follows that faith justifies, only considered as having that property; i.e. on account of the obedience involved in the idea of it" (*On Hearing the Word*, 247). He clearly rejected the position of Dickinson, for whom "his [Christ's] Righteousness imputed to us is the only Ground of our Justification" (*True Scripture-Doctrine*, 193).

fulfillment of certain conditions of behavior, and "free," inasmuch as "any certain connexion between the endeavours of sinful creatures to obtain eternal life, and their actually obtaining it . . . is a connexion which the free grace, or unmerited goodness of God, has made and established."[32]

For Mayhew, as for other Arminians, however, a fourth tenet of traditional Calvinism, "irresistible grace," was also unscriptural. The position of Dickinson and others that "God hath eternally known and eternally willed the whole future Salvation of each individual Heir of everlasting Life and Glory; and . . . their Salvation, being founded upon the Foreknowledge and Will of God, is like his glorious Nature necessary and infallible" was totally unacceptable. There could be no binding link between the call of divine grace and appropriate human response solely on the basis of divine election. Salvation was available to all who were truly "striving to enter in at the strait gate," not just to a chosen few, and men and women were clearly capable of rejecting God's gracious invitation. In *Striving to Enter* (1761), Mayhew conceded that "there is grace accompanying the dispensation of the gospel, sufficient to render it effectual to the salvation of those who hear it." But that was only on the provision that "they are really desirous of, and endeavor after it." So "we see from hence the wonderful goodness and mercy of God; inasmuch as he has given us the strongest assurances of pardon and eternal life, on such terms as, by his offered grace, we may all comply with, if we really desire to do it."[33]

Given the inherent impermanence of any human desire, however noble, it was also quite possible, therefore, for anyone to relapse, even after responding in true faith and obedience. Hence Mayhew's denial of the fifth point of Dortian Calvinism—the necessary "perseverance [in saving faith unto death] of the saints." For Dickinson, "Perseverance in Grace" was a "necessary Consequence" of biblical doctrine and a clear manifestation of God's "everlasting Love." But in his *Practical Discourses* (1760), Mayhew sought to remind his hearers "of these representations in the holy scriptures; which show the possibility and danger of awakened sinners, yea, of partially reformed ones, returning, after a time, to their vicious courses; and dying at last in their iniquities." So while it was important for him to affirm that "all who really desire and strive to obtain eternal life, will certainly obtain

---

32. Mayhew, *On Hearing the Word*, 255, 219; *Seven Sermons*, 148; James Jones, *Shattered Synthesis*, 155; Mayhew, *Striving to Enter*, 44. For a helpful definition of Pelagianism, as of many other theological terms used here, see Gonzales, *Essential Theological Terms*, esp. 128–29. The Synod of Dort defined "faith" as "the gift of God . . . because he who works in man both to will and to do, and indeed all things in all, produces both the will to believe and the act of believing also" (cited in Ferm, *Readings*, 404).

33. Dickinson, *True Scripture-Doctrine*, 25; Mayhew, *Striving to Enter*, 67, 77.

it," and thus to foster assurance and dispense with unnecessary doubts and fears, he also accepted the corollary of that proposition—that salvation depended at least partly on one's own efforts. "If it should be objected," he wrote in his sixth sermon *On Hearing the Word* (1755), "that this doctrine leads men to trust to their own righteousness; I answer it is very reasonable they should do so, in one sense . . . Certainly then good men may so far trust to their own righteousness, as to believe it will be available with a gracious God, thro' the Mediator; so as to procure eternal life for them."[34]

Over the course of his seventeen-year publishing career, Mayhew thus openly, repeatedly, and quite systematically rejected every major tenet that had traditionally defined Calvinist orthodoxy in face of the Arminian challenge. Predecessors like Balch and Briant may have laid the groundwork and been earlier pioneers in stating similar views. But no New England Congregationalist before Mayhew had advanced such positions so fully or so definitively. Although it cannot be shown decisively that Mayhew explicitly rejected the Calvinist doctrines of irresistible grace or the perseverance of the saints before the early 1760s, the evidence of his extant works would suggest that he reached most, if not all, of his Arminian positions by the time that he published *On Hearing the Word* (1755). His theology was consistently Arminian from at least the second year of his ministry at West Church, in 1748, if not before. One of the key differences between Mayhew and his more cautious colleague, Chauncy, was that when the latter arrived at quite similar conclusions, it was to take him much longer to find sufficient personal assurance and public confidence to assert them.

Chauncy's Mid-Life Crisis

On April 14, 1754, when Chauncy wrote to his cousin Nathanael, who was then a minister in Durham, Connecticut, he was just two years into a decisive seven-year period that apparently led to a complete reorientation of his theology from Calvinism to Arminianism and beyond. But he was already indicating ill-defined problems with the Calvinist doctrine of original sin. He had been reading the work of John Taylor, a contemporary English dissenter of what Lippy described as "pronounced Arminian sympathies," whose *Scripture-Doctrine of Original Sin* (1740) denied traditional Calvinist notions of imputed guilt (from Adam to the whole of humanity) and thus

---

34. Dickinson, *True Scripture-Doctrine*, 59; Mayhew, *Practical Discourses*, 354; *Striving to Enter*, 49; *On Hearing the Word*, 167. When the Synod of Dort treated the "doctrine of the perseverance of the saints," it spoke of the "certainty thereof, which God hath most abundantly revealed in his Word" (cited in Ferm, *Readings*, 406).

total depravity. But while Chauncy expressed his "great value" of Taylor, he thought him "very much mistaken in his doctrine of original sin, and in his performance of the Epistle of Romans." He also informed his cousin of his wish "to let you see what I have written upon Paul's Epistles," which showed that "the commonly received [i.e. Calvinist] opinions are quite remote from the truth." By 1768 Chauncy already had three "dissertations" virtually ready for publication on the topics of sin and the Fall, but these would be finally released, with two others, only in the 1780s. Only after public controversy was sparked in New England by the publication of *Winter Evening's Conversation* (1757) by Samuel Webster, minister of Salisbury, Massachusetts, which openly advocated Taylor's views, was Chauncy prompted to give the first indications of the theological struggles that were leading him not only into Arminianism, but ultimately well beyond.[35]

Wright and Wilson have documented the continuing growth of Arminianism in New England in the 1750s and 1760s despite the strong Calvinist opposition evident in persistent disciplinary proceedings against clergy and in vigorous theological controversy. In works like Gay's 1759 Dudleian Lecture at Harvard, *Natural Religion,* Arminians also became bolder and more assertive in expressing their views of the inherent dignity, even virtue, of humankind. "Taylorism" not only encouraged their rejection of traditional notions of inherited sin and guilt, but facilitated the adoption of analytical Bible study methods, which led some who deployed them, like Chauncy, to arrive at hitherto unorthodox positions. Edwards came to see Taylor's ideas as so threatening that he was prompted to write his own overwhelming response in *Great Christan Doctrine of Original Sin Defended* (1758). The more moderate minister of First Church, Salem Village, Peter Clark, took up the same cause in a much less substantial treatise, *Scripture-Doctrine of Original Sin* (1758) and it was Clark's work that provoked Chauncy into public controversy for the first time since the Great Awakening. Even so, Chauncy's caution remained palpable. He chose to publish anonymously in the form of "a letter to a friend" and his *Opinion of One that Has Perused the*

---

35. Chauncy to Nathaniel Chauncy, April 14, 1754, reprinted in Fowler, "President Charles Chauncy," esp. 335; Chauncy, "Sketch of Eminent Men," 163; Webster, *Winter Evening's Conversation.* See Taylor, *Scripture-Doctrine*; *Paraphrase with Notes.* On Taylor and his "Arminian sympathies," see Lippy, *Seasonable Revolutionary,* 60; Wright, *Unitarianism in America,* 76–78. Griffin helpfully defined Taylor's views on sin in the following terms: "Taylor argued that Adam and Eve had begun their lives not in a state of righteousness, but on a primitive moral level; that therefore the fall was a falling short of righteousness, not a falling from it; and that their guilt is not transferable, since guilt can only be personal. Instead of the traditional theory he argued that humans are born neither righteous nor sinful, but capable of being either, as they improve or neglect 'the Goodness of God'" (*Old Brick,* 121, citing Smith, *Changing Conceptions,* 10–36).

Summer Morning's Conversation (1758) was hardly the kind of contribution to the debate over Taylorism that might have been expected following a period of radical theological reformulation. Chauncy began by stating that his "expectations . . . were considerably raised, when [he] heard, that the Rev. Mr. Clark, a Gentleman noted for piety, good sense, learning and candor, as well as for Calvinistical Orthodoxy, had undertaken to answer the *Winter evening's conference about original sin*." Moreover, while he ended up criticizing Clark's work, rather than Taylor's or Webster's, the two main grounds on which he chose to do so were ostensibly thoroughly orthodox:

> The first is, that this Gentleman, so far as I am able to judge, has unhappily said that, which renders it impossible the doctrine of the imputation of Adam's guilt to his posterity should be true, I mean in the full sense in which it is maintained by Calvinists. The second is, that tho' he wears the appearance of a friend to the doctrine of imputed guilt, as held by Calvinists, yet he has deserted this doctrine, nay, given it up, as it maintains that mankind universally, infants as well as others, are liable to the damnation of hell-fire, on account of Adam's first sin.[36]

In stating his second main criticism of Clark, however, Chauncy could not forbear expressing agreement with a departure from strict Calvinist doctrine. By contending that those who died before reaching the age of accountability were not liable to eternal damnation in hell, Clark was apparently undermining the traditional understanding of original sin, which included the imputation of Adam's guilt to all humanity. "'Tis not a secret thing," Chauncy wrote, "in the opinion of Calvinists, that infants, as well as others, are justly liable, viewed as the children of Adam, to the damnation of hell," and Clark had failed to uphold that teaching. But although he noted it, Chauncy personally endorsed this departure from stringent orthodoxy. He could not "blame this Gentleman for hoping the best concerning the future state of infants: Nor do I find any fault with him." Compared with the forceful language and controversial style of some of Chauncy's other works, such remarks were cautiously phrased. He expressed a wish at one point, for example, that "this Gentleman, notwithstanding his hoping so well of those

---

36. Wright, *Unitarianism in America*, 72–5; Wilson, *Benevolent Deity*, 154–91, passim; Gay, *Natural Religion*; Edwards, *Great Christian Doctrine*; Peter Clark, *Scripture-Doctrine*; Chauncy, *Opinion of One*, 3, 5. See, further, Lippy, *Seasonable Revolutionary*, 61–2. Among those dismissed for Arminian "heresy" in the 1750s were John Bass of Ashford, Connecticut, in 1751, and John Rogers of Leominster, Massachusetts, in 1758. By far the most significant Calvinist theological apologist was Edwards, not only in *Great Christian Doctrine*, but in his *Careful and Strict Enquiry*. Chauncy explicitly recorded his indebtedness to Taylor's exegetical methods in *Mystery Hid*, xi–xii.

who die in infancy, had gone particularly and largely into a reconciliation of the Calvinistical doctrine, as opposed by his Antagonist, with the perfections of God." Yet even as Chauncy voiced that wistful hope, he implicitly acknowledged his own theological misgivings. "There is yet opportunity" [for such reconciliation], he wrote, "and he may hereby greatly serve the cause of orthodoxy, by removing away the greatest stumbling-block in the way of its being embraced." It would be twenty-seven years before Chauncy finally felt able to express his own thorough reinterpretation of the doctrine of original sin in *Five Dissertations* (1785). In the meantime, having signaled at least a serious question, if not a major rejection of orthodox Calvinism in 1758, his published theological positions moved in a perceptibly more Arminian direction from the 1760s onwards.[37]

The primary work in which this first became clear was Chauncy's *Twelve Sermons.* (1765), which marked a major shift from his previous views on the nature of faith, Christian salvation, and the relationship between divine grace and human good works. It is obvious from Chauncy's many critiques, especially of *Letters on Theron and Aspasio* (1759), that *Twelve Sermons* was initially provoked by the teaching and New England ministry of the Scottish nonconformist theologian, Robert Sandeman, and particularly by his espousal of a minimalist understanding of faith as mere intellectual conviction. But the full title of Chauncy's sermon collection reveals much broader aims and objectives, and within that ambitious agenda there were four central themes, of which two were ostensibly orthodox. He thus continued to advocate a strong view of God's sovereignty and of the primacy of divine grace in human salvation. Chauncy began *Twelve Sermons* with clear and very traditional-sounding arguments that people were "universally sinners, in the eye of law" and that if they were to enjoy God's saving favor, they needed justification, whereby God must "approve, accept, vindicate or adjudge [them] as just." He contended that "all works, whether of Jews, Pagans, or Christians," were "excluded from justification, law, rigid law, being the rule of tryal," and that "nothing but the interposition of grace [through the mediatorial work of Christ]" could "deliver them from the power of the grave." If divine law, like good works, could not save, it nonetheless had two key purposes, both of which Chauncy again defined in very conventional terms:

> The first is contained in those words, The law "was added because of transgressions, till the seed should come to whom the

---

37. Chauncy, *Opinion of One*, 16–17, 19. Chauncy also suggested, 27, that holding Clark's view on infant salvation with integrity should be no bar to continuing in pastoral office.

promise was made"—The second is thus expressed, "The law was our school-master to bring us unto Christ, that we might be justified by faith."[38]

It was only when Chauncy turned to a third theme of defining faith that the full extent of his newly revealed Arminianism started to become apparent. For genuine Christian faith not only involved much more than Sandeman's simple intellectual acceptance of gospel truth. Chauncy argued that it could not even rest entirely on a heartfelt reliance on Christ. Instead, it "must be . . . such a persuasion of the truth, as shall be effectual to conform our hearts and lives to the will of God, and the example of our Savior and master, Jesus Christ." So "the faith which denominates . . . a justified believer, must contain in it, in God's estimation, repentance, the new-birth and gospel-obedience." Although Chauncy understandably did not highlight the fact, this was a very different interpretation of the definition of faith than he had embraced during the Great Awakening. Chauncy had earlier taken the traditional Puritan view that holiness of life would follow saving faith, or that sanctification would be evidence, but never a means, of justification. Now he included "gospel-obedience" as part of faith itself. He recognized that in doing so he was laying himself open to criticism. "It will probably, be tho't by some," he wrote, "that I have been greatly deficient in not making the essence of faith, as justifying, to consist in the soul's relyance on Christ, or trusting in his righteousness, as the only pleadable title to life . . . In answer whereto I would say, I know of no text, in all the bible, that gives this idea of faith."[39]

---

38. Chauncy, *Twelve Sermons*, 10, 3, 5, 27, 47, citing Gal 3:19, 24; Sandeman, *Letters on Theron and Aspasio*; Walker, "Sandemanians of New England," 139. For a summary of Sandeman's teachings, see Lippy, *Seasonable Revolutionary*, 84. According to the full title of *Twelve Sermons*, Chauncy sought to cover nothing less than *the Following Seasonable and Important Subjects, Justification Impossible by the Works of the Law. The Question Answered, "Wherefore then Serveth the Law?" The Nature of Faith, as Justifying, Largely Explained, and Remarked on. The Place, and Use, of Faith, in the Affair of Justification, Human Endeavours, in the Use of Means, the Way in Which Faith Is Obtained. The Method of the Spirit in Communicating the "Faith, by Which the Just Do Live." The Inquiry of the Young Man in the Gospel, "What Shall I Do that I May Have Eternal Life?" With Interspersed Notes, in Defence of the Truth, Especially in the Points Treated On, in the above Discourses.*

39. Chauncy, *Twelve Sermons*, 111, 112, 113n. In 1742, Chauncy defined faith as "the produce of that internal work of his [God's] upon the mind of the sinner, whereby, the eyes of his understanding being opened, he has such a view of the suitableness of the gospel method of salvation in general, and of the loveliness of christ in particular, his all-sufficiency to be his saviour, as that he is persuaded and enabled to embrace him as such, giving himself up to him, to be instructed, governed and saved by him" (*Outpouring of the Holy-Ghost*, 16).

A last major theme to emerge from *Twelve Sermons* was thoroughly consistent with Chauncy's radical redefinition of faith, for he also advocated a much more synergistic understanding of the whole process of Christian salvation than in his earlier writings. Just as he had come to see obedience as a constituent part of the saving faith that would lead to justification, he stressed the importance of the use of appropriate means, not only to prepare for spiritual regeneration and salvation, but in some sense to achieve it. "Sinners ... may do a great many things in religion," Chauncy argued, and

> what makes these endeavours of sinners most of all reasonable, and fit, is the consideration, that they may, of the mercy of God, thro' Jesus Christ, turn out, in the end, to their spiritual and everlasting advantage. And this leads me to say ... that tis "ordinarily" in concurrence with "these endeavours" of sinners, that God bestows his Spirit to "begin," as well as carry on, the work of faith in their hearts.

Chauncy's views on this topic are not always clear, and despite their apparent consonance with earlier Puritan ideas of "preparation," he seemed almost painfully aware of the dangers of moving too far toward any suggestion that people might in any way earn their salvation. So even as he urged the importance and saving significance of Christian obedience and good works, he also underlined the supremacy of divine grace. But the result was a typically Arminian compromise. On the one hand, Chauncy argued in the last of his *Twelve Sermons*, "no doings of ours are to be look't upon, as the reason, or consideration, upon which the gift of [eternal] life is made. In this sense, all works of righteousness, done by us, are totally useless." On the other, "faith, conversion" are "not only spoken of, in the inspired writings, as 'the work of God,' but a work that he begins, maintains, carries on, and compleats, with the 'concurring agency of men themselves,' in the use of various means wisely adapted to the purpose."[40]

In subsequent works issued prior to the full revelation of Chauncy's radical theological re-orientation in the 1780s, it is significant to note that the doctrinal content is often virtually indistinguishable from that of earlier products of his Calvinist orthodoxy. Preaching at the funeral of Foxcroft in 1769, for example, Chauncy upheld his late ministerial colleague as a model of saving faith, "fixing his dependence, not on his own worthiness, not on any works of righteousness which he had done, but on the mercy of God, and the atoning blood, and perfect righteousness, of Jesus Christ the Savior." In his 1772 series of sermons about Communion, *"Breaking of Bread,"*

---

40. Chauncy, *Twelve Sermons*, 210, 215–16, 334, 338–39. See, further, 101–2n. On Puritan "preparationism," see esp. Norman Pettit, *Heart Prepared*.

he summoned his congregation to self-examination for a similar purpose: "Have you any hope of the pardoning mercy of God, but through the merit of his blood, that blood of his, this institution is a memorial of?" Chauncy later reminded First Church, in classically Calvinist terms, of the only true source of salvation:

> whatever our sins may have been, and whensoever committed, whether before or after a profession of Christ, and eating and drinking in his presence, they come within the reach of offered, and promised forgiveness, and shall certainly, upon our repentance, be pardoned for the sake of Christ, and on account of that atonement he has made for the sins of men.

The central truth, according to the fifth eucharistic discourse, was that "the gospel of the blessed God has provided, through Christ, and promised, pardoning mercy to repenting sinners, however many, or heinous, their sins may have been."[41]

Yet despite such orthodox affirmations, after 1765 Chauncy's preaching regularly combined more traditional teaching with expressions of the clearly Arminian soteriology that he first outlined in *Twelve Sermons*. In *Discourse Occasioned by the Death of the Reverend Dr. Joseph Sewall* (1769), he once more defined faith as "not an empty speculation," for example. "It is that faith," he contended, "by which 'the just do live,' and that is an abiding, habitual, powerful principle of all holy conformity to the will of God, both in heart and life, in a way of suffering as well as doing." In 1770, he reminded his hearers that divine grace was normally synergistic with positive human initiative, for "tho' it is God ultimately who protects, helps, and saves; yet, he ordinarily does this by the intervention of second causes, adapted in their nature to the purpose." On a similar note, Chauncy informed those present at his Thursday Lecture sermon in Boston on August 3, 1773 that "the faith which constitutes men christians in truth, and love to their fellow-brethren in Christ . . . are so far connected together in the sacred books, as to lead us most obviously into the thought, that they are, and ought always to be, inseperable concomitants."[42]

Based on his published works, there is thus clear evidence that Chauncy's theological position had shifted decisively from orthodox Calvinism to Arminianism by the mid-1760s. He apparently reached such conclusions by 1760 in his private studies, but that was still up to twelve years

---

41. Chauncy, *Discourse Occasioned by the Death of the Reverend Thomas Foxcroft*, 27; "Breaking of Bread," 32, 67, 147.

42. Chauncy, *Discourse Occasioned by the Death of the Reverend Dr. Joseph Sewall*, 11, alluding to Heb 10:38; *Trust in God*, 10; *Christian Love*, 29.

later than Mayhew. Moreover, his refusal to issue an outright denial of the reformed doctrine of total depravity, for example, or explicitly to renounce other key tenets of Calvinist doctrine either as early or as openly as Mayhew, placed Chauncy very much at the moderate end of the Arminian spectrum for some fifteen years after his younger colleague's death in 1766.

Despite his subsequent reputation among historians as an early adopter and advocate, with Mayhew, of theological heterodoxy, some of Chauncy's later statements on the doctrine of sin, which were virtually indistinguishable from those of his earlier Calvinist period, are particularly telling. In an ordination sermon of 1766, for example, *Duty of Ministers,* Chauncy summarized "the whole christian scheme of redemption" in remarkably familiar terms, beginning with original sin:

> It's occasion; the undone state of the lapsed sons of Adam: It's original rise; the free favor of the infinitely benevolent Deity: and the method of its execution; the advent of God's only begotten Son into our world, to take on him our nature, and accomplish the work laid out for him, as expedient in order to the purchase and bestowment, not only of pardon, justification, and a glorious immortality beyond the grave; but of that "meetness" for these blessings, without which they could neither be dispensed or enjoyed.

As late as his penultimate published sermon, *Accursed Thing* (1778), Chauncy continued to write of sin in a manner that might have gladdened the heart of the most rigid adherent to the Calvinist doctrine of total depravity. "Mankind are under the law of God . . . ," he reminded his congregation in the midst of Boston's revolutionary turmoil, "and when they transgress this law, they are chargeable with sin." But how did Chauncy understand the true "nature" of human transgression? "It carries in its idea rebellion against the most rightful authority . . . ," he continued, "Nor is sin an accursed thing in its nature only, but in its effects and consequences also . . . . " Then, in terms that would not have been out of place in the most stringent of Puritan jeremiads, Chauncy outlined sin's terrible results:

> 'Tis this that has blinded our understandings, perverted our judgments, stupified our consciences, corrupted our passions and affections. 'Tis this that has deprived us of our original glory, sunk our natures, and from creatures but little lower than the angels, reduced us to a level with the beasts that perish. 'Tis this that has commenced a war in our faculties, disturbing the peace of our minds, and filling them with tumult and vexation, intestine jars and horrid inward recoilings . . . whenever the

judgments of God have been abroad in the earth, 'tis sin that has brought them down . . . 'Tis this that guards the heavenly paradise as with a flaming sword, so that there is no admission for sinners, continuing such, into that blessed place."[43]

Only in the 1780s, when he released his most radical works, did Chauncy finally unveil a reinterpretation of the traditional doctrine of original sin that brought his position more fully in line with that of other Arminians. In *Five Dissertations* (1785), Chauncy did not deny it to be "an undisputed truth . . . not only that the human race descended from Adam as their first progenitor, but that existence was communicated to them in his LAPSED state." But he qualified that with another significant denial: "We do not come into existence with a morally corrupt or sinful nature," he argued, "nor . . . is our nature, as transmitted to us, so destitute of all capacity for that which is morally good, as that a native total corruption of heart becomes hereupon universal, without the exception of a single descendant from the one man Adam." Instead, Chauncy interpreted such inherited corruption as relating to two elements of the human condition which did not entail total depravity, namely, "subjection universally to a life of vanity and sorrow, ending in death," and "such imperfection of nature as renders it impossible, upon the foot of mere law . . . [to] attain to a righteousness that could avail to . . . justification before God." In other words, Chauncy disclosed in his early eighties, human beings came into the world mortal and imperfect as a result of Adam's sin, but not morally depraved. They could not be said to be guilty of any other sin than those which they subsequently went on to commit. Moreover, because grace remained paramount, "mankind may, in consequence of the advantage they are placed under by means of Christ, obtain the gift of pardoning mercy, notwithstanding their personal sins . . . And . . . they might be prepared, not only for the bestowment of this gift, but the enjoyment of an eternal reign in happy life after death."[44]

Just three years before his death, Chauncy thus continued to uphold the centrality of the mediatorial work of Christ to the divine plan of salvation and he plainly maintained that "deliverance from the bondage of sin, however great it has been, or however early contracted, is obtainable upon the foot of grace through Jesus Christ." But in an even more dramatic departure from Calvinist orthodoxy, he also confirmed that he now thought the extent and application of Christ's atoning sacrifice to be truly universal. That

---

43. Chauncy, *Duty of Ministers*, 6; *Accursed Thing*, 7–8, 9–10. Chauncy's last published sermon was *Sermon Delivered at the First Church*, although several other works were issued in the interim.

44. Chauncy, *Five Dissertations*, 129, 191, 133, 137.

more radical change of position will be considered, with others, in chapter 3, which will also give further attention to key differences between the two ministers' theological positions, to how and when they came to express them, and to the underlying factors that help explain them.[45]

---

45. Ibid., 237.

— 3 —

Challenging the Boundaries of Orthodoxy

Unitarianism and Universalism

ON DECEMBER 10, 1780, John Eliot, the second son of Andrew Eliot, friend and colleague of Chauncy and Mayhew, who had succeeded his father as minister of Boston's New North Church, wrote to his ministerial colleague, Jeremy Belknap, who was then serving in Dover, New Hampshire. In the course of a very conversational letter, Eliot mentioned "a droll affair" about Belknap, which he thought necessary to "find room to mention." The latter had apparently been preaching "before the Association of Ministers," and in the process "threw out so many heretical hints [tha]t you was obliged to appear as a candidate for a moderate reproof." Eliot was clearly worried about his friend, but he also had other concerns:

> "Be ye wise as serpents," says our great Master, &c. It will not do to vent these sentiments at present. (You know what I mean, the pudding, as Dr. Chauncy calls it.) People's minds are not ripe enough . . . They are not able to distinguish between [th]e restitution of all things upon his [John Murray's] plan, and the other scheme which employs the attention & arrests the assent of so many of [th]e wise & learned of [th]e modern New England clergy.[1]

Two months later, Eliot addressed similar topics in another, longer letter to Belknap. By that stage the pioneering English universalist preacher Murray had been ministering in Massachusetts for more than five years. Murray taught a simple form of universalism, based on the main premise of Welsh revivalist James Relly, as summarized by Griffin, that "since Christ

---

1. Eliot to Belknap, December 10, 1780, in Belknap et al., "Belknap Papers," *CMHS* 6/4, 199–202, esp. 201, citing Matt 10:16.

had already atoned for all our sins, the debt to God was satisfied and sinners therefore faced no more punishment." He had obviously attracted something of a following in Boston which Eliot dismissed as "the young, gay, volatile part." Eliot also admitted that he had previously thought that Murray's ministry might provide a useful opportunity to introduce Chauncy's universalism of more "substance." But he no longer supported Belknap's view on that. Eliot saw no need for Chauncy's manuscripts to be published immediately. More to the point, nor did Chauncy, he said, who shared Eliot's judgment of Belknap as "erroneous."[2]

Such reservations are remarkable in view of the fact that just two years later Chauncy finally began to make his universalism public with the joint publication, together with his First Church assistant from 1778, John Clarke, of *Salvation for All Men* (1782). This republished the views of previous authors, including Jeremiah White, the chaplain to Oliver Cromwell; David Hartley, the eighteenth-century philosopher; and Joseph Nicoll Scott, an independent minister and physician. The work also contained a preface by Chauncy in which he specifically criticized Murray's teachings as possibly "as hurtful to civil society as to religion." In a December 19, 1782 letter to his friend Ebenezer Hazard, Belknap sought to explain why the work had been issued in such a form. It was not only a response to Murray, he wrote. It reflected growing universalist convictions and concerns that had previously "been kept as a secret among learned men." Following repeated applications to Chauncy, *Salvation for All Men* "came forth as a forlorn hope, or, rather, as a scouting party, to make discoveries and try the temper of the public." When the response proved very mixed, Chauncy decided to state his own views more explicitly in an anonymous nineteen-page letter to "the Friend to Truth," *Divine Glory* (1783). Finally, having committed himself to open publication, he unveiled the three major works that he had kept under wraps for years: *Benevolence of the Deity* (1784), *Mystery Hid* (1784), and *Five Dissertations* (1785). These publications soon revealed the full extent of Chauncy's theological heterodoxy, which involved not only a thorough re-interpretation of his earlier Calvinism, but open advocacy of the universal salvation of all humanity as a result of the divine benevolence of a sovereign God.[3]

---

2. Griffin, *Old Brick*, 171; Eliot to Belknap, February 1781, in Belknap et al., "Belknap Papers," *CMHS* 6/4, 202–8, esp. 204, 202.

3. Chauncy and Clarke, *Salvation for All Men*, iii; Belknap to Ebenezer Hazard, December 19, 1782, in Belknap et al., "Belknap Papers," *CMHS* 5/2, 169–74, esp. 171–72; Chauncy, *Divine Glory*; *Benevolence of the Deity*; *Mystery Hid*; *Five Dissertations*. Eliot's initial caution stemmed from a number of considerations. He was worried that "many serious, good Xtians" would be offended by an apparent departure from orthodoxy, and

The fact that Chauncy did not release these works until sixteen years after he had extensive drafts of them, and some twenty-five years after he first reached the radical positions that he unveiled in them, has already been noted as one of the most striking features of his biography. The delay obviously raises questions about Chauncy and his motivations. It also focuses attention on a crucial period of intellectual change and transformation, when both he and Mayhew were moving well beyond the shift to Arminianism. For it was during the 1750s, if only privately in Chauncy's case, that both challenged, even transgressed, the boundaries of Calvinist orthodoxy in even more fundamental ways. More, it was right in the middle of that decade that Mayhew caused the biggest theological firestorm of his career by raising very public questions of the Christian doctrine of the Trinity.

---

that those "not learned in other languages, or mighty in the Sc[ri]p[ture]s" would not understand Chauncy's ideas. He did not think Murray's influence very great "among men of thought" and he believed that his ministry had, if anything, prejudiced people against universalism. In the longer term, Eliot predicted that "by prudence, or what in my apprehension is styled Christian policy, we may persuade men." Many of "the first divines in New England" had already progressed to "the faith of an universal salvation" and with appropriate wisdom and "necessary caution," more might follow. In the meantime, those who had already come to a knowledge of "universal restitution" could afford to bide their time. This was "an object of speculation affording great comfort to rational enquirers, but by no means necessary to be commonly known." Eliot took the view that "Men will have their own ways of thinking: There are Deists in England. Dr. Chauncy says that the present is the worst time which could ever happen, for men's minds are too much absorbed in politics to attend unto anything else. . . . The pudding is a word which he uses when persons are nigh not acquainted with our sentiments, thus styling the MSS. A word that happen[ed] to come uppermost once when he wanted to know the sentiments of an absent gentleman, — Doth he relish the pudding?" (Eliot to Belknap, February 1781, in Belknap et al., "Belknap Papers," *CMHS* 6/4, 202–8, esp. 202–4, 206–7). In a 1782 letter to Belknap, Eliot also indicated something of the growing tensions resulting from Chauncy's suppression of his views. Relating how Chauncy grew indignant with laymen questioning Oliver Everett about his theology prior to his settlement at New South Church earlier that year, Eliot commented: "It was lucky [th]e dispute turned upon [th]e article of [th]e Trinity & exhausted [th]e patience of [th]e Council, for this was only a prelude to other matters w[hi]ch would have set us all aghast. We might have been obliged to eat [th]e pudding, bag & all" (Eliot to Belknap, February 1, 1782, in 222–7, esp. 225–6). Eliot later described the initial backlash following the publication of *Salvation for All Men*: "Dr. Chauncy & Clarke have let the cat out of [th]e bag . . . Instead of pleasing the rational part of the town & country, such I mean as are even friendly to this subject as a matter of speculation, it is thought by them that it will admit of very bad consequences, and that this time was the improper to start such a controversy" (Eliot to Belknap, September 30, 1782, in ibid., 234–38, esp. 236–37).

Questions of Trinitarianism

Traditional Trinitarianism was a key assumption, if not a major preoccupation, for the first generations of New England Puritans. Acceptance of the basic tenets of the *Westminster Confession* (1646) and their distillation in the *Westminster Shorter Catechism* (1647) was a *sine qua non* not only for ordained ministers, but for those among whom they ministered. Moreover, the commitments to distinctively reformed doctrines which those documents encapsulated were built on Nicene, Trinitarian foundations that had been central to ecumenical Christian orthodoxy since the fourth century. All were expected to affirm that "There is but one [God] onely, the living and true God," and that "There are three Persons in the Godhead, the Father, the Son, & the holy Ghost; and these three are one, true, eternall God, the same in substance, equall in power and glory." The more extensive affirmations of the *Westminster Larger Catechism* (1647) were also common knowledge, or at least desired to be. It was a standard Puritan conviction, however widely shared from the pulpit, that "The Scriptures manifest that the Son, and the Holy Ghost are God, equall with the Father, ascribing unto them such Names, attributes, works, and worship, as are proper to God onely."[4]

Belief in the full divinity of Christ was an essential part of this theological heritage and it was taught from earliest childhood. The bestselling *New England Primer*, which was first published as early as the 1680s to help children learn to read, often included catechetical instruction. The 1727 edition contained founding First Church minister John Cotton's catechism, *Spiritual Milk for Boston Babes*, as an appendix. Among its questions and answers was the following exchange about the person and work of Christ:

> Q. What is the wages of sin?
>
> A. Death and Damnation.
>
> Q. How look you then to be saved?
>
> A. Onely by Jesus Christ.
>
> Q. Who is Jesus Christ?
>
> A. The Eternal Son of God, who for our sakes became Man, that he might redeem and save us.

---

4. Westminster Assembly, *Shorter Catechism*, 6; *Larger and Shorter Catechisme*, 3. As McGrath has noted, "the Nicene creed—or, more accurately, the Niceno-Constantinopolitan creed—of 381 declared that Christ was 'of the same substance' with the Father. This affirmation has since come to be widely regarded as a benchmark of Christological orthodoxy within all the mainline Christian churches" (*Christian Theology*, 277).

> Q. How doth Christ redeem & save us?
>
> A. By his righteous life and bitter death, and glorious resurrection to life again.

Its Trinitarian doctrine was just as direct:

> Q. Who is God?
>
> A. God is a Spirit of himself, and for himself.
>
> Q. How many Gods be there?
>
> A. There is but One God in three Persons, the Father, the Son, and the Holy Ghost.[5]

When Thomas Shepard composed his *Short Catechism* (1654) intended "for the private instruction of the younger sort" where he ministered in Cambridge, Massachusetts, he immediately followed an extensive list of God's "Attributes" with a comprehensive summary of traditional Trinitarianism. His conclusion? "Although nothing is more difficult to conceive, then [sic] how there should be Three Persons in one God, yet there is nothing more clear in all the scriptures then [sic] it is so." God had "revealed this mystery to man" to foster human worship and spiritual fulfillment and to encourage fear of sin. God's intention was that "we are to adore this mystery and to believe that it is so, & not too curiously to dispute and question how it can be so." Perhaps to avoid such questioning, or perhaps because the "mysteries" of Trinitarian theology were deemed so foundational to New England theological tradition that they did not require systematic exposition, the published sermons of the first generations of Puritan preachers reveal few works specifically devoted to expounding or defending the doctrine of the Trinity. In that sense, Wright justly observed that while it was "a part of Puritan theology," it "never took up much of the attention of the first settlers. Neglect of it was an established custom." But from at least the 1730s, there is also evidence that some of the same ministers who dared to raise questions of, or state objections to, specifically Calvinist doctrine were beginning to express doubts and reservations about traditional understandings of the Trinity.[6]

---

5. Cotton, *Spiritual Milk*, in *New-England Primer Enlarged*, 6–7, 1.

6. Shepard, *Short Catechism*, 2–8, esp. 8; Wright, *Unitarianism in America*, 203. On the still rather obscure origins of the *New England Primer*, see Avery, "Origins and English Predecessors." The *Early American Imprints* collection contains just two works with the word "Trinity" (as a theological term) in their titles published before 1720. The only notable one is Cotton Mather, *Christian Conversing*.

Benjamin Kent's 1735 voluntary dismissal from the church of Marlborough, Massachusetts following a series of heresy charges upheld by ecclesiastical council was noted in the previous chapter. So was the fact that his doctrinal offenses extended beyond Arminianism to include "unsound and dangerous Opinions" about the Trinity. Exactly what they were remains unclear, especially since his only publication, *Sermon Preached* (1734), was devoted to a strong defence of the divinity of Christ against Arian and other heterodoxies. But the theologically diverse council of ten churches, which was tasked with investigating complaints against Kent, thought the "Doctrine" on which "the greatest Truths and Duties of our holy Religion, as Christians, are founded" of such importance that its members unanimously placed their negative judgment of his views on the Trinity first on their list of findings against him.[7]

On January 26, 1736, when Robert Breck was ordained minister of Springfield, Massachusetts, he publicly delivered a "Confession of Faith," which included the affirmations that "there is but One God, who is over all, blessed forever; yet, . . . in the Unity of the Godhead there are three Persons, the Father, the Son, and the Holy Ghost; who are the same in Substance, and equal in Power and Glory." He also stated that "this is a Doctrine of pure Revelation, so I look upon it to be of the highest Importance in Religion, and that on which the greatest Truths of the Gospel do depend." But Breck did not reach that point without having to answer a series of charges, not least of which was his alleged refusal to acknowledge the full inspiration of 1 John 5:7: "For there are three that bear record in heaven, the Father, the Word, and the Holy Ghost: and these three are one." Giving testimony about the young ordinand to the council that eventually approved Breck's ordination, Thomas Clap reported a lengthy conversation with Breck in January 1734 about his teaching the previous month. Breck had allegedly not only confirmed charges that he had "denied some Places of Scripture to be of divine Inspiration," including 1 John 5:7. He told Clap "that Dr. [Edward] Wigglesworth had given up that Text . . . and laid no weight upon it at all." Clap thought that "that was a very important and fundamental Point: For if Christ was not God, he could not be able to make Satisfaction to divine Justice for Sin." But although Breck later confessed a very different position before the council that eventually approved his ordination, he first confused and compounded the issue. There was "no need of any Satisfaction to divine Justice for Sin," he argued, for "GOD might consistent with his Justice forgive Sin without any Satisfaction at all."[8]

---

7. *At a Council of Ten Churches*, 1, 3; Kent, *Sermon Preached*, esp. 18–21.

8. Breck, "Confession of Faith," in Cooper, *Work of Ministers*; *Narrative of the*

The 1740s and early 1750s saw continuing evidence of anti-Trinitarian opinion. The change may have simply reflected the advent of a new minister whom the town's nineteenth-century historian described as "severe and somewhat dogmatical." But it is noteworthy that after replacing the New Light enthusiast Solomon Prentice in 1750, three years after his dismissal from the church in Grafton, Massachusetts, Aaron Hutchinson found it necessary to supplement its rather vague founding covenant commitment to "the Lord Jehovah . . . our God." The key additions were an explicit affirmation of the Trinity buttressed by a robust recognition of biblical authority "to be understood 'in that view as exhibited to us in the well-known Westminster Catechism." When the church at Leominster drew up its covenant under new minister John Rogers in 1743, members affirmed their simple dedication "to the Lord Jehovah, (to the Father, Son and Holy Spirit)" and committed to "take Him for our eternal portion." But seventeen years later, its members made a similar clarification to Hutchinson's for more explicit reasons.[9]

In July 1757 an ecclesiastical council of representatives from fifteen churches upheld a series of heresy charges against Rogers. The matters on which he was found wanting went beyond typically Arminian positions. Rogers had denied "the doctrine of original sin, both the imputation of the guilt and the corruption of our nature." He had propagated "an unsound and unscriptural notion" of regeneration. He was "confused" about "the doctrine of conversion" and expressed "most indecent and unchristian reflections, on the shorter catechism of the venerable Assembly of Divines, at Westminster." But the "first article" to vex council members was even more offensive to them. "Respecting . . . that fundamental doctrine of Christianity of the true Divinity or Godhead of Jesus Christ," members "unanimously judge[d], that the aggrieved brethren had just reason to be dissatisfied with him concerning it, and it appeared to the majority of this council, that the aggrieved brethren had just ground of suspicion, that the Rev. Mr. Rogers did not hold or believe the essential Divinity of Christ as it is revealed in the Divine Word." After months of ecclesiastical political wrangling, Rogers was eventually dismissed from Leominster in January 1758, to be replaced by Francis Gardner, who was ordained on December 22, 1762. Meanwhile, on February 4, 1760, the church had already adopted a new covenant which embodied a theological precision that seemed designed to prevent any

---

Proceedings, 55. The ecclesiastical council that passed judgment on Kent included Ebenezer Gay, as well as the orthodox Calvinist Boston ministers, John Webb and William Cooper.

9. Frederick Pierce, *History of Grafton*, 181, 168; Stebbins, *Centennial Discourse*, 82.

repetition of Rogers's errors. Its first clause was: "We do avouch the Lord to be our God, whose name alone is Jehovah, Father, Son and Holy Spirit three persons in one God who is over all blessed forever, to fear him and cleave to him in love, and serve him in truth, with all our hearts."[10]

In support of his claims that 1 John 5:7 and another passage from John 8 lacked "Divine Inspiration," Breck was not only reported to have made specific reference to the views of Harvard Professor Wigglesworth. The account of his questioning by Clap includes two vague mentions of a work by the eighteenth-century English independent minister, Jeremiah Jones. Clear indications of the origins of such ministers' understandings of the Trinity otherwise remain as elusive as their exact nature in the immediate sources. But two thinkers who have been widely recognized for their significant influence on more rationalist eighteenth-century New England clergy are the Church of England cleric and philosopher Samuel Clarke, especially through his *Scripture-Doctrine of the Trinity* (1712), and English dissenting minister Thomas Emlyn, author of *Humble Inquiry into the Scripture-Account of Jesus Christ* (1702).[11]

Much like those of Taylor, who later followed a similar model in his analysis of traditional teachings on original sin, Clarke's conclusions were based on comparative exegesis of relevant biblical texts. Following a tripartite examination organized under the categories "Of GOD the FATHER," "Of the SON of GOD," and "Of the Holy SPIRIT of GOD," he presented no fewer than fifty-five "more particular and distinct Propositions" intended to "set forth at large" the resulting *Scripture-Doctrine of the Trinity*. In the third part of his work, Clarke then related his findings to the Church of England's *Book of Common Prayer*, concluding with a summary of "the principal Passages in the Liturgy . . . relating to that Doctrine" of the Trinity. Scholars have debated Clarke's Trinitarian and Christological views. Wright and others bluntly described his conception of the personhood of Christ as "Arian,"

---

10. Stebbins, *Centennial Discourse*, 81–97, passim, esp. 84, 96; Wright, *Unitarianism in America*, 203–4. See, further, Wilder, *History of Leominster*, 156–88, on events surrounding Rogers's ministry and dismissal. He went on to be minister of a breakaway congregation at Leominster, which operated from 1762 until his resignation in 1787. *SHG*, 9:189–98 offers the most detailed and reliable account of Rogers's life and ministry.

11. *Narrative of the Proceedings*, 4–5, 55, 57; Clarke, *Scripture-Doctrine of the Trinity*; Emlyn, *Humble Inquiry*. In citing the authority of an unspecified Jones to support his unconventional views on John 8 and 1 John 5:7, Breck was clearly referring to Jeremiah Jones, *New and Full Method* (1727). Jones's main treatment of the two passages is found in 1:111 of the 1798 edition, where he argued that the absence of those texts from the "Syriack Version" of the New Testament lent weight to its authenticity and authority.

or, at least, "semi-Arian." Timothy Yenter and Ezio Vailati have offered a more nuanced interpretation that reflects Clarke's stated views more closely:

> Unlike the Arians, Clarke affirmed that the Son is co-eternal with the Father and not created . . . From this it also follows that, *contra* the Socinians, the Son existed before the conception of Jesus. Unlike the Sabellians, Clarke denied that the Son was a mode of the Father . . . Clarke's claimed ignorance . . . made him reluctant to declare that the Father and the Son were the same divine substance, but the Son is endowed by the Father with all of the power and authority of the Father. He also called the manner of the Son's generation from the father . . . "ineffable." What Clarke affirmed was that each member of the trinity was a person (which for Clarke always means "intelligent agent"), but that only the Father had the attribute of being self-existent.

Yenter's and Vailati's resulting conclusion that Clarke's "views might best be described as subordinationist" is clearly supported by evidence in his works.[12]

Emlyn's earlier and much less substantial publication, *Humble Inquiry*, cost him just over two years in a Dublin jail from 1703 to 1705 for the common-law offense of libel in the form of blasphemy. He eventually recovered from his imprisonment to achieve acclaim and influence among more highly placed English critics of Trinitarian orthodoxy, including Bishop Benjamin Hoadly, Locke, and Clarke, of whom he subsequently wrote a memoir. The densely packed arguments of *Humble Inquiry*, for which Emlyn became most famous, sought to demonstrate, based on sundry texts from the New Testament, the highly controversial and thoroughly heterodox thesis that Christ neither claimed, nor was justly attributed with, full divinity as co-equal and consubstantial with God the Father. In purely pragmatic terms, Emlyn saw Trinitarianism as an irrational obstacle to Christian evangelism. As a matter of theological principle, he not only argued that Christ himself recognized his subordinate position to God, but he claimed the support of prominent churchmen, including the Latitudinarian Archbishop of Canterbury, Tillotson, and the Arminian, Daniel Whitby, for that view. He cited

---

12. Taylor, *Scripture-Doctrine of Original Sin*; Clarke, *Scripture-Doctrine of the Trinity*, 1–83, 84–196, 197–239, 240–378, esp. 240, 379–480, esp. 379; Wright, *Unitarianism in America*, 201–2; Yenter and Vailati, "Samuel Clarke (Revised)." Their interpretation of Clarke's views is quoted here in the interests of brevity and conciseness. It is clearly supported by *Scripture-Doctrine of the Trinity*, 279, 292–301, 304–12. See, further, on Clarke, Ferguson, *Eighteenth Century Heretic*. A "subordinationist" view of Christ is here understood as one in which Christ is seen as subordinate to the first person of the Trinity, God the Father.

biblical as well as credal sources in support of the position that Christ did not lay personal claim to divinity. Like Clarke, Emlyn conceded that God had granted Christ authority as mediator between God and humanity, but only in a relationship of subordination. As such, Emlyn wrote

> under the serious impressions of those great relations in which the blessed Jesus stands to me, whom I credit as my great teacher; whom I desire to admire and love as my gracious endeared benefactor, beyond father and mother, or friends, &c. whom I reverence as my Lord and ruler, and solemnly expect as my final glorious judge, who is to come in his own, and in his Father's glory; and in the mean time deal with God thro' him, as my only Mediator and Intercessor.

It was such considerations that led him "earnestly" to "profess, that 'tis not without grievous and bitter resentments, that I should be employed in writing things, which by so many well-meaning Christians will be misinterpreted, to be derogatory to the honour of this great Redeemer." But Emlyn was convinced that Christ was not "the supreme independent God, but only one who is so inhabited and commissioned and enabled by him who is so."[13]

The impact on more critically minded eighteenth-century New England thinkers of Clarke's and Emlyn's conclusions, not to mention the exegetical methods used to arrive at them, is clear from a variety of sources. During his visit to the college on September 24, 1740, George Whitefield heard rumors about some of the possible reasons why Harvard students like Rogers, who graduated in 1732 and was thus a near-contemporary of Kent (1727) and Breck (1730), might have strayed from Calvinist orthodoxy. "Tutors neglect to pray with and examine the Hearts of their Pupils," the evangelist wrote in his journal for that day. "Discipline is at too low an Ebb: Bad Books are become fashionable amongst them:—Tillotson and Clark are read instead of Sheppard [sic], [Solomon] Stoddard and such like evangelical Writers." Although he did not deny the prevalence of what he agreed were "new Books of Morality with Infidelity, w[hi]ch has sensibly hurt some," Colman sought to calm Whitefield's fears and assure him that New England's "Colleges supply us with many worthy Ministers." Others went further and checked the library records to ascertain that undergraduates had shown little interest in borrowing works by Tillotson or Clarke for years. But at least one student clearly was reading them. In 1741 Jonathan Mayhew copied a passage from Tillotson into his commonplace "Book of Extracts." His nineteenth-century biographer Bradford also reported that

---

13. Emlyn, *Humble Inquiry*, 53, 21; "Memoirs" in Whiston, *Historical Memoirs*; Gibson, "Persecution of Thomas Emlyn," esp. 529–30.

"at this [Harvard] period," it appeared "from an imperfect journal, and a book of extracts from Locke, Clarke, and others" that Mayhew "adopted rules for his reading and future conduct, in which he speaks of the importance of method, and of reflecting on what is read."[14]

Mayhew's published works, which contain citations from a wide range of sources, are even more revealing of the extent to which he drew on Latitudinarian and other Church of England, as well as dissenting, authors. In his first publication, *Seven Sermons* (1749), for example, Mayhew not only quoted directly from Clarke; he also cited Bishops Joseph Butler and Hoadly in addition to Locke and the Baptist, James Foster. Other Anglican clerics whose writings he referred to in later works included Bishops Anthony Ellys, Edward Stillingfleet, John Sharp, Thomas Sherlock, and William Warburton. Many of Mayhew's citations of Church of England sources are predictably found in polemical contributions to the debate over the American Episcopate controversy, in which he regularly quoted sermons delivered by prominent clerics to the Society for the Propagation of the Gospel in Foreign Parts (SPG), as well as those of his leading American opponents, especially East Apthorp. Citing a largely non-doctrinaire sermon on the death of King William III, Mayhew made just one mention of Thomas Emlyn. But he quoted directly from works by Clarke on at least two separate occasions and listed him with other luminaries, including Locke, Newton, Butler, and Hoadly, as an exemplary writer and thinker. He also included Clarke's fellow Latitudinarian Tillotson in a similar reference. Thus while Mayhew nowhere noted the opinion or influence of any particular theologian in his controversial comments on the Trinity, it is clear that he not only read, but admired and quoted from, English thinkers who were questioning established doctrines in a variety of areas, including Trinitarian theology. Another possible influence indicated by a handwritten transcription in Mayhew's unpublished papers was the older anti-Trinitarian work, *Brief Notes on the Creed of St. Athanasius*, which was published anonymously in London in 1694.[15]

---

14. Whitefield, *Continuation*, 55; Akers, *Called unto Liberty*, 28, citing Colman to Whitefield, n.d.; Edward Wigglesworth, *Letter to the Reverend Mr. George Whitefield*, 30–31, citing Brattle, "To the Author of the Vindications," 1–2, esp. 2; Mayhew, "Extracts, 1741," MP, 10; Bradford, *Memoir*, 21. There is no evidence of an extant "imperfect journal," nor are there any citations from Locke or Clarke in Mayhew's "Book of Extracts." But the latter does contain sixteen "general Rules for the Improvement of Knowledge." The second half of William Brattle's letter, "To the Author of the Vindications," was published in the *Boston Gazette*, June 22–29.

15. Mayhew, *Seven Sermons*, 14, citing Clarke, *Discourse Concerning the Unchangeable Obligations*, 58; 37–38, citing Locke, *Works*, 1:312; 84–5, citing, without attribution, Hoadly, *Sixteen Sermons*, 98–99; 105–6, citing an extended passage from Butler,

Mayhew and the Arian Question

While he strived to affirm both in the face of strenuous opposition, it has already been seen how Mayhew's cooperative, Arminian soteriology threatened to undermine Calvinist doctrines of the sovereignty of God and the saving power of Christ's atonement. But he attracted even greater controversy for his understanding of the person of Christ, which later scholars, including Rossiter, Bernard Bailyn, and Jonathan Clark, have followed critical contemporaries in interpreting as decisively "Arian."[16]

Fifteen Sermons, 276–78; 108, apparently referring to James Foster, "Of the Power and Providence of God," in *Discourses*, 1:165–93; 123–24, citing Butler, *Fifteen Sermons*, 244–45. Of the bishops listed, for example, Mayhew cited Ellys, *Sermon Preached*, 16, in *Two Discourses Delivered October 9th*, 1760, 60–61n, esp. 61n; Stillingfleet, *Discourse concerning the Idolatry*, 142–43, in *Popish Idolatry*, 37; Sharp, *Works*, 5:182–83, in *On Hearing the Word*, 35–36; Sherlock, *Several Discourses*, 229–32, passim, in *On Hearing the Word*, 319–20n; Warburton, *Alliance between Church and State*, in *Remarks on an Anonymous Tract*, 14. Another reference to a specific work by Clarke is in Mayhew's *Divine Goodness*, 19, where he cited "Sermon XIV. Of the Goodness of God" in *Sermons on the Following Subjects*, 1:321–45. He listed leading Anglican clerics as exemplary in *Christian Sobriety*, 326; *Letter of Reproof*, 32; *Snare Broken*, 35. In *Sermon Preached at Boston*, 22, Mayhew referred to Emlyn, *Works*, 3:131–53. The anonymous anti-Trinitarian work, *Brief Notes on the Creed of St. Athanasius* is in *MP* 124. On the American Episcopate controversy see esp. Cross, *Anglican Episcopate*; Bridenbaugh, *Mitre and Sceptre*; Gerardi, "Episcopate Controversy Reconsidered."

16. Bailyn applied the label "nondoctrinaire Arianism" to Mayhew, whom he thought influenced by "such Christian rationalists as Samuel Clarke," espousing "a flat repudiation of the divinity of Christ" ("Religion and Revolution," 112). Jonathan Clark described Mayhew as "by temperament, an extremist, an indignant and militant Arian" (*Language of Liberty*, 366). While noting that "Mayhew never progressed far toward any theory of the Trinity," Akers helpfully contrasted Arianism with Trinitarian orthodoxy as follows: "The orthodox clung to the Athanasian Creed, which taught that the three persons of the Trinity were all 'coeternal and coequal.' Arians maintained that the Son was subordinate to the Father, yet had existed before the creation and the incarnation"(*Called unto Liberty*, 116–17), See *Called unto Liberty*, 115–22, for Akers's general characterization of the allegedly anti-Trinitarian views expressed by Mayhew in the mid-1750s. Rossiter described Mayhew as both "the forerunner of American Unitarianism" and "recognized as New England's most outspoken Arian," who "preached a gospel that rejected flatly the five points of Calvinism" and espoused "a humanistic, liberal, rational, 'natural religion'"("Life and Mind," 541–43). Among older works viewing Mayhew as a champion of liberal theology and/or a precursor and/or pioneer of Unitarianism, see, for example, Allen and Eddy, *History of the Unitarians*, 178–80; Cooke, *Unitarianism in America*, 60–66; Haroutunian, *Piety Versus Moralism*, 11–13; Morais, *Deism in Eighteenth Century America*, 61–63. Akers rightly noted that Bradford, *Memoir*, "sought to present Mayhew as an American patriot and a pioneer of the Unitarian movement" (*Called unto Liberty*, 235). Sprague's decision to include Mayhew in his Unitarian volume of *Annals*, 8:22–29, assumed a bold, but ultimately questionable, theological judgment, which he sought to justify, e.g., 23–24, 28–29, with a passing reference to Mayhew's alleged Arianism and by citing extracts from *On Hearing the Word*. This was

Mayhew's problems with credal Trinitarianism were first publicly aired in 1755 in his sermon "Of the Nature and Principle of Evangelical Obedience," published in *On Hearing the Word*. In a wide-ranging discussion of "the nature of this obedience, so as to distinguish it from the obedience of a mere Moralist, and of a Theist; and also from that of good men, who lived under the Jewish dispensation," his immediate focus was on the "various duties" that he saw resulting from "the Christian doctrine of a Mediator." Mayhew's initial comments on "the rule and authority" of Christ to which Christians were subject were fairly non-controversial. He stressed that "Christ gives laws to men; not merely as a prophet, or divine messenger," but as "Head" of the church. Mayhew even argued that "our obedience is more immediately due to the Son, than to the Father." It was when he added a key qualification about "the supreme authority and dominion of God, the FATHER Almighty," that his Christology became much more problematic for orthodox readers. For Christians did not "set" this "aside," in Mayhew's view; nor did they attempt "to divide, really destroy, the Monarchy of the universe, which is still in HIM alone."[17]

Instead, he claimed the support of the apostle Paul in Philippians 2 for the argument that "all the homage and obedience which we pay to the Son, should thus be referred to, and terminate in, the Father." In that sense, like Clarke and Emlyn, Mayhew's view of Christ was ultimately subordinationist. One of his primary and most provocative concerns in a New England context where Christ's divinity was deemed an essential theological doctrine was that:

> Christians ought not, surely, to pay any such obedience or homage to the Son, as has a tendency to eclipse the glory of God the Father; who is without Rival or Competitor. The Dominion and Sovereignty of the universe is necessarily one, and in ONE;— the only living and true GOD, who delegates such measures of power and authority to other Beings, as seemeth good in his sight; but "will not give his [peculiar] glory to another."

According to Mayhew's almost hierarchical understanding of the godhead in *On Hearing the Word*, which he never fully expounded elsewhere:

> Our blessed Saviour does indeed assert the rights and prerogatives of his own crown; but never usurped those of His Father's: On the contrary, He constantly and uniformly tells us, that his

---

clearly a strategic decision on Sprague's part. *Annals of the American Unitarian Pulpit* was the eighth of the nine-volume *Annals* series, of which volumes 1 and 2 were devoted to "Trinitarian Congregational" clergy.

17. Mayhew, *On Hearing the Word*, 256–57, 265–67.

authority was given to him of the Father; and is exercised in subordination to His will; not independently of it. He claims no authority, besides what he claims by virtue of the Father's grant, and the commission which he received from Him.[18]

Christ's role was especially that of mediator between God and humankind, and, as such, he was subordinate to the first person of the Trinity. Mayhew stressed this last point so as to justify Christian obedience to Christ without impugning "the Unity, and the supreme glory and dominion of God, the FATHER." He also wished to remove "a great stumbling-block both to Jews and Mahometans," by preserving the Father's "Unity and Supremacy amongst Christians." But his explanatory footnote on this evangelistic focus contained the most controversial of all Mayhew's statements about the Trinity in *On Hearing the Word* (1755). He began with the modest-sounding disclaimer that he was not "bold enough to meddle" with "the metaphysical abstract nature, or essence of the Deity." It was his following commentary on "the Temerity of the Athanasians" to whom he dismissively left "Disquisitions of this kind, and denunciations of God's vengeance against those who do not affect to be wise, or are not willing to believe, above what is written," that caused most offense. The main problem was its overarching emphasis on the inherent unity of God:

> I can, for my own part, freely acquiesce in St. Paul's doctrine, in the most obvious sense of his words, *viz*. That "tho' there be that are called Gods, whether in heaven or in earth; (as there be gods many, and lords many), but [yet] to us there is but ONE GOD, the FATHER—and One Lord, Jesus Christ."—1 Cor. 8. 4—"There is ONE GOD, and One Mediator betwixt GOD and men, the Man Christ Jesus"—1 Tim. 2, 5. Who the only true GOD is, we may farther learn from our Saviour's prayer, John 17. begin. [*sic*] "These things spake Jesus; and lift up his eyes to heaven, and said, 'FATHER, glorify thy Son—This is life eternal that they might know THEE, the ONLY TRUE GOD, and Jesus Christ, whom THOU hast sent.'"[19]

In the other major passage in his works, where Mayhew focused on his understanding of the person, as well as the work of Christ, his goal was to encourage a proper *Christian Sobriety* (1763) in the young men for whom his collection of eight sermons by that name was intended. He openly rejected the views of "the learned Socinus and his followers," but he was at pains "to prevent any wrong inferences" from New Testament verses that

---

18. Ibid., 267–68, citing Isa 42:8 and/or 48:11.
19. Ibid., 268–69, citing, more specifically, John 17:1, 3.

seemed to equate the divinity of Christ with that of "the FATHER," especially in creation. Instead, he sought to remind his hearers of "two or three" other "passages," which appeared to facilitate a less demanding way of "explaining those in which Christ is stiled God." Again, Mayhew stressed the unity of God and the mediatorial role of Christ, laying particular weight on 1 Corinthians 8:4-6. While he joined it with a strongly Arminian affirmation that Christ "died . . . not only for a few particular persons, as some seem to imagine, but 'died for all,'" Mayhew unreservedly upheld the traditional doctrine that Christ "came to make an atonement for the sins of the world." In stressing the full humanity of Christ, he also explained the fact that "he is sometimes called God" by urging that "GOD, even the FATHER, did, in a very particular and eminent, a transcendently glorious and inexpressible manner, dwell in our Lord Jesus Christ, manifesting his glory in, by and thro' him." But Mayhew declared the manner or "mode" of this "divine inhabitation in Christ" to be an unknowable mystery. He rejected the title of "God the Son," as opposed to "the Son of God," as unscriptural. In a later, controversial footnote, where he referred to Christ as "the Logos," Mayhew also seemed to deny a traditional understanding of the Christian incarnation and to make such a differentiation between the first two persons of the Trinity that he confirmed serious doubts about his commitments to their substantial unity or to Christ's divinity:

> The scripture informs us that the Logos had a body prepared for him, and that he partook of flesh and blood, that he might "thro' death destroy him that had the power of death, that is the devil." But that he took into personal union with himself, an human soul, my Bible saith not; nor that there is any other true God, besides "his Father and our Father, his God and our God."[20]

Perhaps even more than the more diplomatic Chauncy, whose analogous rationale for adopting similar hermeneutical methods will be explored later in this chapter, once he had drawn his exegetical conclusions, Mayhew felt no compunction in transgressing traditional, reformed, credal, or confessional boundaries. He was especially dismissive of the strongly Trinitarian Athanasian Creed. "Some contend, and foam, and curse their brethren, for the sake of the Athanasian Trinity," he wrote in *On Hearing the Word* (1755), "till 'tis evident they do not love and fear the ONE living and true God as they ought to do." In a direct parody of some of the phraseology of the Athanasian Creed, Mayhew's anti-Catholicism also emerged, when

---

20. Mayhew, *Christian Sobriety*, 57–59, 66, citing 2 Cor 5:15, 59–60; *On Hearing the Word*, 417–18n, citing Heb 2:14 and alluding to John 20:17.

he mocked Trinitarian formulae by applying them to the Virgin Mary. "It would be no great surprize to me," he noted sarcastically:

> to hear that the Pope and a general Council, had declared the B. Virgin to be the fourth, or rather the first Person, in the Godhead, under the title of God, or Goddess THE MOTHER; adding that neither the Persons are to be confounded, nor the substance divided: that the Mother is eternal, the Father eternal, the Son eternal, and the Holy Ghost eternal; but yet that there are not four Eternals, but one Eternal; that this is the catholic faith, which except a man believe faithfully, he cannot be saved.

Mayhew was bound to attract considerable opposition for even questioning, never mind criticizing, Trinitarian orthodoxy. But the provocative tone of such passages undoubtedly added to orthodox animus against him.[21]

The West Church minister subsequently became known as one of the pioneers, or at least forerunners, of American Unitarianism. But his refusal to specify his understandings of Christ's personhood or of the relationship between him and "God the Father" with greater clarity leaves insufficient evidence to label his Christology decisively "Arian." Unlike Samuel Clarke, whose teachings he otherwise mirrored quite closely, Mayhew nowhere explicitly affirmed that Christ was co-eternal with God, but there is no proof that he regarded the second person of the Trinity as a created being who was less than eternal. Writing in defence of his *Observations* about the SPG in 1763, Mayhew also denied he ever rejected the deity of Christ. He openly admitted that he had voiced his "disbelief, and even contempt of certain metaphysical and scolastic, unscriptural and ridiculous definitions or explications of the trinity, which some men have given." But he dismissed the implication that he "ever denied, or treated in a bold or ludicrous manner, the divinity of the Son of God, as revealed in scripture." While his doctrinal departures from orthodoxy are unmistakable, Mayhew's theology of the godhead thus remains somewhat unclear. The label "subordinationist" seems to capture his understanding of Christ's role most accurately, but it does not stipulate how Mayhew defined the nature of his personhood, which he ultimately refused to clarify.[22]

Much less questionable is the concern, even outrage, that was provoked among orthodox Calvinists by Mayhew's anti-Trinitarian comments. In early 1757 Jonathan Edwards, who was then serving as a missionary in Stockbridge after being dismissed from his church in Northampton, wrote to both Foxcroft of First Church and Edward Wigglesworth at Harvard in

---

21. Mayhew, *On Hearing the Word*, 403, 418n. See also 254, 269n.
22. Mayhew, *Defence of the Observations*, 111.

attempts to ensure that what he called "Dr. Mayhew's late book," and especially "that marginal note of his, wherein he ridicules the doctrine of the Trinity," did not go unanswered. On February 11, he expressed the almost apocalyptic view to Foxcroft that "the guilt of the land (which already is great, and awfully testified against by heaven at this day) will be greatly increased by the neglect, if none should now appear to attempt a full vindication of the doctrine of Christ's divinity." He had already encouraged Boston printer Samuel Kneeland to reprint a copy of a work by Joseph Bellamy, which he sent "to defend the great doctrine of justification by Christ's righteousness (which has been especially impugned by Dr. [Jonathan] Mayhew)." Now he wished to see a vigorous response to Mayhew's "most open denial of the divinity of our Savior, and endeavoring to root the doctrine out of the country." With that in mind, he enclosed an open letter to Wigglesworth of the same date, in which he recalled earlier correspondence with Foxcroft expressing his "sentiments . . . concerning the call of God to ministers . . . , or others whose business it was to teach the doctrines of Christianity, to appear publicly on this occasion in defense of this doctrine." Foxcroft had replied that the matter had been raised with the Harvard Board of Overseers, but that nothing was "concluded to be done." Edwards's new proposal was that Wigglesworth himself, who was "set for the instruction of our youth in divinity in the principal seminary of learning," not only take on the task of responding to Mayhew, but also rebut the arguments of Emlyn's *Humble Inquiry*, which had recently added fuel to anti-Trinitarian flames in New England following its local publication "by one that calls himself a layman" in 1756.[23]

Wigglesworth's answer to Edwards has only survived in part, but he clearly declined such a mission. Ebenezer Pemberton had already offered a vigorous defense of traditional Christological doctrine in his 1756 publication, *All Power in Heaven*. The cautious Wigglesworth reported that "the worthy ministers" in Boston lecture sermons "were generally vindicating the divinity of Christ." He had no desire to stir up further theological strife. Mayhew's and Emlyn's views were meanwhile causing wider controversy among more educated Congregationalists. On March 17, 1756, future American president John Adams recorded a conversation with two friends in Dedham, who were both exercised about Mayhew's Christology. Jason Haven, who had just been ordained minister of the town, told him "very civilly that he supposed I took my faith on Trust from Dr. Mayhew," Adams

23. Edwards to Edward Wigglesworth, February 11, 1757, *WJE* 16:697–700, esp. 698–9; Edwards to Foxcroft, February 11, 1757, *WJE*, 16:694–7, esp. 695; Emlyn, *Humble Inquiry*. The work by Bellamy to which Edwards referred was *The Law, Our Schoolmaster*. See, further, Akers, *Called unto Liberty*, 118–22;

reported. Haven "added that he believed the doctrine of the satisfaction of J[esus] C[hrist] to be essential to Cristianity [*sic*], and that he would not believe this satisfaction, unless he believed the Divinity of C[hrist]." Also present was a "Mr. Balch," who "observed that he would not be a Christian if he did not believe the Mysterys of the Gospel. That he could bear with an Arminian, but when, with Dr. Mayhew, they denied the Divinity and Satisfaction of J[esus] C[hrist] he had no more to do with them."[24]

As such topics of theological controversy preoccupied everyday New Englanders, the polemics also continued in print. Following the release of the "catholic and judicious discourse of Mr. Pemberton . . . , prefaced by Dr. Sewall and Mr. Prince, the two oldest ministers of the town," the irenic Wigglesworth "thought it was now time to have done, and wait in silence till we saw whether any thing would be replied." He blamed the Boston publication of Emlyn's *Humble Inquiry* on "the printers, who live very much by disputes, observing that the people's passions were up, that any thing on that subject would fetch a penny, and that every thing was supposed to be pointed at Dr. Mayhew." This was why they "continued printing little things with pompous advertisements about them in the news papers, week after week." The sort of notice that Wigglesworth had in mind was probably the colorful announcement in the *Boston Weekly News-Letter* of May 13, 1756 of the publication of an English work entitled *That Jesus Christ is God by Nature*, which its printers, Green and Russell, advertised as "attempting [by conclusive Scripture Arguments] to subvert the Doctrine of the Arians." In releasing this work to the public, its Boston publishers made no secret of their view that "that old Arian Doctrine, (which in former Times has been subverted and crush'd) seems of late to be creeping in among us." Their intention was that the reader "may here receive Satisfaction, and never more deny or dispute his [Christ's] Divinity, but consent to and maintain this Important Article of the pure Gospel of Jesus Christ."[25]

Two further, more significant, attempts to refute the arguments of Mayhew and Emlyn emerged in 1757 and 1758, with the publication of *Supreme Deity of Our Lord Jesus Christ* by Edwards's son-in-law, Aaron Burr, and of *Sermons upon the Following Subjects* by Bellamy, which contained

---

24. Extracts of Edward Wigglesworth to Edwards, n.d., in Joseph Clark, *Historical Sketch*, 182–84; Pemberton, *All Power in Heaven*; John Adams, *Diary and Autobiography*, 1:14-15, March 17, 1756. "Mr. Balch" was probably Nathaniel Balch, a Boston hatter, who figures a number of times in Adams's papers. See, further, for example, Adams to James Warren, December 17, 1773, in *Papers of John Adams*, 2:1-2, esp. 2 n. 2.

25. Extracts of Edward Wigglesworth to Edwards, n.d., in Joseph Clark, *Historical Sketch*, 183; *Boston Weekly News-Letter*, May 13, 1756, 2, advertisement for *That Jesus Christ is God*, a work often attributed to Hanley, and originally published in London in 1726 as *Two Letters to a Very Eminent and Learned Gentleman*.

what Akers described as "a masterful sermon" entitled "The Divinity of Christ." Despite such controversy, Mayhew clearly remained undaunted, even when shunned by other Boston ministers. In the third edition of the King's Chapel minister's *Sermons on Particular Occasions* which was published sixty-six years after Mayhew provoked so much controversy with *On Hearing the Word*, James Freeman's Unitarian colleague and annotator, Jedidiah Morse, not only reported that Mayhew had been "the principal means of the republication of Emlyn's *Inquiry*," he cited a letter from Mayhew's daughter, Elizabeth Wainwright, in which she claimed to possess "many sermons" confirming his assertion of "the unity of God in the most unequivocal and plain manner, as early as the year 1753" and another from John Adams of May 15, 1815, in which he identified Mayhew as a Unitarian in 1750. Yet Morse's qualification of that statement seems closer to the mark. He described the West Church minister as belonging to "the school of Clarke" and as one who "admitted, not only the pre-existence, but the atonement of Christ."[26]

Chauncy's Universalism (1782–87)

Chauncy was also identified by the ministerial biographer William Sprague as Unitarian and scholars have often questioned his Christology, but the relative orthodoxy of his understanding of the Trinity will be demonstrated in the next chapter. Much less questionable is his major shift to a

26. Burr, *Supreme Deity*; Bellamy, "The Divinity of Christ," in *Sermons*, 1–42; Akers, *Called unto Liberty*, 121; Freeman, *Sermons*, 235, 236, 238, 241. See John Adams, *Works*, 10:237–39, for the May 15, 1815 letter from Adams to Morse. A modern edition is available in the Founders Online [Early Access] collection. "Sixty five years Ago," Adams wrote, "my own Minister the Reverend Lemuel Briant, Dr Jonathan Mayhew of the West Church in Boston, The Reverend Mr Shute of Hingham The Reverend John Brown of Cohasset, and perhaps equal to all, if not above all, The Reverend Mr Gay of Hingham; were Unitarians." "Early Access" transcriptions in the Founders Online collection are only cited where it has not been possible to check them against original documents or microfilm reproductions and they are not available in published volumes of *Adams Papers*. It is acknowledged that such texts remain subject to subsequent editorial revision. MP 132 contains unidentified and undated notes on the treatment of Mayhew by Boston ministers. Labeled "proofs of coldness to Dr. Mayhew," these included: a "Petititon signd [sic] by Dr. Sewall & Mr. Prince with Two of His Majestyes Council At the board of overseers of Harvard College to have Dr. Mayhew expelled for a marginal note"; a general refusal to "dine in public" with members of his ordaining Council; not attending Mayhew's lecture of December 1755 following "the Great Earthquake" in November; Ebenezer Pemberton of Old South Church telling Mayhew's barber to "stay at home & mind his business," rather than hearing the minister speak; and the "great pains the clergy in gen[era]l have taken to prejudice the people against Dr. Mayhew."

thorough-going, universalist soteriology, which Chauncy apparently made by 1760 but only fully revealed in his final works of the 1780s. In advancing his sophisticated case that the whole of humankind could ultimately expect to be saved, Chauncy was a significant early advocate of one of the two major streams of revisionist theology that was to find institutional expression in New England from the early nineteenth century onwards, when Congregationalist churches became Unitarian Universalist in significant numbers.[27]

Chauncy's long period of silence on his position before the 1780s has been explained in various ways. Lippy's argument that the cautious Chauncy was always careful to act "seasonably," even when releasing radical reformulations of traditional Christian doctrine, goes to the heart of the major explanations. Political debates tended to trump theological ones in the immediate pre-revolutionary period, it is contended, and Chauncy wished to avoid unnecessary controversy. But his caution may also have reflected another factor which scholars have previously neglected, namely his pastoral situation and personal circumstances at First Church.[28]

Ever since its founding in 1630 and especially through the early ministries of influential Puritans John Cotton (1633–52) and John Norton (1656–63), First Church had been a bastion of New England orthodoxy and it was not quick to introduce changes in doctrine or polity. Lippy pointed out that while it had "long held to the principle of strict congregational independency," the congregation became more inclusive under Foxcroft and Chauncy. It finally adopted the provisions of the 1662 "Half-Way Covenant," which allowed the baptism of the children of church attenders who had not formally entered into official membership, in 1731, and it provided for the baptism of all professing adults in 1736. However, in taking such steps, members were simply adopting what had long become standard practice elsewhere in New England. Until Foxcroft died in 1769, Chauncy also found himself working more than four decades alongside a senior minister whose sermons demonstrate a consistent commitment to Calvinism throughout his lengthy pastorate (1717–69).[29]

In 1741, for example, Foxcroft wrote a glowing preface to Dickinson's staunch defense of key tenets of orthodox Calvinism in *True Scripture-Doctrine*. Even in the midst of the Great Awakening, which he consistently supported, he saw no "Sign of the Times" that looked "more favorably, and

27. Sprague, *Annals*, 8:8–13.

28. Lippy, *Seasonable Revolutionary*, 131. See, further, Wright, *Unitarianism in America*, 187–89.

29. Lippy, *Seasonable Revolutionary*, 8; Richard Pierce, "Records of the First Church," 39:161, 172–73; Collins, *This Is Our Church*, 166. On the 1662 "Half-Way Covenant," see esp. Morgan, *Visible Saints*.

promise[d] better to us, than the restoring of a Zeal for Protestant Principles in Religion, for those Divine and ancient Truths which are the peculiar Glories of the Gospel." Despite "the Multiplicity of valuable useful Sermons printed among us," Foxcroft thought that "the grand Principles of the Everlasting Gospel" were "generally not allow'd their due Consideration," nor "so distinctly stated & so fully inculcated" as their importance demanded. He cited earlier works by Cotton Mather, which made a similar complaint, and having praised Dickinson's defense of "Eternal Election, Original Sin, Grace in Conversion, Justification by Faith, And the Saints Perseverance," he closed his preface with the Latin tag "*Sit Anima mea cum Puritanis.*" [30]

Nine years later, in his sermon, *Humilis Confessio* (1750), Foxcroft specifically targeted the key point of difference between traditional New England doctrine and the kind of Arminian position that Chauncy came to adopt. His stated goal in expounding Isaiah 64:6 and Philippians 3:8–9 was to counter Catholic error by "REPRESENTING The commonly receiv'd PROTESTANT Sense & Use of two Scripture-Passages, which depreciate all our personal Righteousness, under the Comparison of filthy Rags, and of despicable Dung." Foxcroft described "the principal Scope, as well as of the Prophet, as the Apostle," as "to renounce all Pretensions to Justification by Works, and disavow every Plea from righteous Self in point of reconciling or ingratiating Worthiness before the Sovereign Lawgiver." As late as 1764, in an unpublished sermon on the text, "faith, which worketh by love" from Galatians 5:6, which urged the importance of good works as evidence of Christian sanctification, Foxcroft presented a forthright account of the classic Reformation doctrine of justification by grace through faith alone.[31]

Although there is no proof of such a motivation, Chauncy's delay in publicizing his Arminian positions until at least 1765 could surely have been influenced by his colleague's (and perhaps his congregation's) strong adherence to more traditional doctrine. His relationship with Foxcroft must have come under strain after they published widely differing views of the Great Awakening in the early 1740s. While Chauncy carefully established himself as the revival movement's major critic, in *Apology in Behalf of The Revd Mr. Whitefield* (1745) and elsewhere, Foxcroft was a faithful defender of the Awakening and its leading evangelist. He did not hesitate to point,

---

30. Foxcroft, "Preface," in Dickinson, *True Scripture-Doctrine*, iv, xi, xiii, ii–iii, citing Cotton Mather, *Theopolis Americana*, 43, 46–47, 49, and x-xi, citing Cotton Mather, *The Minister*, 29–30. "*Sit Anima mea cum Puritanis*" can be literally translated "May my soul be [or rest] with the Puritans." On the history of First Church, see, further, Ellis, *History of the First Church*.

31. Foxcroft, *Humilis Confessio*, title page, 2; Sermon preached Oct. 21, 1764, in FP, Sermons file.

with Chauncy, to some of the dangers of overzealous enthusiasm. One of the reasons why he was so encouraged by a resurgence of the kind of reformed doctrine defended by Dickinson lay in its potential to protect "the Strong and Zealously affected" and "to guard them against the Extreams of censorious Rigour, Antinomian Jangling, & Enthusiastick Delusion." But Foxcroft also did much to promote Whitefield's ministry and he vigorously supported the work of Edwards. Yet despite such marked differences, fragmentary evidence of the immediate, inter-personal dealings between Chauncy and Foxcroft shows no obvious lack of mutual respect or ministerial cooperation at First Church.[32]

In addition to Chauncy's apparent deference to his senior colleague, their relationship may have been aided by a "catholick Congregationalism," discerned by Corrigan, that inclined Foxcroft to seek unity over conflict in "'some smaller things.'" Even while singing the praises of Calvinist "Scripture-Doctrine," he went out of his way to disclaim any intent to be "understood absolutely to confine real Christianity, or a valid Ministry, to Those fully in this Scheme of Principles; Exclusively of all that dissent from any Article of it." Foxcroft allowed specific latitude over a key tenet of reformed doctrine that Chauncy was to find increasingly problematic in later years. As early as 1741, he recognized that "the most controverted" issue was "Predestination." But he approved the comments that he cited from the works of dissenting hymn-writer Isaac Watts and the Cambridge divine, John Edwards, for their "Candour and extensive Charity" in conceding that those ignorant of the doctrine of "ELECTING Love," and even those "of the Arminian Persuasion" in general, might find themselves among God's chosen or be "holy" or "good Men."[33]

---

32. Foxcroft, *Apology*; "Preface," in Dickinson, *True Scripture-Doctrine*, xii. See, further, Foxcroft, *Some Seasonable Thoughts*, 43. Foxcroft was a close friend and strong supporter of the leading theologian and New England promoter of the Great Awakening, Jonathan Edwards, whom he also served in a significant capacity as editor and literary agent in Boston. The online edition of Edwards's *Works* includes no fewer than 181 references to Foxcroft spread over ten volumes, including eighteen letters from Edwards to Foxcroft which are published in *WJE*, 16. For evidence of cordiality of "the immediate, inter-personal dealings between Chauncy and Foxcroft," see five undated notes from Chauncy to Foxcroft in *FP*.

33. Corrigan, *Prism of Piety*, 31, citing Wadsworth, *Mutual Love*, 5; Foxcroft, "Preface," in Dickinson, *True Scripture-Doctrine*, v–vi, citing Watts et al., *Faith and Practice*, 1:251 and *Veritas Redux*, 1:xii, by the rigid English Calvinist, John Edwards, whom Foxcroft also described as a "Bigot to Orthodoxy." Corrigan linked Foxcroft with Appleton, Colman, Pemberton, and his predecessor at First Church Benjamin Wadsworth, as "catholick Congregationalists," who were "influenced by [English] latitudinarian thought" (*Prism of Piety*, esp. 31).

If Foxcroft's Calvinism exerted a restraining influence on the naturally cautious Chauncy, making him more hesitant to reveal marked departures from it until the final few years of his senior colleague's ministry, his moderation may have helped ease relations between the two ministers notwithstanding their obvious disagreements over revivalism. In his funeral sermon, Chauncy certainly praised Foxcroft generously for his personal qualities as well as his pastoral and intellectual gifts. Despite the challenges of ill health, Foxcroft "made it his care to govern his resentments," Chauncy noted, "keeping them under the restraints of reason and religion." In general, he described Foxcroft as "a stranger to all the arts of intrigue and dissimulation," a man of "serious," but "pleasant and affable" "conversation," a witty, but not offensive person, and above all, "a real good christian," who lived true to his orthodox faith, relying "on the mercy of God, and the atoning blood, and perfect righteousness, of Jesus Christ the Savior."[34]

Yet whatever Foxcroft's allowance for Chauncy's or others' theological idiosyncrasies, to the extent that he knew of them, there is no reason to believe that either he or the congregation of First Church would easily have tolerated the universalist ideas that Chauncy came to embrace before Foxcroft's death. In that sense, as others, Chauncy's decision to wait another thirteen years before revealing them publicly is understandable, especially given the radical scale of his departure from traditional New England doctrine. So is the rather tentative nature of his first universalist publication, *Salvation for All Men* (1782), co-authored with John Clarke and intended as an opening "scouting-party" in the form of a brief compilation from the writings of three earlier English authors. The fact that this work appeared at all has already been attributed to the immediate stimulus, even provocation, of the ministry and teaching of John Murray, which Chauncy targeted quite specifically in his preface.[35]

Murray was born in 1741 into a strict Calvinist family in the south of England. But he was persuaded by the teachings of Relly to convert to universalism as early as 1760, when he was living in London and attending Whitefield's "Tabernacle." Following a series of personal crises, he emigrated to America in 1770, and for the first four years after his arrival was based in Good Luck, New Jersey, where he found both a sympathetic welcome and a calling to preach in the meeting house built by the evangelical farmer,

---

34. Chauncy. *Discourse Occasioned by the Death of the Reverend Thomas Foxcroft*, 22–28, esp. 27.

35. Belknap to Ebenezer Hazard December 19, 1782, in Belknap et al., "The Belknap Papers," *CMHS* 5/2, 169–74, esp. 172. Griffin, *Old Brick*, 171–74, offers the most nuanced account of Murray's indirect influence, negative, as well as positive, in first discouraging and then encouraging Chauncy to break his universalist silence.

Thomas Potter. Murray's ministry proved so popular that he was soon able to spread his message to Philadelphia, New York, Newport, Boston, and Portsmouth, New Hampshire. After 1775 he transferred the center of his operations to Massachusetts, where he eventually became full-time pastor of one of the first avowedly universalist congregations in New England, at Gloucester in 1779. Although he also continued a supplemental ministry of itinerant preaching and teaching, he spent his last sixteen years at a church in Boston before his death in 1809. Murray was not the first to teach universalist ideas in the American colonies. From the seventeenth century onwards, others had shared their visions of universal salvation in various communities, including Samuel Gorton and his followers in Rhode Island, John Rogers and the Rogerenes in Connecticut, and in Pennsylvania, the German Baptist "Dunkers," Conrad Beissel and his Ephrata Society, and the physician and mystic, George de Benneville.[36]

What made Murray so significant was that he was the first to attract really widespread attention with a universalist message. By deploying biblically allusive, but rarely explicit, discourse on the theme, he initially seems to have cloaked his most controversial teachings. But once established in Gloucester, Murray preached them quite openly. Like Relly, from whom he clearly drew key ideas, his overarching theological framework remained fundamentally Calvinist. Their major innovation, as Holifield has pointed out, lay in "universalizing" God's decree of election to salvation, together with the extent of Christ's self-identifying and atoning "union" with humankind. Murray thus considered the concept of union as:

> the key by which we unlock this mystery, [that] the head and members are united, and the iniquity of the members, is visited on the head . . . but if it were just to inflict the penalty of death upon Jesus Christ for our sins, then it becomes just that we should live through him, hence as he died for us . . . , so he is now our life.

---

36. On Murray, see (in chronological order): Murray, *Records of the Life*; Eddy, *Universalism in America*, 1:105–266, passim; Allen and Eddy, *A History of the Unitarians*, 388–407; Russell E. Miller, *The Larger Hope*, 3–44, passim; Marini, *Radical* Sects, 68–69; Howe, "How Human an Enterprise"; Hoogenboom. "Murray, John"; Holifield, *Theology in America*, 220–23. On Relly, see Clymer, "Life and Thought of James Relly," reprinted, with minor changes, as "Union with Christ," 116–40; Hill, "Relly, James (1721/2–1778)." On early American universalism generally, see Eddy, *Universalism in America*; Allen and Eddy, *History of the Unitarians;* Cassara, *Universalism in America*; Robinson, *Unitarians and Universalists*; Bressler, *Universalist Movement in America*; Holifield, *Theology in America*, 218–33. See also Marini, *Radical Sects*, esp. 68–75, 83–86, 122–27; Hatch, *Democratization of American Christianity*, passim.

Murray contended that Jesus was "from everlasting ordained to be the Saviour of all." Through federal participation in the first man, Adam, who fell from grace, the whole of humanity must suffer the consequences of sin, even Christ. Yet he, as the perfect "second Adam," with whom humankind was spiritually united, had justly paid the price in his self-sacrificial death on the cross. All had, therefore, been saved through this universal act of atonement. All had been justified before God and would ultimately enjoy full spiritual rebirth in union with Christ in his resurrection. The problem was that not everyone recognized this truth. So Murray distinguished between those who came to Christian faith in their earthly lives, who would immediately be redeemed, and those who did not. The latter would suffer "condemnation," "shame," "labour," "uncertainty," and "fear," he argued, before they came to enjoy the full benefits of redemption after "the day of the Lord" following Christ's second advent, when their true redeemed status would be finally revealed and recognized.[37]

Murray was not alone in preaching a universalist message in the 1770s and early 1780s. Elhanan Winchester, who began ministry as an itinerant Baptist in 1770 in Massachusetts, made his own position public in 1781 with a "discourse" delivered to the Baptist congregation in Philadelphia where he was pastor. But Winchester's major ministry as a universalist teacher came after 1782, when Chauncy had already begun to reveal his views. Other early universalists to impact New England included Isaac Davis of Connecticut and his family and Caleb Rich and Adams Streeter of Massachusetts, who also had an itinerant ministry in the 1770s and went on to serve as ministers of independent Christian "societies" at Warwick, Oxford, and elsewhere. But for Chauncy, Murray was the major challenge, and for two main reasons. His universalist position differed from that of the First Church minister and, much like some of the Great Awakening preachers against whom Chauncy had inveighed in the 1740s, Murray appeared to threaten prevailing social order by fostering antinominianism. "The doctrine of Universal Salvation has, in this and some other towns, been held forth by a stranger," Chauncy and John Clarke wrote of Murray, "who has, of himself, assumed the character of a preacher, in direct contradiction . . . to the whole tenor of the New-Testament-books, from their beginning to end." Chauncy's basic theological point of contention was simple. Murray taught that "a man may go to heaven, notwithstanding all the sins he has been

---

37. Murray, *Letters and Sketches*, 1:45–46, 3:362, 2:46; *Universalism Vindicated*, x–xi; Holifield, *Theology in America*, 220–23, esp. 222. Relly's most influential publication was *Union*. A concise summary of Murray's theology is to be found in Allen and Eddy, *History of the Unitarians*, 392–94, citing Murray, *Letters and Sketches* and Relly, *Union*. See also Murray, *Some Hints*; Russell E. Miller, *The Larger Hope*, 40–42.

guilty of in the course of his life" and this represented not only a serious doctrinal error. It encouraged moral license:

> Such a doctrine looks very like an encouragement to Libertinism, and falls in with the scheme of too many in this degenerate age, who, under the pretence of promoting religion, undermine it at the very root. It is certainly fitted to this end, and has already had this effect upon many, especially of our younger people, who, by means of it, have lost all sense of religion, and given themselves up to the most criminal excesses! If this kind of preaching is encouraged, it may prove as hurtful to civil society as to religion.[38]

Chauncy's and Clarke's initial counter to Murray's ideas and their dangers, *Salvation for All Men* (1782), may have been little more than a collection of quotations from Jeremiah White, Hartley, Scott, and others. But its subject matter was so controversial that it soon provoked some seven rejoinders from orthodox Calvinists, among which Joseph Eckley's *Divine Glory Brought to View in the Condemnation of the Ungodly* (1782) apparently prompted Chauncy's next excursion into such turbulent theological waters. *Divine Glory* (1783) rejected Eckley's arguments as inconsistent both with the goodness and justice of God and with traditional Calvinism. But like *Salvation for All Men*, it ultimately proved just part of an opening salvo to the full-scale presentation of universalist theology that Chauncy unveiled in his three final, major publications, *Benevolence of the Deity* (1784), *Mystery Hid* (1784) and *Five Dissertations* (1785). Reflecting the obvious sensitivity of their subject matter, both *Benevolence of the Deity* and *Mystery Hid* were published in London and the latter, like *Salvation for All Men*, was anonymously attributed to "One who wishes well to the whole Human Race." Scholars have rightly distinguished between Chauncy's socially more elitist universalism and the populist works of Murray and similar contemporaries. They have paid less attention to the differences in his ideas and his sources. In presenting somewhat simplistic categorizations of its adherents' views and unduly focusing on the extent to which they explicitly echoed Murray's

---

38. Winchester, *Seed of Woman*; Chauncy and Clarke, *Salvation for All Men*, ii–iii. On Elhanan Winchester, see the general accounts of Allen and Eddy, *History of the Unitarians*, 408–23; Sweeney, "Elhanan Winchester." On Isaac Davis, Caleb Rich, and Adams Streeter, see Peter Hughes, "The Davis Family," "Caleb Rich," and "Adams Streeter"; Marini, *Radical Sects*, 71–75; Allen and Eddy, *History of the Unitarians*, 423–26 (on Rich and Streeter); Robinson, *Unitarians and Universalists*, 313–14 (on Rich). Allen and Eddy noted that "within ten years from the time of his [Murray's] settlement in Gloucester, seven other preachers of Universalism had arisen in America, and if we also count Rev. John Tyler, an Episcopal rector in Norwich, Conn., there were eight" (*History of the Unitarians*, 398).

indebtedness to Relly and his doctrine of "union," some have also tended to exaggerate the diversity of late eighteenth-century universalism in general.[39]

While their views differed in other ways, for example, both Rich and Davis shared Murray's central commitment to a doctrine of universal salvation by divine grace in and through the mediating and atoning work of Jesus Christ. First a Congregationalist, then a Baptist, before pastoring his own universalist congregation, Rich derived his ideas primarily from a series of intense mystical experiences in the 1770s, together with intensive personal Bible study, according to his colorful autobiographical testimony. He came to the view that "all men who were created in Adam and fell with or died in him would infallibly be restored and made alive in Christ" years before he actually met Murray. Seeing universal salvation as an act of grace accomplished in and through Christ, Rich became convinced that:

> The resurrection of our Lord from the dead was to eternal life, to an inheritance incorruptible undefiled and fadeth not away; and that the first Adam and every individual of his posterity from the beginning of this world to the end, did as truly and positively pass with and in Christ from death to life and became heirs of that inheritance: as that by one man sin entered into the world, and that death had passed upon Adam and all his race who became heirs with him and by nature children of wrath; even so Christ was made manifest in due time utterly and completely to destroy the devil and all his works.

In his one published work, Isaac Davis focused on a similar idea of redemption, arguing, as Stephen Marini has shown, that while Adam's fall produced "a natural, spiritual, and eternal death" for the whole of humanity, "the full imputation of sin onto Christ," who made substitutionary atonement for it, "established the infinite justice of God and gave pardon to all sinners."[40]

---

39. In addition to Eckley, *Divine Glory*, Lippy, *Seasonable Revolutionary*, 112, noted the following Calvinist responses to *Salvation for All Men*: Edwards Jr., *Brief Observations*; Gordon, *Doctrine*; Hopkins, *Inquiry Concerning the Future State*; Samuel Mather, *All Men*; Thacher, *That the Punishment*. The work of Edwards Jr. was written in response to "the doctrine of universal salvation, as lately promulgated" in the city of New Haven. Key source materials for Chauncy's *Salvation for All Men*, were drawn from Jeremiah White, *Restoration of All Things*; Hartley, *Observations*, esp. 2:382–437, passim; Scott, *Sermons*, 2:329–79, passim.

40. Rich, "Narrative of Elder Caleb Rich," esp. 187, 195–96; Marini, *Radical Sects*, 71, citing from Davis, *What Love*. Among more recent historians, Marini is notable for stressing points of difference among early American universalists. He offered the following broad-brush characterizations, for example: "Murray was Calvinistic, Rellyan, doctrinaire, and imperious; Winchester was Arminian, restorationist, rationalistic, and irenic. Murray's theology was fundamentally Christological while Winchester's

The doctrine of Elhanan Winchester, who has been widely hailed, with Murray and Hosea Ballou II, as the second of three "founders" of American universalism, was significantly shaped by his reading of German pastor Georg-Klein Nicolai's *Everlasting Gospel* (1753) and of the works of the universalist Church of England clergyman, Sir James Stonhouse, author of *Universal Restitution: A Scripture Doctrine* (1761). But those who have neglected key points of commonality with the thought of Murray and other late eighteenth-century universalists have given an unbalanced presentation of his ideas, especially when they have simply labeled his theology "Arminian" or over-emphasized Winchester's notions of punishment for sin after death. Winchester developed an elaborate eschatological system which only provided for the full realization of universal salvation after a period of up to fifty thousand, or even two and a half billion, years' punishment for those who declined God's offer of redemption before they died. But even a cursory reading of one of Winchester's fullest expositions of his universalism in *Universal Restoration* (1792) reveals, for example, that he saw the major "principles upon which the doctrine of the Restoration is founded" in remarkably "Murrayite" terms.[41]

Starting from the basic presupposition that a Creator God must be universally benevolent, Winchester thus placed Christ's atonement at the heart of his theology:

> Christ died for all; for though the universality of his death is not expressly asserted, in every text where it is mentioned that he died, it must always be understood; because it is never denied in

was rooted in eschatological speculation" (*Radical Sects*, 68–74, esp. 71).While there are elements of truth in these statements, they are also somewhat simplistic. Robinson seems closer to the mark with his general observation that "the shades of Universalist belief among Murray, Winchester, and de Benneville differ slightly" (*Unitarians and Universalists*, 54).

41. Winchester, *Universal Restoration*, xlv, and see esp. 93–148, "Dialogue III"; *Holy Conversation*, 50–51; Stonhouse, *Universal Restitution*. Nicolai's work was published in Pennsylvania under the pseudonym Paul Siegvolck. See *Everlasting Gospel*. On Stonhouse, see Berry, "Stonhouse, Sir James." Allen and Eddy, for example, described Winchester as an "Arminian" at the time that he embraced universalism, focused on his elaborate, eschatological scheme, and contended that "Mr. Winchester's theology had little in common with that of Mr. Murray" (*History of the Unitarians*, 420–22). Bressler suggested that "Winchester came to Universalism 'from a very moderate Calvinism, if not downright Arminianism'" (*Universalist Movement in America*, 16, citing Ballou II, "Dogmatic and Religious History," 97). By contrast, Robinson wrote of Winchester's "Calvinist evangelicalism" in his brief account (*Unitarians and Universalists*, 51–54, esp. 54). Holifield described Winchester's theology as "a mixture of Arminian and Calvinist ideas" (*Theology in America*, 224–27, esp. 225).The best exposition is that of Parry, "Between Calvinism and Arminianism."

any place, and is plainly, and pointedly declared in those which I have quoted.

In response to the obvious follow-up question, "When shall the world believe, and know that Christ is the Son of God?" he then expounded an almost Rellyan vision of union with Christ, although this was framed in his own distinctive, eschatological terms. Winchester looked forward to a day "when the great marriage of the Lamb shall be celebrated," when "the Church shall be perfected in one," and "when Christ shall give that glory and honour to his Bride, which the Father gave to him, and shall thus unite her to himself, in an indissoluble union." It would be then, he prophesied, that "the world" would "know him, whom to know is life eternal." Moreover, although he rejected traditional Calvinist understandings of a limited atonement for the sins of the elect, Winchester, like Murray, did not take the full Arminian position that salvation, even if universal in application, was in any way contingent on the good works of humanity. The "unchangeableness of God," which was another founding principle of his doctrine of restoration, implied that divine "counsels" were "immutable," including God's purpose to save humankind. In that sense, Winchester's vision of universal salvation by divine decree was much closer to that of Murray's "universalized" Calvinism than some historians have tended to allow.[42]

Winchester's central argument was pretty straightforward:

> If God will have all men to be saved, or restored, and to come to the knowledge of the truth, if it is his good pleasure, which he hath purposed in himself, in the dispensation of the fulness of times, to rehead all Things in Christ, both in heaven and on earth; if he hath sworn, that unto him every knee shall bow, and every tongue shall swear; and if he worketh all things after the counsel of his own will, and is determined to perform all his pleasure, which he is able to do; and with him nothing that he pleases is impossible: I say, if all these things are true, (as who, that believes the Scriptures, can deny?) then, is not the doctrine of the Restoration true . . . which God, in the counsel of his will, hath purposed, and is determined to perform?

Chauncy's doctrine of universal restoration or salvation was more complex. In drawing on White, Hartley, Scott, and others, his sources were more sophisticated. He also, like Winchester and to some extent Mayhew, was prepared to adopt a relatively innovative hermeneutic in developing his

---

42. Winchester, *Universal Restoration*, 99, 100–101, 104–5. See also, among Winchester's other works: *Seed of the Woman*; *Outcasts Comforted*; *Attempt to Collect*.

biblical theology. But some of his conclusions clearly echoed those of other early universalists.[43]

Inasmuch as Chauncy claimed to be doing nothing more nor less than uncovering the true meaning of scripture, except in *Benevolence of the Deity*, the interpretive focus of his last major works was largely biblical and exegetical. Yet as Nathan Hatch has pointed out in an important article, because he relied so heavily on "the right of private judgment in handling Scripture," Chauncy's biblicism, like Mayhew's, also represented a significant departure from the traditional hermeneutical approach championed by "Protestants from Luther to Wesley." The Reformation principle of *sola scriptura* ("by Scripture alone"), which had been consistently upheld to justify the rejection of Catholic and other heresies, had been traditionally balanced by a parallel Protestant commitment to the authority of established theological and/or confessional orthodoxy. But inspired by such examples as Samuel Clarke and Taylor, the "'free, impartial, and diligent' method of examining Scripture," which Chauncy had privately pursued since the 1750s, was relatively free of such constraints. Much like Mayhew, who advanced a subordinationist Christology based on his own biblical understanding, and openly rejected the formulations of the Athanasian Creed, the First Church minister freely plowed his own expository furrow. In addition to his redefinition of the doctrine of original sin, which has already been considered, the results finally unveiled in the 1780s thus included a radically heterodox commitment to universal salvation. In keeping with what Hatch has justly discerned as his "rational biblicism" and a growing "individualization of conscience" reflected in the work of other key figures, including Winchester, Chauncy's argumentation in *Five Dissertations* (1785) and *Mystery Hid* (1784) was studiously based on detailed biblical exegesis. But he often deployed it to discard, not defend, traditional Protestant doctrine.[44]

Chauncy shared Murray's, Rich's, and Winchester's underlying presuppositions of a human fall from grace that was fully reversed by the atoning sacrifice of Jesus Christ. He thus continued to uphold the centrality of the mediatorial work of Christ to the divine plan of salvation and maintained that "deliverance from the bondage of sin, however great it has been, or however early contracted, is obtainable upon the foot of grace through Jesus

---

43. Winchester, *Universal Restoration*, 106–7.

44. Hatch, "Sola Scriptura," esp. 61–63, 66–67; Mayhew, *On Hearing the Word*, 403, 418n. In a preface to one of his last works, Chauncy explicitly acknowledged his "obligations" to Taylor. It was the latter's "example and recommendation that put [him] upon the studying the scriptures in that free, impartial, and diligent manner," he wrote, "which led [him] into these sentiments" (*Mystery Hid*, xi-xii). "Biblicism" is here understood simply as commitment to biblical authority.

Christ." But he now thought the extent and application of Christ's saving work all-inclusive. Through one act of supreme self-sacrifice, Christ had "made ATONEMENT, not only for the original lapse, but for all the sins this would be introductory to, and might be the occasion of being committed by any of the sons of men, in any part or age of the world." Chauncy's departure from traditional, orthodox soteriology found further expression in other ways. He argued, for example, that "the appointment of Christ to be the Saviour of men, took rise from the grace of God," not to "pacify God's wrath" or "to move compassion in him towards sinners." But like Murray's and Winchester's, his universalism was grounded in the fact that he no longer, if he ever truly had, conceived Christ's death as a sacrifice on behalf of a limited number who were pre-ordained or "elected" by God for salvation. According to *Five Dissertations* (1785), as in the full exposition of his universalism, *Mystery Hid* (1784), "the whole human race, in consequence of a divine constitution, occasioned by the obedience of the one man Jesus Christ, are as certainly under the advantage of a deliverance from death, as they were subjected to it in consequence of a counter-constitution, occasioned by the offence of the one man Adam."[45]

As *Divine Glory* (1783) made clear, therefore, the root of Chauncy's universalism lay in his revised understanding of the atonement. "I agree with you," he informed Eckley:

> in opposition to all the CALVINISTS that ever wrote upon the subject, that nothing could be a greater insult on the weakness and misery of mankind, than to offer them all salvation, unless there was a foundation laid for the bestowment of it. And I further acknowledge, "the obedience and death of Christ" are the moral ground of that general proclamation which is made in the gospel, and the pardon which is offered unto all men.

In that sense, "the doctrine of universal redemption necessarily infers [i.e. implies] universal salvation"—an argument that Chauncy expounded through detailed consideration of relevant biblical passages and summarized in six key propositions in *Mystery Hid*:

I. "From the time that sin entered into the world by the first man Adam, Jesus Christ is the person through whom, and upon whose account, happiness is attainable by any of the human race";

II. "The obedience of Christ, and eminently his obedience to death, when he had assumed our flesh, in the fullness of time, is the

---

45. Chauncy, *Five Dissertations*, 237, 245, 246, 136.

ground or reason upon which it hath pleased God to make happiness attainable by any of the race of Adam";

III. "Christ died, not for a select number of men only, but for mankind universally, and without exception or limitation" . . . [and] "if Christ died for all, the scheme we are establishing perfectly falls in with the great design of his death";

IV. "It is the purpose of God, according to his good pleasure, that mankind universally, in consequence of the death of his Son Jesus Christ, shall certainly and finally be saved";

V. "As a mean in order to men's being made meet for salvation, God, by Jesus Christ, will, sooner or later, in THIS STATE OR ANOTHER, reduce them all under a WILLING and OBEDIENT SUBJECTION to his moral government";

VI. "The scripture language, concerning the REDUCED, or RESTORED, in consequence of the mediatory interposition of Jesus Christ, is such as to lead us into the thought, that THEY are comprehensive of MANKIND UNIVERSALLY."[46]

One of the most intriguing aspects of Chauncy's universalist theology is thus an inherent tension between a rather deterministic commitment to universal salvation as a result of Christ's redemption of all humankind by an act of sovereign grace and a more voluntaristic understanding of the innate freedom of women and men to "work out" and even, in some sense, to achieve their own salvation. Propositions IV and V of *Mystery Hid* leave little room for doubt, for example, that Chauncy believed, like Murray and Winchester, in the salvation of humanity by divine *fiat*. In a speculative and even more complex exposition than Winchester's, he accordingly devoted considerable time and attention to outlining a potentially multiple-stage scheme of redemption whereby human beings would be repeatedly presented with God's offer of salvation in this life and even in hell until they eventually accepted it. Yet precisely because Chauncy thought such acceptance inevitable, in espousing the doctrine of universal atonement, he effectively ended up endorsing ideas more normally associated with Calvinist notions of unconditional election and irresistible grace.[47]

46. Chauncy, *Divine Glory*, 7, citing Eckley, *Divine Glory*, 8; *Mystery Hid*, 17, 19, 20, 22, 170–71, 237.

47. Chauncy, *Mystery Hid*, 22, 170–71. Chauncy argued, for example, that "a second period of the reign of Christ will commence at the general resurrection [of the dead], when, as head of the kingdom of God, he will open a new dispensation, with respect to both the righteous and the wicked. As to the righteous, whom he has already, or in the first period of his mediatory reign, reduced under subjection to the moral government

The irony is that in *Mystery Hid* (1784), as in *Divine Glory* (1783) and *Five Dissertations* (1785), Chauncy simultaneously extended the process of repudiating and/or reinterpreting central tenets of Calvinism that he had most explicitly begun in 1765, with *Twelve Sermons*. He had no hesitation in listing "the doctrines of election and reprobation; of the eternity of hell-torments; and of the partial design, and final effect, of the mediatory interposition of Jesus Christ" among "horrible absurdities . . . which Protestants receive for revealed truths." It has already been shown how Chauncy replaced a classical, reformed understanding of original sin, over which he had long been equivocating, with a revised doctrine (in *Five Dissertations*) that humanity was mortal and imperfect, but not morally depraved as a result of Adam's fall from grace. In *Mystery Hid*, he likewise redefined "imputed righteousness" as a moral quality that required human agency, rather than a simple gift of God, and he offered two concepts of election—one with a corporate application to the whole church and the other applying solely to special individuals predestined to come to Christian faith before death. Yet even as he advocated a seemingly irresistible understanding of divine grace in universal salvation, Chauncy also reiterated his Arminian stress on the importance of good works to achieve righteousness before God. Thus in his other major, three-part work of the 1780s, *Benevolence of the Deity* (1785), he went to considerable lengths to stress the importance of human free agency. [48]

---

of God, he will, at his second coming, bestow upon them the reward of good and faithful servants . . . And as to the wicked . . . they, while the righteous are reigning in life and glory, shall be sent by the Lord Jesus Christ, in execution of his mediatory trust, to the place of weeping, and wailing, and gnashing of teeth; not to continue there always, but till the rebellion of their hearts is subdued, and they are wrought upon to become the willing and obedient subjects of God." Chauncy also allowed for the possibility of further resurrections and periods in hell, if necessary, for those who remained unrepentant, but he was confident that "all men will finally be happy" (*Mystery Hid*, 219-20, 404, 9).

48. Chauncy, *Mystery Hid*, 362-63. Instead of a traditional Calvinist understanding of "imputed righteousness," Chauncy stressed that "it ought always to be kept in mind, that righteousness is as truly a moral good quality, as sin is a moral evil one. They are both connected with personal agency, and absolutely dependent on it . . . That part therefore of the advantage through Christ, which consists in our being made righteous, and in this way becoming qualified for an happy reign in life, after we are delivered from death, essentially supposes the use of means, and such too as are proper to be used with moral agents, in order to their being formed, agreeably to their natures, into righteous persons, or, what means the same thing, a meetness for an eternal reign in happy life" (*Mystery Hid*, 85-86). See, further, Chauncy, *Five Dissertations*, 309. Chauncy redefined "the terms Elect, Chosen, [which] are often used in the New Testament, with respect to the whole body of Christians, as signifying nothing more than their being selected from the rest of the world, and admitted into the visible kingdom of God, in order to

Chauncy's central aims in this last work were "to remove away . . . objections, wipe off . . . aspersions, and set forth the benevolence of the Deity, in its true glory." He sought to define the sense in which he attributed that quality to God, to show how the natural order provided evidence of it and to answer objections against it, especially those based on empirical observation of the world's disorders and those deriving from the problem of moral evil. The result was largely a work of natural theology, which relied much less on biblical exegesis than many of Chauncy's other publications. But *Benevolence of the Deity* (1785) was also an exercise in Christian apologetics, which attempted to demonstrate how ascribing "the general notion of goodness" to God was perfectly consistent with earthly reality and the human condition as Chauncy understood them. Scholars have rightly pointed out that the promotion of human happiness was central to his vision of divine benevolence. "A principle disposing and prompting to the communication of happiness" was, in fact, "the first idea that enter[ed] into its composition." So Chauncy could conceive of no "constitution . . . more worthy of the Deity . . . than that which supposes him to exist, not only with the powers of intelligence and volition, heightened in degree of perfection beyond all bounds; but with the principles also of self-love, and benevolence, heightened in like manner, disposing him to seek his own, and the happiness of others."[49]

When he came to expound on the relationship between divine benevolence and human happiness, therefore, Chauncy predictably voiced similarly strong objections to the Calvinist doctrine of eternal reprobation as in *Mystery Hid* (1784). "A more shocking idea can scarce be given of the Deity," he argued, "than that which represents him as arbitrarily dooming the greater part of the race of men to eternal misery." Yet he saw this as "the true import of the doctrine of absolute and unconditional reprobation" and found it nothing short of scandalous to

> make the infinitely benevolent God the grand and only efficient, not only in the bestowment of good, but even in the abuse of it;

their being under peculiar advantages that they may be fitted for eternal life." But he also allowed for another biblical usage "to signify particular persons infallibly selected for salvation" and further asked: "why may we not understand by them those, whom God knew would be wrought upon, in this present state, under the government of Jesus Christ, and therefore fixed upon them as the persons that should, in the next state, be glorified by him? though not to the exclusion of others; as has already been said, and need not be again repeated." (*Mystery Hid*, 230–31). Chauncy freely conceded to Eckley that "could those pious worthies [New England's Calvinist forefathers] (for such I really esteem them) return to this world, they would reprobate your doctrines as earnestly as they would mine. Universal redemption, which you allow, they never admitted as an article of their faith" (*Divine Glory*, 5).

49. Chauncy, *Benevolence of the Deity*, ix, 11, 25.

and [to argue] that he has so laid his plan . . . that its final result should be the everlasting damnation of a great number of the creatures his hands have formed.

Not only was everlasting damnation inconsistent with divine benevolence and the promotion of human happiness, the whole Calvinist doctrine of predestination robbed people of the genuine free will that Chauncy thought a matter of common perception, as well as an essential prerequisite to the exercise of moral virtue. Inasmuch as a rigid scheme of predestination would frustrate freedom of choice, it would thereby diminish human well-being, because "the most exalted happiness, it is possible we should enjoy, is that which is connected with, and dependant on, a free, but wise and good, use of that power [of exercising free will]."[50]

Chauncy's advocacy of free agency was thus a strong feature of his universalist publications of the 1780s. But his parallel and indeed primary commitment in those works to universal salvation by divine decree also led him into an intellectual impasse, which he tried, but ultimately failed to resolve decisively on more than one occasion. In *Divine Glory* (1783), for example, Chauncy openly stated the logical consequence of his universalist soteriology. "Inasmuch as the saviour of the world has atoned for the sins of every creature, and God earnestly desires the salvation of all," he contended, "it is inconceivable that any should perish everlastingly. His infinite power, wisdom and goodness forbid such a dishonourable supposition." Since people were also "free agents," the obvious question was how their freedom could be preserved. But here Chauncy's answer was as vague, as it was speculative. "Though free," he continued, "yet surely, infinite power, guided by infinite wisdom, and excited by infinite goodness, may devise such a scheme, as shall bring all men into a state of moral subjection, without breaking in upon their liberty."[51]

Despite its obvious difficulty, Chauncy did not hesitate to address the same issue at the beginning of *Mystery Hid* (1784). His opening assumptions were that God would not have brought men and women into existence "unless he intended to make them finally happy," and that "it cannot well be supposed," given God's infinite intelligence and wisdom, that "he should be

---

50. Chauncy, *Benevolence of the Deity*, viii, 32, 142. See *Mystery Hid*, 4, 14, 21, 122–23, 168–69, 249–50, 322–24 for often vigorous criticisms of the doctrine of eternal reprobation.

51. Chauncy, *Divine Glory*, 8–9. Despite his stated objections to Calvinist doctrine, when expounding 1 Tim 2:4, which refers to a God, "who will have all men to be saved, and to come unto the knowledge of the truth," Chauncy argued explicitly that the idea that this divine will "must issue in their everlasting salvation . . . falls in with the Calvinian doctrine respecting this point" (*Divine Glory*, 9).

unable to project, or carry into execution, a scheme that would be effectual to secure, sooner or later, the certain accomplishment" of that benevolent intention. So how could anyone have genuine free will? Again his answer, while somewhat more complex in this instance, remained elusive, even evasive:

> Should it be suggested, Free agents, as men are allowed to be, must be left to their own choice . . . The answer is obvious, Their Creator, being perfectly benevolent, would be disposed to prevent their making, or, at least, their finally persisting in, . . . wrong choices . . . Should it be said further, Such free agents as men are may oppose all the methods that can be used with them, in consistency with liberty, and persist in wrong pursuits . . . This is sooner said than proved. Who will undertake to make it evident, that infinite wisdom, excited by infinite benevolence, is incapable of deriving expedients, whereby moral agents, without any violence offered to their liberty, may certainly be led . . . into such determinations, and consequent actions, as would finally prepare them for happiness? It would be hard to suppose, that infinite wisdom should be finally outdone by the obstinacy and folly of any free agents whatsoever. If this might really be the case, how can it be thought, with respect to such free agents, that they should ever have been produced by an infinitely benevolent cause? If the only good God knew . . . that some free agents would make themselves unhappy . . . why did he create them?[52]

Chauncy was a deeper and better educated theologian than other early universalists. His biblical exegesis was more sophisticated and he applied it with some rigor, as he sought to break free from the theological constraints of predestinarian Calvinism. But in the final analysis, when faced with the intractable tensions of simultaneously upholding divine grace and human free will, Chauncy found himself resorting to complex eschatological speculations about the fate of those who died without faith and to summary affirmations, however questioning, of an ultimate divine sovereignty that could somehow work to protect and preserve human free will rather than overpowering it. In that sense, his universalism betrayed greater internal inconsistencies than Winchester's or Murray's. At the same time, because he laid so much emphasis, as they did, on the primacy of divine grace, the radical universalist theology of the septuagenarian and octogenarian Chauncy had more in common with the reformed orthodoxy of his earlier years than scholars have often allowed. His theological revisionism is also open to its

---

52. Chauncy, *Mystery Hid*, 1–3.

own revisionist re-interpretation in another sense. For Chauncy saw his universalism not as a "novel doctrine," published solely in the interests of reform or innovation, but as a biblically inspired attempt to redefine Christian essentials in order to remove unnecessary "stumbling blocks" to belief and so restore their credibility.[53]

Scholars who have largely viewed Chauncy's theology in proleptic terms—as an evolutionary stage en route to nineteenth-century Unitarian universalism—have thus done his thought an injustice. For despite his late universalism and his reinterpretation of Calvinist doctrines, he remained a biblicist, Christocentric thinker to the last, whose fundamental commitment to the primacy of divine grace remains unmistakable. Lippy has argued that theologically, as well as politically, Chauncy was acting to preserve "what he saw as vital to the New England Way" by defending as well as redefining it. However, while Chauncy clearly was attempting to uphold traditional order during the Great Awakening and he showed similar motivations during the American Episcopate controversy and later, Lippy provided no direct evidence from the First Church minister's writings that his major goal in re-conceptualizing important elements of traditional Congregationalist theology was to maintain "the essential structures and categories of Puritan religious thought."[54]

A more promising way of understanding what Chauncy was trying to do in his latter works is to take him at his word and to explore his methods, as well as his conclusions. As his many citations show, Chauncy was influenced quite heavily by the writings of other theologians. But with the exception of *Benevolence of the Deity* (1785), his last major treatises drew mainly on detailed biblical exegesis to develop their conclusions. They were the result of intensive scriptural study and Chauncy explicitly claimed that the findings of his most radical publication were derived from the New Testament. Such a claim is quite consistent with Chauncy's self-proclaimed mandate as minister and theologian "to explain 'the mystery of the gospel,' as it has been manifested . . . in the books of the new-testament." Moreover, the titles of two of Chauncy's last works confirm that that is precisely what he saw himself doing, however heterodox the results. In his 1783 pamphlet, his goal was to show *Divine Glory Brought to View in the Final Salvation of All Men* and when he gave a full presentation of his universalism the following year, he did not offer it as a radically new discovery. It was rather *The Mystery Hid from Ages and Generations, Made Manifest by the Gospel-Revelation,*

53. Chauncy and Clarke, *Salvation for All Men*, i; *Opinion of One*, 19; Hatch, "Sola Scriptura," 62–63. Cf. *Mystery Hid*, vi.

54. Lippy, *Seasonable Revolutionary*, 122, 109. Lippy quoted nothing from Chauncy's works to that effect, instead citing from Walker, *Ten New England Leaders* and May, *Enlightenment in America*.

as this was "opened in the New-Testament writings, and entrusted with JESUS CHRIST to bring into Effect." Right to the end of his writing career, Chauncy can thus be fairly described as a thoroughly biblicist theologian. It was his commitment to the ultimate authority of the Bible, as he saw it, that led him to question, reject and reinterpret traditional doctrines, where he found necessary. Yet the fact that he felt justified in doing so at all reflects another significant element of his theological methodology. For as Hatch has pointed out, the innovative hermeneutical methods of Chauncy's "rational biblicism," unconstrained by a perceived need to conform the results of his exegesis to the doctrines of orthodox tradition, also enabled him to "espouse a Christianity more attuned to the Age of Reason."[55]

In seeking to present fresh interpretations of traditional doctrine that were more in keeping with the intellectual currents of his age, the universalist works of Chauncy's final years thus continued the intellectual trajectory of his Arminian publications of the 1760s onwards. They also reflected a similar motivation and inspiration as Mayhew's daring explorations of anti-Trinitarianism and heterodox Christology in the mid-1750s. But to conclude, as many have done, with the most strikingly progressive endpoints of the two ministers' theological journeys without paying attention to strong themes of continuity with more traditional doctrines, even in their most radical works, easily leads to an unbalanced portrayal of their religious thought as a whole. It also removes an important key to understanding how their ideas could prove so influential. For Mayhew and Chauncy were not only pioneers of transformation, who made significant contributions to breaking new ground theologically. They were also, in some ways, pillars of tradition. Notwithstanding their heterodoxy, their parallel position as significant defenders of the "New England Way," doctrinally as well as ecclesiastically, will be clearly established in the next chapter. In addition to the two ministers' thoroughgoing, albeit revisionist biblicism, the major evidence lies in their ongoing commitments to established homiletic tropes of "sin–salvation–service," in Chauncy's case, to a relatively high Christology, to the defence of traditional, Congregationalist polity, and to a vigorously anti-Catholic theology.[56]

---

55. Chauncy, *Duty of Ministers*, 15; *Mystery Hid*, title page; Hatch, "Sola Scriptura," 62–63. In *Mystery Hid*, Chauncy made at least forty-five references to other works, for example, and in *Five Dissertations*, at least thirty. The publications of such prominent English Arminians as Taylor and Whitby featured prominently in these references, often on biblical and exegetical topics. It is fair to say that Chauncy's biblical exegesis was often shaped by the prior interpretations of others, not least those of Taylor and Whitby.

56. The phrase "sin–salvation–service" is taken from Stout, *New England Soul*, e.g., 41.

— 4 —

Maintaining Tradition

Consistent Puritan Themes

ON JANUARY 17, 1764, Jonathan Mayhew wrote a public letter to John Cleaveland, a Separatist minister in Ipswich, Massachusetts. Cleaveland had recently published *An Essay, to Defend Some of the Most Important Principles in the Protestant Reformed System of Christianity* (1763), which constituted a 108-page attack on Mayhew's *Divine Goodness* (1763). His main target was the doctrine of Christian atonement presented in that work, which Cleaveland thought cast "injurious Aspersions" on Calvinist orthodoxy. Mayhew's response, *Letter of Reproof* (1764), was a rather high-handed and vituperative composition, which clearly bespoke his elitism. He wrote, he told Cleaveland, "not to dispute with, but to chastize and admonish you, for your real good; and to make you an example and warning to others." Mayhew also made it painfully obvious in some of his opening questions and comments that he ultimately regarded a man of Cleaveland's education and social standing as unworthy of his time and attention:

> Can you then possibly think it became you, an obscure person from another province, and one so unletter'd as you are; an outcast from the college to which you was a disgrace; for some time a rambling itinerant and promoter of disorders and confusions among us; so raw and unstudied in divinity; one hardly ever heard of among us, but in the frequent reports of your follies and extravagances, and at length set up as a minister to an assembly of separatists;—Can you possibly think it became you to turn author on this occasion; and to take this supposed necessary work of defending the most important principles of the protestant religion against me out of the hands of our Divines

of indisputable ability? What unaccountable vanity and infatuation was this![1]

Yet although *Letter of Reproof* showed such obvious signs of personal offense and indignation, Mayhew's main agenda was ultimately doctrinal. Cleaveland had impugned his soteriology, alleging that it included the notion that "'there was no absolute necessity for the sacrifice of Christ to make atonement, or to satisfy divine justice, in order to God's forgiving the sins of men consistently with his moral goodness.'" Mayhew was keen to protect himself against charges of theological heterodoxy in such a central doctrinal area and to preserve whatever reputation he retained. So before denying that he ever advanced the position that Cleaveland attributed to him, he appealed directly to the example of "eminent protestant Divines . . . even Calvinistical Divines," in support of it. In that sense, *Letter of Reproof*, though hardly one of Mayhew's most notable works, provides a vivid example of an ongoing concern, often neglected by scholars, which he and Chauncy shared to demonstrate reformed orthodoxy long after they had both publicly embraced Arminian ideas. This was also reflected in key themes in their works, which demonstrate their continuing allegiance to Puritan tradition, even while sometimes departing from it.[2]

"Sin–Salvation–Service"

Despite the obvious heterodoxy of some of their theological ideas, both Mayhew and Chauncy focused, like other more rationalist preachers of the post-Great Awakening period, on traditional homiletic themes of "sin–salvation–service" that Stout has identified as unifying features of Congregationalist preaching throughout the seventeenth and eighteenth centuries. Mayhew may have rejected the doctrine of total depravity in a strictly Calvinist sense, but he did not pull many rhetorical punches when addressing

---

1. Mayhew, *Letter of Reproof*, title page, 3, 4, citing Cleaveland, *Essay*. Akers suggested that in his subsequent *Reply*, Cleaveland "struck the most telling blow of the controversy by suggesting that Dr. Mayhew had not written in the spirit of the Gospel"(*Called unto Liberty*, 132). For consideration of Mayhew's elitist and hierarchical sociopolitical and even cosmological vision, see chapter 5.

2. Mayhew, *Letter of Reproof*, 7, citing Cleaveland, *Essay*, 9; among "Calvinistical divines," Mayhew singled out, 7–8, Twisse, *Vindiciae Gratiae*, 198. He quoted from Twisse's work in the original Latin, but patronizingly offered English translations of cited passages "for the sake of you, Mr. Cleaveland, and my other English readers." On Twisse, see, for example, Hutton, "Thomas Jackson, Oxford Platonist, and William Twisse, Aristotelian." See Mayhew's defense against accusations of Arianism in *Defence of the Observations*, esp. 111, which was considered in the previous chapter.

the sins and shortcomings of either his West Church congregation or the world in which they lived. Exploring the possible "special grounds and reasons of God's displeasure against us, and of his contending with us in so terrible a manner" as the Boston fire of 1760, he spoke, in remarkably jeremiad terms, of communal "pride," addiction to "luxury," selfishness, greed "of gain, without a due and proportionate regard to the welfare of the public and of our neighbour," and of "formality in our religion" in particular. "Many atrocious sins, and flagrant abominations, are found in the midst of us," Mayhew thundered. "Probably none of us can intirely acquit ourselves of having contributed to it [the event of the fire], by our own particular miscarriages." He was in little doubt that "the end of our being thus visited and chastized, is our reformation" and he was not afraid to indicate where reforms might be necessary. Similar concerns to identify sin and to urge moral improvement, wherever possible, are common throughout his works.³

Chauncy's open redefinition of original sin did not appear publicly until the release of *Five Dissertations* in the mid-1780s. But however his private position changed before then, the First Church minister was no less vigorous as an aged Arminian than as a young Calvinist in his denunciations of the perceived evils of his congregation or of New England society in general. To add to earlier examples, in his Artillery Election sermon of 1734, one of the key applications that Chauncy drew from a military defeat reported in the biblical Book of Judges was that "Nations and cities should learn . . . the dreadful evil and danger of sin; and be afraid to go on commiting [sic] it, hardening themselves against GOD, least [sic] he should be provoked in his holy and righteous providence, to bring them to ruin." At a Thursday Lecture in December 1741 which became one of his earlier Great Awakening publications, Chauncy stressed the salvific significance of preaching traditional themes of sin and judgment:

> sinners . . . should be plainly and faithfully told of that wrath of God, which is revealed from heaven against such persons as they are . . . And the terrors of God ought the rather to be set in array against them, because it is, in this way, ordinarily, that sinners are awakened out of their security, and put upon endeavours to get into a state of safety respecting another world.

Thirty years later, in his alternative election sermon after the removal of the General Court from Boston to Cambridge, an openly Arminian Chauncy

---

3. Stout, *New England Soul*, 37, 41–43, 92, 148, 180, for "sin–salvation–service" as a cluster of common homiletic themes for Congregationalist ministers in the seventeenth and eighteenth centuries, notwithstanding theological differences; Mayhew, *God's Hand*, 21, 23, 25–27.

lauded Puritan ancestors whose theology he had once shared. He highlighted their humility in entertaining "exalted apprehensions of this favor of the 'high and lofty one who inhabiteth eternity'; and as low ones of themselves, in consideration of their own comparative nothingness, much more of their sinfulness, whereby they had exposed themselves to the righteous resentments of heaven." In turbulent times, Chauncy thought it vital to continue to remember that "our sins are the worst enemies we have. They are, properly speaking, the true moral cause of all that we now suffer, or have reason to fear."[4]

Mayhew's emphasis on the need for moral improvement in sinful humanity is equally inescapable from *Seven Sermons* (1749) through *On Hearing the Word* (1755) to *Practical Discourses* (1760). For the West Church minister, faith and works were inseparable: "Christianity . . . is not only a rule of faith," Mayhew argued, "but of practice also; it is as certain that we are obliged to obey it, considered in the latter of these respects, as that we are bound to believe it, considered in the former." As "a practical science" constituting "the art of living piously and virtuously," the Christian religion taught "a doctrine according to Godliness, not a doctrine of licentiousness." So "the great aim of it" was "to make us fear and love God, and work righteousness." Because the "grand concern of mankind" was "to act with propriety as the subjects of God's moral government," Mayhew also understood his ministry in such terms. "Since the substance of christian duty consists in the love of God and of our neighbour, and in the practice of morality," he contended in one of his earliest published sermons, "this shows us what a gospel-minister's preaching ought chiefly to turn upon." While Mayhew also gave significant attention to more abstract, doctrinal issues, a consistent focus of his teaching was thus on the need to work out one's salvation through a life of dedicated and morally virtuous service.[5]

Scholars have rightly seen such moralism as evidence, with Mayhew's alleged rationalism, of Enlightenment influences and his discourse clearly underlines the impact of an Arminian theology of salvation on his understanding of Christian ethics. But it is also redolent of more traditional pastoral concerns to urge proper "preparation" for conversion and a subsequent process of Christian sanctification. On the assumption that virtuous behavior and gospel obedience were necessary concomitants to justification by faith, Mayhew placed the onus very much on his hearers to do their part. "Our making a wise and diligent improvement of this present life," he wrote

4. Chauncy, *Character and Overthrow*, 10; *Gifts of the Spirit*, 9; *Trust in God*, 8, citing Isa 57:15, 29.

5. Mayhew, *On Hearing the Word*, 78, 83, 75–76; *Practical Discourses*, 303; *Seven Sermons*, 154.

in *Practical Discourses* (1760), was "the only opportunity which we have, or may expect, in order to work out our salvation." By highlighting not only the dangers of sin, but the need for redemption and the demands of Christian service, Mayhew did all in his power to urge his congregation to seize the day. In that sense, his perceptions of the gravity of sin and evil, combined with his emphasis on the resulting human need for divine mercy, link his theology more closely with his Puritan heritage than has sometimes been allowed.[6]

Even while urging his hearers to strive "to enter in at the strait gate" in a sermon on Luke 13:24, Mayhew spoke, just five years before his death, in terms that echoed the theology of New England's founding fathers:

> It is in this view that mankind are considered in the gospel; the very foundation of which is laid in, and the whole superstructure built upon, the supposition that mankind in general are in such a state of sin, condemnation and ruin.

This negative view of the human condition led Mayhew to affirm that "however free the grace of God is, it is manifest that he has required something of us in order to our salvation. And our Lord . . . enjoins us to strive to this end." Morally upright behavior was not only reasonable and advantageous to society; it was also necessary to avoid spiritual death and destruction. For Mayhew, "the greatness of the punishment of those who die impenitently under the gospel" was undeniable and it was "not inconsistent with the most perfect goodness, especially in certain cases, to punish wicked men." Yet there was an alternative for those prepared to work hard and trust God for divine deliverance. Salvation had been "revealed thro' Jesus Christ," and its recipients would be "not the righteous, but sinners; not men, considered in a state of innocency, who would need no such salvation, but apostate, degenerate and guilty creatures, justly obnoxious to the wrath of God."[7]

Chauncy's emphases on the sinfulness of humanity and the resulting need for redemption remained similarly unmitigated by his shifts from orthodox Calvinism to Arminianism and even to full-blown universalism. In his very first published sermon, the First Church minister described life as "a Probation season for eternity" and taught that "the Terms of Salvation are bro't down to our present fallen State: and nothing more is absolutely requir'd of us, but FAITH in JESUS CHRIST, as the SON of the living GOD."

---

6. Mayhew, *Practical Discourses*, 73. See Phil 2:12. James Jones wrote of Mayhew, for example, that "faith existed to serve morality; religion became simply a resource for human effort" (*Shattered Synthesis*, 160). Haroutunian, *Piety Versus Moralism*, e.g., 53–54, adopted a similar interpretation.

7. Mayhew, *Striving to Enter*, 11, 23; *Divine Goodness*, 66–67.

Twenty-five years later, after he had already declared his Arminianism in *Twelve Sermons*, Chauncy not only reminded those present for the ordination of Penuel Bowen of "the whole christian scheme of redemption," which he described in remarkably orthodox terms, but he urged fellow preachers that "they should mainly insist upon the method of salvation by Jesus Christ." As he sought to encourage all who heard or later read his revolutionary jeremiad, *Accursed Thing* (1778), to turn away from the sins that were impeding military progress, Chauncy also stressed the ultimate remedy. Because "the Lord Jesus Christ" had "taken upon him the curse of sin . . . ," he said hopefully, "this will inspire us with zeal and vigor, in the use of all means, that we may obtain, through him, redemption from the curse of the law and the wrath of God." When Chauncy finally unveiled the full inclusiveness of his soteriology in *Divine Glory* (1783), a key argument was that Christ's "universal redemption" entailed the "universal salvation" of humanity.[8]

Chauncy's Christology

Just as Chauncy consistently urged the centrality of Christ and his atonement to Christian salvation, he also upheld a relatively high Christology. There is no convincing evidence that he ever embraced an Arian understanding of the second person of the Trinity, or even a subordinationist one, like Mayhew. In his earliest writings, Chauncy affirmed the sinlessness of the "perfectly holy JESUS" and described him as God's "only begotten son," who came to provide a unique way of salvation through the "mediatorial" sacrifice of his death. He stressed that Christ "used Violence with no man" by compelling him to come to faith, although he had both "Sufficiency and infinite Readiness to be a Saviour." He consistently lauded Christ's atonement, including "the glorious purchases of his cross." He stressed that Christian salvation and justification could come solely "on the Account of Christ's Righteousness" and that humanity could only find "safety" and "security" with God through Christ. He upheld a classically reformed understanding of the incarnation as a "wonderful" act of "condescension," whereby "the Son of God, our Saviour and Judge," took "notice of the charities of such poor, imperfect, selfish creatures" and "was pleased to become a partaker of flesh and blood, in fashion as a man . . . like as we are, sin only excepted."[9]

---

8. Chauncy, *Man's Life Considered*, 6–7; *Duty of Ministers*, 6, 17; *Accursed Thing*, 11; *Divine Glory*, 7.

9. Chauncy, *Nathanael's Character*, 8; *Prayer for Help*, 3; *Only Compulsion Proper*, 4, 11; *New Creature Describ'd*, 22; *Ministers Exhorted*, 21; *Earth Delivered*, 24; *Charity*, 20–21. And see *Ministers Cautioned*, 31–32.

As his theology moved publicly in an Arminian direction, Chauncy allowed more room for human cooperation and initiative in salvation. But that did not diminish his Christology. It was "the incarnation of Christ," with "his obedience in our nature even to the death of the cross, which ought always to be esteemed the true and only moral ground of the bestowment of spiritual and heavenly blessings." Christ was "the Saviour it pleased the all-merciful God early to provide for a perishing world, thro' whom alone any of the race of men could be delivered from sin and wrath, and obtain salvation with eternal glory." So even in Chauncy's most Arminian work, the "capital truth" remained that "'Jesus, who is the Christ, died for our offences, and rose again for our justification.'" As a result:

> The sinners . . . that are in a justified state are those only, who are distinguished from others by being believers in Christ. Their faith gives them a discriminating character, which character is connected, by the appointment of God, with that deliverance from wrath, and right to life, which are the gift of grace thro' the atonement by Christ.

The "method of . . . execution" of "the whole christian scheme of redemption" was thus "the advent of God's only begotten Son into our world, to take on him our nature, and accomplish the work laid out for him." Chauncy described "the incarnation of the Son of God" as a "revealed mystery." But he was equally clear that even if "revelation does not go on, and describe the 'modus' of that union between these different natures which denominate them one person," he accepted the classically orthodox and definitely non-Arian doctrine that Christ was "in true propriety, 'the son of man,' as well as 'the son of God.'"[10]

Christ's supreme, saving role remained undiminished in Chauncy's final, universalist soteriology. In *Salvation for All Men* (1782), Chauncy and John Clarke quoted from Jeremiah White on the vital significance of Christ's atonement in God's plan of universal salvation:

> as sin hath reigned universally unto death, so grace shall reign through righteousness as universally, through Jesus Christ our Lord. Grace will triumph at last . . . By taking upon him our sins, and expiating them on the tree, he has reconciled the world unto God, slain the enmity between them, and made provision for an Universal restoration to favour.

---

10. Chauncy, *All Nations*, 11, 5–6; *Twelve Sermons*, 123, citing Rom 4:25, 157; see, further, 151–52; Chauncy, *Duty of Ministers*, 6, 12n. See also *Sermon Preached May 6, 1767*, 28–30, 32–33; *Trust in God*, 11; "Breaking of Bread," 31, 147; *Accursed Thing*, 11.

A year later, in *Divine Glory* (1783), Chauncy reiterated the point that "'the obedience and death of Christ' are the moral ground of that general proclamation which is made in the gospel, and the pardon which is offered to all men." When listing evidence of divine goodness in *Benevolence of the Deity* (1784), he argued that:

> the mission of his own son from heaven, into our world to become incarnate, that he might by being obedient to death, make atonement for the sins of men, and by his exaltation, in consequence of this obedient submission, at the right hand of God to finish the work, he had begun on earth, are the grand means by which this stupendous benevolence of the Deity, in the business of salvation, is carried into effect.

In that sense, "the gift of Christ, through which we have redemption, sprang originally from the love of God." Even in *Five Dissertations* (1785), Chauncy's reconceptualization of the doctrine of original sin did not prevent him from arguing that "mankind may, in consequence of the advantage they are placed under by means of Christ, obtain the gift of pardoning mercy, notwithstanding their personal sins, however many they have been."[11]

An exalted view of the person and work of Christ remained central to Chauncy's final universalist vision in *Mystery Hid*, where all six of the work's main "propositions" were decidedly Christocentric. When he urged the congregation of First Church in his last published sermon to "pay all due honour to the ordinance of the supper . . . in remembrance of him who died for your sins, that, by making atonement for them, he might open a way for the display of God's mercy in their pardon," his advice was consistent with similar statements over nearly sixty years of prior publications. In that sense, Chauncy's continuing Christological orthodoxy frustrates earlier scholarly attempts to link him, like Mayhew and his subordinationist view of Christ, with the origins of the Unitarian, as well as the universalist, movement in New England. Other indicators of Mayhew's and Chauncy's continuity with traditional New England orthodoxy include the basic biblicism which shaped their theological methodology, even when it led to heterodox conclusions, their consistent Congregationalism, and the rigorously Protestant persuasion which lay at the heart of their theology and animated their fierce anti-Catholicism.[12]

---

11. Chauncy and Clarke, *Salvation for All Men*, 11–13, citing Jeremiah White, *Restoration of All Things*, passim, and Rom 5:21; Chauncy, *Divine Glory*, 7, citing Eckley, *Divine Glory*, 8. See 8, 10; *Benevolence of the Deity*, 166, 170; *Five Dissertations*, 137. See 243–47.

12. *Sermon Delivered at the First Church*, 20. Gibbs and Gibbs largely upheld such

"Rational Biblicism"

In eighteenth-century New England, where such an allegiance remained standard almost irrespective of a minister's other theological positions, Chauncy's and Mayhew's general commitment to biblical authority was to be expected. What remains notable is that even their most innovative doctrines were not generally based on more abstract, philosophical processes of argumentation. They were developed on the basis of considered and often very detailed biblical exposition. In the sense that it differed from more conventional approaches both in his exegetical methods and his willingness to reach and state resulting positions that transcended traditional orthodoxy, Chauncy's "biblicism" has already been described, following Hatch, as "rational." Mayhew's has been shown to merit a similar definition. Yet the ministers' strong statements of biblicist conviction also remain clear indicators of their self-conscious continuity, even in more heterodox contexts, with Congregationalist tradition, even when they doctrinally departed from it.[13]

Despite his broad acquaintance with contemporary thought, Mayhew's approach to preaching and to wider Christian ministry was certainly

---

an interpretation of the orthodoxy of Chauncy's Christology, although their analysis, which drew heavily on *Mystery Hid*, was somewhat problematic. By affirming the presence and activity of Christ as the divine "Logos" in the creation, government, and redemption of the world, they persuasively demonstrated how Chauncy maintained a view of Christ's pre-existence to the incarnation that was inconsistent with Arianism. Their conclusion that Chauncy's Christology, in which "Christ is 'truly God' and 'truly man,'" was "not Arian but unequivocally Chalcedonian" was also compelling. But their parallel claim that, for Chauncy, the incarnate Jesus was "a special creation of the Logos" who did not "possess absolute or essential Deity," was not only inconsistent with their earlier observation that "Chauncy affirmed the identity of the preexistent Logos, the crucified servant, and the exalted and reigning Lord." Like their misleading characterization of Chauncy as a "liberal evangelical," it was simply unsubstantiated by their evidence ("'In Our Nature,'" esp. 227, 228, 224, 233). See also Gibbs and Gibbs, "Charles Chauncy."

13. Hatch, "Sola Scriptura," 62–3. In his comprehensive survey of colonial and revolutionary New England preaching, Stout highlighted the continuing importance of *sola scriptura* as a guiding theological and homiletic principle in the eighteenth century. "As always," he argued, "church members agreed to honor their minister's voice only if it conformed to the 'Scripture rule' as codified in the doctrines of the Westminster Confession of Faith and the polity of *The Cambridge Platform*. Eighteenth-century congregations studied that Word and honored its precepts as closely as their parents had." Among ministers, Stout likewise discerned an "enduring loyalty to *Sola Scriptura*," not only as "a matter of personal conviction, formal training, or aesthetic preference," but as a ministerial "badge of entry into the Congregational churches." He contended that "historians have too often ignored the enduring primacy of *Sola Scriptura* on the rationalist mind" and argued that even in revolutionary "political preaching," the "most important" ideas "reached all the way back" to its "principles" (*New England Soul*, 150, 154, 227, 285).

based on his understanding of biblical principles. "I must now declare, once for all," he wrote in the preface to *On Hearing the Word* (1755):

> That I will not be, even religiously scolded, nor pitied, nor wept and lamented, out of any principles which I believe upon the authority of Scripture, in the exercise of that small share of reason which God has given me: Nor will I postpone this authority, to that of all the good Fathers of the Church, even with that of the good Mothers added to it!

Mayhew saw his primary ministerial calling, therefore, as that of a faithful Bible expositor. "Christian teachers in after ages," he wrote in his first publication, "are (or at least ought to be) only commentators upon the scriptures: and we cannot suppose their commentaries have greater weight and authority than the text itself." Biblical warrant should extend to every area of the Christian life, with a goal of "strictly adhering to the Holy Scriptures in doctrine, discipline, worship and practice." Mayhew was confident that "a common rule of faith, worship, and discipline" had been "transmitted . . . in the writings of the new testament; and is sufficient now, for the regulation of the church."[14]

Mayhew's hermeneutical approach to biblical interpretation was thus avowedly literalist. "The most literal and obvious sense of scripture, should ever be adhered to," he promised in *Expected Dissolution* (1755), "till we see some plain and positive reason for departing from it." The "declared design" of "the scriptures of truth" was ultimately to lead to salvation, even as they guided believers "into the way of peace." So when Mayhew delved into the Bible, as he did in all his works, he ultimately found a very traditional understanding of religion. It consisted in:

> knowing God and Jesus Christ; in understanding his word and will; in believing what God has revealed; in loving him above all things; and an habitual care to keep his commandments, in hope of eternal life; not as of merit in us, but as the "gift of God through Jesus Christ our Lord."

When he rejected traditional doctrines—favouring an Arminian over a Calvinist understanding of the process of salvation, for example, or a subordinationist over a strictly Nicene Christology, Mayhew went out of his way, like Chauncy, to demonstrate proper biblical justification for his preferences.[15]

14. Mayhew, *On Hearing the Word*, iii; *Seven Sermons*, 79, 75; *Discourse on Rev. XV*, 46.

15. Mayhew, *Expected Dissolution*, 18; *Striving to Enter*, 17; *Practical Discourses*, 319–20, citing Rom 6:23.

Mayhew's fourteen sermons *On Hearing the Word*, which represent his major defense of Arminianism, constitute a sustained series of biblical expositions designed to show that "Christianity . . . is not only a rule of faith, but of practice also," and that "the scripture doctrine of our salvation by Grace" confirms rather than overthrows "the necessity of obedience." Even when rejecting the title "God the Son" for Christ and seeking to show that the phrase "Son of God" did not entail equal divinity with the only "true God" but a more subordinate status, Mayhew did so on the basis of close examination of key texts. As has been seen, his general treatment of Christology, like his vigorous critique of Trinitarianism, was so heavily reliant on detailed biblical exegesis that his conclusions really stood or fell by it. Yet Mayhew's biblicism was as unbound by perceived needs to sustain traditionally orthodox positions as Chauncy's. His was a similarly "rational," somewhat individualistic, biblicism and he was even more outspoken than his First Church colleague in departing from the formulations of classical or even credal orthodoxy. Mayhew had particularly strong words for the Trinitarianism of the Athanasian Creed, for example, denouncing its "Temerity," judgmentalism and metaphysical speculativeness.[16]

A similarly strong biblicism is evident throughout Chauncy's works. In one of his earliest sermons, *Early Piety Recommended* (1732), Chauncy commended "the Word of God" as "the best and most sutable rule, by which to govern our selves in the business of religion." He also urged that "all our views, all our hopes, all our encouragements and dependances in and from religion, be regulated by the Word." Five years later, Chauncy defined "the Godly man" as one who "so believes the faithfulness and veracity of God, as to rely on his word, confide in the truth and depend on the fulfilment of his promises." But in singing the praises of "the first fathers of this country, who were, perhaps, a set of as holy men as the world ever saw," he made clear in *Gifts of the Spirit* (1741) that even their "authority" should be subject to that of "reason and scripture." At the height of Great Awakening excesses, Chauncy was in no doubt as to the best source of discernment. There was "a rule by which you may judge of persons, whether they are enthusiasts, meer pretenders to the immediate guidance and influence of the Spirit," he told the members of First Church in 1742. "And this is, in general, a regard to the bible, an acknowledgment that the things therein contained are the commandments of God. This is the rule in the text." Chauncy had a high view of the calling and status of church ministers, but like Mayhew he was very clear that they too were men under authority. So they "should take

---

16. Mayhew, *On Hearing the Word*, 78, 123, 267–69, esp. 269n.; *Christian Sobriety*, 59–60. See, further, *On Hearing the Word*, 417–18n.; Hatch, "Sola Scriptura," 62–63.

heed to their Doctrine, that it be sound, in Opposition to that which is false and erroneous. It should be the pure, uncorrupted Word of God." "To the Law and to the Testimony," he warned his colleagues in 1774. If "what we say does not agree herewith, there is no Light nor Truth in it," because "the HOLY BIBLE" was "that one only test of all religious Truth."[17]

In the political arena, one of the main reasons why *Civil Magistrates Must Be Just* (1747) was that "they are ... obliged to be ... just, in virtue of the will of the supreme legislator, made known in the revelations of scripture." And when analyzing claims to any form of special revelation or insight, there was just one acid test. "The divine Spirit, in enlightening men's minds, lets them into the knowledge of no truths, but those that are contained in the sacred books of scripture," Chauncy wrote in *Twelve Sermons* (1765). So scriptural justification ought "to be the grand question in all supposed illuminations, manifestations, suggestions, and discoveries from the Spirit." In a 1766 ordination sermon written several years after the intensive period of study that led to his radical theological re-orientation, Chauncy gave a clear indication of the kind of intellectual restraints under which he intentionally operated. "It is not ... any part of the work of ministers, in these days, to publish 'new revelations' ...," he warned. Their "proper work is, to explain 'the mystery of the gospel,' as it has been manifested by Jesus Christ, and his Apostles, in the books of the new-testament." This view was grounded in Chauncy's apparently unshakable conviction of the absolute reliability and infallibility of the Bible. "The inspired writings only are exempt from error and defect," he wrote in his *magnum opus* of patristic scholarship, *Compleat View of Episcopacy* (1771), "and ... those of the most eminent men ... are to be ... examined by the only touch-stone of religious truth, the perfect and unerring word of God, and approved of so far only as they are found to agree herewith."[18]

Because Chauncy set such a standard for himself, when it came to justifying the conclusions of his theological treatises of the 1780s, there was only one reliable source of authority, however heterodox his interpretations of it. "What I ... now offer to the world is ... fetched ... solely from the fountain of revealed truth, the inspired oracles of God," he claimed when introducing *Mystery Hid* (1784). As a result, "those only ... are proper judges in this debate, who have made the sacred writings in general, and the apostolic writings in particular, especially the writings of the apostle Paul, their careful and diligent study." Chauncy's final published work, *Five*

17. Chauncy, *Early Piety Recommended*, 21, 25. See 22–24; *Prayer for Help*, 2; *Gifts of the Spirit*, 36, 39; *Enthusiasm Described*, 7; *Ministers Exhorted*, 18. See *Ministers Cautioned*, 9–10.

18. Chauncy, *Civil Magistrates*, 46; *Twelve Sermons*, 301, 304; *Duty of Ministers*, 15; *Compleat View of Episcopacy*, 347.

Dissertations (1785) displays evidence of a similar biblicism. Not only did he ground his reformulations of the doctrine of original sin in detailed biblical exegesis. He explicitly pointed out that "it is with me one of the strongest evidences of the divinity of the Scriptures, that this [from Genesis 3], and other ancient promises and predictions, are so worded, that the scheme of salvation, as it has been gradually unfolding till these last days, is very obviously, however comprehensively, pointed out in them."[19]

In short, throughout their pastoral and theological careers, Mayhew and Chauncy claimed to maintain the high view of scriptural authority that Chauncy recommended to his colleagues in *Duty of Ministers* (1766):

> "What saith the scripture?" should be their [ministers'] grand inquiry. To this sacred text they should constantly repair; receiving nothing, delivering nothing, for revealed truth, but what they have found there. They are, by office, "stewards of the mysteries of God"; and where should they go, but to his written word, for the knowledge of them? They are no where infallibly contain'd, but in this sacred book. The BIBLE therefore, the BIBLE, I say, should be the guide of their thoughts, the only rule of their faith: And they should make it evident by their preaching, that this has engrossed their time, and chiefly engaged their labor in their studies.

The Bible was crucial for all kinds of reasons. It was "the light he [God] has given the world, in the revelations of scripture . . . by which we are let into the knowledge of the gospel method of 'redemption thro' Jesus Christ." It was the major source and justification for their theological innovations. It was also, they believed, the only true source of the Congregationalist polity which they defended, in different ways, with equal vigor, becoming, in the process, its primary apologists of the 1760s and 1770s.[20]

Committed Congregationalism

Notwithstanding his willingness to depart from received orthodoxy in other areas, Chauncy ranked as one of the most stalwart defenders of the established New England church order. But unlike the Essex minister John Wise, who conducted the major defense against "Presbyterianizing" tendencies within Congregationalism of a previous generation, or Mayhew, who also debated the missionary role of the SPG in the 1760s, Chauncy's focus was consistently on the general question of episcopacy, which he pursued in two

---

19. Chauncy, *Mystery Hid*, vi, viii–ix; *Five Dissertations*, 102.
20. Chauncy, *Duty of Ministers*, 15–16, citing 1 Cor 4:1; *Twelve Sermons*, 283.

main types of publication. Between 1762 and 1771, Chauncy issued two studies intended for a more scholarly readership, *Validity of Presbyterian Ordination* (1762) and *Compleat View of Episcopacy* (1771). He also wrote three more controversial works directly addressing the American Episcopate controversy: *Letter to a Friend, Containing Remarks* (1767), *Appeal to the Public Answered* (1768) and *Reply to Dr. Chandler's "Appeal Defended"* (1770). His motivations for releasing these last three works were clearly political, as well as theological.[21]

Chauncy initially had personal reasons for studying the question of episcopacy. In 1729, not long after beginning ministry at First Church, he had officiated at the wedding of his first wife's sister, Jane Hirst, and the lawyer Addington Davenport. However, soon afterwards, they both converted to the Church of England. Davenport traveled to England in late 1732, where he took orders in the Church of England. He was appointed missionary at Scituate by the SPG and returned to New England to take up that position in 1733. He went on to become Lecturer of King's Chapel in 1737 and the first Rector of Trinity Church, Boston, in 1740. What seems to have irked Chauncy most about the couple's conversion was Davenport's alleged reason for it. He had apparently become convinced, Chauncy wrote to Stiles in 1768, "that it was a certain fact, that Episcopacy, in the appropriated sense, was the form of government in the church from the time of the Apostles and down along through all successive ages." Chauncy "imagined" that his family "connection" with Davenport "would naturally lead [him] into frequent conversations upon this point." So to "be thoroughly qualified for a debate," the ever-diligent minister entered into what he described as "four years of harder study than ever I went through in any part of my life in reading the Fathers, and all the books I could find upon the Episcopal controversy, on both sides, in all the libraries in town, and that at Cambridge." On May 30, 1734, little more than a couple of years into this process, the *Boston Weekly News-Letter* duly advertised the forthcoming publication by subscription of his *A Compleat View of the First Two Hundred Years after Christ Touching Episcopacy*. Chauncy failed, however, to secure the necessary level of subscriber support. Thirty-four years later, he informed Stiles that he still had all the unpublished materials to hand. Only in 1771, after he had commanded attention with other anti-episcopal works in the heat of the American Episcopate controversy, was Chauncy finally able to see his magnum opus in print.[22]

21. See esp. Wise, *Churches' Quarrel*; *Vindication*; Mayhew, *Observations*, *Defence of the Observations*, *Remarks on an Anonymous Tract*. For a recent reinterpretation of Wise, see Oakes, "Beyond the 'Democrat' and 'Conservative' Dichotomy."

22. Griffin, *Old Brick*, 29–30; Foote et al., *Annals of King's Chapel*, 1:480–2; *SHG*,

Chauncy's purposes in his general studies of Presbyterian/Congregationalist ordination and episcopacy were basically to uphold the validity of the former and to deny the biblical necessity or early patristic precedent for the latter. His first publication on the topic, *Validity of Presbyterian Ordination*, which was delivered as Harvard's 1762 Dudleian Lecture, was intended to show precisely what its title implied. "The design of the present discourse," wrote Chauncy, was "to vindicate the New-England churches in their method of ordination by presbyters . . . to the purposes of the gospel ministry," and in its first part, he sought to argue:

> That the apostles of Christ, in settling the churches, constituted (besides the order of deacons) no more than one order of standing pastors; That these pastors, in their day, were called sometimes bishops, sometimes presbyters, and promiscuously pointed out by either of these names; and finally, that these bishops or presbyters were endowed with all the ordinary powers that were to be exercised in the church of Christ, particularly with that of ordination.

Much of the remainder of Chauncy's work was devoted to rejecting the case for episcopacy, before he attempted to show how "the protestant churches abroad, in common with our's, far from owning the *jus divinum* ["divine right"] of episcopacy, assert a parity between bishops and presbyters, allowing the latter, equally with the former, to perform the work of ordination." Befitting the occasion, Chauncy concluded with "a few words to the young gentlemen" of Harvard, urging adherence to New England's Congregationalist traditions. He also added an appendix to the publication on the letters of the apostolic church father, Ignatius of Antioch, who had often been cited in support of a separate order of the episcopate.[23]

Chauncy's authorities in *Validity of Presbyterian Ordination* (1762) were both biblical and historical. His clearly stated assumption was that "episcopal-ordination . . . must be considered necessary, if so at all, by the

---

6:304–8; Chauncy, "Sketch of Eminent Men," 161–62; "Advertisements," *Boston Weekly News-Letter*, May 30, 1734, 2. According to Griffin, the Davenports converted to Anglicanism the year after Chauncy had officiated at their wedding in 1730. In *SHG*, 6:305, Shipton states that their conversion was not until the fall of 1732. Samuel Sewall reported on November 25, 1732, that "Couz. Addington Davenport Goe on Board Capt. Sheperdson To sale for England. On the 12th Instant I hear he partook at the Church of England in Dr. Cuttler's Church & on the 19th. He & his wife went to church there. It is said he goes to take Orders to be a Church of England Parson" (Sewall, "Extracts," 71).

23. Chauncy, *Validity of Presbyterian Ordination*, 7, 13–14, 74, 87, 91–118. Here and elsewhere, Chauncy clearly understood "presbyter," from New Testament Greek usage, as simply meaning church elder or pastor.

revelations of God, and in fair and legible characters too." So he contended on scriptural grounds, for example, that "gospel-presbyters . . . are true scripture bishops and cloathed with authority to do everything that is done in the business of ordination." But Chauncy also made the historical arguments that "those ecclesiastical superiorities and inferiorities which have, for a long time, been visible in the christian world, were unknown in the first and purest ages" and that "Ignatius only excepted, the fathers, within the first two centuries, unitedly concur in speaking of bishops and presbyters much in the same language with the sacred scriptures." The appendix on Ignatius was designed to show that the letters credited to him were essentially unreliable as historical sources.[24]

In *Compleat View of Episcopacy* (1771), which was finally issued in an attempt to see off demands for an Anglican bishop in the American colonies, Chauncy significantly expanded on the historical aspects of his argument to produce an impressive volume of eighteenth-century scholarship which drew on the most authoritative sources in patristics studies available to him. The result was a laborious, comprehensive, and detailed analysis of relevant texts "from the FATHERS of the CHRISTIAN CHURCH, until the Close of the Second Century," designed to show "concerning BISHOPS and PRESBYTERS," to quote from the work's full title, "that they esteemed these ONE and the SAME ORDER of Ecclesiastical Officers." The main church fathers that Chauncy addressed included Barnabas, Dionysius Areopagita, Hermas, Clement of Rome, Polycarp, Ignatius, Justin Martyr, Irenaeus, and Clement of Alexandria. But he predictably devoted most attention to Ignatius, developing a much longer treatment of his works than in *Validity of Presbyterian Ordination* (1762). The model of episcopacy that he opposed was that of a diocesan bishop of a superior order to that of presbyters or pastors with an "EXCLUSIVE RIGHT OF GOVERNMENT," "SOLE POWER OF ORDINATION," "SOLE POWER OF ORDINATION," and "the power of CONFIRMATION." Chauncy associated such a model with the dangers and excesses of Catholicism and the ultimate conclusion of his scholarship was that it was historically as well as biblically unwarranted. "I may venture to say, with the highest assurance," he concluded:

> that he [the reader] will be in no danger of calling in question the authority of the new-testament books, for want of testimonies . . . , though he should utterly reject EPISCOPACY, in the impleaded sense, as having no support, either in point of RIGHT, or PRACTICE, from any thing he may have met with in the writers within the first two ages of the Christian church.[25]

24. Ibid., 13, 64, 68.
25. Chauncy, *Compleat View of Episcopacy*, title page, ix, xii, xiii, 474. Chauncy devoted nearly 30 percent of this work, 187–318, to Ignatius alone.

Chauncy's other three publications on issues of church polity were all written as contributions to the ongoing debate, in which Mayhew was the main New England protagonist until his premature death in 1766, on the desirability and possible legitimacy of appointing a Church of England bishop to the American colonies. In that sense, Chauncy assumed his friend's mantle, although Mayhew's polemical concerns had first been stirred by the activities of the SPG and its apparent design to episcopize New England under the guise of indigenous missionary work.

The broader historical background to Mayhew's engagement in such controversies, especially over the establishment of an American episcopate, has been well documented by Arthur Cross, Carl Bridenbaugh, and others. It will not be repeated here. Rossiter has made the most concise summary of the main events surrounding his involvement:

1. a newspaper article published in Boston in February, 1763, which seized upon the death of an Anglican missionary in Braintree as an excuse for attacking the practice of the Society for the Propagation of the Gospel of placing its missionaries in settled towns;

2. a return to these aspersions by . . . East Apthorp, missionary in Cambridge, entitled *Considerations* [1763]. . . ;

3. a quick retaliation by Mayhew, *Observations* [1763];

4. a series of replies to Mayhew, three from America, one from England;

5. two further rejoinders by Mayhew, *Defence of the Observations* [1763] in reply to the most important American attack, [and] *Remarks on an Anonymous Tract* [1764] in answer to the British pamphlet;

6. a final pamphlet by Apthorp [*Review of Dr. Mayhew's Remarks* (1764)], in which he reviewed the entire controversy and got in a few last blows for the Church of England and the Society. Mayhew thought it unworthy of an answer and put an end to this war of words by ignoring it.[26]

---

26. Rossiter, "Life and Mind," 537–38, edited for stylistic consistency. The works referred to by Rossiter are the following: "J.B.," "To the Printers, &c.," described by Bridenbaugh, *Mitre and Sceptre*, 219, as "a sort of sardonic obituary describing the career of . . . Ebenezer Miller"; Apthorp, *Considerations*; Mayhew, *Observations*; Aplin, *Verses*; Browne, *Remarks*; Caner, *Candid Examination*; Secker, *Answer*; Mayhew, *Defence of the Observations* and *Remarks on an Anonymous Tract*; Apthorp, *Review of Dr. Mayhew's Remarks*. See further on Mayhew and the American Episcopate controversy: Cross, *Anglican Episcopate*, 145–60. Cross also noted the later "broadside,"

It is important to note that throughout most of his three controversial works of 1763–4 Mayhew's major concern was the activities of the SPG. He especially targeted the society's interference in the religious life of New England by its support of Anglican missionaries and churches with a "formal design," as he saw it, "to root out Presbyterianism &c. and to establishing both Episcopacy and Bishops in the colonies." Gifted controversialist that he was, Mayhew generally eschewed any broader theological critique of episcopalianism. His primary focus was on the SPG's failures to honor the terms of its original 1701 charter and on Apthorp's and others' alleged misrepresentations of the ecclesiastical situation in New England. He began the second section of his *Observations* by quoting the whole preamble to the charter. He then argued that "if the society have applied any part of their fund to support and encourage the peculiarities of episcopacy in any such places [where established Congregationalist ministry already existed], they have applied it in a manner not warranted." As Mayhew understood the terms of the SPG's founding document, it knew of:

> no distinction amongst christians, except that of protestants and papists: Its grand object, a truly glorious one, is, to promote christianity, considered in opposition to atheism, infidelity and popery; not episcopacy and the liturgy of the church of England, in opposition to presbyterianism, &c.[27]

One of Mayhew's primary points of contention, therefore, which he continued to pursue in both *Defence of the Observations* (1763) and *Remarks on an Anonymous Tract* (1764), was that although leaders of the SPG had "done much, according to the true intent of their charter, as it has been represented . . . . they have also done much beside, or beyond that intent, by supporting and propagating the church of England, in opposition to other protestant churches, at a great expence, where their charity was not needed." In other words, the missionary society had acted, Mayhew contended, "to support and strengthen the episcopal party, and gradually to bring us into the bosom of the church [of England]."[28]

Concomitant with this central critique of the SPG, Mayhew also sought to counter false accounts of the religious state of New England generally and the broader threat of a Church of England episcopate to the American colonies. In addressing such topics, his committed Congregationalism

---

Anon., "Advertisement," and observed that Secker's work "appeared anonymously, but was later discovered to have been written by Archbishop [of Canterbury] Secker" (ibid., 150–51). It was included in the third edition of Secker, *Works*, 6:340–402.

27. Mayhew, *Observations*, 103, 17–18, 22–23, 28.

28. Mayhew, *Defence of the Observations*, 31; *Remarks on an Anonymous Tract*, 35.

was unmistakable. Countering Apthorp in *Observations* (1763), Mayhew reminded his readers that

- "the first settlers ... were such as came hither chiefly on account of their sufferings for non-conformity to the church of England";
- Congregationalist doctrines were orthodox and "very agreeable to the doctrinal articles of the church of England";
- "our churches seem to have a proper legal establishment"; and
- such was the spiritual vigor of New England that "the people ... are all in general professed Christians." Indeed, there was "no such monster as an Atheist known amongst us; hardly any such person as a Deist."

Mayhew repeated such points in *Defence of the Observations.* (1763), forcefully contending that there was "a real and effectual establishment of religion made by the laws of this province," which was Congregationalist. But this was "perhaps, the most generous and catholic one that was ever made in any country," since it allowed for such widespread religious toleration. Mayhew was relatively undogmatic in his opposition to the Church of England. He conceded, for example, that he was "far from being zealous against all forms of prayer," that "the bishops are now generally persons of moderation; lovers of civil and christian liberty," and, more generally, that "ministers or churches differing widely in opinion about an hierarchy, discipline, and modes of worship, may yet be equally orthodox." But he also made his personal preferences very clear. He was convinced that

> the most detestable hypocrisy in the sight of God and wise men, is that which is shewn in a zeal for rites and ceremonies, for external modes and forms; especially uninstituted ones, the inventions of men, while the zealots are comparatively negligent of the weightier matters of the law and gospel. Of which kind of hypocrisy there has unquestionably been much more amongst us, since the Society [SPG] was instituted than before.[29]

29. Mayhew, *Observations*, 39, 41, 43, 44, 70, 93; *Defence of the Observations*, 60, 100–1; *Remarks on an Anonymous Tract*, 26. Mayhew likewise professed that "no treatment which I have, or may receive from persons of a narrow, contracted way of thinking, shall discourage me from standing up to the utmost of my power, in vindication of our religious liberties, and our congregational church order; which, in my humble opinion is more scriptural and liable to fewer inconveniences, than any other now in the world; tho' there are others for which I have a great veneration" (*Defence of the Observations*, 143n). He earlier affirmed that "notwithstanding he [i.e., Mayhew] is in principle and profession an anti-episcopalian; yet he sincerely loves and honors all virtuous, candid and moderate men of all denominations among Christians; by no means excepting those of the episcopal communion; with several of whom he has a personal

Mayhew had no hesitation in stating his general objection "against the church of England," as well as his potential regret "from a regard to what I suppose a more scriptural way of worship, to see that church prevail here." But his arguments became much more specific when confronted, as he was in *Answer to Dr. Mayhew's Observations* (1764) by the Archbishop of Canterbury, Thomas Secker, with a concrete proposal for the introduction of American bishops. Despite Secker's assurance that this plan was not intended to "infringe or diminish any privileges and liberties enjoyed by any of the laity," Mayhew had grave doubts in two main areas. First, he did not trust the durability of such intentions. "Let us suppose," he asked,

> that bishops are to be at first sent to America with such limited powers, to reside in episcopal colonies, and to have no concern, but with episcopalians: Have we sufficient ground to think that they and their successors would, to the day of doom, or for a long time, remain contented with such powers, or under such limitations?

Even assuming the goodwill of current British leaders, "may not times alter, and administrations change?" Second, there was the constant danger that "appointing bishops for America, would be a probable means of increasing the episcopal party here," and that with Anglican growth would eventually come Church of England establishment and taxes. In that sense, Mayhew's concerns for religious toleration were overridden by what he saw as the political threat of American episcopacy.[30]

Chauncy's dedication to preserving the ecclesiastical structures of New England Congregationalism was no less decisive in his most polemical writings on church government, in which he pursued similar arguments against two other Church of England leaders, Bishop John Ewer of Llandaff and Chandler of New Jersey, after Mayhew's death in 1766. In a sermon preached at the Anniversary Meeting of the SPG missionary society in 1767, Ewer had had the gall not only to call for bishops in the American colonies, but to criticize the general state of religion there. Chauncy was not the only New England minister to be outraged by these allegations. Andrew Eliot of New North also took up his pen. But the cautious Eliot soon demurred, as he told his English correspondent Thomas Hollis, in case his initiative "interfered" with Chauncy. The result, according to Griffin, was Chauncy's

---

and agreeable acquaintance, which he would be glad to keep up; Nor would he willingly and unnecessarily give offence to any persons of that persuasion" (*Observations*, 175).

30. Mayhew, *Remarks on an Anonymous Tract*, 78, 58 (citing Secker, *Answer to Dr. Mayhew's Observations*, in *Works*, 6:394), 60, 62, 63. See, further, 12–14 on the alleged political threat of American episcopacy.

"best seller," *Letter to a Friend, Containing Remarks* (1767). It was soon followed, in 1768, with *Appeal to the Public Answered*, a spirited and comprehensive 205-page reply to Chandler's *Appeal to the Public* (1767). Over the next couple of years, Chauncy then returned to the kind of full-scale publication war in which he had not really participated since the Great Awakening. Chandler's own rebuttal, *Appeal Defended* (1769), accordingly elicited a 180-page response in the form of *Reply to Dr. Chandler's "Appeal Defended"* (1770). Like *Appeal to the Public Answered*, this last work sought to answer Chandler's arguments in favor of a limited, "spiritual" but not temporal, form of Church of England episcopacy in the American colonies.[31]

The central themes of Chauncy's three most combative anti-episcopal works were consistent. In *Letter to a Friend, Containing Remarks* (1767), he vigorously and filiopietistically defended the state of religion in New England, which Ewer had impugned, and regarded as unnecessary efforts by the SPG and others to expand episcopalianism. But Chauncy also perceived a deeper threat in an expansionist and episcopally aggressive Church of England and, like Mayhew, his theological and practical objections to episcopacy became political. The founders, he argued, had emigrated to New England expressly to find "liberty to worship God agreably to the dictates of conscience." In so doing, they had abandoned "a blind submission to Church-power, arbitrarily exercised" in pursuit of "this undoubted Gospel-truth, namely, that Jesus Christ only is supreme Head and Lord of the christian church." One of Chauncy's main fears was that imported bishops would impinge upon such freedoms, making "use of their SUPERIORITY, as most probably they would, sooner or later, to influence our great men here, and much greater ones at home, to project, and endeavour to carry into execution, measures to force the growth of the Church."[32]

In *Appeal to the Public Answered* (1768), Chauncy's agenda was more explicitly theological: he again sought to counter Chandler's arguments in favor of a separate order of bishops, divinely established by apostolic succession and uniquely empowered to perform such rites as ordination and confirmation. He appealed to familiar precedents drawn from the New Testament and the writings of the early church fathers. But Chauncy also advanced strong criticisms of the declining state of the Church of England

---

31 Andrew Eliot to Thomas Hollis, December 10, 1767, in Eliot, "Letters," 412–21, esp. 418; Chauncy, *Letter to a Friend, Containing Remarks*, responding to Ewer, *Sermon Preached*; Griffin, *Old Brick*, 135. Chandler later sought to continue the debate with *Appeal Farther Defended*, to which Chauncy declined to reply. On Chandler, see Hoyt, *Sketch of the Life*.

32. Chandler, *Appeal Defended*; Chauncy, *Letter to a Friend, Containing Remarks*, 26, 12, 47. See, further, 9, 16, 34, 46.

and of the role of bishops in it. Despite, or more probably because, "Bishops, with the whole Church-Clergy, are CREATURES of the state, and the Church itself a PARLIAMENTARY Church," Chauncy contended:

> The plain truth is, the constitution of the Church, at least in the affair of discipline, is in a miserably defective, if not ruined, state. It greatly wants amendment; and unless it should vastly differ in America from what it is in England, Bishops would be of little service with respect to discipline. The Church may, perhaps, do as well without them, as with them.

Chandler's arguments—that colonial Anglicans needed bishops for practical as well as disciplinary reasons to offer local ordinations and confirmations—were simply specious. Without the financial support of the SPG, which had unnecessarily and disproportionately targeted funds to New England, the colonial church would be in a more parlous position than it already was. Chauncy thought the current situation particularly threatening, because "there never was a time, since the incorporation of the Society for the propagation of the Gospel, wherein such earnest and vigorous efforts were made, both in the Colonies and in England, to obtain the long wished-for blessing, an American-Episcopate."[33]

As in *Letter to a Friend, Containing Remarks*, Chauncy clearly perceived this threat as political as well as ecclesiastical. New England's founders had "fled hither, as to a place of safe retreat from the oppressive power of tyrannising Bishops; chusing rather to expose themselves to external hardships and dangers, sadly grievous, and extraordinarily trying, than wrong their consciences by submitting to meer human impositions in the worship of their maker." So it would be an insult "to the memory of our Progenitors," if Chauncy's generation "should encourage the establishment of that very [prelatical] power which was so injuriously harrassing to them, and may in time be so to us." At the same time, he simply did not believe Chandler's assurances that the current plan for an American episcopate would invest bishops with spiritual authority over colonial Anglicans, clergy in particular, but with no civil powers in society at large. Even as he expressed "fidelity and loyalty to the British Crown" and referred to "that wisely contrived mixture of power, which gives the British-state-constitution the preference to any on the whole earth," Chauncy thus argued that "the Church of England knows no such Bishops as are specified in this plan, nor can they, in consistency with it's constitution, be sent to the Colonies." He quoted extensively

---

33. Chauncy, *Appeal to the Public Answered*, 58, 63, 103. Chauncy also, 111–16, 154–56, vigorously disputed Chandler's claims as to the numerical strength of the Church of England in the American colonies.

from Mayhew to highlight the dangers that would likely result from the introduction of episcopal power, including a general rise in Anglican adherence, the possible establishment of the Church of England in the colonies, the imposition of a Test Act and church taxes, and a growth in Episcopalian political influence. "We are as fully persuaded, as if they had openly said it," Chauncy concluded, "that they have in view nothing short of a COMPLETE CHURCH HIERARCHY after the pattern of that at home." Such a prospect was deeply threatening both to church and state, especially in a situation, in 1768, where "'most of the Colonies' think themselves as nearly touched in their CONSTITUTIONAL RIGHTS by the late Parliamentary proceeding, as by the STAMP-ACT itself; and they are every day groaning out their complaints; though they are resolved to do it in those ways that are legal."[34]

Two years later, in *Reply to Dr. Chandler's "Appeal Defended"* (1770), Chauncy returned to similar arguments within the context of a devastating rebuttal in which he systematically dismantled Chandler's positions in every section of *Appeal Defended*. He rejected the notion that episcopacy by divine right was ever part of the authentic ecclesiology of the Church of England and sought to adduce historical evidence from the English Reformation to that effect. He repeated his denial of the doctrine of apostolic succession, as Chandler understood it, and his contention that managing large dioceses "destroys their [bishops'] capacity to serve the ends, designed by CHRIST in the institution of their office." Chauncy still saw "THE PROPAGATION OF EPISCOPACY" at the heart of Anglican designs and openly expressed his concerns that "the present struggles of the Missionaries and others to introduce [it] into America, originate from ambitious designs for establishing an opulent hierarchy in this Country, with prelatical distinction and power." But his ultimate fear remained the prospect of an established Church of England that would be a political threat to colonial freedoms:

> It is strange the Doctor, while arguing for nothing more than that limited Episcopate he had proposed, should endeavour to do it upon a plan that would make it reasonable, that the church of England should exist here IN ALL RESPECTS, and in ALL ITS PARTS, as it does at home. But he ought to know, that in order to this, something more than "a fair and full toleration" would be necessary. There must be an ESTABLISHMENT . . . And if the

---

34. Ibid., 94, 154, 96, 198–99, 149, 161–78, passim (citing Mayhew, *Remarks on an Anonymous Tract*, 57ff.), 202, 110. According to "Test act," *Encyclopedia Britannica*, this was "any law that made a person's eligibility for public office depend upon his profession of the established religion." Chauncy's reference is clearly to the English Test Act of 1673, which made the holding of all public offices conditional on communicant membership of the Church of England.

state interposes to constitute a Colony Episcopate, it must be under their patronage, guidance and controul, as to the exercise of its powers. And what is this, in real meaning, but an establishment?[35]

In that sense, as in his other, more controversial, anti-episcopacy writings, a key objective for Chauncy in *Reply to Dr. Chandler's "Appeal Defended"* was to present political, as well as religious and theological, objections to the appointment of Anglican bishops. Yet in so doing, he was not advancing radically new ideas of freedom or independence from metropolitan institutions. He was upholding New England tradition and the legacy of its founders. It was out of "regard to the memory of our Progenitors" and a concern to protect the freedoms that they had secured, as well as his ecclesiological convictions, that Chauncy was motivated to defend Congregationalist polity against the threat of episcopacy. Similar concerns were operative in Chauncy's and Mayhew's political thought, as will be seen. Seeing themselves in the vanguard of a global battle against the heretical and enslaving evils of Roman Catholicism, they also shared a wider agenda to counter any force, religious or otherwise, that appeared to threaten New England's Protestant traditions and identity. Anti-Catholicism and especially the fear of Catholic absolutism or "arbitrary" power (see chapter 5) were part and parcel of Mayhew's and Chauncy's political worldviews, as of the "Real" and mainstream Whig ideology that helped shape them. But their theological opposition to Catholicism deserves prior consideration in its own right.[36]

Anti-Catholicism

Mayhew's anti-Catholicism was more fully and systematically developed than Chauncy's; his writings were more overtly political in places and he took the opportunity, in his 1765 Dudleian Lecture *Popish Idolatry*, to offer the kind of sustained theological critique of Catholicism that Chauncy never did, even in his anti-episcopal works. But Chauncy made his own rigorously Protestant positions clear enough in consistent references throughout his massive corpus to show that he shared Mayhew's aggressive opposition. They were far from alone in this. Jonathan Clark has emphasized the religious and political importance of English anti-Catholicism from the sixteenth through the nineteenth centuries. This was a prominent trope in seventeenth-century New England Puritanism and, in the early

35. Chauncy, *Reply to Dr. Chandler's "Appeal Defended,"* 73, 106, Appendix, vii, 174–75, 177.
36. Chauncy, *Appeal to the Public Answered*, 154.

eighteenth century, Thomas Kidd identified anti-Catholicism, along with "international Protestantism" and "British nationalism," as significant factors in helping shape "a post-Puritan identity in New England society" in the aftermath of the new colonial settlement of the 1690s.[37]

One of Chauncy's major objections to Rome emerged in an earlier work, *Only Compulsion Proper* (1739), where he expounded a key text as an inducement to rational and moral persuasion in matters of religion, not physical compulsion. What Chauncy found most problematic about a Catholic interpretation of Luke 14:23 ("Compel them to come in") was that it was seen as "a Divine Warrant to make Use of Force and Violence in the Affairs of Conscience and Salvation." He was unsparing in his critique of the "Church of Rome," for which it had been "the grand Engine," he argued, "to make Men Proselytes to their Way of Worship." Church leaders had even "barbarously murder'd Men's Bodies, at the same time, pretending the greatest Love and Charity to their Souls." Like other New England Congregationalists, Chauncy also viewed the problem in graphically eschatological terms. The Roman Catholic Church was nothing less than that "Beast exceeding dreadful," prophesied in Daniel 7:19. According to a standard Puritan apocalyptic identification, which he clearly shared, it was the woman of Revelation 17:5-6, "whose Name is, THE MOTHER OF HARLOTS, AND ABOMINATIONS OF THE EARTH," and who was "drunk with the Blood of the Saints, and with the Blood of the Martyrs of Jesus." Such was this church's corruption that it had spread similar persecution and intolerance among Protestants, although Chauncy was thankful that "the Principles of Liberty are every Day gaining Ground in our Nation." The Roman "synagogue of Satan" was headed, in the form of the Pope, by "the MAN OF SIN" or the "anti-christ," another key eschatological figure, who "began to make his appearance," especially from the third century onwards, when Catholic declension grew apace, "though it was in a gradual way that he attained to that exaltation in dignity and power, as to be 'above all that is called god.'"[38]

Elsewhere in his works, Chauncy identified Rome with political as well religious forces of evil and tyranny. But many of his objections to

---

37. Jonathan Clark, *Language of Liberty*, 238; Kidd, *Protestant Interest*, 18. On late seventeenth- and early eighteenth-century anti-Catholicism, see especially Stanwood, *Empire Reformed*. On the English background, see, for example, Christianson, *Reformers and Babylon*; Hibbard, *Charles I and the Popish Plot*. On eighteenth-century English anti-Catholicism, see Haydon, *Anti-Catholicism*.

38. Chauncy, *Only Compulsion Proper*, 3, 12, 13–15; *Reply to Dr. Chandler's "Appeal Defended,"* 67; *Compleat View of Episcopacy*, viii–ix, citing Rev 2:9, 2 Thess 2:3–4. Citing John 17:12, and 2 Thess 2:7, Chauncy contended that "the grand corruption of christianity, under the Roman 'son of perdition,' is spoken of in that language, 'the mystery of iniquity'" (*Duty of Ministers*, 8). See, further, *Appeal to the Public Answered*, 28.

Catholicism were explicitly doctrinal. In the heat of the Great Awakening, Chauncy felt free to cite religious enthusiasm as a "source of infinite evil" on a par with "POPERY" generally as a "mother" of "blasphemies and abominations." His problems with Rome were also very specific. In a funeral sermon of 1745, he gave a long list of them:

> The Church of Rome has invented Pilgrimages, Penances, Processions, and numberless other Superstitions; adding them to those Exercises of Piety the Scripture has pointed out: Yea, they have introduced the Virgin Mary, and an hundred other Saints both dead and alive, as so many Mediums of Approach to the divine Majesty, to the great Dishonour, if not Exclusion, of JESUS the one Mediator between God and man. And what Multitudes of poor deluded People are there, who think themselves, and would be tho't by others, eminently devout and pious, because they are religiously strict in these and such like Observances.

Chauncy also criticized the Catholic doctrine of purgatory. Following the death of his colleague Foxcroft's wife, he preferred the view that the spirits of faithful Christians like her ascended immediately into God's presence after death rather than that they went "to a Place of Purgation, in order to their being fitted for the paradisaick [sic] State."[39]

Perhaps because of his own later Arminianism, Chauncy did not generally belabor the major Protestant objection to Catholicism—that it credited undue efficacy to good works in the process of human salvation. But in commending "charity to the distressed members of Christ" in a 1757 funeral discourse on verses from Matthew 25, the still avowedly Calvinist Chauncy argued that "blessedness" at the final judgment would have nothing to do with charitable acts. "The church of Rome may think highly of the value of good works," he contended, "hoping to be bid, at the judgment, to inherit God's heavenly kingdom, on account of the worthiness of them . . . But they certainly mistake his [Christ's] meaning." In fact, any notion that such works could be "meritorious of heavenly blessedness is an absurdity too gross to be entertained by any, who are allowed the free use of their reason, and the word of God." In his major declaration of Arminianism, *Twelve Sermons*, Chauncy later contented himself with the most general of critiques. Doctrines and practises like "the worship of God by images; the use of living and dead saints as mediators with heaven, particularly the Virgin Mary," and "the conversion of the bread and wine, in the sacrament, into the real body and blood of Christ" were "more palpable absurdities" than

---

39. Chauncy, *Enthusiasm Described*, 15; *Comelius's Character*, 8; *Blessedness of the Dead*, 10.

anything of "pagan" origin. He also returned to his earlier criticisms of Roman persecution and absolutism, with which he linked teachings that "this same church . . . is infallibly right in establishing these monstrous errors."[40]

The other key doctrinal area on which Chauncy offered significant anti-Catholic commentary has already been noted. In his forty-year preoccupation with issues of church polity, his main concern was to counter the problems, as he perceived them, of Episcopalianism. But in *Compleat View of Episcopacy* (1771), his reinterpretation of key patristic sources led him to reject Catholic notions of episcopacy even more strongly than episcopalian ones, especially the doctrine of apostolic succession. One of Chauncy's major criticisms of Chandler was that he "did not think it proper to prove the only thing that here needed proof, viz. that authority can be conveyed mediately from CHRIST" through an uninterrupted series of Catholic bishops. New England's Congregationalist churches cared nothing about such a doctrine, he contended, "as they know they have power from CHRIST to constitute officers for all the purposes of the gospel-ministry, should it so happen, that the line of succession, in regard of Presbyters, as well as bishops, had been interrupted and broken." Chandler's position was all the more ridiculous because the Church of England's own teachings denied the authenticity of the Catholic Church for "NINE HUNDRED YEARS past." Chauncy's mockery was unstinting:

> That which is no true church, nor has been any thing like it for a thousand years past; yet conveys true, regular offices and powers! An anti-apostolic church imparting genuine apostolic orders! The synagogue of satan becomes the sacred repository, wherein the power of ordination to holy offices, in CHRIST's church, for more than ten centuries, principally rested, and was almost only to be found! The church of Rome, which, by apostacy hath cut itself off from the body of CHRIST, hath nevertheless his spirit and authority dwelling in it.

His general conviction was unshakable that the Roman Church's "trumpery, which was absolutely unknown in the apostolic age" had now rendered it both "superstitious and corrupt."[41]

Mayhew's critique of Catholicism was as political as it was theological; like Chauncy, he often conflated the two, but his doctrinal concerns were paramount. In the aftermath of the Boston earthquakes of November 1755, when expounding on a general "Obligation to fear and worship God," Mayhew not only found it necessary to urge that "God's holy word ought

---

40. Chauncy, *Charity*, 7–8; *Twelve Sermons*, 289.

41. Chauncy, *Reply to Dr. Chandler's "Appeal Defended,"* 58, 62, 66–67; *Compleat View of Episcopacy*, 90.

to be the rule of the worship, service and obedience which we pay to him," but to warn against "superstitions and idolatries," of which Catholic abuses were the most dangerous. Because, like Chauncy, he identified Rome with the anti-Christian "Babylon," the "mother of harlots and abominations" of Revelation 17, Mayhew understandably counseled Congregationalist Bostonians to keep their distance. "We ought not to go wholly over to that apostate church . . . ," he warned, "we ought not to conform to, or symbolize with her, in any of her corruptions, and idolatrous usages: but to keep at as great a distance from them as possible."[42]

Although Mayhew had strong words for Anglican error and episcopacy in his writings against the SPG, even there he made a clear distinction between "the Christian religion" and "atheism, infidelity and popery." One of his major charges against the missionary society, as against the Church of England in general, was its apparent toleration of Catholicism. He was "persuaded," he informed Archbishop Secker and the readers of *Remarks on an Anonymous Tract* (1764), "from the very nature of divers popish tenets, that roman catholics cannot be safely tolerated in the free exercise of their religion, in a protestant government." In some of the fiercest and most apocalyptic anti-Catholic rhetoric found anywhere in his works, Mayhew thus inveighed against "cruel, blood-thirsty and rebel-hearted roman-catholics," who "had hardly any opposition made to them, or any thing to fear in England, either from law or gospel." It was "by such-like means," he ranted, citing the apocalyptic language of Revelation 17 and 18, that

> the Scarlet Whore, with whom the Kings and great men of the earth have committed fornication, at certain seasons got fairly mounted on her horned beast, and rode, with cup of abominations in her hand, almost triumphant thro' England: Seeming to want only a little more time, and a favourable concurrence of circumstances, by means of foreign or domestic broils and jarrings, to shew her execrable, infernal face in its most hideous attitudes, and to exert a bloody, fiery, diabolical strength; the utmost consequences of which, no one could foresee, but all had great reason to dread![43]

Mayhew's theological objections to Catholicism were particularly prominent in his final years—especially around the time of his 1765 Dudleian lecture at Harvard, which was published as *Popish Idolatry*. He prepared very carefully. An unpublished collection of "Hints and References

---

42. Mayhew, *Discourse on Rev. XV*, 44–46.

43. Mayhew, *Observations*, 73, *Remarks on an Anonymous Tract*, 71, 74–75. And see 72–73.

Alphabetically Disposed," dated December 28, 1764, contains ample references to key works, along with brief comments on topics ranging from "Adoration" to "Superstition," all seemingly related to his problems with the Church of Rome. Another notebook from the same year, containing "Notes on the Church of Rome," focuses more narrowly on the theme of idolatry. But in the course of eight densely packed pages it extends to a wide range of other points of contention, among which he listed:

> Infallibility, Supremacy, Idolatry, Transubstantiation, purgatory, lying wonders, Frauds, Persecutions, usurpation on Princes, Inquisition, corrupt rapacity and immorality, forbidding to marry, to abstain from meats, Pilgrimages, praying for the dead, religious orders of men and women, Praying in an unknown tongue, forbidding the Scriptures to be read in the vulgar tongue, Penances, compensations, dispensations, mental reservations, absolutions, their principle of no faith to be kept with heretics, the opprobrious noise given by them to all good Ch[ris]tians, robbing the people of the Scriptures, and of the Cup in the Lord's Supper, thinking to make up, by giving them 5 whole sacraments instead of the half one taken away.[44]

In his second notebook, Mayhew was clearly identifying sources and rehearsing arguments that would later appear in *Popish Idolatry* (1765). He defined idolatry itself, for example, "not in an explicit renunciation of the true God, and worshipping other beings as such, exclusively of him; but in paying them religious worship at least in conjunction with him; and such as is due only to him. (1) To the virgin. (2). To the bread and wine. (3). To the saints, real or pretended. (4). To Images & pictures. (5) To relicks. (6) To the Pope. (7) To the cross." Mayhew outlined the implications of Roman Catholic idolatry in very broad terms:

1. What is idolatry.—Babylon

2. This is allowed, enjoined and universally practised in the C[hurch] of R[ome].

3. No sin more plainly forbidden, or severely censured, in the Bible.

4. Therefore the S[ai]d Ch[urch is] so far from being the only true, that she is the most corrupt ch[urch] in the world, if indeed she may be called a church.

---

44. Mayhew, "Hints and References Alphabetically Disposed," *MP* 87; "Notes on the Church of Rome," *MP* 119.

His problems with the Church of Rome were comprehensive, even all-embracing. "What can be said in opposition to a church so abounding in errors & corruptions as that of Rome," Mayhew argued, "tho' it may be sufficient to make her appear odious to all seasonable men, unprejudiced men, must yet come so far short of her demerits, that it will bear no greater a proportion, than that of a drop to the ocean." Thus "the controversy," as Mayhew delineated it, extended so far as to threaten basic human sense-experience. It was

> not merely a defence of reason against the grossest fanaticism, of the holy Scripture against the most absurd legends, of the worship of one God in Spirit & truth, in opposition to that of a thousand idols, with all the pomp & pageantry of heathenism; of our laws & rights as members of civil society, against the claims and encroachments of ecclesiastical persons, who would bring us into the most ignominious bondage; but it is the defence of the right [of] our natural senses, of the rights, if I may so express it, of seeing, hearing, tasting, smelling, touching; all which popery would deprive us of, as a means of enslaving us to the dictates of what they call the ch[urc]h. Such is the nature of the nature of this dispute!"[45]

In *Popish Idolatry* itself, Mayhew's argument was much more focused and specific. Noting that his two predecessors as Dudleian Lecturers had addressed the topics of papal infallibility and Catholic supremacy, he recognized such limitations from the outset and offered his "learned audience . . . nothing more in a single discourse, tho' long, than a general idea of popish idolatry; an imperfect sketch, the outlines of it." Having summarized what he took to be Catholic teaching on four different kinds of worship and on the doctrine of transubstantiation, Mayhew began by arguing that since this was held to justify the worship of consecrated Communion elements and since it was "as plainly absurd, self-repugnant, and impossible to be true, as any one that can be imagined," the "more sincerely any believe transubstantiation, and worship the eucharist as God; the more sottish is their idolatry." Proceeding to what he called "the worship of saints and angels, as practiced in the same church," Mayhew drew upon Catholic sources, as well as Protestant interpretations of them, to contend that: "that service and respect, whether it be called honor only, or worship, which the church of Rome pays to saints and angels, is unwarranted by reason, contrary to scripture, and properly idolatrous." He deployed similar arguments against "the worship of pictures and images," concluding that "to make and worship any picture or image of Christ, considered as God, which is what they chiefly

45. *MP* 119.

intend here, is idolatry; and directly contrary to the second commandment," notwithstanding sophisticated Catholic doctrinal distinctions. But it was in Mayhew's closing observations that he finally unleashed the full force of his invective against Roman Catholicism. "If then, the church of Rome be grossly idolatrous in the several respects aforesaid . . . it follows, that she is so far from being the only true church, and chaste spouse of Christ, that she is a most corrupt one, a filthy prostitute, who hath forsaken her first love, and is become, indeed, the 'mother of harlots.'"[46]

Defenders of "Orthodoxy"

Mayhew had good reason to believe that his problems with Rome would be shared by dissenters of pretty much every doctrinal stripe in New England. But he was keen to defend his theological orthodoxy in other settings. When faced with charges made by Henry Caner in *Candid Examination of Dr. Mayhew's Observations* (1763), he freely admitted that his "religious sentiments" were "in some respects, different from those of the generality of our forefathers." But he vigorously disputed Caner's allegations of heretical Christology and he upheld his allegiance to "what our pious fore-fathers considered as the most essential branches of christianity." Because none of his writings seriously departed from New England Calvinist tradition for the first four decades of his ministry, Chauncy could long and legitimately have made the same claim. Even after he had composed his most revisionist works, his refusal to release them publicly allowed him to shift to moderately Arminian positions without attracting undue criticism. As late as 1758, he wrote of the desirability of serving "the cause of orthodoxy" and he continued to praise the piety of New England's founders long after that. In 1768, he was clearly aware that what became his *Five Dissertations* would not "comport with what is called orthodoxy," but it would still be more than a dozen years before any of them was released.[47]

Only when his most provocative writings were finally published in the 1780s did Chauncy openly admit that his now universalist soteriology differed from "the ORTHODOX sentiments of our country." Even so, he continued to decry what he called "modern fatalism" and suggested that "our fathers, who were esteemed the standard of ORTHODOXY, would have

---

46. Mayhew, *Popish Idolatry*, 5, 10, 17, 19, 30, 38, 41, 43–44, citing Rev 17:5.

47. *Defence of the Observations*, 108, 110n; Chauncy, *Opinion of One*, 19; "A Sketch of Eminent Men," 163. See, further, *Defence of the Observations*, 107–12, passim, and Caner, *Candid Examination*, 47–48, for implied charges of Christological heresy against Mayhew.

reprobated" it, "though they might not have fallen in with" his own "doctrine of a final restitution." With the publication of *Benevolence of the Deity* (1784), Chauncy finally felt free to speak out strongly against the doctrine of eternal reprobation that he had privately rejected for years and to mock those who embraced it as "divines" who "would be looked upon as the only orthodox ones among their brethren." In the "Conclusion" to his fullest exposition of universalism, *Mystery Hid* (1784), he went further, describing as "gross absurdities" and "palpably wrong and dishonourable ideas of God" not only what was "taught in the church of Rome," but "some of the doctrines which Protestants receive for revealed truths." Among them he singled out traditional Calvinist understandings of "election and reprobation; of the eternity of hell torments; and of the partial design, and final effect, of the mediatory interposition of Jesus Christ."[48]

Yet even as the seventy-nine-year-old Chauncy decisively rejected doctrines he had advocated for years, his final source of authority remained constant:

> And as it is from the BIBLE, that we are furnished with this evidence [of universal salvation]; as it is in this sacred book, that the infinitely benevolent God is represented as having set foot a scheme for the recovery of the whole race of Adam, which scheme he will go on prosecuting by his Son Jesus Christ, on whose blood and righteousness it was founded, till he has instated them all in the possession of everlasting happiness;—how thankful should we be for the scripture-revelation?

Chauncy's universalist theology, which remained Christocentric and continued, despite his rejection of Calvinist election, to rely heavily on the sovereignty of divine grace to "instate" all into universal salvation, was also profoundly shaped by the deep, albeit critically innovative, commitment to biblical revelation that he shared with Mayhew. Equally persuasive evidence of their continuing theological traditionalism has emerged in the two ministers' focus on traditional homiletical topics of "sin–salvation–service," in Chauncy's Christology, in their consistent commitment to the defense of Congregationalist polity, especially against incursions from the Church of England, and in the anti-Catholicism that informed their sense of identity as loyal defenders of New England's heritage. Chapter 5 will explore their political vision, to which this last concern was also central.[49]

---

48. Chauncy, *Divine Glory*, 4, 17; *Benevolence of the Deity*, 132; *Mystery Hid*, 362–63.
49. Chauncy, *Mystery Hid*, 358.

PART 2

Conservative Revolutionaries

— 5 —

Engaging the Public Square

Ministers in Politics

WHEN JONATHAN MAYHEW WROTE a lengthy letter to Massachusetts Governor, Sir Francis Bernard, on December 18, 1761, he had good grounds to be anxious. Almost exactly a month earlier, on November 17, he had entertained two Pokanauket native Americans as overnight guests in his Boston home. James Tallman, the father of one of Mayhew's indentured servants, had arrived in town with Judah Olson to present a petition to the General Court, which was then in session, and they had gone straight to Governor Bernard's house, where he had received it personally. The two men were short of money and Mayhew agreed to give them two dollars for their journey home. But another aspect of their circumstances troubled him so much that he subsequently made further enquiries. The native Americans were without funds, they claimed, because they had paid the governor two dollars to accept their petition.[1]

On December 8, Mayhew shared his concerns about Bernard's alleged gratuity with two close friends, a deacon of West Church and a member of the Royal Council, one of whom offered the possible explanation that the governor had received the money on behalf of Provincial Secretary Andrew Oliver. But the matter did not remain in confidence, and three days later Mayhew was visited by the deputy registrar of the Vice-Admiralty Court,

---

1. A draft of Mayhew's letter to Francis Bernard of December 18, 1761 is to be found in *MP* 61, which constitutes two notebooks containing eleven letters and sundry "remarks" relating to the incident with Bernard and others. Its full title is "Letters to a friend. A circumstantial Narrative of what passed betwixt the Author and an Indian relating to a certain petition and two dollars, etc. With Remarks." The letter was also reprinted in Bradford, *Memoir,* 217–24. For reliable secondary accounts of the circumstances surrounding Mayhew's letter of December 18, 1761, see Akers, *Called unto Liberty,* 153–61; Mullins, "Father of Liberty," 172–82. See, further, Mullins, "'A Kind of War.'"

William Story, who informed him that news of his report of Bernard's dealings had already reached high places. After Mayhew confirmed the details and refused to retract, Story reported back to Bernard, who dispatched Oliver to call on Mayhew at 9 a.m. on December 9 and summon him to a meeting with the governor within the hour. Mayhew discovered that this was to be neither a private nor a pleasant conversation. Having invited Oliver and Lieutenant Governor Thomas Hutchinson into the room to serve as witnesses, Bernard denied the story of his gratuity and effectively accused Mayhew of a slanderous defamation of character, for which he demanded "satisfaction." When Mayhew showed himself unwilling to recant or apologize, Bernard angrily reproached him for not only spreading a lie, but abusing "British liberty" and admiring the government of Oliver Cromwell. After one and a half hours of hostile exchanges, Bernard informed Mayhew that he would take further advice on how to proceed in light of his intransigence. A week later, on December 16, Hutchinson paid a visit in an abortive attempt to act as mediator. The following day, Mayhew's friend Harrison Gray informed him that Bernard was suggesting private arbitration. Mayhew eventually learned from his brother Zechariah, who had interviewed Tallman in Martha's Vineyard, that the two native Americans had mistaken the governor's identity and given the gratuity to one of his servants; however, there is no record that Bernard and Mayhew ever formally resolved their differences.[2]

Instead, Mayhew continued to uphold his position, not only in his letter of December 18, 1761, but in a private, sixty-four-page memorandum containing sundry documentation on the matter to an unnamed friend. The general tone of "A Circumstantial Narrative" was predictably defensive, but it offered fascinating insights into Mayhew's political views. He speculated, for example, that the real cause of Bernard's anger was his resentment of the minister's denunciations of Charles I and other Stuart monarchs in *Discourse Concerning Unlimited Submission* (1750), of his "notions of civil liberty," and of parts of a 1760 funeral sermon remembering Chief Justice Stephen Sewall. In his letter to the governor, Mayhew took particular offense at "another angry expression," that he allegedly "adored the Oliverian [i.e., Cromwellian] times"—a charge which he rejected, although he could not help casting ironic aspersions on Bernard's own views:

> But I now beg leave to add, that I am as far from adoring those times of confusion and religious madness, as your Excellency is from adoring the times of the Jameses and Charleses, when arbitrary power was carried to such enormous lengths, that hardly

2. *MP* 61.

any wise and honest man could, with freedom and safety, speak his thoughts. And, surely, Your Excellency is far from adoring such wretched and despotic times as those.³

Although he arguably oversimplified their positions, Mullins contrasted the differences between Bernard and Mayhew as those between "Court versus Country, Tory versus Whig." Another dimension of the conflict, which he and Akers acknowledged, but underplayed, was the obvious religious tensions between the high-church Anglican governor and the dissenting Congregationalist minister. Yet Mayhew clearly thought them central. He suggested in "A Circumstantial Narrative," for example, that the governor, who was a member of the SPG, did not like Mayhew's opposition to the Church of England's "39 Articles of Religion," to Anglican liturgy, or to the establishment of an Anglican episcopate in the American colonies. He also stated, in his letter of December 18, 1761, that rather than "the Oliverian times," he adored "HIM alone, who was before all times, even from everlasting to everlasting; who always does right, and can never do wrong." Mayhew clearly linked religious and political concerns when he went on to observe:

> If I adored any times, they would be those of the glorious revolution, when the nation was almost miraculously rescued from tyranny, and its liberties, by the bill of rights, &c., were established upon the present basis; which I pray God may be immutable.⁴

Even in such a practical piece of correspondence, Mayhew's references to such "liberties" were also shaped by his theology. "I am confident you have no desire," he told Bernard:

> to obtain and establish such a universal influence over the tongues or pens of his majesty's loyal subjects, as is not warranted by law; such an one as is not consistent with the genius of the British government; in short, such an one as true Britons neither will nor ought to be under, so long as they enjoy both tongues and pens, and their liberties.

---

3. Ibid.; Mayhew to Bernard, December 18, 1761, in Bradford, *Memoir*, esp. 222, and *Discourse Occasioned by the Death of The Honourable Stephen Sewall*. Akers rightly noted that Mayhew also prepared a second letter to the governor, which he never sent, and after receiving clarification about the initial incident from his brother, he "admitted privately that there had been no bribe involved in the case" (*Called unto Liberty*, 158, 160).

4. Mullins, "Father of Liberty," 180–82, esp. 180; *MP* 61; Mayhew to Bernard, December 18, 1761, in Bradford, *Memoir*, 222–23.

Yet while laying claim to the freedom of expression guaranteed by the British constitution that he valued so highly, Mayhew made it very plain that his understanding of such a right and privilege was also biblical. "I beg . . . that you would not entertain so hard a thought of me," Mayhew continued, citing 1 Peter 2:16, "as to suppose, that I 'use liberty for a cloak of maliciousness'; against which I have often cautioned others." Such biblicist rhetoric is common in Mayhew's writings, but its presence in this and similar contexts is particularly striking given the lack of attention to spiritual considerations in many scholarly assessments of Mayhew's, as of Chauncy's, political opinions and exchanges.[5]

Rejecting Mayhew "as the exemplary Liberal revolutionary," even while portraying Chauncy as "the greatest Liberal of all" in his own theologically rationalist, but sociopolitically reactionary terms, Heimert recast both within a more traditionalist framework. But with few exceptions, including Corrigan's comparative study with its focus on their quest for "wholeness and balance," the vast majority of scholars have focused on Mayhew's and Chauncy's Whig influences. In an influential article responding directly to Heimert's central thesis in *Religion and the American Mind*, Bailyn amplified earlier portraits of Mayhew as a revolutionary precursor and forerunner, redefining his major political muse as not only Whig, but "Real Whig" ideology. Later scholars to interpret Mayhew's thought in similar terms, with some variations of emphasis, have included Mark Noll, Mullins, Chris Beneke, and Howard Lubert. In foregrounding such sources, historians have stressed important elements in Mayhew's political thought. But with the notable exceptions of Heimert, Corrigan, and Lubert, who focused on Mayhew's more general attitudes to religion and society, recent scholars have tended to overlook more moderate political themes, as well as more traditional religious elements, even in discourse suffused with biblical content and rhetoric.[6]

5. MP 61; Mayhew to Bernard, December 18, 1761, in Bradford, *Memoir*, 221. In citing 1 Pet 2:16, Mayhew was pleading for much more than a simply individualistic or solely political right to say what he wanted. As will be argued in the next chapter, a traditional Puritan notion of spiritual freedom to serve God and others underlay and informed his libertarian discourse.

6. Heimert, *Religion and the American Mind*, 290, 418; Corrigan, *Hidden Balance*, 7; Bailyn, "Religion and Revolution"; Noll, *America's God*, 79–80, 138–40; Mullins, "'A Kind of War'"; Beneke, "The Critical Turn"; Lubert "Jonathan Mayhew." See Bailyn, *Pamphlets*, 206–11, where he offered an assessment of Mayhew's influence by Real Whig ideology. "Earlier portraits of Mayhew as a revolutionary precursor and forerunner" included Baldwin, *New England Clergy*, e.g., 44–45, 90–92; Rossiter, "Life and Mind"; Akers, *Called unto Liberty*. In seeking to synthesize "the history of ideas with biographical and political narrative," Mullins followed Bailyn's interpretation most faithfully. He portrayed Mayhew as "a revolutionary in religion as well as politics," who departed

Although his political views have mostly been interpreted in more general, rather than Real Whig terms, the same can be said, with equally few exceptions, of Chauncy. His principal biographer, Griffin, followed historiographical tradition in placing such convictions front and center in his subject's opposition to the prospect of an American episcopate, to the Stamp Act, to other British taxation, and eventually to military measures of the 1760s and 1770s. While recognizing Chauncy as a creative innovator

from Calvinist orthodoxy, was "the first American openly to reject the Trinity," and consistently promoted the "Country Whig political ideology," of which he offered "the first great restatement by an American" in *Discourse Concerning Unlimited Submission*. Mullins departed from some previous scholars in locating the deepest roots of Mayhew's thought in an Enlightenment worldview first acquired at Harvard. In urging the primacy of Real Whig ideology, as well as Enlightenment rationalism in shaping Mayhew's political ideas, Mullins's thesis posed problems of internal consistency, to which he offered a potential solution by suggesting that the former led Mayhew to embrace the latter. He also advanced a radically libertarian and individualistic view of Mayhew's understanding of liberty, which was central, he argued, to the "liberal consensus" that was "Mayhew's greatest contribution to the intellectual origins of the American Revolution and to the Republic he did not live to see" ("Father of Liberty," "Abstract," 2, 4, 253–7, esp. 253, 256). Since 2005, Mullins has returned to his subject, not least in an article focusing on Mayhew's dispute with Bernard in late 1761. In a detailed account of that incident, he sought to show how it not only resulted from previous tensions between Bernard and Mayhew, it encapsulated, even provoked, Mayhew's agitation against the British authorities over such issues as the American Episcopate controversy, support for a new, non-Anglican society to promote the evangelization of indigenous peoples, and, ultimately, violent opposition to the Stamp Act. Mullins thus saw the "Indian Affair" as "an example of the ideologically driven politics that led to the constitutional crises that characterized the decade from 1765 to 1775." It also "contributed to those crises by propelling Mayhew into the popular opposition aligned against Bernard's administration," and, in the process, the Boston minister's true, egalitarian, and radical Whig sentiments fully emerged ("'A Kind of War,'" esp. 53). Of the other two scholars to devote significant attention to Mayhew in more recent years, Beneke sought to place *A Discourse Concerning Unlimited Submission* within the more narrow context of growing anti-British sentiment and activism in mid-eighteenth-century Boston and Lubert offered a broader reinterpretation of Mayhew's political thought as a "conservative revolutionary." Beneke took issue with historians who had seen Mayhew's 1750 sermon on the hundredth anniversary of King Charles I's death as a precursory presentation of Whig arguments that would ultimately pave the way for the American Revolution. It was better contextualized, he argued, 41, within the setting of "local political and religious conflicts," including the 1747 Knowles Riot, flourishing "rumors of an impending colonial bishopric," and pending imperial replacement of the Massachusetts currency ("The Critical Turn," esp. 41). Extending his analysis well beyond one sermon to offer a broader interpretation of the Boston pastor's political views, Lubert likewise stressed a less proleptic interpretation of Mayhew's ideas. While clearly maintaining their radical Whig sources and implications, especially in *Discourse Concerning Unlimited Submission* and Mayhew's incendiary sermon of August 1765, Lubert also highlighted their continuing sociopolitical traditionalism ("Jonathan Mayhew," esp. 589). "Real Whig" ideology is defined below.

in some areas, Lippy also stressed more traditionalist aspects of his social and political vision and he offered a much more substantial account than Heimert's scattered sketch of a reactionary who only grudgingly embraced revolution in the mid-1770s. But Lippy failed to show how this "seasonable" revolutionary's identification with the patriot movement from 1774 was ultimately motivated by his quest for "a lost ideal . . . of human liberty." His discovery of more conventional motives behind the First Church minister's anti-authoritarian rhetoric of the 1760s and 1770s also neglected evidence of its obvious Whiggery. Noll addressed the latter more fully. But while he claimed that Chauncy's sociopolitical traditionalism entailed a "defense of New England" that was "infected by none of Bernard Bailyn's 'contagion of liberty,'" he did little to explain his distinction between the minister's general Whig principles and the more militant ideology attributed to Mayhew and others. Together with a consistent failure to integrate the spiritual with other dimensions of the two leaders' political worldviews, such considerations highlight the need for a more balanced and nuanced interpretation.[7]

7. Griffin, *Old Brick*, e.g., 134-44; Lippy, *Seasonable Revolutionary*, 100, 103-4, esp. 104; Heimert, *Religion and the American Mind*, e.g., 244, 246-49, 382-84, 431-32; Noll, *America's God*, 141-43, esp. 143. Lippy viewed the First Church minister's opposition to the Stamp Act as "an effort to maintain intact the structures of political authority which he believed had been operative prior to its passage." In the American Episcopate controversy, he thought Chauncy motivated by a continuing desire "to structure a church and to worship according to traditional Puritan precepts" while defending the "religious and political liberties of New England." Even during the revolutionary period, Lippy did not see Chauncy driven by a more radical vision of a newly independent nation, but by concerns for "the transmission of those social and political patterns which he perceived as integral to a developing American identity and self-awareness" (*Seasonable Revolutionary*, 72, 82-83, 103-4). In the sense that he sought to square more traditionalist with more progressive elements of Chauncy's political vision, Noll's account is arguably more balanced than Lippy's. But he also largely ignored the prevalence of libertarian rhetoric in Chauncy's earlier writings. Beginning with the loyalist commentator, Peter Oliver, who viewed the venerable First Church minister six years before his death as a prime instigator of revolution, earlier historians almost universally echoed Baldwin's verdict that Chauncy was a single-minded rebel, "who dwelt long upon the nature and advantages of a balanced government," who was "outspoken in laying the evils of the day upon the general Court," and who was "one of the most ardent and influential in the American cause" (*New England Clergy*, 43). According to Oliver, "Among those who were most distinguished of the Boston Clergy were Dr. Charles Chauncy, Dr. Jonathan Mayhew & Dr. Samuel Cooper; & they distinguished theirselves in encouraging Seditions & Riots, untill those lesser Offences were absorbed in Rebellion" (*Origin and Progress*, 43). Perry Miller viewed Chauncy as a "courageous and devoted" patriot, who "fought for tangible ends, for freedom from taxation and for habeas corpus," and as "a liberal in theology, an advocate of the rights of man, and a champion of Americanism in all its phases" (*Jonathan Edwards*, 326, 322). See, further, Rossiter, *Seedtime of the Republic*, 233, 328. With Heimert, Noll, and to a lesser extent Lippy, Corrigan has been the other major scholar to highlight more traditionalist elements

Whiggery in Perspective

Although no historian has thoroughly pursued it in the context of the two ministers' political views, an important distinction informing this discussion has already emerged. At its heart lies the simple assumption, widely endorsed by historians, that the "mainstream" Whiggery often attributed to Chauncy and the Real Whig ideology ascribed to Mayhew, especially since Bailyn, were closely related, but by no means identical. Equally significant, when addressing spiritual themes in Mayhew's and Chauncy's political writings, is the parallel premise that in the highly religious cultures of late seventeenth-century and eighteenth-century Britain and colonial America, Whiggism of any description, whatever its practical agenda, itself embraced and was to some extent defined by significant religious concerns. In that sense, to argue, as Bailyn did, that the Whig "determinants of revolution" were solely "political" is to misrepresent Whiggery itself, especially in the case of church leaders, whose rhetoric, even when most political in orientation, often confounds modern attempts to impose anachronistic distinctions between "sacred" and "secular" realms of discourse.[8]

The historical emergence of Whiggism has been well documented. The political philosophy dated from the English "Exclusion Crisis" of 1679–81, which led to the Glorious Revolution of 1688 and to the succession of the Protestant King William III and Queen Mary II. In response to the threat and then reality of a Catholic king, James II, with perceived absolutist tendencies, Locke, the English politicians and republican theorists James

---

of Chauncy's political thought. But he was more concerned with offering a broad outline than addressing the specific questions that have preoccupied other historians. For Corrigan, as already noted, "'mutual dependency' was the key to Chauncy's vision of government." In analyzing Chauncy's social views, Corrigan acknowledged the First Church minister's traditionalism. Like Mayhew, "Chauncy often wrote in defense of social deference," he contended, "and of the static character of social order, arguing that society was divided into 'spheres' or 'stations,' the boundaries of which were not to be crossed." But Corrigan also stressed that "equality of opportunity made vertical mobility an integral part of the social system in the colonies in the eighteenth century," and that "Chauncy and Mayhew believed that perfectibility in nature came through the cultivation of one's potential, and that advancement in one's worldly circumstances was possible in the same way" (*Hidden Balance*, 64–65, 88, 90–91).

8. Bailyn, "Religion and Revolution," 85. Bailyn's general argument that "it is a gross simplification to believe that religion as such, or any of its doctrinaire elements, had a unique political role in the Revolutionary movement" is especially unconvincing given his prior observation that "the whole of American culture was 'religious' in the sense that common modes of discourse in both ordinary life and high culture were derived from Protestant Christianity." It is argued here that such religiously derived "common modes of discourse" included, to some extent, those of Whig and Real Whig ideology, which Bailyn interpreted in entirely non-religious terms.

Tyrrell and Algernon Sidney, and others took up their pens to counter the "divine right" monarchism and doctrine of non-resistance advocated by Robert Filmer, especially in his posthumously published *Patriarcha Non Monarcha* (1680). The results were distinctive visions of an emergent Whig philosophy born out of a shared "historical and ideological context" defined by Lee Ward as anti-Catholicism, revulsion against republicanism, and fear of the recurrence of civil war. Yet Tyrrell's more traditional social vision, Lockean liberalism, and even, to some extent, Sidney's republicanism united in their advocacy of a contract theory of government, of parliamentary sovereignty under the supremacy of the King-in-Parliament (but not alone), of the British "mixed constitution," of vigorous Protestantism, of toleration for Protestant dissent, and of opposition to Catholicism, especially a Catholic monarchy.[9]

This moderate Whiggery, here termed "mainstream," maintained strong allegiance to the constitutional order resulting from the Glorious Revolution. It also came to constitute a dominant political philosophy during the period, often known as the "Whig supremacy," from the Hanoverian succession of 1714 under George I until at least the early 1760s. Its core convictions were even shared by the "Court" and "Country" factions which periodically battled for power and influence in eighteenth-century Britain. Those two parties primarily disagreed over other issues, including the maintenance of constitutional equilibrium and the strengths and weaknesses of emerging economic structures and practices.[10]

Within this wider historical context, Bailyn's seminal demonstration of the influence of Real Whig on American revolutionary ideology focused especially on the works of leading Country figures in what Caroline Robbins had defined as a third "generation" of eighteenth-century "Commonwealthmen," including John Trenchard, Thomas Gordon, Robert Molesworth, Henry Bolingbroke, and the latitudinarian Bishop Hoadly. Bailyn freely recognized that the force of Real Whig ideas could easily be "mistaken because

---

9. Ward, *Politics of Liberty*, 100–103 (esp. 101), 14, 306–7 (esp. 306). See esp. Filmer, *Patriarcha*; Tyrrell, *Patriarcha Non Monarcha*; Locke, *Two Treatises*, first published in 1680; Sidney, *Discourses*. Ward defined a "mixed constitution" as "balancing the various classes, interests, and estates of the realm in a system of shared legislative power including king, Lords, and Commons" (*Politics of Liberty*, 306). According to Burgess, Filmer's *Patriarcha Non Monarcha* was "perhaps written . . . about 1630, though it remained unpublished until 1680" ("Filmer, Sir Robert (1588?–1653)"). Ward has contended that "Sidney founded a strain of Whiggism that was deeply opposed to the principle of [royal] prerogative and an independent executive." Instead, he "advocated a distinctly modern form of republicanism infused with the principles of radical natural rights theory"(*Politics of Liberty*, 156).

10. Ward, *Politics of Liberty*, 306–7.

on the main points of theory the eighteenth-century contributors to this tradition were not original." In fact, "their key concepts—natural rights, the contractual basis of society and government, the uniqueness of England's liberty-preserving 'mixed' constitution—were commonplaces of the liberal thought of the time." But while they strongly upheld mainstream constitutional tenets, in publications like Trenchard's and Gordon's *Independent Whig* (1721) and *Cato's Letters* (1724), Real Whigs stridently critiqued the eighteenth-century English political establishment under Prime Minister Robert Walpole and other ministers. "Cassandras of the age," according to Bailyn, they saw political corruption, conspiracy and decline pretty much everywhere they looked in Georgian England. They "'stressed the danger to England's ancient heritage and the loss of pristine virtue.'" They saw government "corruption," "luxury," "conspiracy," and even "slavery" threatening basic English liberty, virtue, and constitutional rights. They called for major reforms to remedy these ills.[11]

11. Bailyn, *Ideological Origins*, 34–54, 45–46 (citing McKillop, "Background of Thomson's *Liberty*," 87), xiii. See, further, David Mayer, "English Radical Whig Origins," esp. 162–63, 164–68, citing Pocock, "Machiavelli, Harrington, and English Political Ideologies." In her groundbreaking study, *Eighteenth Century Commonwealthman*, Robbins identified three generations of English "Real Whigs" avowing what Mayer described as "a consciousness of kinship with civil-war-period republican political writers, such as Milton, Harrington, and Sidney" ("English Radical Whig Origins," 162). Among key "Real Whig" works, see esp. Trenchard and Gordon, *Independent Whig* and *Cato's Letters*; Hoadly, *Measures of Submission*; Hoadly, *Original and Institution*; D'Anvers, *The Craftsman*; Molesworth, *Account of Denmark*. Key Real Whig writings against standing armies included Trenchard, *Short History*; Trenchard, *Discourse of Standing Armies*; Trenchard, *Standing Armies*. See, further, Bolingbroke, *Works*. According to Bailyn, Hoadly also produced "extreme statements of Whig political theory" in addition to his many theological writings (*Ideological Origins*, 37). As Rodgers has argued of Bailyn's understanding of "ideology," "by 1973 Bailyn . . . recast the argument of his *Ideological Origins* . . . Between formal ideas and social experience was a middle stratum of mind that 'crystallizes otherwise inchoate social and political discontent,' mobilizes 'disconnected, unrealized private emotions,' elevates 'to structured consciousness' confused and mingled urges, that in short constructs a revolutionary mentalité" ("Republicanism," 19–21), See esp. Bailyn, "Central Themes," esp. 11, drawing heavily on Geertz, "Ideology." Mayer noted that the Real Whigs also "used the terms 'Independent Whig,' 'True Whig,' and 'Honest Whig' to describe themselves." In deliberate contradistinction from "contemporaries in the mainstream of British political discourse," one of their key political objectives was to counter the undue cabinet or "court" influence of senior government leaders, especially during the tenure of Walpole. As remedies to such "corruption," Real Whigs of a "country" persuasion set great store by the balance of powers inherent in a properly functioning, mixed British constitution, where Members of Parliament were free to exercise due supervision of the executive. They sought the reform of Parliamentary elections and procedures and they were strong advocates of religious liberty and toleration. They argued that every Englishman should have the right to be ruled by laws approved by a government in

Although Real Whig ideology had little practical impact in its original British context, Bailyn persuasively showed how its ideas were enthusiastically circulated and widely adopted, especially from the 1760s, by leading American colonial protesters (and eventually revolutionaries) against the perceived injustices of imperial rule. Especially influential in the reception of such ideological commitments was the negative, critical, even paranoid style in which they were expressed. As they "dwelt endlessly on the evidences of corruption they saw about them and the dark future these malignant signs portended," their "obsessive," fearful, and ever more extreme discourse found a ready audience among colonists outraged by British taxation and other measures who were "seeking justification for concerted opposition to constituted governments." Scholarship has expanded exponentially since Bailyn's pioneering work of the 1960s, with major studies urging the revolutionary significance of other philosophies and ideologies, including different streams of republicanism and, more recently, a new synthesis of Lockean liberalism. In 2010, Alan Gibson noted a growing historiographical "consensus" around "the conciliatory and catholic but also diffuse claim" that the political thought of America's founding era was "best understood as an amalgam of liberalism, republicanism and perhaps other traditions of political thought." But Bailyn's work remains influential and Mayhew has consistently been seen as a key adopter and advocate of Real Whig ideology in America.[12]

---

which he was properly represented and they wished to see that right extended to all at home or abroad. Their calls for political reforms also extended to full press freedom and an end to standing armies ("English Radical Whig Origins," 162-63, 162n, 166–67). The masculine "Englishman" is used quite deliberately in this footnote, since the Real Whigs showed no concern for women's emancipation or suffrage.

12. Bailyn, *Ideological Origins*, 43–52, esp. 46, 48, 52; Gibson, *Understanding the Founding*, 134–35. Ward portrayed American "revolutionary constitutionalism" in terms of "laboratories of Radical Whiggism" (*Politics of Liberty*, 396–425). Commenting on the general historiography, Shain contended that as recently as the 1950s, when there was a noted resurgence of interest in revolutionary political philosophy led by twentieth-century "neo-Whig" historians, "there was only one claimant to the role of reigning 18th-century political philosophy: the still vibrant philosophy of liberal individualism" (*Myth of American Individualism*, xiv–xvii, esp. xiv). This liberal consensus was subsequently displaced by a republican one in the 1970s and 1980s, with the other two leading studies of that school, Wood, *Creation of the American Republic*, and Pocock, *Machiavellian Moment*, offering complementary, but also somewhat disparate interpretations of revolutionary and post-revolutionary thought from Bailyn. Ward suggested in 2004 that "the state of the debate" was "one of stalemate," with scholars quite widely accepting that both liberal and republican interpretations of American revolutionary origins and development had substance (*Politics of Liberty*, 6). Gibson's similar observation was made, *inter alia*, in the context of his account of the emergence from the 1990s of a "Neo-Lockean Synthesis" in such works as Greenstone, *Lincoln Persuasion*, and Zuckert, *Natural Rights Republic*, 137–41).

Bailyn's demonstration of Mayhew's dependence, in *Discourse Concerning Unlimited Submission* (1750), on Whig works by Hoadly and Gordon and on the English pamphlet *Letter to a Clergyman* (1746) is compelling. Alongside clearly Lockean themes (see chapter 6), he also showed the influence of such ideas in Mayhew's previously unpublished "Memorandum" of an August 25, 1765 sermon on liberty, in *Snare Broken* (1766), and in other works. But Bailyn went further. He not only thought such writings steeped in Real Whig thought and so "the fulfillment and application" of the 1750 *Discourse*. He proleptically, and so problematically, placed "the American Revolution itself" in the same category. Although Bailyn occasionally adverted to mainstream Whig themes in Mayhew's writings, he paid little attention to them, still less to more traditionalist positions, and he totally discounted the influence of the minister's profound religious beliefs. Drawing on two main sources, which Bailyn himself highlighted, this chapter affirms the significance of Real Whig themes in Mayhew's political thought. It also offers, through analysis of other works, a more rigorous interpretation of his and Chauncy's sociopolitical views that gives due recognition to other influences and sources, including their pervasive spiritual content.[13]

Real Whig Rhetoric

Real Whig rhetoric had long been part of the dissenting Protestant, anti-Catholic polemical tradition in which Mayhew and Chauncy enthusiastically participated. Yet in raising fears of state and church "tyranny" under despotic powers, Mayhew adopted a notably conspiratorial view of British intentions during his 1763-4 controversy with East Apthorp over Church of England plans to establish an episcopate in the American colonies. Focusing on the corrupt institutions at the heart of Georgian England and the threats which they allegedly posed to New England, Mayhew had little doubt that the work of the SPG in establishing and supporting new Church of England congregations in areas already well served by Congregationalists had dark, ulterior motives. These missionary efforts had "all the appearance of entering wedges; or rather of little lodgments made in carrying on the crusade, or

13. Bailyn, *Pamphlets*, 208-9, 211, citing Hoadly, *Measures of Submission*; Coade, *Letter to a Clergyman*; Trenchard and Gordon, *The Independent Whig*. See also Bailyn, "Religion and Revolution," 121. Perhaps based on the work's title page, Bailyn described the authorship of *Letter to a Clergyman* as "anonymous" (*Pamphlets*, 208). Mayhew's sermon "Memorandum" is found in *MP* 91, and reprinted in Bailyn, "Religion and Revolution," 140-43. A modern edition of Mayhew, *Snare Broken* is reprinted in Sandoz, *Political Sermons*, 1:231-64. A modern edition of Mayhew, *Discourse Concerning Unlimited Submission* is reprinted in Bailyn, *Pamphlets*, 212-47.

spiritual siege of our churches, with the hope that they will one day submit to an episcopal sovereign." It seemed "at least probable . . . that this has long been the formal design of the Society; and that it is the true plan, and grand mystery of their operations in New-England." In response to a defense of Anglican strategy by Secker, Mayhew appealed to the lessons of the past to justify his fears of arbitrary episcopal rule: "It is . . . pretty evident from our history," he argued, "that in arbitrary reigns, and foolish and wicked administrations, the bishops have commonly been the most useful members, or instruments, that the crown or court had, in establishing a tyranny over the bodies and souls of men."[14]

Such a view of what the writer of a letter to the London *St. James's Chronicle* described in June 1766 as "the Stamping and Episcopizing our Colonies," rendering them "only different Branches of the same Plan of Power," lay at the heart of the somewhat paranoid Real Whig perspective on metropolitan political strategy held by Mayhew and like-minded New England contemporaries. Similar ideological currents flow strongly through his correspondence with the prominent English Whig, Thomas Hollis, which extended for the last seven years of his life. After August 16, 1759, when Mayhew wrote a letter of thanks for the English activist's first anonymous and then open donations of books by Sidney, Puritan poet John Milton, and others, the West Church minister corresponded regularly with Hollis until his death. Three major themes in their letters were a shared commitment to a Real Whig political philosophy, which shaped their interpretations of contemporary events in Britain and North America; fierce anti-Catholicism; and their fears of the prospect of a Church of England episcopate in the colonies.[15]

For Hollis, who declared himself "ever an open and most declared Whig, who adored the Revolution, and the House of Hanover because of it, and their merits," Sidney, Milton, and the seventeenth-century English Parliamentarian "honest" Edmund Ludlow were "Heroes." After briefly outlining Milton's political "principles," as he understood them, the London activist had no hesitation in stating that "it is to Milton, the divine Milton, and such as him, in the struggles of the civil wars and the Revolution, that we are beholden for all the manifold and unexampled Blessings which we now every where enjoy; and Mr. President Holyoke for his Liberty and his [Harvard] College." Mayhew had a similar pantheon. In his very first

14. Mayhew, *Observations*, 57; *Remarks on an Anonymous Tract*, 12.
15. Homologistes (pseud.), "To the Printer of The S: J. chronicle," cited, without attribution, by Bailyn, *Ideological Origins*, 97, and Bradford, *Memoir*, 372; Mayhew to Hollis, August 16, 1759, in Mayhew and Hollis, "Thomas Hollis and Jonathan Mayhew," 109–10. On Hollis, see esp. Robbins, "Strenuous Whig."

letter to Hollis, he declared himself "indebted for Sidney's most excellent *Discourses on Government*, and the admirable Milton's EIKONOKLASTES." He was also confident that others shared his preferences. "His political notions, and sentiments concerning Milton . . . ," Mayhew assured Hollis about Holyoke, "are not materially different from your own. These are indeed the principles which, God be thanked! generally prevail in New England."[16]

Many of the books that Hollis sent to Boston were chosen precisely as means of advancing his Whig agenda. Mayhew responded warmly to these gifts and reciprocated with some of his own. He esteemed Caleb Fleming's *Palladium . . . Or Historical Strictures of Liberty* (1762) as "an excellent Performance." He offered favorable commentary on "the New Edition of the admirable Sydney" and on "the New Edition of Locke upon Government and . . . the *Philosophical Survey*." Among American works, Hollis hailed James Otis's *Rights of the British Colonies Asserted* (1764), which a friend thought embodied all "the great and generous Principles of government, that is of public good, which ever warmed Milton, Locke, or any patriot head." Mayhew also forwarded Hutchinson's *History of the Massachusetts-Bay* (1764), although he had concerns that while the author "in many . . . places . . . appears very full in the principles of liberty, civil and religious," in others, "he seems . . . to favor the interposition and power of the civil Magistrate in merely ecclesiastical Affairs, more than I can see reason for."[17]

---

16. Hollis to Mayhew, August 27, 1760, in Mayhew and Hollis, "Thomas Hollis and Jonathan Mayhew," 114–17, esp. 116–17; Mayhew to Hollis, August 16, 1759, in ibid., 109–10, esp.109; Mayhew to Hollis, March 19, 1761, in ibid., 118–20, esp. 118. Hollis understood Milton's political "principles" in the following terms: "That Government, at least our government is by compact. That a King becoming a Tyrant, and the compact thereby broken, the Power reverts again to the Constituents, the People, who may punish such Tyrant as they see fit, and constitute such a new form of government as shall then appear to them to be most expedient. It is true indeed that that form of Government which he and many other able honest men inclined to on the death and punishment of the Tyrant Charles was a Commonwealth; which the Army that Hydra-beast prevented; forcing the Nation thereby, against its bent, after numberless vexations, to call back that riot-Prince Charles the second. But Milton nor the warmest Commonwealth's man, never thought of altering the antient [sic] form of Government till Charles the first had sinned flagrantly and repeatedly against it, and had destroyed it by his violences"(Hollis to Mayhew, August 27, 1760, in ibid, 116–17).

17. Mayhew to Hollis, November 21, 1763 in ibid., 140–41; Mayhew to Hollis, October 17, 1764, in ibid., 158–59, esp. 159; Hollis to Mayhew, March 4, 1765, in ibid, 164–66, esp. 165–66; Mayhew to Hollis, December 18, 1764, in ibid., 161–64, esp. 163. For further details of books listed as exchanged in first or most recent editions between Hollis and Mayhew, see Anon, *Philosophical Survey of Nature*; Fleming, *Palladium*; Hutchinson, *History of the Colony of Massachusetts Bay in New England*; Locke, *Two Treatises*, 6th ed. (1764); Otis, *Rights of the British Colonies*; Sidney, *Discourses Concerning Government* (1763 ed.).

When Mayhew and Hollis exchanged views about contemporary political issues, their perspectives were so shaped by such sources that they tended to see many more signs of danger than sources of encouragement in the unfolding of national and international events. "The several Political Publications sent me, confirm the Apprehensions which I have all along had concerning the P---e," Mayhew wrote of the 1763 Treaty of Paris, which marked the end of the Seven Years' War (1756–63), and he "almost tremble[d] for the Consequences. May God unite the Hearts of all wise and good men;—all who love liberty and Great-Britain, and hate French ambition and S[cotc]h Politicks." Hollis shared Mayhew's fears of an unduly generous British settlement with France, but found potential in the likely political appointment of a mutual hero, even if only as the result of government expediency. "It seems probable," he informed Mayhew in April 1764, that

> Mr. [William] Pitt will be made Secretary of State in no long time, and some others of the opposition be permitted to take share in places; not from any fear the Ministry are under of them, or noble pursuit in which they wish to employ Mr. Pitt, but solely in hopes thereby to still all popular clamour: And in that way it is possible they might stifle clamour till the next general war, when woe to Britan [sic], who, by its leaders, at the close of the last, has seemed to renounce the very providence of the Almighty.

Mayhew's emotional investment in such events was high. He found Hollis's "account . . . of the political state of Affairs in England . . . extremely afflictive." Although he saw nothing in his "natural temper, inclining to melancholy, or a dejection of spirits," news on both sides of the Atlantic filled him, in true Real Whig fashion, with "very gloomy apprehensions." So he was moved to prayer:

> May HE that governs the world, avert the evils which there is so much cause to fear! If England cannot at this day be justly called the Land of Patriots, it is not destitute of some glorious ones: among whom I cannot help reckoning you as one, even though you are so averse from appearing to have any concern in the public, national Affairs. God increase the number, and give them at once all needful magnanimity and prudence! How it is in England I do not so well know; but here, I have reason to suppose, that there are many who might adopt—. . . *Video meliora proboque, Deteriora sequor.*[18]

18. Mayhew to Hollis, November 21, 1763, in Mayhew and Hollis, "Thomas Hollis and Jonathan Mayhew," 140–41; Hollis to Mayhew, April 4, 1764, in ibid., 144–47, esp. 146; Mayhew to Hollis, received August 23, 1764, in ibid., 148–51, esp. 150. The Latin

A major factor in Mayhew's and Hollis's anxious vision of British and colonial American politics related to their further fears that the kind of arbitrary power which they saw evident in "French ambition and S[cotc]h Politicks" might come to impinge upon British liberties ecclesiastically, as well as politically. They also thought the two dangers connected, especially when contemplating the threat of a Church of England episcopate in the colonies and the rise of Catholicism at home and abroad. The conspiratorial view of British intentions which featured in Mayhew's public contributions to the American Episcopate controversy was reflected in his private correspondence. He first raised the issue in April 1762, when he reported apprehensions that there was "a scheme forming for sending a Bishop into these parts; and that our Governor, Mr. Bernard, a true church-man, is deep in the plot." Despite Hollis's sanguine attempts to put his fears to rest, Mayhew's resulting "uneasiness" subsequently played out in letters to Hollis over a period of more than three years, although nearly all their correspondence on the matter concerned practical and editorial issues connected with the West Church minister's three publications directly addressing the controversy.[19]

The anti-Catholicism of the Mayhew–Hollis correspondence is yet more strident. Commenting on a London reprint of Mayhew's critique of the SPG in *Observations* (1763), together with East Apthorp's *Considerations* (1763) which had initially provoked the work, Hollis noted "the strange impropriety of [the SPG's] Episcopal Propagators attempting the conversion of foreign Protestants to Churchism, when their own People at home were perverting yearly to Popery, by hundreds and thousands, and ten thousands." For Hollis, this was "the sore of sores, by which to gaul at Pleasure

---

citation is from Ovid, *Metamorphoses*, VII, 20–21 and can be translated, "I see and approve of the better, but I follow the worse." Knollenberg suggested that "P——e" might be an elision for "Prince, referring to George III" or "Peace, referring to the Peace Treaty of Paris of 1763" (ibid., 141n) The context clearly supports the latter.

19. Mayhew to Hollis, November 21, 1763, in ibid., 140–41, esp. 141; Mayhew to Hollis, April 6, 1762, in ibid., 127–31, esp. 128–29. For Hollis's "attempts to put [Mayhew's] fears to rest," see, for example, Hollis to Mayhew, July 28, 1762, in ibid., 131–33, esp. 131. For correspondence concerning Mayhew's publications on the American Episcopate controversy, see Mayhew to Hollis, April 27, 1763, in ibid., 136–38; Mayhew to Hollis, November 21, 1763 in ibid., 140–41, esp. 140; Hollis to Mayhew, December 6, 1763, in ibid., 142–44, esp. 142–43; Hollis to Mayhew, April 4, 1764, in ibid., 144–47, esp. 145–47; Mayhew to Hollis, received August 23, 1764, in ibid., 148–51, esp. 148–50; Mayhew to Hollis, June 24, 1764, in ibid., 153–54; Mayhew to Hollis, October 17, 1764, in ibid., 158–59; Hollis to Mayhew, November 6, 1764, in ibid., 160; Mayhew to Hollis, December 18, 1764, in ibid., 161–64, esp. 161–62; Hollis to Mayhew, March 4, 1765, in ibid., 164–66, esp. 165; Hollis to Mayhew, April 22, 1765, in ibid., 166–67; Mayhew to Hollis, May 13, 1765, in ibid., 167–68, esp. 168; Mayhew to Hollis, August 8, 1765, in ibid., 172–74, esp. 173; Mayhew to Hollis, September 26, 1765, in ibid., 178–80, esp. 178.

and beyond expression our Prelates and Commendamists, when touched by a master" and he gave Mayhew a litany of evidence of the dire rise of "the foulest-Hydra Popery" in England. A few months later, after the appearance of *Answer to Dr. Mayhew's Observations* (1764), which Hollis confidently attributed to Archbishop Secker, he remarked that since the latter's "elevation to the Primacy," he had "left Popery unnoticed, widespreading, intolerant, overturning Popery, and yet prosecuted with bitterest severity, [Peter] A[n]net, a poor old speculative Philosopher." This was hardly surprising, in Hollis's view, from one who "shewed no hearty affection to Liberty of any sort, nor those men who loved it" and "trod with glee the mired Court paths." The English Whig was especially troubled by the "Conduct of the Church of England in respect to Papists and Popery," which seemed "to have been always strange or wicked, and never more strange nor wicked than at this time," although he was comforted that this also left the church's leaders open to attack in the cause of liberty by such as Mayhew.[20]

In 1764-5, Hollis repeatedly returned to anti-Catholic themes. He passed on the gossip of "A Tradesman of character" that "a Popish Priest boasted to him, openly, in his shop, that he alone had converted 1500, read 1500 persons, in this Town, to the Catholic faith." He described Apthorp's *Considerations* as "certainly a serious and though impudent yet not unartful Performance of a Roman Catholic," which "ought to have been answered by the Clergy on the Establishment." The reason it had not been, he thought, was because "the Dignitaries, from Laziness and Commendam," wished "to keep all matters in their Department, those relating to Popery especially, as still, unnoticed, untalked of as possible." After hearing that "Papists are admitted in the civil, perhaps I should write military Government of C[anada] (under the command of a military [governor]) to bear civil offices, as Justice of the Peace, etc., and Popish Priests to act as Surveyors of the Country, etc.," Hollis warned Mayhew and other "Men of New England" of the "need to look sharp at these backfriends." In a sense, Hollis's warning was unnecessary. The anti-Catholicism in Mayhew's letters, which centers on his 1765 Dudleian lecture at Harvard, *Popish Idolatry*, is less frequent, but clear.[21]

20. Hollis to Mayhew, December 6, 1763, in ibid., 142–44, esp. 143–44, citing Mayhew and Apthorp, *Observations*; Hollis to Mayhew, April 4, 1764, in ibid., 144–47, esp. 146; Hollis to Mayhew, April 22, 1764, in ibid., 147–48, esp. 148. A "commendam" was "the custody of an ecclesiastical benefice in the absence of a regular incumbent" and "the tenure or enjoyment of the revenues of a benefice held as above" (*OED Online*). By "Commendamists," Hollis seems to have in mind senior clerics benefiting from the latter.

21 Hollis to Mayhew, October 10, 1764, in ibid., 157–58, esp. 158; Hollis to Mayhew, March 4, 1765, in ibid., 164–66, esp. 164; Hollis to Mayhew, June 24, 1765, in ibid., 170–72, esp. 170.

In the midst of his research for that presentation, Mayhew shared the view, in February 1765, that "the Progress of Popery in England is extremely alarming." Mayhew's assessment of the dangers of Rome echoed fears of expansionist Anglicanism already manifest in his engagement with the American Episcopate controversy and in another letter to Hollis three months later, he made the connection directly. "When I delivered the Discourse before referred to, in our College Chapel, against Popery, I could scarce refrain," he wrote, "from some strictures on another church, so zealously propagated among us of late years." But in this case, Mayhew saw discretion as the better part of valor. "On the whole, [I] thought it more adviseable to refrain." Although Mayhew had fewer doctrinal problems with low-church Anglicanism than with Roman Catholicism, he clearly came to see the Church of England as well as the Church of Rome as threatening New England's religious and political freedoms. He was determined to resist both churches with all the intellectual armory that he could muster, but Catholicism was ultimately the major enemy. Planning to send Hollis a copy of *Popish Idolatry*, he expressed doubts about its wider influence, despite the pains taken in writing it. He was confident that the lecture would "discover" his "great detestation of popery," although he had earlier observed that "it is but a small part of that Mystery of Iniquity, that can be laid open and exposed in a Discourse of one hour."[22]

Consistent with their anti-Catholicism, one of the major reasons why the growing tension between Britain and the American colonies over new taxation measures, especially the Stamp Act, so aggravated Mayhew and Hollis was their common fear of arbitrary power threatening basic colonial freedoms. In that sense, as others, the Real Whig convictions which informed their approach to developments as diverse as the settlement of the Seven Years' War or the American Episcopate controversy decisively affected their approach to metropolitan attempts to exercise more active rule in New England and exact greater revenues in the process. "The Colonies are universally and greatly alarmed at the Measures lately taken respecting them," Mayhew wrote to Hollis on August 8, 1765. "These Measures appear to me extremely hard and injurious," he explained. "If long persisted in, they will at best greatly cramp, and retard the population of, the Colonies, to the very essential detriment of the Mother country. And what may, in time, be the consequence of raising a general and great disaffection in the people of this large Continent, no one can certainly foresee." Mayhew then stated a key premise: "But you and I, Sir, are at least clear in this point, that

22. Mayhew to Hollis, December 18, 1764, in ibid., 161–64, esp. 163 (postscript dated February 9, 1765); Mayhew to Hollis, May 17, 1765, in ibid., 169; Mayhew to Hollis, May 13, 1765, in ibid., 167–68.

no people are under a religious obligation to be slaves, if they are able to set themselves at liberty."[23]

Over the next nine months, Mayhew's letters were replete with commentary on the hardships and dangers of recent British fiscal impositions, and his language naturally gravitated toward Real Whig extremes. "The Colonists ... almost one and all consider this [the Stamp Act], and the power lately given to the Admiralty-courts, whereby the right of being tried by Juries is in a great Measure taken from them, as instances of grievous oppression," he informed Hollis on August 19, 1765, "and scarce better than right down tyranny." He followed that dramatic judgment with a graphic account of violent protests in Boston that month. Mayhew saw virtually prophetic fulfillment of one of Trenchard's and Gordon's *Cato's Letters* (1724) in such contemporary events. He greatly doubted "the expediency of Great-Britain's waging war with her American Colonies, as it were, only for the sake of carrying this odious Act into execution; and thereby hazarding either their destruction, or their intire loss to, and revolt from her." The reality was that "the people in the Colonies, are far, very far indeed, from desiring to be independent upon Great-Britain; and nothing, I believe, could make them even willing for it, but what they esteem hard cruel and oppressive Treatment." Just over a month later, Mayhew repeated that assessment. Reporting on the opening of the Stamp Act Congress in New York at the beginning of October 1765, he noted that while he personally saw "the inexpediency and great danger of any forcible, riotous and illegal proceedings, in opposition to parliamentary authority, even though the Colonies should be oppressed," he also deemed "People in the Colonies . . . resolved to run all hazzards [sic] rather than submit." A key assumption was that "nothing worse can happen to us than such slavery." Writing in November 1765, Hollis echoed Mayhew's concerns, informing his friend that he had been "extremely concerned, afflicted at the present sad, melancholy state of affairs betwixt England and her Colonies," but still expressing the hope that "Mr. Pitt will again, in a short time come into Government, and with such latitude of Power as every honest man wishes, an Assertor of Liberty, and a friend to the House of Hanover."[24]

As the Stamp Act crisis continued into 1766, Mayhew's fears and forebodings remained unabated. He observed that "the great uneasiness in the Colonies, occasioned more especially by the Stamp Act," had not "subside[d], but rather increase[d]." He thought that Hollis's gifts of books

23. Mayhew to Hollis, August 8, 1765, in ibid., 172–74, esp. 173.

24. Mayhew to Hollis, August 19, 1765, in ibid., 174–76; Mayhew to Hollis, September 26, 1765, in ibid., 178–80; Mayhew to Hollis, October 1, 1765, in ibid., 180–81; Hollis to Mayhew, November 18, 1765, in ibid., 181–82.

would "answer valuable purposes in these Colonies," and would "do so more and more, to the common advantage of Great Britain, unless wrong-headed politics, and arbitrary measures should intirely interrupt and destroy the commercial intercourse between the Mother country and the Colonies; which God forbid!" Based on Hollis's intelligence about recent changes in the British government, his opinion of the "Circumstances" of "the whole Brittish [sic] empire" had also deteriorated to the point where he described them as not only "very deplorable," but "in imminent danger of coming into much worse, under the hands of such Operators, and a pensioned, bribed H[ouse] of C[ommo]ns and H[ouse] of L[ords]." However, by April 8, Mayhew's outlook had become more positive, even hopeful. He had heard unconfirmed rumors of a major reversal in British policy, although it was not until the following month, soon after Hollis wrote encouraging him to "Rejoice in the Repeal of the Stamp Act" and lauding Pitt as its author, that Mayhew was able to preach *Snare Broken* in a May 23 celebration at West Church. When he hastily sent Hollis a copy dedicated "to that Right Honorable Personage, who was so strenuous an Assertor, and able Vindicator of the oppressed Liberties of America," he accordingly entreated his friend "to take special Care of that which is directed to Him." Nearly a month later, when Mayhew was about to suffer the stroke that led to his death in July 1766, Hollis wrote to report that "Political measures continue the same ... things are far from going right according to Your and my Ideas." But by the time it arrived in Boston, Hollis's communication was probably too late to influence Mayhew's outlook on that or any other issue. How much he would have maintained the positions which he shared with Hollis after 1766 obviously remains unknown. But their major significance for at least the last sixteen years of Mayhew's life clearly emerges from his correspondence, as well as from other writings.[25]

Mainstream Mayhew

The main problem with focusing solely on such themes, as Bailyn did, is that they cannot fully explain more mainstream Whig elements in Mayhew's thought. Such a narrow portrayal of the West Church minister also fails to do justice to more traditionalist aspects of his sociopolitical and religious outlook, which reveal connections with an older, sometimes Puritan,

25. Mayhew to Hollis, January 7, 1766, in ibid., 183–85, esp. 183–84; Mayhew to Hollis, April 8, 1766, in ibid., 185–87, esp. 185; Hollis to Mayhew, May 8, 1766, in ibid., 187–88, esp. 187; Mayhew to Hollis, May 1766, in ibid., 188; Hollis to Mayhew, June 19, 1766, in ibid., 189–91, esp. 191.

heritage that scholars have often neglected. In some areas, especially Mayhew's rampant anti-Catholicism, where more moderate Whigs followed a long tradition in transatlantic Protestantism, these two shortcomings actually coincide. In all, Mayhew's worldview had much in common with that of the more temperate and cautious Chauncy. His loyalty to the British constitution and monarchy as key defenses of New England's religious and political interests not only echoed that of centrist Whigs on both sides of the Atlantic, it reflected the views of many contemporary New England leaders and of recent forebears responding to changes in political structures in the early 1690s following the Glorious Revolution and the collapse of the Dominion of New England government (1686–89). Mayhew's political thought also remained firmly grounded within a more traditionalist religious framework, and his inherently Puritan understanding of liberty was foundational to that. His conventional views of society, including his hierarchical understanding of civil authority, belie anachronistic attempts to redefine or reinvent him as any kind of democratic egalitarian.[26]

On one occasion, Mayhew personally apologized in case he had "verge[d] a little nearer to what is commonly called politics" in one of his discourses, "than is ordinarily convenient or suitable for the pulpit." But no fewer than eight of his twenty-three published works can be labeled political in the sense that they quite specifically addressed public issues of the day. Three others embraced related themes as part of Mayhew's defense of the New England Congregationalist establishment against the threat of an American episcopate. In addition, a funeral sermon occasioned by the death of Judge Sewall prompted Mayhew to write about the qualities that he found praiseworthy and desirable in the magistracy. From these and other writings, in which the West Church minister offered more general social commentary, the overarching weltanschauung to emerge is one which valued a structured, traditional social order, where educated and refined gentlefolk exercised authority and received due deference from those in less exalted stations. This order was further informed and infused by a vision of a vigorously Protestant New England church and state which served as a bastion and protector of basic English liberties, guaranteed by a mixed constitution, in which the British royal family played a crucial role.[27]

26. For a cogent, brief account of events surrounding the Glorious Revolution and its colonial American repercussions, see Dunn, "Glorious Revolution and America." On the Revolution in New England and the 1692 Massachusetts Charter, see Lovejoy, *Glorious Revolution in America*, 235–50, 340–53.

27. Mayhew, *Two Discourses Delivered October 25th. 1759*, 36. Mayhew's overtly political works include *Discourse Concerning Unlimited Submission; Sermon Preached at Boston; Sermon Preach'd; Two Discourses Delivered November 23d. 1758; Discourse*

While he was as much concerned with the tone as with the content of Mayhew's discourse, Heimert correctly identified the social traditionalism of Mayhew's views of society. For the West Church minister, everyone had "his station, whether high or low; as every member of the natural body, in the regular discharge of its particular office, contributes to the good and perfection of the body." This reflected a natural order, in which there was "variety . . . & particular arrangement of the creatures and works of God." The young men to whom he addressed his sermons on *Christian Sobriety* in 1763 were thus advised to be "serviceable, and a real ornament" to "society" in their "station" by living "soberly, righteously and godly in the world," according to the demands of their social position. Following the commotion surrounding the Stamp Act and its repeal a couple of years later, Mayhew saw a need to "apply ourselves with diligence, and in the fear of God, to the duties of our respective stations." He also regretted that "even the poor, and laboring part of the community . . . have had so much to say about government and politics, in the late times of danger, tumult and confusion, that many of them seemed to forget, they had any thing to do." According to his elitist understanding of public "reputation," it was the opinions of the "best judges, the greatest masters," that counted, not those of "vast, ignorant multitudes, who had neither skill, taste nor judgment in them." Education was vital and Mayhew regretted

> the unhappiness of a great part of mankind that they do not sufficiently consider this natural weakness, ineptitude and awkwardness of human reason before cultivation; but sit down contented with their imaginary sagacity and promptness of understanding, without using the proper means to qualify them for judging of things that may come under their consideration.

In the same spirit, he did not hesitate to make his snobbish and vituperative *ad hominem* attack after John Cleaveland had dared to question his theological orthodoxy (see pages 110–11). Mayhew only really considered himself open to judgment by social and intellectual equals, and he saw relatively few of them.[28]

Such a stratified and somewhat rarified social vision permeated the West Church minister's general political thought, although it was tempered

---

Occasioned by the Death of King George; *Two Discourses Delivered October 9th, 1760*, and *Snare Broken*. See, further, *Discourse Occasioned by the Death of The Honourable Stephen Sewall* and, on the American Episcopate controversy, *Observations*; *Defence of the Observations* and *Remarks*.

28. Heimert, *Religion and the American Mind*, e.g., 47–48, 169–70, 254–55, 274–75, 290–91; Mayhew, *Christian Sobriety*, 272–73, 244; *Divine Goodness*, 30; *Snare Broken*, 41–42; *Seven Sermons*, 31; *Letter of Reproof*, 4.

by a religiously inspired realism about the limitations of even the most exalted personages. "There is, as there ought to be, a wide difference of rank and circumstance amongst mankind, in this world," he observed in *Sermon Preached at Boston* (1751) following the death of Frederick, Prince of Wales. Even so, it was a "common and shameful . . . practice to extol persons of mean accomplishments and little worth, merely because they possess great power and wealth and external dignity." In his election sermon of 1754, Mayhew thus urged "the Legislators and political Fathers" of New England

> as you fear God, whose ministers you are; as you love the country, whose welfare depends upon you; as you regard that good name, which is as precious ointment, and rather to be chosen than great riches; as you have any concern for posterity, even your own; as you would enjoy the blessed peace of a good conscience, in life and death; and in fine, as you would be found of our common judge in peace, in the day of his appearing . . . to be faithful in the discharge of that trust which is devolved upon you by God and man; to let no unworthy views influence your conduct; but in all things to consult and prosecute the common good.[29]

Like Whigs of all descriptions and many early to mid-eighteenth-century New Englanders generally, Mayhew strongly supported the virtues of the British mixed constitution, of which monarchy was a key element. He fiercely opposed Catholicism and Catholic powers on political as well as religious grounds, and he missed no opportunity to praise Protestant princes, where he saw good reason for doing so. As early as *Seven Sermons* (1749), where he berated ecclesiastical "tyrants" who "throw their chains and fetters upon the mind, which . . . was born free; and which ought not to be in bondage to any man: but only to the Father of Spirits," he also wrote mockingly of how "Sovereign princes must think themselves honoured in having the liberty to kiss the toe of an old Monk, who calls himself Christ's Vicar." In *Discourse Concerning Unlimited Submission* (1750), Mayhew gave thanks that "one may, in any part of the british dominions, speak freely . . . both of government and religion; and even give some broad hints, that he is engaged on the side of Liberty, the BIBLE, and Common Sense, in opposition to Tyranny, PRIEST-CRAFT, and Non-sense, without being in danger either of the bastille or the inquisition." Yet even in this *locus classicus* of Mayhew's Real Whiggery, Bailyn admitted that the West Church minister advanced "principles of government and of the limits of civil power" that were "commonplaces of Whig thought" and had long "formed the substance

---

29. Mayhew, *Sermon Preached at Boston*, 37, 25; *Sermon Preach'd*, 24–25.

of annual election sermons delivered before the Assemblies of Massachusetts and Connecticut and published by order of those governments."[30]

Mayhew thus began his provocative defense of the execution of Charles I and of the right of rebellion against the "tyranny and oppression" of such a corrupt ruler in a notably deferential tone. He opened his exposition of one of the standard biblical texts cited in support of civil obedience, Romans 8:1–8, with a conventional summary of key points of "the apostle's doctrine, in the passage thus explained":

> THAT the end of magistracy is the good of civil society, as such:
>
> THAT civil rulers, as such, are the ordinance and ministers of God; it being by his permission and providence that any bear rule; and agreeable to his will that there should be some persons vested with authority in society, for the well-being of it:
>
> THAT which is here said concerning civil rulers, extends to all of them in common . . .
>
> THAT disobedience to civil rulers in the due exercise of their authority, is not merely a political sin, but an heinous offence against God and religion:
>
> THAT the true ground and reason of our obligation to be subject to the higher powers, is the usefulness of magistracy (when properly exercised) to human society, and its subserviency to the general welfare:
>
> THAT obedience to civil rulers is here equally required under all forms of government . . . :
>
> (From whence it follows, THAT if unlimited obedience and non-resistance, be here required as a duty under any one form of government, it is also required as a duty under all other forms; and as a duty to subordinate rulers as well as to the supreme.)

---

30. Mayhew, *Seven Sermons*, 57–58; *Discourse Concerning Unlimited Submission*, "Preface," 2; Bailyn, *Pamphlets*, 207. Bailyn contended that "in the principles it expresses," *Discourse Concerning Unlimited Submission* was "a cliché of Whig political theory." While conceding that "it was widely agreed that resistance to tyranny was justified," Bailyn further argued that Mayhew was more stringent in arguing that "'subjects in general' were the 'proper judges [of] when their governors oppress them, and play the tyrant,' . . . that everyone was "bound' to rebel against evil governors, and that failure to do so was 'to join . . . in promoting the slavery of . . . society'" (*Pamphlets*, 206–7, citing Mayhew, *Discourse Concerning Unlimited Submission*, 39n, 30).

AND lastly, that those civil rulers to whom the apostle enjoins subjection, are the persons in possession; the powers that be; those who are actually vested with authority.

Mayhew also vigorously defended "the english constitution" as "originally and essentially free." The "ancient Britains [sic]" were "extremely jealous of their liberties," he argued, and he saw "frequent instances and proofs of the same glorious spirit . . . remaining in their posterity ever since."[31]

Far from being the result of a lawless rebellion, Mayhew saw Charles I's dethronement and execution as the legitimate results of a properly functioning British constitutional process. It was through the effective workings of the tripartite, English governmental structure that "the LORDS and COMMONS" in Parliament had "almost unanimously opposed the king's measures for overturning the constitution," thereby "changing that free and happy government into a wretched, absolute monarchy," and initiated the necessary military action. Such "resistance" was thus a vindication, not a violation of the system. "Here," Mayhew argued, were

> two branches of the legislature against one;— two, which had law and equity and the constitution on their side, against one which was impiously attempting to overturn law and equity and the constitution; and to exercise a wanton licentious sovereignty over the properties, consciences and lives of all the people.

He continued this theme in later works. In 1754, he praised "the form of our government" as "justly the envy of most other nations," and he gave thanks, four years later, for blessings relating to "the civil state of the nation in general; as the preservation of the British government." Mayhew even contended that it would be "highly criminal" to "raise or countenance any kind of rebellion, or sedition" when enjoying the "happiness of living under such a free, mild government as the British."[32]

Unafraid to contend for a general right of rebellion or to defend the deposition and execution of Charles I, Mayhew was also, for the most part, a committed monarchist, who repeatedly expressed his praise for and loyalty to the British royal family under testing circumstances. He vigorously denied "the hereditary, indefeasible, divine right of kings, and the doctrine of non-resistance, which is built upon the supposition of such a right." But even when vigorously opposing annual celebrations of Charles I's supposed

---

31. Mayhew, *Discourse Concerning Unlimited Submission*, 41, 9–12, 45n. For helpful analysis of the political theory of the Massachusetts election sermons, see esp. Counts, "Political Views"; Plumstead, *Wall and Garden*, esp. 3–37.

32. Mayhew, *Discourse Concerning Unlimited Submission*, 44–46; *Sermon Preach'd*, 19; *Two Discourses Delivered November 23rd. 1758*, 7 (and see 8–9), 48.

"martyrdom" in 1750, Mayhew was at pains to stress New England's "happiness to live under the government of a PRINCE who is satisfied with ruling according to law; as every other good prince will." In view of that, he contended, "it becomes us . . . to be contented, and dutiful subjects." More extravagant expressions of royalism pepper many of his later works. For his sermon following the death of Frederick, Prince of Wales in 1751, Mayhew made full use of Psalm 118:9 to urge critical discernment of royalty. There had, after all, been "many princes in the world . . . who could not be trusted at all" and "all human power" was "but a poor refuge" from the inevitable storms and "tumults" of life. But having done so, he felt free to praise the late prince as one who was "likely" not just to "fill," but to "adorn the British throne," a true "heir, not only of the authority and highest titles, but of the princely qualities, of his royal ancestors." Chief among those, here as elsewhere for Mayhew, were Frederick's Protestant heritage and credentials as a member of "the illustrious House of Hanover," "the Patrons and Bulwark of Liberty," to which, he noted, New England had shown "stedfast loyalty." Unlike "those strange men, who had rather be ruled by a papist, and Italian tyrant, than a protestant Prince, under the restriction of salutary laws," the West Church minister thus lauded the Prince of Wales for his "due abhorrence of popery and arbitrary government, as being both of them contrary to reason and christianity."[33]

Mayhew echoed such themes in later works from the mid to late 1750s. He argued that "for several late reigns," British subjects, including New Englanders, had been "blessed with Princes too just & good to encroach upon the rights of their subjects." He described George II as a "steady defender" of "the laws of liberty," "a true protestant, and a friend to the natural rights of mankind, especially to those of his own subjects," and he left it to his own congregation to "judge, how great the blessing is, of having the life of a good protestant King." In a typical exhortation, which conflated the benefits of enjoying a monarchy that was both Protestant and protective of the British constitutional heritage, Mayhew urged his hearers to

> Consider, for example, how miserable we should have been, if instead of having the life of a good protestant King preserved to us; if instead of having the British laws and government, and our civil and religious liberties, continued as they are; that good King had been taken away, and a bad one succeeded him; (especially the worst, a thorough Roman-catholic, whose evil conscience, whatever he might swear to the contrary, would still

---

33. Mayhew, *Discourse Concerning Unlimited Submission*, 35, 54–55; *Sermon Preached at Boston*, 13–14, 19, 23, 28–29.

oblige him to distress, if not to destroy, his protestant subjects—for the good of their souls!) if the free and happy government of Great-Britain had been overturned, and arbitrary sway, and papal tyranny, had been established in its room.[34]

In sermons delivered and published in 1758–60 to mark "the Success of His Majesty's Arms" in the Seven Years' War, it is not surprising to find Mayhew lauding victory for the forces of true [Protestant] religion over those of Catholic tyranny and error. But the strength of his anti-Catholic venom remains remarkable. "It were next to madness to imagine, that the nation could ever be safe and happy under a roman catholic prince," he argued in 1758. "A romancatholic [sic] King" was "one of the greatest curses righteous heaven c[ould] send upon Great Britain," because "while such a King reigns," Mayhew contended, "the most fundamental laws of the kingdom are no security to the subject, either with respect to liberty or property, religion or life; unless it be to popish subjects: Who indeed may live, and increase, and flourish abundantly, under that same baleful influence which blasts all good men." When he celebrated the reduction of Quebec the following year, Mayhew took it for granted that had the French "at length got the upper hand, we should doubtless have been deprived of the free enjoyments of the protestant religion." One of the greatest blessings flowing from recent military successes was that "we shall be delivered from the ravages and barbarities of . . . faithless Frenchmen." Mayhew struck a similar theme in his thanksgiving sermon of 1762, where he referred to the perils of "a roman-catholic country," together with all the "errors, superstitions and idolatries of the church of Rome." If New Englanders had been subject to such a "lot," he argued, "we should probably, the most of us, have been enslaved to those delusions, and the papal tyranny to this day."[35]

Examples of corrupt Catholic royalty were not hard to find, not least "his Most Christian Majesty" the King of France, who had threatened Protestant Hanover and other parts of Europe in addition to occupying Canada before its liberation by British forces. As Mayhew surveyed that ongoing military struggle and its consequences in *Two Discourses Delivered October 25th. 1759*, he could not ignore the threat that New Englanders themselves might be "deprived of the free enjoyments of the protestant religion; harrassed, persecuted and butchered, by such blind and furious zealots for the religion of Rome." But such had been the progress of British arms that he ventured so far as to express a millennial optimism that the time when

34. Mayhew, *Sermon Preach'd*, 19; *Two Discourses Delivered November 23rd. 1758*, 9, 11, 33.

35. Mayhew, *Two Discourses Delivered November 23d. 1758*, title page, 10–11; *Two Discourses Delivered October 25th. 1759*, 47, 43; *Divine Goodness*, 71.

God's "unalterable purpose, in due time, tho' gradually, to consume and destroy the beast and the false prophet" of Catholic power might be fulfilled.[36]

Mayhew's opposition to the Stamp Act of 1765 led him into a major personal controversy (see chapter 7). Yet after its repeal, while his respect for British justice may have been diminished, his loyalty to the Crown and at least one of its ministers remained unshaken. Written as a "Thanksgiving-Discourse," *Snare Broken* (1766) was dedicated to Prime Minister William Pitt, an "ILLUSTRIOUS PATRON OF AMERICA" and "a principal Instrument in the hand of GOD, of saving GREAT BRITAIN and her Colonies from impending ruin." Basing his argument on British constitutional standards, Mayhew took it "for granted," not only that "the colonies had great reason to petition and remonstrate against" the act as "an infraction of" their "rights, and tending directly to reduce us to a state of slavery," but that "an act of that sort was very hard, and justly grievous, not to say oppressive." Yet "however unconstitutional, oppressive, grievous or ruinous" the Stamp Act had been, or "fatal in its tendency," Mayhew's major concern was to laud the fact that "his Majesty and the Parliament have been pleased to hearken to the just complaints of the colonies." So he made a careful distinction between "our gracious Sovereign or the Parliament; who must not be supposed to have any evil designs against the colonies" and "some evil-minded individuals in Britain," whom he suspected of engineering the legislation to cause division between the colonies and the mother country, thus aiding and abetting Catholic powers, not least "the Houses of Bourbon and the Pretender."[37]

In general terms, Mayhew hailed the repeal of the Stamp Act as living proof that "'our soul is escaped as a bird from the snare of the fowlers; the snare is broken and we are escaped'; tho' not without much struggling in the snare, before it gave way, and set us at liberty again." He had no hesitation in condemning the excesses of extremists. But he saw appropriate resistance in the American colonies and in Britain, along with the change of policy to which it led, as entirely providential in origin. In such a view of history, inherited, in a direct line of succession, from Mayhew's Puritan forebears, the repeal was, therefore, cause for rejoicing as well as thanksgiving. But it also provided an occasion "to add the obedience of our lives, as the best sacrifice that we can offer to Heaven." Mayhew applied this with particular force to the political arena, where he urged "a respectful, loyal and dutiful manner of speech and conduct, respecting his Majesty and his government" and the paying of "due respect in all things to the British Parliament." He declared himself

36. *Two Discourses Delivered October 25th.* 1759, 10, 47, 49 (and see 61).
37. Mayhew, *Snare Broken*, title page, iii–iv, 5, 7–9.

> well apprised of the firm attachment of these colonies in general, and of our own province in particular, to the King's person, and to the protestant succession in his illustrious House; for the preservation of which, there is hardly a native of New-England, who would not, upon constitutional principles, which are those of liberty, chearfully [sic] hazard his life; or even more lives than one, if he had them to lay down in so good a cause.

Mayhew had "not the least suspicion of any disaffection . . . to his Majesty." Even so, he took occasion to observe that "the duty of subjects to Kings, and to all that are in authority, is frequently to be inculcated by the ministers of the gospel, if they will follow the example of the apostles in this respect." Such a duty could only be magnified given the "recent and memorable proof of his Majesty's moderation, his attention to the welfare of his people, and readiness, so far as in him lies according to the constitution, to redress their grievances, on reasonable and humble complaint."[38]

It would be mistaken to conclude from such counsel that Mayhew did not see a continuing need to act to preserve liberty, whenever it was deemed under threat. Just the previous year, in *Popish Idolatry* (1765), he had described Roman Catholicism as not only a corrupt and heretical institution, but a threat to basic human rights—civil as well as religious. New England's "controversy" with that corrupt body involved nothing less than

> a defence of our laws, liberties, and civil rights as men, in opposition to the proud claims and encroachments of ecclesiastical persons, who under the pretext of religion, and saving mens souls, would engross all power and property to themselves, and reduce us to the most abject slavery . . . Popery and liberty are incompatible; at irreconcilable enmity with each other.

In *Snare Broken,* he repeated such concerns in a British context:

> If Britain, which has long been the principal support of liberty in Europe, and is, at least was, the chief bulwark against that most execrable of all tyrannies, Popery, should in destroying her colonies destroy herself; (Heaven forbid it!) what would become of those few states which are now free? what, of the protestant religion?

Hence the necessity "for those who would preserve and perpetuate their liberties, to guard them with a wakeful attention; and in all righteous, just

---

38. Mayhew, *Snare Broken*, 8 (citing Ps 124:7), 23–25. After one of his sermons had been associated with it, Mayhew, 7, pulled no punches on extremist resistance to the Stamp Act.

and prudent ways, to oppose the first encroachments on them." In Mayhew's global vision of the battle between the forces of Protestant liberty and Catholic oppression, both political and religious, the fate of New England was linked not only to that of the mother country, but of the whole civilized world. The very preservation of true religion could be at stake should Mayhew's worst fears be realized—that Europe might "fall before the Grand Monarch on this side of the Alps" (i.e. the King of France), and Protestantism be overcome by "the Successor of the apostle Judas, and Grand Vicar of Satan" (i.e. the Pope).[39]

Together with vigorous support for English Protestant "liberties," such an apocalyptic fear that "one universal" Catholic "despotism" could "swallow up all" was clearly a significant element of the Real Whig ideology that heavily influenced Mayhew's political thought. But his anti-Catholicism, monarchism, and British constitutionalism were widely shared, if not always so forthrightly expressed, by more moderate Whigs and other contemporaries. They also had deeper roots in British Protestantism, in early New England Puritanism, and in the seventeenth- and early eighteenth-century colonial American world, where, as Kidd and Owen Stanwood have argued, anti-Catholic and pro-British constitutional rhetoric became especially influential following the Glorious Revolution and resulting colonial, political settlements. It is precisely such connections that make it impossible to categorize Mayhew solely, or even primarily, as an eighteenth-century Real Whig without disconnecting him from his more immediate heritage and from more traditionalist currents of Protestant thought and discourse so clearly echoed in his works. Mayhew's concerns to uphold general Whig values and to defend and advance New England's Protestant cause had much in common with those of the more cautious Chauncy, whose moderate Whiggery was grounded in a similar vision of the general sociopolitical order.[40]

Chauncy's Constitutional Caution

On May 30, 1770, Chauncy spoke to city leaders at a time of crisis. He delivered his election sermon, *Trust in God*, less than three months after the Boston Massacre, when "the opened earth in one of our streets, in the month of march last, received the streaming blood of many slaughtered, and wounded innocents." He addressed people for whom "the removal of the GENERAL

39. Mayhew, *Popish Idolatry*, 48–49; *Snare Broken*, 22, 34.

40. Ibid., 22; Stanwood, *Empire Reformed*, 20, 115–26; Kidd, *Protestant Interest*, 17–18.

COURT [from Boston to Cambridge] . . . unhappily excites in our breasts . . . sensations of grief." He recognized that "the face of providence is angry and threatning" and that "our mother-country is in a state of great perplexity, difficulty, and confusion." He acknowledged, more particularly, that

> new [Townshend] duties have been imposed on us, and without any to represent our persons in parliament, or to act in our behalf; new officers have been appointed . . . ; in consequence of which our trade was never before so incumbered with difficulties . . . we have, in a measure, been treated as tho' we were rebels; otherwise what occasion could there be for this metropolis to be, as it were, garrison'd with the King's troops, to the infinite hurt of the morals of its inhabitants, and to their being in a variety of ways insulted, injured, and abused?

But what was the major counsel of this leading Boston minister, later portrayed by historians as a leader of the "black regiment" of pro-revolutionary, Whig clergy? Despite such a dire and threatening situation, it was to urge caution.[41]

The sixty-five-year-old Chauncy encouraged his listeners to follow the example of "pious progenitors," by whom he meant Massachusetts founders, and to trust in God to work out everything for the best. This was not the first time that New Englanders had suffered at the hands of oppressive authorities, and God had consistently delivered them. So they should look to themselves and seek moral improvement, because "our sins . . . are . . . , properly speaking, the true moral cause of all that we now suffer, or have reason to fear." Chauncy also gave voice to familiar expressions of monarchist loyalism. "Our prayer to the GOD of heaven is, that the [Hanoverian] succession may abide forever!" he said. "Notwithstanding the base and false representations which have occasioned his Majesty, and many of his ministers, to look upon us with a jealous and angry eye," King George III had "no subjects, in any part of his extended dominions, that would more readily venture their lives and fortunes in defence of his person, the succession in his royal house, and his government within the bounds of the english constitution, than we in the MASSACHUSETTS-PROVINCE."[42]

Over a long career, Chauncy wrote much about the political challenges of his day and he was consistently prepared to speak out against related excesses and hypocrisies. He ultimately embraced the Patriot cause with some enthusiasm and his Whiggery was widely recognized, especially during the revolutionary period. In a popular ballad dating from circa 1774,

---

41. Chauncy, *Trust in God*, 35, 32, 22, 23.
42. Ibid., 6, 29, 20, 37.

Chauncy was famously described as "a zealous Whig, than Wilkes more big" and libertarian themes were more prominent in his writings from the mid-1760s onwards. But his Whiggism was generally more moderate than that of Mayhew, and from the 1730s through the early 1770s most of his works are more easily reconcilable with a general tendency to protect and preserve the sociopolitical status quo than to protest against or overturn it. The need for traditional social order and hierarchical structures in both church and state, which concerned Mayhew, especially preoccupied Chauncy at times of social and/or ecclesiastical upheaval. His traditional loyalty to British constitutional values persisted beyond the outbreak of revolutionary hostilities and it was buttressed by his theological conceptions of the primacy of spiritual over all other forms of liberty and of an overarching divine providence in which New England's Protestant traditions held a vital place.[43]

In his earliest sermon on a publicly political occasion, for the Artillery Election of June 3, 1734, Chauncy predictably expounded on Judges 18:27–8 to urge the general security goal that "our TOWN and LAND may be both put and kept in a sutable posture of defence." Although he thought that "our militia . . . is not so large and honorable, as it might and ought to be," he noted with pleasure "the reviving of a martial spirit in our land." But Chauncy was ultimately most concerned with ensuring the spiritual defenses which he thought necessary to secure New England. Five years later, in *Only Compulsion Proper*, Chauncy struck notes of royalism and English patriotism that he echoed consistently over the years, requesting God "to protect the Persons, and prolong the Lives of his present Majesty, his Royal Highness, with the rest of the Royal Family, on whom, under God, the Nation depends for their Enjoyment of this Blessing of Liberty, on which depends every Thing else that is dear and valuable to them." Yet while Chauncy's rhetoric undoubtedly showed periodic evidence of greater militancy, especially in the pre-revolutionary and revolutionary periods, his monarchist Anglophilia and continuing concern to protect national liberty did not overtly reflect the Real Whig ideology of Gordon, Trenchard, or similar figures.[44]

43. Chauncy's description as "a zealous Whig" originated in a line from "Boston Ministers: A Ballad," also cited by Baldwin, *New England Clergy*, 93n: "That fine preacher, called a teacher / Of Old Brick Church the first, / Regards no grace, to men in place, / And is by tories curst, / At young and old, he'll rave and scold, / And is, in things of state, / A zealous Whig, than Wilkes more big / In Church a tyrant great." According to "Boston Minister: A Ballad," this is the first of eight verses in the second part of the original ballad. See, further, "Boston Ministers, A Ballad–First and Second Parts." "Old Brick" was a familiar nickname of Boston's First Church. "Libertarian" is here understood, in a very general sense, as upholding and/or concerned with human liberty, however defined.

44. Chauncy, *Character and Overthrow*, 11, 14, 13, 10; *Only Compulsion Proper*, 16.

During the Great Awakening in the 1740s, Chauncy saw itinerancy and the expansion of lay ministry into unfamiliar roles as especially disruptive threats to social order, including in the church. "Government is as necessary in Church as State," he warned the ministers of Massachusetts in 1744, "tho' the Ends to which it is designed, and the Manner of Administration may be different." Then he added:

> Nor should they [ministers] suffer the keys of the Kingdom of Heaven, in this, or any other Use of them, to lie by neglected, where Persons break in upon the Rules of Decency, or otherways walk in a disorderly Manner... 'Tis Discipline, my Fathers and Brethren, not the meer Name, but the vigorous and impartial Execution of the Thing, that must preserve and establish our Churches.

On a similar note, he told the people of Old Brick at the height of revivalist enthusiasm, "'Tis not... the pretence of being moved by the SPIRIT, that will justify private christians in quitting their own proper station, to act in that which belongs to another. Such a practice as this naturally tends to destroy that order, GOD has constituted in the church, and may be followed with mischiefs greater than we may be aware of."[45]

Much like Mayhew's, Chauncy's anti-Catholicism reflected his Whiggery as well as his vigorous Protestantism, and it was particularly prominent when he had occasion to speak about military victory over the forces of Catholic France, as he did in thanksgiving for the reduction of Cape Breton in 1745. Allied to this defense of the sociopolitical status quo and New England's heritage, at least until American independence, was a vigorously pro-British royalism. In a sermon occasioned by the Jacobite Rebellion at Boston's Thursday Lecture in February 1746, Chauncy looked back to 1688 and hailed "the glorious King WILLIAM, under God, the great Deliverer of the Nation from POPERY and SLAVERY," as well as New England's "REVOLUTION" against Sir Edmund Andros that had followed England's Glorious Revolution. He viewed the attempted enthronement of the Catholic James Stuart, aided and abetted by those "natural and inveterate Enemies of ENGLAND," the "Kings of FRANCE and SPAIN," as a development that tended "directly and surely..., in the natural Course of Things, to... utter ruin; the

---

A significant indicator that Chauncy's Whiggery was more moderate and mainstream than Mayhew's is that Real Whig citations are remarkably absent from his works. His sole references to Hoadly, for example, are to a work on church polity, *Reasonableness of Conformity*, 388–89, 326–27, 338–39, 349, 57–58, cited in *Validity of Presbyterian Ordination*, 28, 59–62, 67; *Reply to Dr. Chandler's "Appeal Defended,"* 23–24; *Compleat View of Episcopacy*, x–xi.

45. Chauncy, *Ministers Cautioned*, 36–37; *Enthusiasm Described*, 12.

Subversion of the Constitution, the depriving the People of their just Rights and Liberties, as Englishmen and Protestants, and the putting them under a Government which knows no Rule but that of meer Will and Pleasure." It was generally "the Way of popish Princes, bigotted [*sic*] to the Religion of Anti-christ" to make "use of their Power and Influence to extirpate the true Protestant Religion." So before concluding in prayer that God would protect his People's "Rights and Liberties," he described the present King George II as "the Head of a Kingdom, its rightful and lawful Sovereign, with whose Ruin the Ruin of a whole Nation is inseperably connected." Chauncy was in no doubt that George "really received the Kingdom from God, and in a Manner truly wonderful, and in which the Pleasure of God was indubitably made known." By contrast, Stuart was "a known avowed Enemy to that Constitution, and those Liberties both civil and religious, which our present King has all along defended and protected." The threat of the Pretender thus presented a direct challenge, in both church and state, to the English Protestant liberties that Chauncy held so dear.[46]

In his 1747 Massachusetts election sermon, *Civil Magistrates*, Chauncy had his first public opportunity to present his political outlook more extensively. Except for more controversial comments about the hardships of ministers on limited incomes, the result was a pretty conventional exposition of Congregationalist governmental theory. His basic argument was simple. "There is a certain order among mankind, according to which some are entrusted with power to rule over others" and "those who rule over others must be just, ruling in the fear of God." Chauncy saw the origins of government as "founded on the will of God" as well as "in the reason of things." Because of sin, it was "necessary" for people, "for their mutual defence and safety, [to] combine together in distinct societies, lodging as much power in the hands of a few, as may be sufficient to restrain the irregularities of the rest, and keep them within the bounds of a just decorum." Although the need for government was commanded by God, there was no divine mandate for any particular form of it, or for any single manner of

---

46. Chauncy, *Counsel of Two Confederate Kings*, title page, 28, 23, 30, 24, 43, 31, 32, 37. In a similarly anti-Catholic strain, Chauncy elsewhere prayed for Cape Breton that "all proper Care be taken, that the pure Gospel of Christ be preached in this part of the Dominion of Antichrist. May the Man of Sin, that Son of Perdition, be no longer acknowledged as Christ's Viceregent. May all Graven Images be pulled down, all Superstition removed, and the Religion of our Lord Jesus Christ, as it is contained in the bible, be upheld and practiced there" (*Marvellous Things Done*, 22). He also hoped that God would not "suffer the Man of Sin, that Son of Perdition, who hath exalted himself into the Seat of Christ, to be again acknowledged and adored, by a [British] Nation who have declared their Abhorrence of worshipping him, instead of the Son of God" (*Counsel of Two Confederate Kings*, 41).

vesting rulers with authority. The general purposes of civil governance were, however, patently manifest:

> for the general good of mankind; to keep confusion and disorder out of the world; to guard men's lives; to secure their rights; to defend their properties and liberties; to make their way to justice easy, and yet effectual, for their protection when innocent, and their relief when injuriously treated; and, in a word, to maintain peace and good order, and, in general, to promote the public Welfare, in all instances, so far as they are able.[47]

Within such a teleological framework, Chauncy defined "just" rulers as those who were "positively righteous," who did not abuse their power and enacted and administered appropriate laws with justice and impartiality. They should be good creditors and "preserve and perpetuate to every member of the community, so far as may be, the full enjoyment of their liberties and priviledges, whether of a civil or religious nature." They should take particular care to preserve people's religious freedoms or, at least, "such as may consist with the public safety." They should defend the state, "promote the general welfare and prosperity of a people," especially morally, and "rule in the fear of God." They should remember the example of pious ancestors, "the worth of learning, and the advantage of a liberal education," as well as the providence and judgment of God, to which they were accountable. Chauncy regretted, in somewhat jeremiad terms, that "religion is not in such a flourishing state, at this day," informing assembled officials that "it needs the countenance of your example, and the interposition of your authority, to keep it from insult and contempt." He expressed a particular concern for the welfare of ministers, and urged rulers to make better provision for the clergy's and others' economic wellbeing by doing their utmost to stabilize currency values. Griffin suggested that Chauncy's financial special pleading almost prevented his sermon from being published. But in otherwise echoing the content of many similar election sermons, *Civil Magistrates* can have done little more to upset local authorities than his subsequent political works.[48]

In two "letters to a friend" of 1755, Chauncy's comments on a victory at Lake George and a defeat in Ohio during the French–Indian War were typically providentialist, as well as Anglophile and anti-Catholic. They also showed a willingness to criticize British leadership, where necessary. The conquest of the French at Lake George had been "the greatest Action, in its

---

47. Chauncy, *Civil Magistrates*, 7, 9, 11, 13.

48. Chauncy, *Civil Magistrates*, 14, 17, 23, 28–29, 33, 36, 42, 44, 49, 55–56, 60, 38–39, 41, 21–22; Griffin, *Old Brick*, 102.

kind, that ever happened in North-America." It gave Chauncy confidence that "we shall soon be able ... under the smiles of providence, to bring down the pride of the American French, and make them glad to be at peace with us upon any terms." Even so, "the burden laid upon the New-England colonies" was "far beyond what they are able to bear, if Great-Britain does not interpose for our help." So he called for "support from our mother-country." The Ohio defeat had been "a terrible evil." Yet it might ultimately prove a providential link "in that chain of causes, by which Heaven may intend to chastise the French, curb their insolence, drive them out of the encroachments they have made on us, and reduce them to a necessity of keeping within their own boundaries without disturbing us in the possession of ours." An important key would be the actions of British leaders, who would be well advised to appoint more officers from New England, to protect New Englanders from unnecessarily harsh disciplinary procedures, and to fund their war effort with hard cash. "American irregulars, in an American war, are full as necessary as British regulars," Chauncy contended. Moreover, "New-England in general, and the Massachusetts-Province in special, are the chief, I may say the only, sources that may be rely'd on for a supply of effective men to carry into execution any future designs against the French."[49]

When speaking at the ordination of Joseph Bowman for missionary work in 1762, Chauncy took the opportunity to infer further providential significance from recent victories over the French in the Seven Years' War. "By crowning the British arms, in these American lands, with success beyond even our biggest expectations," he contended, God had "opened a wide door for sending the gospel to the Gentiles inhabiting here." More particularly, "the providence of God, by so succeeding his Britannic Majesty's Arms as to put Canada into English hands, seems evidently to point our view to these [northern and eastern] tribes of Indians." Chauncy's interpretation of the repeal of the Stamp Act in 1766 was equally providentialist. But his thanksgiving sermon on that occasion also gave him scope to express some of the most Anglophile, loyalist, and royalist statements in all his writings. Chauncy acknowledged that there had been problems with the act. But in repealing the legislation, "the supreme authority in England, to which we inviolably owe submission" had revealed its true colors. It was clear that "the affectionate regard of the American inhabitants for their Mother Country,

---

49. Chauncy, *Second Letter*, 2, 16, 3, 14; *Letter to a Friend* (*Ohio-Defeat*), 5, 9, 11. Guyatt defined "providentialism" in broad terms as "the belief that God controls everything that happens on earth" (*Providentialism*, 5). It is acknowledged, with Guyatt, that this was a fairly commonly held assumption in eighteenth-century colonial America. Specific attention is periodically drawn to it, where it seems a particularly striking feature in the thought of Chauncy or Mayhew.

was never exceeded by any Colonists, in any part, or age of the world," and justly so. Their affection for King George III was especially strong. There were, in fact, "no subjects, not within the realm of England itself, that are more strongly attached to his person and family, that bear a more sincere and ardent affection towards him, or that would exert themselves with more life and spirit in defence of his crown and dignity."[50]

Although he acknowledged recent strains in the imperial relationship, two years after the repeal of the Stamp Act Chauncy reaffirmed the loyalism and royalism of American colonists in one of his anti-episcopacy writings, *Appeal to the Public Answered* (1768). He conceded that Episcopalians were "'equal' . . . to the other denominations of men in the Country," but they were definitely not "superior" among those "who esteem themselves as strongly bound to fidelity and loyalty to the British Crown, upon 'the principles of Christianity,' as well as from 'present interest and inclination.'" He wrote warmly of that "wisely contrived mixture of power, which gives the British-state-constitution the preference to any of the whole earth." He again welcomed that "the dispute, relative to the STAMP-ACT, has been happily terminated." Yet in responding to some of the ancillary detail, as well as the main substance of a work revealing plans for the introduction of an Anglican episcopacy into America, he questioned Thomas Chandler's statement that "the greatest harmony subsists between our Mother-country, and most of the Colonies." Once more appealing to those British "CONSTITUTIONAL RIGHTS," which he valued so highly, Chauncy wrote of colonies "every day groaning out their complaints," but still determined to act loyally "in those ways that are legal."[51]

Like many other New England leaders, Chauncy's loyalty remained strong but by the late 1760s it was under strain. His consistent commitment to the "Mother-country" as a source and defender of New England's interests, including the sociopolitical status quo, remained undiminished. But Chauncy was as keen to ensure that the Church of England did not export an alien episcopacy that might threaten colonial liberties as he was to protest against perceived threats to the colony's interests from new imperial legal and/or taxation measures. As has been seen, his vigorous opposition to an American episcopate, expressed in three polemical works of 1768–70, was politically as well as religiously motivated. Such was his mistrust of

50. Chauncy, *All Nations*, 46, 29; Chauncy, *Discourse on "The Good News,"* 7, 16, 30. Chauncy also urged New Englanders to "make our religious grateful acknowledgments to the supreme Ruler of the world, to whose super-intending providence it is principally to be ascribed, that we have had 'given us so great deliverance'" (ibid., 27). See ibid., 11–13n, for Chauncy's views of the possible consequences of the Stamp Act.

51. Chauncy, *Appeal to the Public Answered*, 96, 199, 110, citing Chandler, *Appeal to the Public*, passim.

the British ecclesiastical authorities that even the prospect of a "spiritual" Church of England bishop, with no temporal powers, of the kind advocated by Chandler, was too much for him.[52]

Despite such obvious concerns to protect New England from undue British encroachments, whether in church or state, the more moderate, less conspiratorial rhetoric of the First Church minister's political commentary justifies Noll's refusal to identify Chauncy with the Real Whig ideology that Bailyn found so influential in the revolutionary and pre-revolutionary periods. Yet Noll's emphasis on a decisively more Whig and providentialist tone in some of Chauncy's statements between 1766 and 1783 seems misplaced. As early as 1746, he wrote, for example, of "English Liberties, whereby we are distinguished from every other People under Heaven" and of "those invaluable Privileges which we enjoy as Protestants." In his 1747 election sermon, Chauncy defended "the liberties and privileges of the subject" and referred to "the invaluable priviledges of Englishmen." Deploying a long-standing Protestant trope, he equated Catholic ecclesiastical and political power with "slavery" in the mid-1740s. On the premise that "civil government, is not a contrivance of arbitrary and tyrannical men, but a regular state of things," he wrote of the need for godly Protestant rulers to preserve "order and rule in society." Chauncy's providentialism likewise was just as strong in his earlier works as in his post-Stamp Act writings. With Mayhew and other Congregationalist ministers of his time and place, Chauncy conceived of a universe in which every aspect of life, both private and public, was under God's superintending purview and control. He may have argued quite forcefully for the importance of human free will, especially from the late 1750s, but he saw providence at work everywhere he looked—locally, nationally, and internationally.[53]

To cite just a few examples of Chauncy's early national and even global providentialism, he noted the fate of the city of Laish in the Book of Judges to warn New Englanders in 1734 against the dangers of sin lest God should "be provoked in his holy and righteous providence." The reduction of Cape

52. Chauncy, *Letter to a Friend Containing Remarks*; *Appeal to the Public Answered*; *Reply to Dr. Chandler's "Appeal Defended."* With others already cited, Griffin, *Old Brick*, 135–58, passim, helpfully highlighted the significance of connections between colonial fears of ecclesiastical oppression under imposed Anglican bishops and of growing imperial control threatened by British measures to assert authority over colonists through legislation such as the Stamp Act (1765), the Townshend Acts (1766), and eventually both the Tea Act (1773) and the Coercive or "Intolerable" Acts (1774).

53. Noll, *America's God*, 141–43; Bailyn, *Ideological Origins*; Chauncy, *Counsel of Two Confederate Kings*, 24, 28, 43, and see 30, 35, 37; *Civil Magistrates*, 32, 35, 8. For examples of Chauncy's providentialism in interpreting people's personal lives, see *Man's Life Considered*, "Dedication"; *Nathanael's Character Display'd*, 27–28; *Joy*, 22; *Civil Magistrates*, 53; *Blessedness of the Dead*, 30; "Life of the Rev. President Chauncy," 171.

Breton in 1745 followed "the Direction of Providence . . . that so many Things were remarkably ordered all along in favour of it, and so as finally to bring it to an happy Issue." So did the protection of Novia Scotia ten years later "under the smiles of providence" after "the seasonable arrival of Admiral Boscawen." It was the same "providence of God" that gave English forces victory in the Seven Years' War. When Chauncy described the repeal of the Stamp Act as "principally to be ascribed" to the "super-intending providence" of "the supreme Ruler of the world," he was thus continuing a long-established theme. The First Church minister's 1770 ascription of the support and protection of New England's founding fathers to "marvellous protections afforded to them by God Almighty" is less indicative of the particularly "providential nature of Chauncy's Whig views" from the mid-1760s onwards than of a consistent, longer-term understanding of divine supervision of the affairs of nations which reflected a Puritan historical vision dating back to the seventeenth century and beyond. Chauncy maintained such a perspective into the revolutionary period, when he not only discerned providential victories for the American cause, but saw both parties in the conflict "made use of in the providence of God to chastise one another" for their sins.[54]

What Noll has seen as Chauncy's increased Whig providentialism is, therefore, best linked with other themes in a basically conventional, sociopolitical worldview which contained libertarian elements by virtue of Chauncy's allegiance to mainstream Whig values, as well as to a lofty vision of New England's Protestant British heritage. His concern to protect civil and religious "liberties" was of a piece with his desire to conserve an established order that he thought guaranteed them. When he saw such freedoms at risk, he was prepared to speak out against forces threatening them, whether legal, ecclesiastical, or fiscal, especially when they were connected with the dangers of Catholic absolutism or related phenomena, like Church of England hierarchicalism. At a time when it was far from popular to do so, Chauncy was even ready to defend the rights and dignities of those such as African slaves, who were denied all autonomy, and of indigenous peoples subjected to cultural assimilation by zealous missionaries (see chapter 6). But his religious and political lodestar in doing so remained consistent. Slavery should be ended because it was "a dishonor to Englishmen, who esteem it their distinguishing glory, that they enjoy the fullest reasonable liberty," as well as a clear violation of the Christian ethic. A primary reason not to alienate or endanger "Indian-Natives" by imposing English culture

---

54. Chauncy, *Character and Overthrow*, 10; *Marvellous Things Done*, 13; *Letter To a Friend (Ohio-Defeat)*, 13; *All Nations*, 29; *Discourse on "The Good News,"* 27; *Trust in God*, 14; *Accursed Thing*, 15, and see 24; Noll, *America's God*, 141.

on them was likewise to protect them from "the religion of Rome" and from being "indoctrinated in the principles of Popery."[55]

Creative Traditionalists

Much like Mayhew's, Chauncy's political worldview thus reflected older traditions than scholars have often credited. Both espoused a fairly traditionalist, hierarchical view of society, which set great store by the "stations" in which people found themselves and by the education that they had received. Although they allowed for justifiable acts of civil rebellion *in extremis*, both held a high view of civil authorities and of the duties owed to them. Both embraced a providentialist understanding of colonial and international history and politics, in which Britain and New England were divinely ordained forces for good. Both were deeply loyal to the values and structures of the British mixed constitution and to the monarchy which remained central to it. Last but not least, both saw themselves as defenders of New England's "Protestant interest," both political and religious, and they believed that the traditional liberties which it upheld were crucial not only to the progress of Christian civilization, but to the welfare of all humankind.

In such ways, Chauncy's and Mayhew's political views had as much commonality as scholars have often attributed to them, but for different, rather more complex, reasons than a simple categorization of them both as Whigs. They did indeed maintain the key commitments to British constitutionalism and monarchism, to anti-Catholicism, and to measured religious toleration shared by most Whigs in the eighteenth century Atlantic world. But their worldviews were not only more traditionalist, providentialist, and profoundly religious than historians have generally allowed, their Whiggery itself took different forms. In Mayhew's case, the strong influence of Real Whig ideology is undeniable from at least his second publication to his last, while Chauncy's views are best described in more mainstream terms. At the same time, because their related discourse defies the imposition of firm distinctions between sacred and secular, it is often impossible to separate the political from the religious views of two ministers who devoted the whole of their adult lives to pastoral ministry. As we turn to consider their "languages of liberty," chapter 6 will explore a crucial example of such ambivalence and ambiguity in Chauncy's and Mayhew's usage of one of the most significant, but also elusive, terms in colonial and revolutionary America.

55. Chauncy, *Appeal to the Public*, 117, 125–26. In *Idle-Poor Secluded* and *Charity*, Chauncy also defended the rights of the poor in general. Yet with his advocacy of voluntary poor relief for the helplessly indigent, but of work for those capable of it, he arguably pursued an even safer sociopolitical line.

— 6 —

Fighting the Cause

Languages of Liberty

IN JULY 1766, CHARLES Chauncy was in unusually ebullient mood. Four months earlier, King George III had given Royal Assent to the repeal of the Stamp Act by the British parliament. Following receipt of this "good news from a far Country," July 24 had been formally declared "A Day of Thanksgiving to Almighty GOD throughout the Province of the Massachusetts Bay in New-England . . . appointed by his Excellency, the GOVERNOR of said Province." Taking Proverbs 25:25 as his text, Chauncy was effusive in stressing the magnitude of the repeal's significance. Even the people of Israel could not have been "more pleased with the royal provision in their day, which, under God, delivered them from their bondage in Egypt," he contended. The Stamp Act had "greatly alarmed" the colonists' "fears, and troubled their hearts." Now that it no longer remained in force, the situation had changed so dramatically that

> It was to them as "life from the dead." They "rejoiced and were glad." And it gave strength and vigor to their joy, while they looked upon this REPEAL, not merely as taking off the grievous restraint that had been laid upon their liberties and privileges, but as containing in it an intention of continued indulgence in the free exercise of them. Tis in view of it, that they exult as those who are "glad in heart;" esteeming themselves happy beyond almost any people now living on the face of the earth.

Chauncy went on to expand on the nature of New England's freedoms and how they had been threatened. He also revealed his understanding of some of their biblical limitations in the process. The resulting discourse not only had a direct bearing on his own conceptions of liberty, it directly mentioned a dramatic series of events in the life of Jonathan Mayhew, which led the West Church minister to present a much more systematic definition.[1]

In a bid to help recoup costs incurred during the Seven Years' War, the Stamp Act, which took effect in November 1765, required many printed materials to be produced on paper from London carrying an embossed revenue stamp. This effectively imposed a new tax in the colonies, to be collected in British currency, and enforced by imperial Admiralty Courts. According to Edmund and Helen Morgan:

> The highest tax, £10, was placed ... on attorney licenses. Other papers relating to court proceedings were taxed in amounts varying from 3d. to 10s. Land grants under a hundred acres were taxed 1s. 6d., between 100 and 200 acres 2s., and from 200 to 320 acres 2s. 6d., with an additional 2s. 6d. for every additional 320 acres (1.3 km2). Cards were taxed a shilling a pack, dice ten shillings, and newspapers and pamphlets at the rate of a penny for a single sheet and a shilling for every sheet in pamphlets or papers totaling more than one sheet and fewer than six sheets in octavo, fewer than twelve in quarto, or fewer than twenty in folio . . .

Following the 1764 Sugar Act, which had already provoked strong American protests, the Stamp Act gave rise to concerted colonial political resistance, not least in the form of the New York Stamp Act Congress of October 1765, when twenty-seven delegates from nine colonies gathered to draft a set of formal petitions stating why Parliament had no right to tax them. The resulting "Declarations of the Rights and Grievances of the Colonists" stated fourteen points of colonial protest. As well as addressing specific problems with the act, the document asserted the general principle of "no taxation without representation," arguing that since the American colonists possessed English rights, but were not represented in the British parliament, only duly elected colonial assemblies had the right to tax them. The statement was sent to London with separate petitions to the king and to both Houses of Parliament.[2]

In addition to more formal protests, the Stamp Act also provoked significant civil unrest in the form of street demonstrations in a number of colonies, including New York, Rhode Island, New Hampshire, and both Carolinas, as

1. Chauncy, *Discourse on "the Good News,"* title page, 16.

2. Morgan and Morgan, *Stamp Act Crisis*, 72, 107–19; Stamp Act Congress, *Proceedings*, 15–16, 17–24. The third of the "Declarations of Rights and Grievances" stated: "That it is inseparably essential to the Freedom of a People, and the undoubted Right of Englishmen, that no Taxes be imposed on them, but with their own Consent, given personally, or by their Representatives."

well as Massachusetts. Boston saw some of the most violent actions. On August 14, 1765, a crowd attacked first the office and then the home of the newly appointed distributor of stamps for Massachusetts, Provincial Secretary Oliver, intimidating him into a public resignation. Twelve days later, a similar raid took place on the home of Lieutenant Governor Hutchinson. By November 1765, the "Sons of Liberty" had emerged as a more or less coordinated, transcolonial mobilizing force, and historians have shown clear evidence that major Boston leaders influenced, if not directly orchestrated, such attacks. Mayhew became personally implicated in the violence at Hutchinson's house by virtue of a sermon on Galatians 5:12–13 which he had delivered at West Church on August 25, reminding those present: "brethren, ye have been called unto liberty." The details of this incident and its aftermath will be more fully explored in the next chapter.[3]

In his thanksgiving discourse for the Stamp Act's repeal, Chauncy was predictably unstinting in his praises for the upholding of "liberties and privileges" to which New Englanders were "natural heirs . . . , by being born subjects to the British Crown" and for local concerns to preserve such an inheritance. But he also offered strong words of condemnation for those "sons of wickedness" who took "occasion from the stand that was made for liberty to commit violence with an high hand," not least in the "villainous conduct" that gave rise to "the outrage at Lieut. Governor HUTCHINSON's house." Chauncy made no mention of Mayhew, but others clearly did. The resulting attempts to defend and distance himself from the charge of rabble-rousing led Mayhew to expound directly on his ideas in a "Memorandum" of a significant part of his sermon of August 1765, as well as in letters to Hutchinson and to a West Church parishioner, Richard Clarke, who was so offended by the incident that he and his family left the congregation immediately. Taking Mayhew's own six-fold definition in his memo as a point of departure, this chapter will compare and contrast his and Chauncy's understandings of the crucial concept of liberty that was central to his provocative sermon. Through a systematic analysis, it will highlight the heavily theological framework that informed their conceptions and thus suggest hitherto neglected dimensions of revolutionary libertarian discourse and its power to motivate sometimes violent resistance.[4]

---

3. On civil unrest surrounding the Stamp Act, see esp. Morgan and Morgan, *Stamp Act Crisis*, 125–64. On its orchestration and the "Sons of Liberty," see ibid., 187–213. See, further, Nash, *Unknown American Revolution*; Maier, *From Resistance to Revolution*, esp. 77–112. Gal 5:12–13 reads: "I would they were even cut off which trouble you. For, brethren, ye have been called unto liberty; only use not liberty for an occasion to the flesh, but by love serve one another."

4. Chauncy, *Discourse on "the Good News,"* 14–15, 25–26; Mayhew, "Memorandum";

Definitions of Liberty

In the account of his August 25, 1765 sermon on Galatians 5:12–13, Mayhew identified and/or briefly defined six common "ac[c]eptations of the word":

1. Philosophical liberty, or freedom of choice & action.

2. Gracious liberty, given in regeneration, and consisting in a will or disposition to do good, in opposition to the slavery of [sin].

3. What is commonly called religious liberty; or that natural right which every man has to worship God as he pleases, provided his principles & practices are [not] prejudicial to others.

4. Liberty, or freedom from the ceremonial law, which law is considered in scripture as a yoke & burthen to those who were under it.

5. That liberty which every man has, in what is commonly called a state of nature, or antecedent to the consideration of his being a member of civil society; consisting in a right to act as he pleases, in opposition to being bound by any human laws; always provided that he violates no law of God, nature or right reason; which no man is at liberty to do.

6. Civil Liberty...

The origins of two of Mayhew's definitions—"gracious liberty" and "liberty ... from the ceremonial law"—are clearly biblical, while the other four also draw on philosophical and/or political sources. But deeper analysis shows that none of the six can be properly understood apart from their relevant theological context and that all were ultimately dependent on the second, which was the most foundational.[5]

---

letter to Thomas Hutchinson, August 27, 1765, reprinted in Bradford, *Memoir*, 420–22; Mayhew, "Letter of Rev. Jonathan Mayhew to Richard Clarke, 1765." Together with his "Memorandum," Mayhew's letter to Hutchinson is found in *MP* 91.

5. Mayhew, "Memorandum," 140–43, 141. Mayhew's notion of "gracious liberty, given in regeneration, and consisting in a will or disposition to do good, in opposition to the slavery of [sin]" depended on a reformed theological understanding of regeneration and salvation as processes which restored freedom of choice to a fallen humanity. His primary sources for the biblical concept of "liberty, or freedom from the ceremonial law" were found in the New Testament Epistles to the Galatians and to the Romans.

Philosophical Liberty

Beginning with *Seven Sermons* (1749), Mayhew consistently maintained a vision of Christianity as an inherently rational religion that reasonable people would naturally and freely embrace, when given the choice. But his fullest treatment of what he termed "philosophical liberty," or "freedom of choice & action," is found in an extended footnote to Sermon IX of *On Hearing the Word* (1755), where he considered the topic of "liberty, as opposed to necessity" in the context of a more general treatment "Of the Nature and Principle of Evangelical Obedience." His views were initially grounded in an empirically pragmatic, philosophical realism that led him to deny that human language about or experience of freedom could be fundamentally misleading or deceptive. The notion of philosophical liberty was linguistically essential, Mayhew argued, inasmuch as "all human language is exactly accommodated to the doctrine of freedom: so that we could neither understand each other, nor ourselves, without the idea of liberty; or a power both of choosing and acting variously, or differently, within a certain sphere, under the same given circumstances." Above and beyond the fact that "all men have . . . the idea of liberty," however, direct human consciousness and experience of freedom made it absurd to deny that it really existed. The concept of philosophical liberty was thus "a natural one; bro't into our minds by daily observation." Humankind could not be "more certain of any one thing, except, perhaps, of our own existence, than that we are free creatures." Mayhew was even prepared to concede that "we are more certain of this fact, that we are free, from daily experience; than we can be of the truth of Christianity." For to reject such a certainty, or "first principle," would lead to an epistemological "abyss," an "endless labyrinth of doubts, from whence no clue can extricate us."[6]

But Mayhew's deeper theological convictions also led him beyond such common-sense, empiricist considerations. In cosmological terms, he accepted an Aristotelian understanding of God as the "first Mover" in a universal chain of cause and effect, and he affirmed God's status as "a free Being" with the attribute of "active power." Such an attribute must also be communicable to humankind and this had serious moral consequences. Mayhew saw "a close, an intimate connexion, betwixt the ideas of blameworthiness and liberty; so that the former cannot be without the latter . . .

---

6. Mayhew, *Seven Sermons*; *On Hearing the Word*, 294–303n, esp. 294n, 295n, 296n, 300n, 298n. For more general observations on human liberty, see *Seven Sermons*, 52–53, 58; *Two Discourses Delivered October 9th. 1760*, 27; *Christian Sobriety*, 22; *On Hearing the Word*, 284. Mayhew's extended footnote in *On Hearing the Word*, 294–303n, was reprinted in Bradford, *Memoir*, 155–64.

Nor can a man calmly and cooly [sic] think any action really culpable, or him that did it, of ill-desert, without presupposing, that he was a free being." Therefore, a denial of philosophical liberty would seriously undermine the doctrine of God's moral perfection. For how could "the great Author of our being . . . resent, or be angry with his creatures for, any thing besides the abuse, or the neglect, of their own freedom and active powers"? "Human liberty" was thus "the true basis of the moral constitution of things." Mayhew readily admitted that for Calvinists, "the doctrine of necessity, if true, would, indeed afford a solution of some of the difficulties respecting fore-knowledge, predestination, and Their mechanical conversion." But as a convinced Arminian, he saw insuperable difficulties in trying to square that doctrine with any acceptable understanding of divine justice. On the one hand, how could a perfectly good and omnipotent deity punish people for actions in which they ultimately had no choice? On the other, how could any counter-claim that "vicious men are justly punished, because they are not actuated by a foreign, external constraint; but will, and chuse to sin, and do it voluntarily" be consistent with a rigorously applied notion of necessity? "Philosophical liberty" was thus not only empirically evident, it was integral to Mayhew's theological conceptions of human moral responsibility and divine justice.[7]

Perhaps because of his Calvinist positions for more than half his career at Boston's First Church, Chauncy's references to philosophical liberty were very limited in his earlier publications. It was only when he finally felt able to unveil a fully Arminian and universalist theology in his most heterodox treatises of the 1780s that he devoted major attention to the topic. A key premise shared with Mayhew was that if human beings were to have proper accountability before God, they must first have freedom of choice. Thus in *Benevolence of the Deity* (1784), Chauncy argued:

> We feel in ourselves a power over our own volitions, and such an one as enables us to direct, suspend, overrule, or put an intire stop to them: Nor, unless we were possessed of this dominion, could we be agents, however great liberty might be allowed us in bringing into event what we have previously willed. It is essential to free agency, and such a use of it as to make us capable of good or ill deserts, that our volitions, upon which our actions follow, should be within the reach of our command.

7. Mayhew, *On Hearing the Word*, 294–303n, esp. 296n, 299n, 300n, 302n. As already noted in chapter 2, Mayhew further argued that "to deny to this great first Cause, the power of imparting to his creatures a measure of freedom; or of making a free creature, who can either chuse and act, or not, within a certain sphere, (how narrow and limited soever that sphere may be) is making much too free with Him"(ibid., 296n).

Since Chauncy saw human well-being as contingent on moral virtue, "the most exalted happiness" was also "connected with, and dependant on, a free, but wise and good, use" of a power to do what we choose; and "had we not this power, we could be happy in no other sense, than that in which all meerly percipient beings are so." In that sense, Chauncy contended, "if there was no free agency, there could be no virtue, nor any of that sublime happiness, which may be the result of it. There could not, in one word, be any such thing as moral government."[8]

A main reason Chauncy rejected the Calvinist scheme of predestination so decisively was because it robbed humanity of genuine free will. But his parallel commitment to God-ordained, universal salvation eventually led him into the theological quandary (outlined in chapter 3) of trying to balance absolute divine sovereignty with human freedom of choice. Commenting on the meaning of a key New Testament passage in *Mystery Hid* (1784), for example, Chauncy considered the possible objection to his argument that "[God] may . . . use proper moral means that all men might be saved; but, as men are free agents, they may mis-improve these means, and bring final ruin upon themselves, notwithstanding God's willingness they should be saved." His response as noted earlier, was speculative and inconclusive:

> I readily own, in answer hereto, that men, as they are free agents, have the power of resisting, or opposing, those means, which God, from his desire of their salvation, may see fit to use with them; which power ought not to be over-ruled, nor indeed can it be in consistency with moral agency... [But] is infinite wisdom, excited by infinite benevolence, and accompanied with infinite power, incapable of devising, and then executing, a scheme, with reference to all men, which shall, in event, without breaking in upon their liberty, or using any means but such as are moral and rational, and therefore adjusted to their character as moral agents, infallibly issue in their salvation?

Chauncy's commitment to universal salvation thus not only undermined his claim to have rejected predestinarian Calvinism, it threatened the validity of his strong affirmations of human free will. In the final analysis, much like Mayhew, although for somewhat different reasons, he could not separate his treatment of even the most basic form of "philosophical" liberty from deeply theological considerations.[9]

---

8. Chauncy, *Benevolence of the Deity*, 132–33, 142, 210.
9. Chauncy, *Mystery Hid*, 166–67. Cf. 1–3.

Religious Liberty

Inasmuch as "religious liberty" constituted "that natural right which every man has to worship God as he pleases, provided his principles & practices are [not] prejudicial to others," it was part and parcel, with civil liberty, of the inherited rights or "prescriptive" liberties that Mayhew frequently described as necessary, constituent parts of life in a properly ordered society, where people were free to judge for themselves. But in mid-eighteenth-century New England, where toleration remained limited and relatively recent, Mayhew appealed to and sometimes reinterpreted his Puritan heritage in order to defend religious freedoms. Although he generally saw Britain as a model and inspiration, he also showed periodic ambivalence towards it, especially during the American Episcopate controversy of the 1760s, when the mother country itself came to seem a threatening source of religious authoritarianism and interference.[10]

Despite the lack of toleration among the first Puritans, which he regretted, religious liberty from British oppression was one of the distinguishing virtues of their "errand into the wilderness," as Mayhew understood it. It was also central to his continuing vision of a free and just society. Towards the beginning of *Seven Sermons* (1749), Mayhew cited apostolic precedent for encouraging "liberty and freedom of thought," quoting one of the key texts which he regularly deployed in that connection. And in his appeal to Galatians 5:1, the West Church minister clearly extended its application from ceremonial liberty in a strictly Pauline sense to a much broader definition of religious freedom. He accordingly began his argument with a clear reference to Judaic legal matters, but pursued his exposition with a strong focus on religious liberty in general:

> Stand fast, says he [the apostle Paul], in the liberty wherewith Christ has made you free: (i.e. assert your freedom from the mosaic law, and all the old jewish institutions) and be not again intangled with any yoke of bondage. (i.e. stand up in defence of your christian liberty, not only against these your judaizing brethren; but also against all others who shall attempt to exercise any kind of spiritual tyranny over you.)[11]

---

10. Mayhew, "Memorandum," 140–43, 141. Shain defined "prescriptive liberties" in the plural, as "an inherited set of rights that were applicable to members of a particular class or a local corporation (often a town or village)—rights to which, as English subjects, Americans believed themselves duly entitled" (*Myth of American Individualism*, 171).

11. Mayhew, *Seven Sermons*, 53, 55–56.

Mayhew defined "religious liberty" in very general terms. It involved "intire liberty of conscience," free from the kind of "restraints and embarrasments, not to say persecutions," that New England's founders once suffered in Britain. It entailed freedom to use different forms of worship and church government, even the episcopal. Mayhew wrote his influential series of polemical works against the introduction of English bishops into America because he viewed Church of England episcopacy as a threat to other liberties. But although he was a committed Congregationalist, he also described himself in one of those same publications as "a warm friend to religious liberty in the largest sense," by whom "mutual forbearance cannot be too much recommended, where the differences are merely of a religious nature, or such as do not affect the liberty, safety and natural rights of mankind." For Mayhew, it was "one of the chief honours of the present age, that the principles of religion, particularly of religious liberty, are better understood, and more generally espoused, than they have, perhaps been, since the days of the apostles." New England's British heritage was central to this. Yet while the West Church minister often expressed his loyalty to the monarchy, as well as his pride in such a constitutional heritage, his understanding of recent history also led to some reservations about the true extent of religious freedoms in Britain.[12]

On the one hand, he thanked God, in his *Discourse Concerning Unlimited Submission* (1750), for British toleration and relative freedom of speech. On the other, he vigorously upheld, like earlier Puritans, the historical contention argued in his election sermon of 1754, that "our ancestors, tho' not perfect and infallible in all respects, were a religious, brave, and vertuous set of men, whose love of liberty, civil and religious, brought them from their native land, into the American deserts." Mayhew could thus dream in that same address of "Liberty victorious! Slavery biting her own chain! Pride brought down! Vertue exalted! Christianity triumphing over imposture! And another Great Britain rising in America!" But he could equally defend his *Observations* (1763) with the assertion that his forebears "came hither chiefly on a religious account:—that they might enjoy intire liberty of conscience, free from those restraints and embarrasments, not to say persecutions, which they suffered there." In that sense, religious liberty entailed much more than the exercise of personal or communal discretion; it was

---

12. Mayhew, *Defence of the Observations*, 48; *Remarks on an Anonymous Tract*, 71; Mayhew, *On Hearing the Word*, 16. See, further, *Divine Goodness*, 72; *Observations*, 80, 175; Mayhew, *Sermon Preached at Boston*, 29; *Two Discourses Delivered November 23d. 1758*, 11.

an apostolic principle that lay right at the heart of Mayhew's conception of Puritan, New England identity.[13]

Chauncy likewise credited God with ultimate responsibility for the establishment and enjoyment of the liberties inherited from New England's English Protestant forebears, especially since the Glorious Revolution. He rarely defined "CHARTER-RIGHTS, not only setting them free from the oppression of church power, but intitling them to distinguishing liberties and privileges, both civil and religious," with great specificity. But he wrote of the value of such freedoms, including that of conscience and a limited measure of religious toleration, throughout his works and he ultimately set such great store by them that he ended by endorsing the American Revolution itself in a bid to protect them. In *Counsel of Two Confederate Kings* (1746), he repeatedly stressed the threat of the Jacobite rebellion to people's "just Rights and Liberties, as Englishmen and Protestants," praying that God would "mercifully save his People from Popery and Slavery; perpetuating to them the Enjoyment of their Rights and Liberties." In *Civil Magistrates* (1747), he cited it as a special duty of just rulers to protect both civil and religious freedoms. Immediately after the repeal of the Stamp Act, Chauncy waxed almost lyrical about "the hopeful prospect it gives us of being continued in the enjoyment of certain liberties and privileges, valued by us next to life itself." They included "being 'tried by our equals,' and . . . 'making grants for the support of government of that which is our own, either in person, or by representatives we have chosen for the purpose.'"[14]

In *Letter to a Friend, Containing Remarks* (1767), Chauncy cited "liberty to worship God agreably to the dictates of conscience" as "the grand motive" in the immigration of the founders. But such rights also had an illustrious lineage as the natural inheritance of those "born subjects to the British Crown," as "additional charter-grants," and as the "righteous due in consequence of what they, and their fore-fathers, had done and suffered in subduing and defending these American lands." The Stamp Act's repeal meant that "instead of being slaves to those who treat us with rigor, we are indulged the full exercise of those liberties which have been transmitted to us, as the richest inheritance, from our fore-fathers." Two years later, in *Appeal to the Public Answered* (1768), Chauncy argued that a major reason why the introduction of English bishops should be resisted was because it would threaten the religious liberty of others if they had any civil powers:

---

13. Mayhew, *Discourse Concerning Unlimited Submission*, ii; *Sermon Preach'd*, 23, 39; *Defence of the Observations*, 48.

14. Chauncy, *Trust in God*, 13; Chauncy, *Counsel of Two Confederate Kings*, 30, 43; *Civil Magistrates*, 33; *Discourse on "The Good News,"* 14.

> Should it be said, we claim liberty of conscience, and fully enjoy it. And why should we confine this privilege to ourselves? . . . we are as willing they [Episcopalians] should possess and exercise religious liberty in it's full extent, as we desire to do it ourselves . . . We desire no other liberty, than to be left unrestrained in the exercise of our religious principles, in so far as we are good members of society. And we are perfectly willing Episcopalians should enjoy this liberty to the full . . . If Episcopalians would rest satisfied, as the other denominations do, with what they apprehend to be PURELY SCRIPTURAL ministers, they would be perfectly upon a par with them, as to the enjoyment of religious liberty in it's fullest extent: But if they must have what they call these scriptural ministers upon a STATE-ESTABLISHMENT, they can have no reason to complain, unless of themselves, if they do not enjoy that liberty which others do; not because they are more favored or distinguished, but because they claim no other religious liberty, than what is granted in the Gospel-charter.

Chauncy repeated such arguments in *Reply to Dr. Chandler's "Appeal Defended"* (1770). Episcopalians were "at full liberty to provide themselves with such spiritual officers, discipline, and worship, as they shall think agreeable to the will of CHRIST," he contended, but not with bishops empowered to intervene in the civil affairs of the colonies. Therefore, "if we oppose Bishops of a contrary species [i.e., with civil powers]," Chauncy concluded, "we oppose no part of that episcopal liberty which is RELIGIOUS; and should great inconveniences be likely to follow from the sending such Bishops, opposition to their mission would, on this account, be highly reasonable, and not the least infringement on RELIGIOUS liberty."[15]

In Chauncy's pre-revolutionary sermon, *Trust in God* (1772), he not only appealed to the memory of godly ancestors, he also remembered the struggles of those who had opposed the oppressive measures of the Dominion of New England Government, because they "'thought themselves INTITLED TO THE LIBERTIES AND IMMUNITIES OF FREE AND NATURAL BORN ENGLISH SUBJECTS, and consequently that NO MONIES OUGHT TO BE RAISED FROM THEM BUT BY THEIR REPRESENTATIVES.'" For the providentialist and still royalist Chauncy, the Hanoverian succession of 1714 under George I had likewise been a "signal interposition" of God to ensure the continuation of "religious and civil liberties and privileges, both of the mother-country and the American colonies." Indeed:

---

15. Chauncy, *Letter to a Friend, Containing Remarks*, 26; *Discourse on "The Good News,"* 14–15, 23; *Appeal to the Public Answered*, 179–81; see ibid., 97, 149; *Reply to Dr. Chandler's "Appeal Defended,"* 104, 163.

> Had it not been for this marvellous appearance of divine providence, in favor of the people in Old, as well as in New-England, they would have been governed, not by law, but by sovereign will, absolute pleasure; that is, in plain words, they would, instead of being free-men, have been made abject slaves.

The moral lesson that Chauncy drew from such a brief excursion into the providential glories of New England history was that "if we would hope, upon just grounds, to be a happy people, and to have continued to us those invaluable rights and liberties that have been transmitted to us from our fathers, we must be imitators of their virtue." [16]

Natural and Civil Liberty

Of all Chauncy's and Mayhew's notions of freedom, that of "civil liberty" would seem most naturally attributable to non-religious origins. Closer analysis of relevant texts again reveals otherwise, although in Mayhew's understandings of "natural," as well as civil, liberty, the strong influence of Locke's Whig liberalism is unmistakable. Mayhew's definition of natural liberty, which he only addressed in his sermon "Memorandum" on Galatians 5:12–13, can be understood entirely in terms of Locke. His notions of civil liberty are more complex, but it is only once their strongly Lockean elements have been clearly established that the role of other sources, especially deeper theological influences, in shaping the West Church minister's ideas emerge decisively.

In general terms, Locke understood liberty as "to be free from restraint and violence from others which cannot be, where there is no Law." Yet freedom was not "a Liberty for every Man to do what he lists: . . . But a Liberty to dispose, and order, as he lists, his Person, Actions, Possessions, and his whole Property, within the Allowance of those Laws under which he is." Inasmuch as the "State of Nature" was "a State of perfect Freedom" for people "to order their Actions, and dispose of their Possessions, and Persons as they think fit, within the bounds of the Law of Nature, without asking leave, or depending upon the Will of any other Man," Locke's "Natural Liberty" involved being "free from any Superior Power on Earth." Mayhew's definition of the same "liberty which every man has, in what is commonly called a state of nature, or antecedent to the consideration of his being a member of civil society" was almost identical. It consisted, he argued, "in a right to act as he pleases, in opposition to being bound by any human laws; always

---

16. Chauncy, *Trust in God*, 15–17n, [esp. 17n, citing Hutchinson, *History of the Colony of Massachusets-Bay* (1764), 361–62], 20, 30.

provided that he violates no law of God, nature or right reason; which no man is at liberty to do."[17]

Locke's conception of civil liberty was really an extension of his idea of freedom in a "State of Nature," based on his understanding of the foundation and formation of governmental structures by compact or mutual consent. A "Community" was free to decide between various forms of government, including democracy, oligarchy, or different types of monarchy, just "as they think good." What he called "the Liberty of Man, in Society," was "to be under no other Legislative Power, but that established, by consent, in the Common-wealth, nor under the Dominion of any Will, or Restraint of any Law, but what the Legislative shall enact, according to the Trust put in it." Mayhew's definition of civil liberty in his sermon "Memorandum" assumed the same Lockean premise that "men, for the sake of common good, and mutual security, give up some part of their natural liberty" to come under "the restraint of laws, some persons to govern, and some to be governed." Once people were "united together in civil Society, or a body politic," it was also necessary that "those laws, by which a nation is governed, are made by common consent & choice; that all have some hand in framing them, at least by their representatives, chosen to act for them, if not in their own persons." What Mayhew defined, following Locke, as the "essence of civil liberty" did not, therefore, "consist in, or depend upon, the number of persons, by whom a nation is governed; but in their being governed by such persons & laws, as they approve of." [18]

Yet while Locke's influence on Mayhew's ideas of "natural" and "civil liberty" was clearly decisive, it was not unique, at least regarding the latter. On more than one occasion, Mayhew directly acknowledged his intellectual debt to the seventeenth-century English philosopher, but he also credited others. In his final published sermon, *Snare Broken* (1766), he wrote in glowing terms of his education in and love of "the doctrines of civil liberty" by classical figures like "Plato, Demosthenes, Cicero and other renowned persons." In addition to Locke, he singled out the influence of Sidney, Milton, and Hoadley [sic]"among the moderns." Even when discussing issues of practical politics, Mayhew also drew on his Puritan, biblical heritage. He had "earlier still learnt from the holy scriptures, that wise, brave and vertuous men were always friends to liberty" and that freedom, therefore, was "a great blessing."[19]

17. Locke, *Two Treatises*, student ed., 306, 269, 283; Mayhew, "Memorandum," 141.

18. Locke, *Two Treatises*, student ed., 269, 354, 283; Mayhew, "Memorandum," 141-2.

19. Mayhew, *Snare Broken*, 35. Mayhew also hailed the influence of Locke in a list of eight "modern" figures (*Christian Sobriety*, 326).

Snare Broken was thus replete with biblical content from start to finish. In thanksgiving for "the REPEAL of the Stamp-Act," Mayhew's last published sermon was really a paean to liberty, as well as a hymn in praise of God's providential care. Taking Psalm 124:7–8 as his text, Mayhew was less rigorous in his expository focus than in some previous sermons, but that did not prevent him from suffusing his whole discourse with scriptural references. In his preface dedicated to William Pitt, for example, he expressed the hope that if the ailing British minister gained "an adequate conception of the universal joy of AMERICA," this might enable him to "take up Your bed and walk,' like those sick and lame persons instantly cured by the word of Him, who came from Heaven to make us 'free indeed.'" He also stated America's prayer that when Pitt "must, according to the common lot of men, however great and good (O may it be late!) cease to plead the cause of LIBERTY on earth, You may in Heaven, as Your reward, enjoy 'the glorious LIBERTY of the sons of God.'" These citations from Mark 2:9/John 5:8, 8:36, and Romans 8:21 were followed, toward the beginning of the discourse itself, by a markedly political definition of civil liberty, following Magna Carta, which included rights to personal autonomy, as opposed to slavery, and to trial by jury. But Mayhew had already described his basic agenda in *Snare Broken* in much simpler, biblical terms: "We only exercise that liberty, wherewith Christ hath made us free," he wrote, citing Galatians 5:1, "being desirous that all other persons and churches should do the same; and not chusing that either they or we should be 'entangled with any yoke of bondage.'" And in distancing himself from unduly violent acts of resistance, he again alluded to the graphic language and imagery of the Bible.[20]

Mayhew could thus view opposition to the Stamp Act in the American colonies and Britain, together with the repeal to which it led, as entirely providential in origin. Having cited Psalm 124:2–8, he went on to argue that if "He who made the world, exercises a providential government over it . . . How much more then is his providence to be acknowledged in the rise, in the preservation, in the great events, the revolutions, or the fall of mighty states and kingdoms?" Describing British taxation measures as a "grievous and heavy burden," Mayhew quoted from Psalm 126 to suggest that "when the Lord turned our captivity," repeal "was received as an emancipation indeed, from unmerited slavery." But it also provoked ongoing obligations to respect legitimate authority structures and he saw a constant need to act to protect freedom, whenever it was under threat.[21]

---

20. Mayhew, *Snare Broken*, title page, iii–viii, esp. vi, vii–viii, 4–5, 2, 7, alluding to 2 Cor 6:15.

21. Mayhew, *Snare Broken*, 11–12, 14, 24.

It was precisely this last concern that prompted Mayhew to engage, in one of the most notable passages in all his works, in the praise of liberty personified as "celestial Maid, the daughter of God." Yet even there, biblical language and literature provided so much of the symbolic and discursive framework for his libertarian discourse that it is impossible to separate his political philosophy from his practical divinity. Mayhew was not remiss in listing key philosophical influences, but he made his prior debt to biblical sources consistently clear. Not only had he learned from Scripture that good men were "always friends to liberty," he had gathered, quite specifically, that "God gave the Israelites a King [or absolute Monarch] in his anger, because they had not sense and virtue enough to like a free common-wealth, and to have himself for their King." He had also grasped "that the Son of God came down from heaven, to make us 'free indeed'; and that 'where the Spirit of the Lord is, there is liberty,'" all of which made him "conclude, that freedom was a great blessing." [22]

In a conflation typical of such discourse elsewhere in Mayhew's works, this remarkable use of language from John 8:36 and 2 Corinthians 3:17 then led him to expound on his love of liberty as a political phenomenon. When threatened by the imposition of the Stamp Act, liberty "seemed about to take her final departure from America, and to leave that ugly Hag Slavery, the deformed child of Satan, in her room." The act's repeal had brought liberty's return, encouraging Mayhew to sing her praises, which he did by once more appealing to religious and scriptural terminology. Speaking of those in Europe who might seek "a safe retreat from slavery in some far-distant climate," he expressed the wish that they would "find one in America under thy brooding, sacred wings; where our oppressed fathers once found it, and we now enjoy it, by the favor of Him, whose service is the most glorious freedom!" He concluded what he later characterized as "this odd excursion" by praying that God would never permit liberty to "forsake" America "for our unworthiness to enjoy thy enlivening presence! By His [God's] high permission, attend us thro' life AND DEATH to the regions of the blessed," Mayhew pleaded, "thy original abode, there to enjoy forever the 'glorious liberty of the sons of God!'" After such high flights of rhetoric, the remainder of *Snare Broken* seems rather plain and down-to-earth. But Mayhew continued with biblical themes right to the end of what has so often been construed as one of his most political works. He urged all, in typically Puritan manner, to "apply ourselves with diligence, and in the fear of God, to the duties of our respective stations" and to "join with heart and hand in supporting the lawful, constitutional government over us." Last but not

---

22. Mayhew, *Snare Broken*, 36, 35, citing/alluding to John 8:36, 2 Cor 3:17.

least, he quoted one of the major texts in his scriptural armory. "If we hope for admission into those eternal mansions of joy," Mayhew enjoined, citing 1 Peter 2:17, "let every one of us, as the apostle Peter exhorts, 'honor all men, love the brotherhood, fear GOD, honor the KING.'" [23]

Such a biblically and theologically based view of the nature and advance of civil liberty was similarly evident in some of his earlier works. To take a particularly striking example, stressed by Lubert, it was primarily through the interpretation of Romans 13:1–8, rather than an immediate appeal to Lockean philosophy or Whig ideology, that Mayhew came to the conclusion in *Discourse Concerning Unlimited Submission* (1750) that "if those who bear the title of civil rulers, do not perform the duty of civil rulers, but act directly counter to the sole end and design of their office; if they injure and oppress their subjects, instead of defending their rights and doing them good; they have not the least pretence to be honored, obeyed, and rewarded." D. A. Lloyd Thomas discerned four main "grounds for justifiable rebellion" in Locke's *Second Treatise*, including a government's failures to "enforce the law of nature," "to further the common good," to maintain public "trust" or to "act within the bounds of positive law." But Mayhew appealed straight to scripture, when he argued that

> Common tyrants, and public oppressors, are not intitled to obedience from their subjects, by virtue of anything here laid down by the inspired apostle. I now add, farther, that the apostle's argument is so far from proving it to be the duty of people to obey, and submit to, such rulers as act in contradiction to the public good, and so to the design of their office, that it proves the direct contrary.[24]

Mayhew was strongly influenced by Locke, and his further dependence, for key elements of the argument of *Discourse Concerning Unlimited Submission* (1750), on works by Hoadly, Gordon, and Coade has already been noted. But the demonstration of such links does nothing to disprove the traditional, biblical content or structure of Mayhew's discourse. Indeed, his understanding of civil liberty, including the right of resistance (further explored in chapter 7), was thoroughly grounded in his interpretation of biblical revelation and Puritan tradition, even when expressed in terms of seventeenth- and eighteenth-century political philosophy. Mayhew's

---

23. Mayhew, *Snare Broken*, 36 (alluding to wording from the Collect for Peace from the Morning Prayer service in the Church of England's *Book of Common Prayer*, 50, as well as citing Romans 8:21), 37, 41–42, 43, 44.

24. Mayhew, *Discourse Concerning Unlimited Submission*, 22–23; Lubert, "Jonathan Mayhew: Conservative Revolutionary," 593–94; Thomas, *Locke on Government*, 62–65.

exegesis of Romans 13:1-8 not only enabled him to offer a biblically based summary of "the apostle's doctrine [of civil obedience], in the passage . . . explained," it facilitated the conclusion that since rulers had "no authority from God to do mischief," the apostle's argument did not entail unlimited submission to them. Apostolic doctrine was thus the major authority for Mayhew's support of active resistance against a monarch become tyrant. He was thankful, in 1750, that New Englanders were not being asked to submit to such a ruler, but he also saw a need both to "prize our freedom" and to honor the biblical injunction of 1 Peter 2:16 not to "use our liberty for a cloke of maliciousness."[25]

In addition to *Snare Broken*, clear evidence of a similar biblical discourse emerges from Mayhew's other statements on liberty in 1765-6. When Mayhew wrote to Hutchinson on August 27, 1765 to disavow any part in provoking the attack on his house by his inflammatory sermon on Galatians 5:12-13 two days earlier, he conceded that he had strongly supported "civil and religious liberty" and that he had spoken of "the late stamp act as a great grievance, likely to prove detrimental in a high degree both to the colonies and to the mother country". But he also sought to convince the lieutenant governor that he had warned against overreacting to it. In his September 3 letter to parishioner Richard Clarke, Mayhew quoted directly from his words on August 25, underlining the biblical, as well as philosophical, foundations of his argument. Having repeated his decidedly Lockean definition of "civil liberty" as a state which presupposed "men to be united together in civil society," as opposed to "a state of nature," and governed by "the restraint of laws," Mayhew turned to exegesis of the Pauline injunction, "Only use not liberty for an occasion to the flesh." In expounding that command, he not only treated the abuse of ceremonial or gracious liberty "in the practice of fleshly lusts, or in any immoral & sinful actions," he dealt directly with the need for civil obedience, appealing to such texts as Matthew 22:21 and Romans 13:5: "We ought to be subject, not only for wrath, or for fear of the wrath of man," he concluded, "but also for conscience sake."[26]

Chauncy's references to civil liberty were equally general. In theological terms, he clearly allowed for the existence of a state of natural freedom, like that of "Adam . . . at liberty, in his original state," before the formation

---

25. Bailyn, *Pamphlets*, 208 (citing Hoadly, *Measures of Submission*; Coade, *Letter to a Clergyman*; Trenchard and Gordon, *The Independent Whig*); Mayhew, *Discourse Concerning Unlimited Submission*, 9–12, 23, 55.

26. Mayhew to Hutchinson, August 27, 1765, in Bradford, *Memoir*, 420–22. See esp. 421. *MP* 91 dates the letter August 27, 1765. See, further, "Letter of Rev. Jonathan Mayhew to Richard Clarke, 1765," 16–20, esp. 17–18; Mayhew, "Memorandum," 140–43, esp. 141, 143.

of society. Subsequent to that, his obvious valuation of the "Blessing of Liberty" knew no bounds. Thus he commended "the Principles of Liberty," "the wiser sons of liberty," "the friends of liberty," and "Patrons of liberty." He described his friend Mayhew as "eminently a friend to liberty both civil and religious" and noted that "his first printed discourses were upon the subject of LIBERTY." Most strikingly, Chauncy was one of the few of his generation to apply his general concern for civil liberty to the terrible conditions suffered by slaves and indigenous peoples. Moreover, in criticizing such injustices, he was self-consciously guided by what he saw as traditional religious, as well as political, values.[27]

At the 1762 ordination of Joseph Bowman to serve as a missionary "Among the Mohawk-Indians, on the Western Borders of New-England," Chauncy urged renewed efforts to share Christian orthodoxy with indigenous peoples and to protect them from Catholicism. But he also spoke out strongly against their cultural assimilation and called for local schooling. In *Appeal to the Public Answered* (1768) he continued the same theme. "The Indian-Natives have certainly been hurt, not served, by being put into the English way of living," Chauncy argued. In viewing such peoples as "Savages," who needed to be "humanised" as well as "christianised," he clearly shared two of the major prejudices of his age. But he saw no "need of what is called civilizing them, in order to their embracing Christianity."[28]

Further to a dispute with Chandler over his inclusion of African-Americans in the number of Anglicans in North America, Chauncy pulled no punches describing the plight of slaves in the same sermon. His underlying assumptions were that "the poor Negroes" were "'sharers with us in the same common nature'" and had "the same natural essential rights." They were "as good by nature as their masters." But their "right to the FREEDOM OF MEN" was "outragiously invaded, while . . . held in ignoble slavery." "It is most horribly shameful," he wrote, "that so many of the human species . . . should be bought and sold as though they were cattle; and dealt with as though they were an inferior order to dogs!" It was particularly dishonorable for those enjoying the benefits of English liberties "to make SLAVES, and in the most abject sense, of such amazing numbers of their fellow-men." Chauncy felt so strongly about this that he described it as "an abomination highly worthy of a Parliamentary interposition" and his ultimate grounds were religious as well as political. "I have often wondered," he continued,

27. Chauncy, *Five Dissertations*, 54; *Only Compulsion*, 16, 15; *Discourse on "The Good News,"* 19, 21n, 31. See, further, *Discourse Occasioned by the Death of the Reverend Jonathan Mayhew*, 27.

28. Chauncy, *All Nations*, title page, 26–27n, 28–29, 32–33n, 34–36nn; *Appeal to the Public Answered*, 125–26.

"nothing has been done in the Colonies to put a stop to the cruelly unjust practice of making slaves . . . ; especially, as they have, for some years, been sighing out the most bitter complaints against all tendencies towards their being enslaved themselves. Is this to act a consistent part? Is it, in any equitable sense, doing to others as they would others should do to them?"[29]

Spiritual Liberty

Since "gracious liberty, given in regeneration, and consisting in a will or disposition to do good" and "freedom from the ceremonial law," which was an essentially Pauline concept, both stemmed directly from Mayhew's understanding of New Testament soteriology, there is no reason to question their status as the most deeply theological in origin and orientation of his six definitions of liberty. However, such concepts were not only crucial to his theological worldview but, through a consistently deployed, biblicist discourse of liberty, informed his libertarian thought as a whole. Textual evidence thus indicates that they were ultimately the most foundational of all Mayhew's categories.[30]

In keeping with his Arminian understanding of free choice, Mayhew was consistent in seeing Christian salvation as an essentially cooperative process. This enabled him to stress the importance of gracious liberty without impugning the philosophical liberty so central to his general conception of the human condition. When speaking "On the Shortness and Vanity of Human Life. Occasioned by the Death of a Young Person" in Sermon XII of *On Hearing the Word* (1755), for example, Mayhew made the optimistic observation that

> Our condition is not desperate: So far from it, that God has made ample provision for our deliverance from this state of bondage, corruption and death, into the glorious liberty of his Sons. For as in Adam we die, so in Christ we may be made alive.

In his *Practical Discourses* (1760), Mayhew defined "moral liberty" as involving "a fixed habit of piety, and obedience to God's commandments," and he later wrote, in the same work, of "a life of irreligion and vice" as "naturally productive of many evils and disquietudes, from which the contrary course of life is free." But while the proper exercise of gracious liberty might entail

---

29. Chauncy, *Appeal to the Public Answered*, 116–17, alluding to Matt 7:12/Luke 6:31.

30. Mayhew, "Memorandum," 141.

disciplined application, it was one of the most hopeful and inspiring implications of Mayhew's thoughts on "divine goodness" that

> When we reflect, that according to the apostle Paul, where sin has abounded, grace does much more abound; and that the same creature [or creation] which was originally made subject to vanity, is to be delivered from the bondage of corruption, into the glorious liberty of the children of God . . . light and comfort arise out of darkness and sorrow.[31]

Mayhew's reference to Romans 8:21 in this passage is representative of a familiar pattern found frequently in his works of citations of and allusions to key New Testament uses of the word "liberty." Other biblical texts deployed in this fashion included John 8:36, 2 Corinthians 3:17, Galatians 5:1 and 5:13, James 1:25 and 2:12, and 1 Peter 2:16. All were central to Mayhew's development of a biblically based, libertarian discourse that framed the whole of his thought about liberty, both religious and political. A key example of how he deployed such texts is his treatment of James 2:12 in Sermons 8–10 of *On Hearing the Word* (1755), which addressed "Justification by Faith," the "Nature and Principle of Evangelical Obedience," and the "Extent of Evangelical Obedience." Mayhew first cited the verse toward the beginning of his sermon on justification, where he saw "an obvious inference" from James's command to "so speak . . . and so do, as they that shall be judged by the law of liberty," that "we cannot now be justified by this law of liberty." He defined the latter as "no other than the gospel-rule of life and manners" and he contended that even on the Day of Judgment, "the law of liberty will not then justify us, unless we have sincerely obeyed it." As such, the gracious liberty which Mayhew had in mind involved more than the spiritual "deliverance from" a "state of bondage, corruption and death, into the glorious liberty of his [God's] Sons," which he discussed elsewhere. It consisted not only in "a will or disposition to do good," but in their practical realization. Mayhew rejected any notion that the "law of liberty" was a "legal dispensation," but he was keen to affirm the importance of "Christian

---

31. Mayhew, *On Hearing the Word*, 436, citing Rom 8:21, 1 Cor 15:22; *Practical Discourses*, 109–10, 134; *Divine Goodness*, 89–90, citing Rom 5:20, 8:21. Mayhew dealt with "ceremonial liberty" in a strictly Pauline sense in his August 25, 1765 sermon on Gal 5:12–13, in which he identified those deemed by the apostle Paul to be troubling the Galatians as "judaizing Christians, who adhered to the cerimonial law, particularly to circumcision; and who insisted on the Gentile converts submitting to the same heavy yoke & burthen." In that context, Mayhew interpreted the words "for, brethren, ye have been called unto liberty" in Gal 5:13 as proof that "the apostle considered liberty in general as a great good, or important blessing; and that he was accordingly justly provoked with the judaizing Christians for usurping on the [ceremonial] liberty of the Gentiles in one instance, by troubling them about circumcision" ("Memorandum," 140, 141).

obedience therein," albeit "with reference to the gospel of Christ." In that sense, notwithstanding Mullins's contentions to the contrary, Mayhew's understanding of spiritual liberty had little to do with later notions of personal freedom "as an individual right." It had much more in common with the traditional Puritan one which Massachusetts founder John Winthrop described as "a liberty to that only which is good, just and honest."[32]

Mayhew made this view more specific in two other places in his works. In the second of *Two Discourses Delivered October 9th. 1760*, he cited another key biblical text, 1 Peter 2:16, which united the ideas of liberty and Christian service. "Let us be admonished," he exhorted his hearers, "to make it manifest, that we have a proper sense of God's undeserved goodness to us, by forsaking all our evil practices; whatever is displeasing in his sight, and serving him in holiness and righteousness according to the gospel of his Son: As free, and not using our liberty for a cloke of maliciousness, but as the servants of God." In his first sermon on *Christian Sobriety* (1763), Mayhew repeated the biblical reference in connection with an even more explicit identification of gracious liberty with freedom to do good. "Are you at liberty to act unreasonably?" he asked the young men in his West Church congregation rhetorically. "Have you a right to reject the truth?" Then he answered his own questions. "You cannot think that you have any such right as this, to do wrong; or that you may 'use liberty for a cloak of maliciousness.'" In that sense, just as in traditional Puritan conceptions, there was a clear, internal tension in Mayhew's understanding of spiritual liberty. On the one hand, the believer was free, because he or she had been released from "the slavery of sin." But this spiritual liberty was only really worth the

---

32. Mayhew, *On Hearing the Word*, 223–24, 436, 260, 275; "Memorandum," 141; Mullins, "Father of Liberty," 253; Winthrop, "Speech to the General Court," 207. The full text of key verses from the King James Bible that Mayhew used reads as follows: John 8:36—"If the Son therefore shall make you free, ye shall be free indeed"; Rom 8:21—"Because the creature itself also shall be delivered from the bondage of corruption into the glorious liberty of the children of God"; 2 Cor 3:17—"Now the Lord is that Spirit: and where the Spirit of the Lord is, there is liberty"; Gal 5:1—"Stand fast therefore in the liberty wherewith Christ hath made us free, and be not entangled again with the yoke of bondage"; Gal 5:13—"For, brethren, ye have been called unto liberty; only use not liberty for an occasion to the flesh, but by love serve one another"; Jas 1:25—"But whoso looketh into the perfect law of liberty, and continueth therein, he being not a forgetful hearer, but a doer of the work, this man shall be blessed in his deed"; Jas 2:12—"So speak ye, and so do, as they that shall be judged by the law of liberty"; 1 Pet 2:16—"As free, and not using your liberty for a cloke of maliciousness, but as the servants of God"; 2 Pet 2:19—"While they promise them liberty, they themselves are the servants of corruption: for of whom a man is overcome, of the same is he brought in bondage."

name if it was pursued within the bounds of "evangelical obedience" and so resulted in good works.[33]

Chauncy's various writings show that he too prioritized notions of spiritual liberty and quite often deployed a similar libertarian discourse shaped by biblical texts, which served to inject scriptural content and to evoke spiritual allusions even in overtly political contexts. His references to spiritual liberty clearly overlapped with those to other types of freedom, and especially to the religious liberty central to the prescriptive freedoms which he valued as part of his New England inheritance. In one of his last works, *Mystery Hid* (1784), Chauncy made it very clear that he continually adhered, even in one of his most heterodox publications, to an understanding of spiritual liberty that the earliest New England Puritans would not have disavowed. Like Mayhew, he espoused a basic conception of Christian freedom as human "deliverance ... into the glorious liberty of the children of God," which he described as "precisely the same thing, in import, with the free gift that is come upon all men unto justification of life." In other words, Chauncy's fundamental notion of Christian liberty was freedom from sin and ultimately death through the mediatorial work of Christ. Humankind had "all along been interested in the gift and grace through Christ ...," he argued, "and in the deliverance from the bondage of corruption into the glorious liberty of children." So true spiritual freedom did not entail doing exactly what one wanted. That would constitute "Licenciousness, which is the Excess in Liberty" and against which Chauncy consistently warned. Instead, the Christian's goal should be "voluntary ... submission; a submission of freedom and love, rather than of constraint."[34]

If spiritual liberty was freedom from sin to serve God and others, as Chauncy maintained, it was obviously crucial to stand firm in it, and he consistently appealed to similar biblical texts as Mayhew did to encourage such resolve. The two main verses were Galatians 5:1 and Romans 8:21 and he used them so often, though sometimes ambiguously, that the centrality of his commitment to spiritual liberty becomes unmistakable. In *Twelve Sermons* (1765), as in *Mystery Hid* (1784), Chauncy specifically cited Romans 8:21 with reference to the freedom resulting from Christian salvation, and he

---

33. Mayhew, *Two Discourses Delivered October 9th. 1760*, 62; *Christian Sobriety*, 26.

34. Chauncy, *Mystery Hid*, 110, citing Rom 8:21 and 5:18: "Therefore as by the offence of one judgment came upon all men to condemnation; even so by the righteousness of one the free gift came upon all men unto justification of life"; 107, also alluding to Rom 5:15: "But not as the offence, so also is the free gift. For if through the offence of one many be dead, much more the grace of God, and the gift by grace, which is by one man, Jesus Christ, hath abounded unto many"; *Only Compulsion Proper*, 15n; *Mystery Hid*, 196. Other key texts cited by Chauncy were Isa 61:1, Luke 4:18, and Gal 5:1.

made similar references in *"Breaking of Bread"* (1772) and *Five Dissertations* (1785). In *Only Compulsion Proper* (1739), which was basically a sermon upholding prescriptive religious liberties, Chauncy urged his readers:

> And as for us, the professed Disciples of Christ, in this Land, Let us stand fast in the Liberty wherewith Christ has made us free. And as we have appeared against the Methods of Force in Matters of Religion, against the Impositions of Men in the Worship of God, let us go on to do so; esteeming it to be our Glory. And let us always plead for the use of Liberty in the Affairs of our Souls; and another World.[35]

Chauncy was keenly aware how biblical texts could be misused for the purposes of argument and in *Seasonable Thoughts* (1743) he explicitly critiqued Joseph Emerson's citation of Galatians 5:1 to urge the practice of itinerancy. But in *Validity of Presbyterian Ordination* (1762), he quoted from the text personally, as he urged New England's churches to hang on to "the right of electing their pastors in the most ample manner of any in the whole christian world." He made similar quotations in *Discourse Occasioned by the Death of the Reverend Jonathan Mayhew* (1766), *Appeal to the Public Answered* (1768), *Discourse Occasioned by the Death of the Reverend Thomas Foxcroft* (1769), and *Reply to Dr. Chandler's "Appeal Defended"* (1770), again referring to religious liberty in a prescriptive sense. Two other texts that Chauncy cited in connection with libertarian themes in *Twelve Sermons* (1765) were Luke 4:18 and James 1:25. Such usage clearly constituted a biblicist discourse that lay at the heart of Chauncy's rhetoric of liberty and when he used such phrases as "Christian liberty" or "Gospel-liberty," or otherwise wrote of spiritual liberty in more general terms, those terms were clearly informed by its resonances. Although Chauncy devoted significant attention to other forms of liberty, in a worldview where spiritual liberty was central they too carried more or less religious significance. Despite the heterodox ideas expressed in his works of the 1780s, the inherent traditionalism of Chauncy's discourse of liberty was consistent with the more conventional elements of his ecclesiological, political, and general theological thought. In the final analysis, just like Mayhew, Chauncy primarily understood the foundation of all liberty in a traditional, Puritan sense as freedom in Christ to serve God and others.[36]

---

35. Chauncy, *Twelve Sermons*, 26–27; *Mystery Hid*, 99, 101, 119, 154; *"Breaking of Bread,"* 35, 37; *Five Dissertations*, 103–4, 135, 203; *Only Compulsion Proper*, 16, citing Gal 5:1.

36. Chauncy, *Seasonable Thoughts*, 65, citing and critiquing Emerson, *Emerson's Exhortation*, esp. 2; *Validity of Presbyterian Ordination*, 9. See also Chauncy, *Discourse*

Languages of Liberty

Previous scholarship has laid much emphasis on more philosophical and ostensibly "secular" notions of liberty, even in ministerial discourse, but it is clearly significant that Mayhew's and Chauncy's major political writings are often saturated not only with biblical content, but with a libertarian discourse directly grounded in a traditional Puritan understanding of "spiritual" liberty for Christian service. This also raises broader questions of an historiography of revolutionary and pre-revolutionary ideology that has tended to prioritize contemporary or classical political sources at the expense of traditional religious ones, despite the undoubted religiosity of so much colonial American culture, especially in New England.

Many have noted the major significance of eighteenth-century ideas of liberty, but relatively few have sought to define them, and their definitions have varied widely. Commenting on general conceptions "in the Anglo-American world," Joyce Appleby assumed that a more modern understanding of "liberty as personal freedom" was not widely held in colonial America. Instead, she argued, "its meaning was [only] precise in particular intellectual contexts, of which there were at least three which speakers might have in mind in the seventeenth and eighteenth centuries." These were a "classical republican definition of liberty," similar to that advanced, in significant variations, by Bailyn (1967), Gordon Wood (1972), and John Pocock (1975); "the liberty of secure possession," which was "negative, private, and limited," and "the liberal concept of liberty," which centered on individual rights and was based on a particular narrative of the origins of government. Other historians who have analyzed colonial conceptions of liberty in some depth, including Michael Kammen (1986), John Phillip Reid (1987), and David Hackett Fischer (1989), have highlighted the importance of various inherited British understandings of liberty, although only Fischer included a spiritual conception in Massachusetts that Appleby, Kammen, and Reid ignored.[37]

Occasioned by the Death of the Reverend Jonathan Mayhew, 39; *Appeal to the Public Answered*, 200; *Discourse Occasioned by the Death of the Reverend Thomas Foxcroft*, 23; *Reply to Dr. Chandler's "Appeal Defended*,*"* 163; *Twelve Sermons*, 230, citing Luke 4:18, and 294, citing Jas 1:25. For "Christian liberty"/"freedom of Christians," see, for example, Chauncy, *Seasonable Thoughts*, 67, 236, citing Bolton, *Some Generall Directions*, 48; *Validity of Presbyterian Ordination*, 107; *Letter to a Friend, Containing Remarks*, 41, 47–48, 53; *Appeal to the Public Answered*, 204; *Discourse Occasioned by the Death of the Reverend Thomas Foxcroft*, 24. For "Gospel-liberty," see *Seasonable Thoughts*, 235, citing Flavel, *Whole Works*, 1:634.

37. Joyce Appleby, *Capitalism and a New Social Order*, 15–22, esp. 19, 16, 15, 17, 20; Bailyn, *Ideological Origins*; Wood, *Creation of the American Republic*; Pocock,

Jonathan Clark (1994) placed religion front and center in his argument that the American Revolution was essentially "a rebellion by groups within Protestant Dissent against an Anglican hegemony." This was, he contended, "a religious and civil war," in which revolutionary Americans primarily conceived and expressed the freedom from hegemonic British power structures which they sought in terms of religious and legal discourses. But there are no indexed references to, still less precise definitions of, what Clark actually meant by "liberty" in his massively revisionist *Language of Liberty*. In the same year, Barry Shain offered an extended "introductory typology" of "the meaning of liberty in the revolutionary era." Building on the work of previous scholars, including Miller (1953), Hatch (1977), Noll (1977), and Stout (1986), Shain also made the bold and unprecedented claim that "spiritual liberty" was actually "Revolutionary-era Americans' most fundamental understanding." Shain's "typology" was grounded in similar attempts at definition by earlier writers and he discerned "eight different meanings of liberty available in 18th-century America." They included "philosophical (freedom of the will), political, spiritual (or Christian), prescriptive, familial (economic independence or autonomy), natural, civil, and individualistic (modern individual autonomy)."[38]

The central thrust of Shain's argument was that instead of being "accurately characterized as predominantly individualistic or . . . classically republican," the "vast majority of [eighteenth-century] Americans lived voluntarily in morally demanding agricultural communities shaped by reformed-Protestant social and moral norms." Through a comprehensive analysis of different understandings of liberty, he also contended that

---

Machiavellian Moment; Fischer, *Albion's Seed*, esp. 199–205, passim; Kammen, *Spheres of Liberty*; Reid, *Concept of Liberty*. On general historiographical trends, see, further, Rodgers, "Republicanism"; Ward, *Politics of Liberty*. See also, Ferguson, "Dialectic of Liberty"; Ferguson, "Literature of Public Documents." A significant scholar to argue more recently that "the late colonial gentry" were neither "bearers of a 'reactionary' liberty nor a 'progressive' one, but . . . essentially adhered to the inherited, privilege-based meanings of liberty and equality paramount in the British world during the century preceding 1764" was Rozbicki ("Between Private and Public Spheres," esp. 294). Rozbicki has since more fully expounded his views in *Culture and Liberty*.

38. Jonathan Clark, *Language of Liberty*, 5, 41; Shain, *Myth of American Individualism*, 151–319, esp. 193, 153, 169, 178–81. For earlier attempts to define spiritual and religious conceptions of liberty in New England, see, for example, Perry Miller, *New England Mind: from Colony to Province*, esp. 132, 168, 171, 377; Hatch, *Sacred Cause of Liberty*, esp. 46–47, 50–51, 63; Noll, *Christians in the American Revolution*, esp. 52–56, 150, 172–73; Stout, *New England Soul*, esp. 296–99, on "liberty's double meaning." See also Noll, *America's God*, 53–92, passim, 214–16, for more recent summaries of Noll's views on connections between Christianity and republicanism, including ideas of liberty.

"spiritual liberty," which freed Christians "from absolute servitude to sin and the necessity of adhering to the tenets of Mosaic law," ultimately "set the standard by which other forms of liberty were judged." This was essential to revolutionary ideology, because "from a reformed-Protestant perspective, only spiritual liberty could prepare a person to exercise corporate political liberty." In that sense, neither a lofty vision of classical republicanism nor the pursuit of individual rights as ends in themselves were major forces behind the revolutionary quest for independence, Shain argued. "As a largely Christian and overwhelmingly rural people, Americans instead understood politics as instrumental in the services of higher religious and other publicly defined goals."[39]

The evidence for Shain's conceptual "typology" is sporadic, and his work is open to criticism on other grounds. But it continues to raise the significant question whether his prioritization of spiritual liberty was justified by the available evidence. In the case of Chauncy and especially of Mayhew, who has so often been linked with debates about the causal significance of religious motivations for revolutionary thought and action, it is significant to note that it was so justified. Even when they advocated overtly political notions of freedom, these two prominent New England Congregationalist leaders primarily conceived liberty in terms that were explicitly biblical in origin and orientation. Their discourse of liberty displays strong evidence of intellectual continuity with that of their Puritan forebears. For Chauncy and Mayhew, spiritual liberty to serve God and neighbor was primary. To what extent other eighteenth-century American leaders shared their conviction remains to be explored, but their examples indicate the potential importance of that exploration.[40]

---

39. Shain, *Myth of American Individualism*, xvi, 193, 212, 272. Shain also defined "spiritual" or "Christian" liberty as "the relative freedom that a Christian enjoyed through Christ from sin and from the necessity of obeying the Mosaic law" (ibid., 180). It was thus an inherently religious and theological concept, traditionally understood in terms of reformed doctrinal statements like the *Westminster Confession* and based on a Puritan understanding of spiritual liberty as what Winthrop called "a liberty to [do] that only which is good, just, and honest" ("Speech to the General Court," 207). This was also combined, Shain contended, with a view, that "godly living by all was a necessary [and publicly enforceable] social standard by which to measure the public good" (*Myth of American Individualism*, 204).

40. Among reviews of Shain, *The Myth of American Individualism,* see Bergman, Review; Bonomi, Review; Zuckert, Review. See Oakes, "Conservative Revolutionaries," 198–205, for analysis of the ideas of liberty held by Mayhew's Boston ministerial colleague, Andrew Eliot, which shows that he similarly prioritized "spiritual" over other definitions of liberty.

— 7 —

Resolving the Big Issue

Submission or Revolution?

ON THE EVENING OF August 26, 1765, amid the gathering storm of the Stamp Act crisis, a crowd gathered at the Boston house of Lieutenant-Governor Hutchinson and proceeded to wreck it. According to an authoritative modern account, "they destroyed windows, doors, furniture, wainscoting, and paintings, and stole £900 in cash, as well as clothing and silverware. They cut down all the trees in the garden, beat down the partitions in the house and had even begun to remove the slate from the roof when daylight stopped them." The leader of the assault, Ebenezer McIntosh, was subsequently arrested, but released by the Sheriff as a result of political pressures. No one was ever formally charged or criminally convicted for the attack. But the influential minister of West Church subsequently sought to clear his name and clarify his position in response to accusations of complicity in the riot.[1]

Mayhew's alleged offense had been to preach a sermon the previous day on Galatians 5:12–13, in which he had so strongly urged his West Church congregation that "ye have been called unto liberty" that some decided to take the law into their own hands. Some years later, in his *History of the Province of Massachusetts Bay*, Hutchinson wrote that "the text alone, without a comment, delivered from the pulpit at that time, might be construed by some of the auditory into an approbation of the prevailing irregularities." He noted that "one, who had a chief hand in the outrages which soon followed, declared, when he was in prison, that he was excited to them by this sermon, and that he thought he was doing God service." Hutchinson also thought that if Mayhew had paid more attention to the second half of Galatians 5:13, including the instruction to "use not liberty for an occasion

---

1. Morgan and Morgan, *Stamp Act Crisis*, 133, 134–35.

to the flesh," this "would have been sufficient to have kept the people within bounds." When prominent parishioner, the merchant Richard Clarke, took offense at his sermon of August 25, Mayhew defended himself as "no encourager of mobs and riots," but acknowledged that Clarke was not alone in representing his discourse "in that odious light." [2]

Mayhew's letter to Clarke is one of four extant documents which Bailyn rightly interpreted as testimony to his efforts "to bring back into balance a reputation he felt had been grotesquely distorted." The others included the "Memorandum" of the offending sermon, a letter to Hutchinson of August 27, 1765, and his last published discourse, *Snare Broken*, delivered at West Church on May 23, 1766, after the Stamp Act's repeal. Mayhew had long and consistently defended the right of rebellion against unjust authorities. His most famous early sermon was devoted to that theme and he continually opposed "unlimited submission." But Mayhew's eagerness to reject any charge that he had personally encouraged lawlessness of any kind after the riot at Hutchinson's house raises interesting questions about how much he was ultimately prepared to sanction practically what he advocated theoretically. Similar issues arise in the case of the politically less militant Chauncy, especially after earlier acts of rebellion like the Stamp Act riots were followed by widespread revolution from 1776.[3]

This chapter will closely examine Mayhew's and Chauncy's views on rebellion and revolution. It will consider how ready they were to translate such opinions into action when faced with the reality, and not just the

---

2. Hutchinson, *History of the Province of Massachusetts Bay*, 123n; Mayhew, "Letter of Rev. Jonathan Mayhew to Richard Clarke, 1765," 19. Akers cited a letter of September 5, 1765 to Archbishop Secker in London, in which Henry Caner, who was then Rector of King's Chapel, Boston, took an even more aggressive view of Mayhew's sermon: "Dr Mayhew has distinguished himself in the pulpit on this Occasion (it is said) in One of the most seditious Sermons ever delivered, advising the people to stand up for their rights to the last drop of their Blood" (*Called unto Liberty*, 205). See also Caner and Cameron, *Letter-book*, 123.

3. Bailyn, "Religion and Revolution," 111–24, 140–43, passim, esp. 115; Mayhew, "Memorandum"; letter to Hutchinson, August 27, 1765, in Bradford, *Memoir*, 420–22; *MP* 91; *Snare Broken*. At the time of writing, Mullins was about to publish an article on Mayhew's controversial sermon entitled "The Sermon That Didn't Start the Revolution." According to Zachary McLeod Hutchins, in a pre-released editorial introduction to the collection in which it was to appear, "while he acknowledges that Mayhew promoted Whig ideology during his tenure in the pulpit, Mullins effectively decouples this prominent preacher from the 1765 violence against royal officials by providing an alternative explanation for the origins and motives of the mob that attacked Hutchinson and by documenting Mayhew's insistence on the duty of restraint in effecting political change. The ritual gathering of Mayhew's nouveau riche congregation did not lead to the coarse behavior and wanton demolition of the Hutchinson mob, Mullins argues, much less the American Revolution" (*Community without Consent*, xv).

possibility, of resisting established authority. It will conclude that attempts by modern historians to claim that Mayhew, who died in 1766, was a proto-revolutionary, while inevitably somewhat anachronistic, have some justification. Yet when his revolutionary ardor was put to the test practically in the aftermath of the Stamp Act riots, what Heimert aptly described as his "aversions to [civil] violence, revivals, awakenings, and popular enthusiasm" combined with his desire to avoid personal disgrace to quench it. Although he paid much less attention to the question in his earlier writings, Chauncy shared Mayhew's commitment to the right to rebel against unjust rulers. When forced to face the realities of putting political theory into practice, he eventually endorsed the American Revolution. But he did so only after some hesitation and neither as early nor as enthusiastically as scholars have sometimes claimed. He also continued to show ambivalence about the consequences. Even after he reached the conclusion that Protestant, British constitutional principles and structures actually justified such a rebellion, he remained troubled, as Mayhew was during the Stamp Act crisis, by the notion of rejecting imperial authority. Both ministers' inherently providentialist understanding of violent conflict, as of world affairs in general, militated against uncritical support for any party, whatever their personal loyalties, especially when allied with their tendency to view all political issues through a biblical and theological lens.[4]

Mayhew and "Unlimited Submission"

Mayhew first and most notably advocated the right of resistance in *Discourse Concerning Unlimited Submission* (1750), where he drew quite heavily on Whig sources (see page 155). In that sense, his sermon taught what Bailyn justly described as "commonplaces of Whig thought," although such principles were also part of his New England Congregationalist heritage. Mayhew's conclusions were based on quite detailed exegesis of a biblical passage, often interpreted to commend civil obedience. His conventional summary of key points of doctrine in Romans 13:1–8 has already been cited (see pages 167–8). As he expounded his text in more depth, he came to two further conclusions that facilitated a less submissive approach to unjust rulers. Considering the "nature" of the apostle Paul's argument for "the duty of submission to the higher powers," he found a crucial limitation:

> we shall find it to be such an one as concludes not in favor
> of submission to all who bear the title of rulers, in common;

---

4. Heimert, *Religion and the American Mind*, 291.

but only, to those who actually perform the duty of rulers, by exercising a reasonable and just authority, for the good of human society. This is a point which it will be proper to enlarge upon; because the question before us turns very much upon the truth or falshood [sic] of this position. It is obvious, then, in general, that the civil rulers whom the apostle here speaks of, and obedience to whom he presses upon christians as a duty, are good rulers, such as are, in the exercise of their office and power, benefactors to society.

In circumstances where civil authorities failed in such duties, therefore, they could no longer expect unqualified support. In fact, where they were guilty of obvious oppression and injustice, they did not have "the least pretence" to expect civil obedience.[5]

Mayhew's allegiance to Lockean principles has been clearly observed in his justification for resisting civil authority and in his prior assumption that "the true ground and reason of our obligation to be subject to the higher powers, is the usefulness of magistracy (when properly exercised) to human society, and its subserviency to the general welfare." At the same time, Mayhew so liberally quoted from, or at least alluded to, works by British Whigs that justifiable charges of plagiarism were made in the Boston press. But biblical theology shaped the main substance of his expository argument from Romans 13:1–8 and he paid keen attention to the passage's literary and historical context, which he interpreted to strengthen his case. Inasmuch as "there were some professed christians in the apostolic age, who disclaimed all magistracy and civil authority in general, despising government, and speaking evil of dignities," Mayhew contended that it was with "persons of this licentious opinion and character that the apostle" was "concerned . . . to show, that they were bound to submit to magistracy in general." Authorities deserving full civil obedience were "good rulers, such as are, in the exercise of their office and power, benefactors to society." But that did not include "common tyrants, and public oppressors," acting "in contradiction to the public good, and so to the design of their office."[6]

---

5. Bailyn, *Pamphlets*, 207; Mayhew, *Discourse Concerning Unlimited Submission*, 20, 22–23.

6. Mayhew, *Discourse Concerning Unlimited Submission*, 10–11, 18, 20, 29. See Lloyd Thomas, *Locke on Government*, 62–65; Locke, *Two Treatises*. *Boston Evening-Post*, April 16, 1750, 1–2, and April 23, 1750, 1–2, highlighted Mayhew's borrowings from Hoadly, offering line-by-line comparisons in parallel columns of passages from *Discourse Concerning Unlimited Submission*, "Preface," 5–7, 7–8, 14–16, 11, 32–33 with Hoadly, *Measures of Submission*, 11, 41, 53, 58–60, 3, 61. Bailyn also cited "the alleged plagiarism" of Coade, *Letter to a Clergyman*, 33–35, in *Discourse Concerning Unlimited Submission*, 45–46, and a further claim of "reliance" on Milton (*Pamphlets*, 697–98).

Mayhew's support for resistance against a tyrannical Charles I was buttressed by his unconditional rejection of Filmerian doctrines of kingship by "divine right," which he found "altogether as fabulous and chimerical, as transubstantiation; or any of the most absurd reveries of ancient or modern visionaries." It was preposterous to speak of violent opposition to or even the dethronement of such a king as "criminal," for such conduct was "but a reasonable way of vindicating . . . liberties and just rights." This was rather a case of "making use of the means, and the only means, which God has put into their power, for mutual and self-defense." The overthrow of Charles could not even be called "rebellion," because "resistance was absolutely necessary in order to preserve the nation from slavery, misery, and ruin." In that sense, the only explanation that Mayhew could offer for the "mysterious doctrine of king Charles's saintship and martyrdom" and related celebrations on January 30 was ultimately the self-interest of the English established church. The king had been "a good churchman" and "a lover . . . of the hierarchy" and he became a martyr, because he "died an enemy to liberty and the rights of conscience," as well as to "dissenters." Thankfully, in 1750, New Englanders were not being asked to submit to such a tyrant, but to "a PRINCE [in King George II] who is satisfied with ruling according to law."[7]

In her dissertation on eighteenth-century Massachusetts election sermons, Martha Counts argued that the defense of resistance against unjust rulers became a growing trend from the mid-1750s through the 1770s. Certain tenets thus became widely accepted by 1776, not least that

> The people had a right to judge for themselves whether or not they were being oppressed; it was their duty to complain of these oppressions; if they received no relief, then they were obliged to stand up and fight. Both the law of self-preservation and their commitment to pursue the common good required the people to do this. If they were to obey the magistrate to further the happiness of society, they had to resist when the magistrate invaded their rights and liberties and perverted the ends of government.

But Counts also showed how the people's "right to resist tyranny and oppression stemmed from the theory" that ministers had expounded in sermons of the first half of the eighteenth century. Mayhew's comments on

---

Discourse Concerning Unlimited Submission attracted further attention and controversy in the press in the February 19, February 26, March 12, March 19, April 2, May 21, June 18, and July 9, 1750, issues of the *Boston Evening-Post*, as well as in the February 27, March 13, and March 20, 1750, editions of the *Boston Gazette,* and in the March 1 and March 22, 1750, issues of the *Boston Weekly News-Letter.*

7. Mayhew, *Discourse Concerning Unlimited Submission,* 35, 40, 44–45, 52, 54.

the theme in *Sermon Preach'd* (1754) were relatively restrained compared with sentiments expressed in *Discourse Concerning Unlimited Submission* (1750), but he continued to defend non-submission vigorously. His main homiletic purposes were the traditional ones of addressing "the source and origin of civil power" and "the great end of government." He accordingly stated that "some of those arguments, by which those who are vested with authority, should be induced to exercise it with fidelity" and concluded with "some reflections, chiefly relative to this Anniversary, and to the present state of the Province." But even as he stressed the difficulty of mentioning "any duty which the gospel inculcates upon the consciences of men, with greater solemnity, than that of paying due honour to Kings, and all that are in authority," he repeated, if more implicitly, a familiar qualification:

> as in all free constitutions of government, law, and not will, is the measure of the executive Magistrate's power; so it is the measure of the subject's obedience and submission. The consequence of which, I shall at present leave others to draw; only observing, that it is very strange we should be told, at this time of day, that loyalty and slavery mean the same thing; tho' this is plainly the amount of that doctrine which some, even now, have the forehead to ventilate, in order to bring a reproach upon the Revolution, upon the present happy settlement of the crown, and to prepare us for the dutiful reception of an hereditary Tyrant.[8]

Based on the Lockean and, he thought, biblical principle of submission to rulers who govern lawfully, and not arbitrarily, Mayhew thus went out of his way to defend the Glorious Revolution of 1688, as well as the Puritan Revolution of the mid-seventeenth century, and to warn against Jacobite forces seeking to re-impose a Catholic Stuart dynasty. Similar preoccupations emerge in other works. While mourning the death of Frederick, Prince of Wales, in 1751, and taking occasion to warn his hearers against placing undue trust in any human ruler, Mayhew nonetheless praised the recently departed prince for having those qualities that properly entitled him to popular allegiance. It was the prince's "good sense," as well as his lineage, that fostered his anti-Catholicism, Mayhew thought, and so "attached him firmly to the protestant interest, and a limited monarchy; such as our own." Seven years later, giving thanks for the victories of Protestant forces in

---

8. Counts, "Political Views," 123–27, esp. 127, 123; Mayhew, *Sermon Preach'd*, 3, 20–21. Among the most prominent other ministers to defend resistance against unjust rulers from the mid-1750s through the mid-1770s, Counts listed Andrew Eliot in 1765, Samuel Cooke in 1770, John Tucker in 1771, Charles Turner in 1773, and Samuel West in 1776, citing Eliot, *Sermon Preached*; Cooke, *Sermon Preached*; John Tucker, *Sermon Preached*; Turner, *Sermon Preached*; West, *Sermon Preached*.

the Seven Years' War, he took a similar opportunity to remind those present of the "melancholly experience" that had resulted from "two princes of the Stewart race." It was their "arbitrary principles and practices, naturally, if not necessarily connected with their religion," which "plainly shew'd that one of the greatest curses righteous heaven can send upon Great Britain, is a romancatholic [sic] King." Mayhew thus saw their forceful removal as an act of God, who "delivered the nation" not only "from the contemptible, tho' royal race above-mentioned," but from the prospect of groaning under "the iron scepter of a confirmed, lawless despotism, and the antichristian yoke of religious persecution."[9]

Mayhew returned to the subject with a more thorough exposition of recent British history in his sermon following the death of King George II in 1760. Here, as elsewhere, his theological perspective was markedly providentialist. God was the ruler "in the kingdom of men, as he gives to the reign of earthly kings either a shorter or longer term, as seemeth good in his sight." In Mayhew's survey of English kings and queens after the death of Elizabeth I, he thus saw "four princes" coming "successively to the throne," whose reigns were "sore visitations of divine providence." James II had represented the culmination of this evil succession—"an open, professed and bigotted roman-catholic; who stuck at no measures in order to introduce the religion of Rome, to despoil the British nations of their ancient liberties, and to entail upon them the two-fold curse of popery and slavery." Charles I had already "involved the nation in a civil war," which had only yielded a positive outcome when many of his subjects had risen up "in defence of public liberty." After the 1660 restoration of the monarchy under Charles II, the pernicious theory of "passive obedience and non-resistance had . . . been . . . the established doctrine, which no one could contradict with impunity." Thankfully, "the brave people who had lately made such efforts in defence of their liberties, would not now tamely submit to arbitrary sway; but again have recourse to some extraordinary means of self-defence." As a result, and by the direct interposition of divine grace, "the glorious REVOLUTION took place," with the accession of William of Orange, "a true protestant and an hero." Mayhew clearly saw such events as a living vindication of his and others' refusal to endorse the kind of "unlimited submission" against which he had spoken so powerfully ten years earlier. God had validated the right of resistance against unjust rulers, ensuring that despite "the repeated efforts of tyranny," "glorious struggles for liberty" had met with success in Britain.[10]

9. Mayhew, *Sermon Preached at Boston*, 29; *Two Discourses Delivered November 23d. 1758*, 10–11.

10. Mayhew, *Discourse Occasioned by the Death of King George II*, 18, 23–26, 29.

As he reflected on "the Success of His Majesty's Arms MORE ESPECIALLY In the intire Reduction of CANADA," Mayhew saw the same providential progress taking place in a wider international context in 1760. He was persuaded not only that God would "at length in a most wonderful manner bring down, humble, and even destroy, that corrupt and apostate, that idolatrous and persecuting church" of Rome, but would facilitate "the establishing of christianity thro-out the world." Such a millennial vision of the global triumph of Protestantism was clearly an inspiration to Mayhew. In correspondence with the English Whig Hollis, both paid keen attention to the signs of the times, as they fretted, for example, about the growth of Catholicism in England. But they also lauded past champions of Protestant liberty, to whom they acknowledged their present indebtedness. For Hollis, as for Mayhew, "unlimited submission" made no sense in the face of despotism. In the case of "a King becoming a Tyrant," like Charles I, Hollis preferred what he understood to be "Milton's principles," which justified his punishment and replacement with a new form of government. Mayhew predictably endorsed such a view, describing the Puritan poet-philosopher's political ideas as thankfully prevalent in New England.[11]

One of Mayhew's major challenges, when faced with the attempted enforcement of the Stamp Act in 1765, was thus that the same British authorities, whose praises he had been singing throughout his ministerial career as champions of the cause of Protestant liberty against Catholic tyranny, now seemed to threaten the freedoms of New England itself. In early August of that year, he reported to Hollis general colonial distress, as well as his personal struggle with the harshness and harmfulness of the new British taxation measures. He also wrote somewhat conspiratorially of the potential dangers of mercantile "slavery" and of a corresponding duty to act in the interests of liberty. Eleven days later, his reportage was much more dramatic. He informed Hollis of the colonists' view of the Stamp Act and related powers as grievously oppressive and almost tyrannical. He described the Boston protests in August 1765, when a mocking effigy of Provincial Secretary Oliver was put on public display, paraded through the streets, and burned—he had been suspected of being a supporter and financial beneficiary of the Stamp Act, along with Lieutenant Governor Hutchinson. Mayhew reported how rioters had "demolished" a new building intended

---

11. Mayhew, *Two Discourses Delivered October 9th, 1760*, title page, 53–54; Mayhew to Thomas Hollis, December 18, 1764, in Mayhew and Hollis, "Thomas Hollis and Jonathan Mayhew," 161–64, esp. 163; Hollis to Mayhew, October 10, 1764, in ibid., 157–58, esp. 158; Hollis to Mayhew, December 6, 1763, in ibid. 142–44, esp, 143; Hollis to Mayhew, August 27, 1760, 114–17, esp. 116–17; Mayhew to Hollis, March 19, 1761, in ibid., 118–20, esp. 118.

to serve as a "Stamp-Office" and attacked Oliver's house. A week before this action took place, he noted that Hutchinson himself had narrowly escaped a similar fate and warned that he anticipated no possible enforcement of the act, except "at the point of the Sword." Mayhew still felt able to assure Hollis that there was no colonial desire for independence, but he clearly implied that this might change, and he worried about the possible consequences which could "prove very fatal to both" parties.[12]

Given how strongly he felt about the injustices of the Stamp Act, it is not surprising that Mayhew decided to throw himself publicly into the debate. He already had a considerable record as a controversialist. But the way that he chose to do so, advertising in advance, according to Hutchinson, that he would be preaching "a political discourse" on Sunday, August 25, was bound to draw attention. And what remains of the sermon, in the form of the incomplete "Memorandum" prepared by Mayhew after the fact, clearly suffices to explain why his discourse might have proved incendiary, despite his protestations. The opening sections are rather dry, even technical in places, addressing finer exegetical points before outlining his six-fold definition of "liberty" (see page 187). But Mayhew's remarks on civil liberty, while also quite theoretical and even abstract to start, soon gather pace and force as they become more specific. "The essence of civil liberty does not consist in, or depend upon, the number of persons, by whom a nation is governed," he argued, "but in their being governed by such persons & laws, as they approve of." By contrast:

> the essence of slavery consists in being subjected to the arbitrary pleasure of others; whether many, few, or but one, it matters not. Still people are real slaves, not in a state of civil liberty, if they approve neither the persons nor laws, by which they are governed, but are obliged to submit to them contrary to their will.[13]

Then Mayhew suddenly and somewhat uncomfortably brought matters closer to home. "People of the same nation may be in very different circumstances with respect to civil liberty," he contended, "some of them enjoying it in as high a degree as can be desired, while others are in a state

---

12. Mayhew to Hollis, August 8, 1765, in ibid., 172–74, esp. 173; August 19, 1765, in ibid., 174–76, esp. 175–76.

13. Bailyn, "Religion and Revolution," 113, citing a letter from Hutchinson to East Apthorp of October 3, 1765; Mayhew, "Memorandum," 142. "Sunday the 25 of August," Hutchinson wrote, "notice being given that he was to preach a political discourse, he [Mayhew] had a crowded audience, which he entertained from this text, 'I would they were even cut off which trouble you for, brethren, ye have been called unto liberty.' Here he stopped, the remainder of the sentence not being to his purpose."

little or nothing better than that of slavery." And what exemplified such a state?

> As, for example, a mother country & her colonies. While she is free, it is supposeable that her colonies may be kept in a state of real slavery to her. For if they are to possess no property, nor to enjoy the fruits of their own labor, but by the mere precunious [sic] pleasure of the Mother, or of a distant legislature, in which they neither are, nor can be represented; this is really slavery, not civil liberty. Only slaves are bound to labor for the pleasure & profit of others; and to subsist merely on what their masters are pleased to allow them, tho' they may possibly have kind masters, who treat them with tenderness & humanity, still they are as really in a state of slavery, as those who have hard & cruel masters.

At this point in his "Memorandum," Mayhew obviously felt the need to give his argument some support. So he noted, parenthetically, that it was "agreeable to the reasonings of the most approved English writers on liberty."[14]

In his fourth section, considering the apostle Paul's injunction to "use not liberty for an occasion to the flesh," the West Church minister further emphasized restraint. "They also use liberty for an occasion to the flesh," he argued, "who under color of it disregard the wholesome laws of Society, made for the preservation of the order and common good thereof." Yet there remained a sting in the tail. "Then it was observed, that some people might perhaps say, as they truly might," Mayhew continued, "that a nation is sometimes actually abused by their rulers to a great degree; and treated as if the people were made only to be subservient to their pride, pleasure and profit." Such a situation was bound to raise questions, not least, "supposing this to be actually the case," the following, to which he gave a brief, but very provocative answer, before petering out altogether:

> the question was then proposed, Whether passive obedience and non-resistance were the duty of such a people; or Whether opposing such rulers, and the execution of unrighteous & oppressive laws, could properly be accounted using liberty for an occasion to the flesh? This was answered in the negative, for the following reasons . . . .[15]

"This was answered in the negative." In other words, a people "enslaved" by financially punitive laws that were not of their own making could

14. Mayhew, "Memorandum," 142.
15. Ibid., 143.

not, according to Mayhew, be justly accused of "using liberty for an occasion to the flesh" if they rebelled against the authorities imposing them. In such circumstances, "passive obedience and non-resistance" were not required. Given the obvious direction of the closing lines of Mayhew's account of his sermon, his decision not to leave a complete account of it is hardly surprising. Had he detailed his "reasons" for justifying civil disobedience or rebellion, he might only have strengthened the case of those who accused him of rabble-rousing and thus provoking the Boston crowd to follow through on earlier plans to attack Hutchinson's house. In that sense, the latter's view that Mayhew could have encouraged more restraint by paying more attention to the instruction to "use not liberty for an occasion to the flesh" seems misguided.[16]

Whatever the truth of the situation, Mayhew obviously connected the riot with his sermon. If he had not, it is difficult to see why he chose to write to Hutchinson on August 27, 1765 to distance himself from the attack. "God is my witness," he wrote, "that, from the bottom of my heart, I detest these proceedings." He had heard reports that some of his "numerous and causeless enemies" had "expressed themselves to-day, as if I approved of these doings; and had, indeed, encouraged them." Yet although he admitted strongly supporting "civil and religious liberty" and denouncing the Stamp Act, Mayhew was keen to assure Hutchinson that "as my text led me to do, I cautioned my hearers expressly against the abuses of liberty." Such were his concerns for scriptural obedience and public order, he informed the lieutenant governor, that "in truth, I had rather lose my right hand than be an encourager of such outrages as were committed last night." Mayhew went as far as to describe the assurances that he gave Hutchinson as "solemn declarations" made so "that though you may have heard something to my prejudice in this affair," the official might rest assured that "I have therein been misrepresented." He concluded with the assertion that "not a single person concerned in this outrage, or of their advisers, is known to me; nor am I a friend to any, farther than to wish them repentance." Hutchinson had heard otherwise, but the lieutenant governor personally indicated to Mayhew that he took him at his word. He "heard the talk of the town" on August 26, but "never doubted" Mayhew's "friendship." "I was sure you abhorred mobs and riots," he continued, "and had no other design than to preserve, in the minds of the people, a just sense of their liberties; and when something further was suggested, I remembered how often I had been misrepresented, aspersed, and injured myself." [17]

16. Ibid., 143; Hutchinson, *History of the Province of Massachusetts Bay*, 123n.
17. Mayhew to Hutchinson, August 27, 1765, in Bradford, *Memoir*, 420–22, esp.

Hutchinson certainly found more reassurance in Mayhew's protestations than West Church member Richard Clarke, although not for want of pastoral attention. Mayhew visited him twice before he left the congregation, and also sent a detailed explanation of his conduct in the form of a letter on September 3, 1765. He acknowledged in that document that Clarke was not alone in viewing his August 25 discourse as incendiary. He recognized that Clarke and his family had every right to leave his church and disavowed any intention to try to persuade them to return. But Mayhew still thought himself "bound as a christian, as far as I am able, when any one who was once a brother, is offended with me, to remove the ground of his uneasiness, and to give him all the satisfaction in my power." With that in mind, he now expressed some regret that he had preached "a sermon, the chief aim of which was to show the importance of Liberty, when people were before so generally apprehensive of the danger of losing it. They certainly needed rather to be moderated and pacified, than the contrary," he conceded, "And I would freely give all that I have in the world, rather than have preached that sermon." He also admitted that he had been provoked into action by popular complaints over ministerial "silence in the cause of liberty" and by allegations of cowardice "at a time when it was almost universally supposed, as it still is, that our common liberties and rights, as British subjects, were in the most imminent danger." Yet even though "the sermon itself . . . was composed in a high strain of liberty," he remained confident that "no person could, without abusing & perverting it, take encouragement from it to go to mobbing, or to commit such abominable outrages as were lately committed, in defiance of the laws of God and man." Why not? The minister's major defense was that he "did, in the most formal, express manner, discountenance everything of that kind."[18]

The main way in which Mayhew sought to dissociate himself from the charge of rabble-rousing was by quoting quite extensively, but also selectively, from his August 25 sermon, as reproduced in the subsequent "Memorandum." He began with the Lockean definition of "civil liberty" noted in the previous chapter. He then dwelt extensively on his exposition of the apostolic command to "use not liberty for an occasion to the flesh," understandably focusing on issues of politics and civil disobedience:

> They use liberty for an occasion to the flesh, who causelessly
> & maliciously speak evil of their rulers; endeavouring to make

421–22; Hutchinson, *History of the Province of Massachusetts-Bay*, 123; Hutchinson, undated letter to Mayhew, reprinted in Bradford, *Memoir*, 422.

18. Mayhew, "Letter of Rev. Jonathan Mayhew to Richard Clarke, 1765," 16–20, esp. 16–17.

> them appear odious or contemptible, or to weaken their influence, and proper authority, in their several stations. [Still more do] they use liberty for an occasion to the flesh, who cause factions or insurrection against the government, under which they live, and who rebel against, or resist their lawful rulers, in the due discharge of their offices. We ought to be subject, not only for wrath, or for fear of the wrath of man, but also for conscience sake. [For government was instituted by God for the good of man]. For this cause pay we tribute also, because civil [rulers] are the ministers of God to us for good, attending continually upon this very thing. We are bound to render unto Caesar the things that are Caesar's, as well as to God the things that are [his]. They [therefore], who rebel & resist, as aforesaid, resist the ordinance of God: And the apostle saith, they shall receive to themselves damnation.[19]

Inasmuch as Mayhew appealed directly here to texts from Romans 13 and Matthew 22, the scriptural, as well as Lockean, premises of his original argument were again inescapable. But he also cited materials not extant in his sermon "Memorandum." He noted that he had "charitably" expressed the hope that local leaders had not sought the provisions of the Stamp Act for financial gain. He said that he had decried the use of "any method, for the defence of our rights & privileges, besides those which are honest & honourable," and that he had ended his controversial sermon "with an ardent wish, that we and all his Majesty's subjects, 'thro'out his extended dominion, might lead quiet & peaceable lives in all godliness & honesty.'" In expostulating with Clarke, Mayhew stressed that he had not been reserved in expressing such views, either on August 25 or on September 1, when he had addressed the topic again at West Church in order to "exculpate" himself "in the most open & solemn manner." His concerns remained so grave that he was even prepared to consider a parliamentary statute as an act of "war" against Great Britain and its libertarian values, which he cherished:

> I still love liberty as much as ever; but have apprehensions of the greatest inconveniences likely to follow on a forceable, violent opposition to an act of parliament; which I consider, in some sort, as proclaiming war against Great Britain. These are the Sentiments of my soul, which I more particularly declared the

---

19. Mayhew, "Letter of Rev. Jonathan Mayhew to Richard Clarke, 1765," 17–18, citing from Rom 13:1–2, 4–5 and Matt 22:21. The words in brackets represent obvious additions to the text of Mayhew's "Memorandum," as reprinted in Bailyn, "Religion and Revolution," 140–43, esp. 143. Mayhew also reordered and paraphrased some of this text in his letter.

last Lord's day, in the fear of God, and with the deepest concern for the welfare of my country, and all the British Colonies, at this most alarming Crisis which they have ever known, whether they do or do not submit to said act. What the end of these things will be, God only knows. To him I lift up my soul for the common good, the public welfare.

Mayhew then ended his letter on a remarkably pastoral note. He prayed for the Clarkes' family situation, asking "God to make us all wiser & better by all that occurs to us in this varying & troublesome world; and finally to bring us to rejoice together in a better, notwithstanding any unhappy differences which have, or may arise between us here."[20]

Mayhew's attempt to separate himself from the seemingly violent consequences of his rhetoric, while continuing to uphold the right to resist unjust rulers, continued into his last published sermon, *Snare Broken* (1766). But there, as he celebrated the repeal of the Stamp Act, he was also able to return to less convoluted pro-British rhetoric. The work's laudatory dedication to William Pitt set the tone. On the basis of fundamental rights, Mayhew took it as read that the colonies had just cause to protest the act as "tending directly to reduce us to a state of slavery." In fact, he argued, "altho' the colonies could not justly claim an exclusive right of taxing themselves, and the right of being tried by juries; yet they had great reason to remonstrate against the act aforesaid on the footing of inexpedience, the great hardship, and destructive tendency of it; as a measure big with mischief to Britain, as well as to themselves."[21]

But if the injustice of the Stamp Act had justified New England's protests against it, Mayhew also retreated from some of his earlier, more militant views now that it had been repealed. The act had indeed been unconstitutional and unjust. There had been a "diversity of humours, sentiments and opinions among the colonists" in response to it, which "occasioned great animosities, mutual censures and reproaches." Mayhew told how "it was hardly safe for any man to speak his thoughts on the times, unless he could patiently bear to lie under the imputation of being a coward, an incendiary, rebel, or enemy to his country; or to have some other odium cast upon him." Since British taxation without representation of the American colonies was a form of slavery, whereby "those who were born free" were "made slaves," Mayhew saw repeal as an act of liberation which found its ultimate origin in divine providence. But he also now made clear that he did not consider the act's problems to have been so severe as to vindicate violent rebellion:

20. Mayhew, "Letter of Rev. Jonathan Mayhew to Richard Clarke, 1765," 18–19.
21. Mayhew, *Snare Broken*, iii–viii, 5–6.

> as to any methods of opposition to that measure, on the part of the colonies, besides those of humble petitioning, and other strictly legal ones, it will not, I conclude, be supposed, that I appear in this place as an advocate for them, whatever the general sense of the colonies may be concerning this point. And I take for granted, that we are all perfectly agreed in condemning the riotous and fellonious proceedings of certain men of Belial, as they have been justly called, who had the effrontery to cloke their rapacious violences with the pretext of zeal for liberty; which is so far from being a new thing under the sun, that even Great Britain can furnish us with many, and much more flagrant examples of it.[22]

In Mayhew's providentialist understanding of history, the repeal of the Stamp Act not only called for thanksgiving, it reinforced the need for civil obedience and respect. Longstanding concerns for the preservation of liberty were accordingly accompanied by standard biblical injunctions, drawn from 1 Peter 2:17, to "fear God" and "honor the king." Recent events had actually vindicated the British monarchy and Parliamentary system of government, not just lawful American protests. So there was no point in bearing grudges over past injustices. Mayhew hoped that there would now be "very few people, if any, in the colonies, who have the least inclination to renounce the general jurisdiction of Parliament over them, whatever we may think of the particular right of taxation." If future problems should arise, there were legal remedies available:

> The colonists are men, and need not be afraid to assert the natural rights of men; they are British subjects, and may justly claim the common rights, and all the privileges of such, with plainness and freedom. And from what has lately occurred, there is reason to hope, that the Parliament will ever hereafter be willing to hear and grant our just requests; especially if any grievances should take place, so great, so general and alarming, as to unite all the colonies in petitioning for redress, as with one voice.

In the meantime, Mayhew argued, his hearers should focus on "leading in a prudent, temperate, wise behaviour" and to pursue the "duty of cultivating a close harmony with our mother-country," as well as "a dutiful submission to the King and Parliament, our chief grievances being redressed."[23]

---

22. Mayhew, *Snare Broken*, 19–20, 14, 12, 7, with allusions to 2 Cor 6:15, 1 Pet 2:16, and Eccl 1:9.

23. Mayhew, *Snare Broken*, 23–27, esp. 26–27, 33, 34. See, further, 44.

It should not be concluded from this counsel, however, that Mayhew did not think it necessary to act to preserve New England's rights and freedoms whenever they were threatened. It was precisely such a concern that led to his poetic tribute to liberty as a "celestial Maid, the daughter of God" (see page 198). But after this outburst, Mayhew's conclusion was much more mundane. He bemoaned the "many unwarrantable jealousies, and bitter mutual reproaches among the people of this town and province" and the fact that some were "blamed as too warm and sanguine, others as too phlegmatic and indifferent, in the common and noble cause of liberty." He also called upon his congregation to pursue the "most prudent, most christian" course of action and "to begin our civil, political life anew as it were, from this joyful and glorious aera of restored and confirmed liberty." Diligence in everyday duties and support for "lawful, constitutional government" thus became paramount. In such ways, *Snare Broken* can justly be characterized, in Bailyn's terms, as "a statement of the social limitations of radical Whig thought" resting on the clear assumption that "a stable social order was the counterpart of political freedom and that a reform of politics need not be associated with social upheaval." Yet because it contributed to Mayhew's quest to clear himself of responsibility for the social unrest following his sermon the previous year, *Snare Broken* (1766) also highlights significant tensions.[24]

On the one hand, Mayhew was firmly committed to the right of resistance against unjust rulers. On the other, he shied away from the consequences when a public furor threatened his own reputation. On the one hand, he was convinced that the rights and liberties enshrined in the unwritten British constitution themselves implied a right of rebellion that justified civil unrest. On the other, he was so troubled by perceived contradictions between constitutional principles and recent government actions that he was prompted to describe the taxation measure as nothing less than an act of "war" against Britain itself. On the one hand, he saw the repeal of the Stamp Act as a providential act of divine deliverance and thus cause for thanksgiving. On the other, he not only viewed the government which had imposed such repressive measures as deserving of civil obedience, he leapt to interpret the act's repeal as a living vindication of the British system of governance.

Evidently, while Mayhew valued a right of resistance in principle and he prized key historical instances of its exercise, he was much more ambivalent when confronted by the harsh realities of its implementation in New England and beyond. Moreover, his struggle was as much philosophical as it was personal, and the question that he found most difficult was the same

---

24. Mayhew, *Snare Broken*, 36, 39–41, 43; Bailyn, "Religion and Revolution," 121.

as that faced by Chauncy during the American Revolution. When allegiance to British constitutional liberties was so foundational to his political worldview, how could he justify rebellion against metropolitan authorities for infringing on rights for which they had served, in his view, as the principal guarantors?

"A Zealous Whig, than Wilkes More Big"?

On May 1, 1770, Chauncy attended an unusual meeting of the Harvard Board of Overseers. He had belonged to this body for most of the forty-three years since he had become a minister at First Church, but it is doubtful whether he had ever been present in more unusual circumstances. Exactly twenty months earlier, in the mounting crisis over resistance to fresh imperial taxation measures following the repeal of the Stamp Act, a thousand British troops had marched into Boston, to be followed, in November 1768, by others who filled the barracks at Castle William. British ships began to patrol the harbor in an attempt to secure a free flow of imports despite a local non-importation agreement. Bostonians understandably chafed under an effective state of military occupation, and, encouraged by more radical groups like the "Sons of Liberty," opposition to Britain's commercial policies grew steadily. A major crisis finally erupted in early 1770, with the tragic events of the Boston Massacre on March 5, when British soldiers fired on a Boston crowd, killing five people. In an attempt to ease political tensions, Hutchinson, by now elevated to the position of governor, had relocated meetings of the Massachusetts General Court from the Boston Town House to Harvard the previous summer. His initial intention had been to return the winter session of 1770 to Boston, but for strategic and political reasons, he was persuaded otherwise.[25]

This delay annoyed some members of the College Board of Overseers, including Chauncy and his colleague at Brattle Street Church, Samuel Cooper, who moved a provocative motion at its May 1 meeting. The resolution would have declared the legislators' residency in Harvard an "Infringement" of the "rights of this Corporation," as well as the cause of significant inconvenience to both faculty and students. Chauncy and Cooper's motion was eventually defeated, but only following "a large Debate," after which Hutchinson himself cast the deciding vote in the negative. A clearer

---

25. On the Boston Massacre, see esp. York, *Boston Massacre*, esp. 3–47. According to Harvard University. *Historical Register*, 13–18 passim, Chauncy was an active Harvard Overseer in the following years: 1728–46, 1748–49, 1751–57, 1759–62, 1764, 1768–70, 1775–76, and 1779.

indication of the strength of feeling at the college then emerged with the passage of a similar resolution by Harvard's other major governing body, the Corporation, expressing "deep concern" over the same issue. Growing opposition to British measures was also reflected in the May provincial election, which resulted in virtually unanimous support for leading Boston Whigs. Hutchinson persisted with his plans to open the General Court at Cambridge on May 30, where an official election sermon was preached by Samuel Cooke of Cambridge. But Boston held its own solemnities, including an unofficial sermon by Chauncy, which has already been noted for its cautious focus on moral improvement in difficult times.[26]

The Boston Massacre was "so shocking a tragedy," Chauncy told those assembled to hear *Trust in God* (1770), as "was never before acted in this part of the world; and GOD forbid it should ever be again!" The relocation of the colonial government to Cambridge "from this its ancient and constitutional seat" caused feelings which obstructed "the motions of that joy, which, upon this occasion, used to be pure and unalloyed." Yet Chauncy could still "bow the knee in humble grateful acknowledgments to the supreme Ruler of the world, that we are not deprived of our RIGHT, in virtue of the ROYAL GRANT, to chuse councellers [*sic*] from among ourselves, whatever representations have been made to those in power, at Home, tending to wrest from us this invaluable right." He observed that "Tis certainly the truth of the fact, however the right of taxation be determined, that we are in a perplext situation." But he eschewed "going out my line, by entering upon a political consideration of what may be thought the true source of those difficulties which make the present, a day of trouble." Instead, he urged continued loyalty to "King and country" even in the face of commercial imperialism and military oppression. Chauncy also appealed, in *Trust in God*, to a singular historical example of resistance to unjust imperial authority that had been vindicated:

> Our fathers, even after they had, in a good measure, subdued this wilderness-country, enlarging their borders, increasing in numbers, and in a plenty of the comforts of life, and, at the same time, adding strength and glory to the British crown, were hardly dealt with by those who had the government in their hands. Their charter rights were trampled upon, and arbitrary methods taken to dispose of their lands, and make them slaves to those who had it in view to tyranize over them. But, as they trusted in God, he made bare his arm for their deliverance. This he did by effecting a glorious revolution in England; glorious in this, among other

26. On the Harvard Board of Overseers' meeting and its immediate background, see Akers, *Divine Politician*, 101–7, esp. 106.

respects, that it changed the line of the Regal succession, settling it on her Electoral Highness, the Princess SOPHIA Dutchess of Hanover, the only remaining PROTESTANT branch of the old royal family, and the heirs of her body, being PROTESTANTS.

In making this appeal to what was widely construed as a peculiar triumph of divine deliverance in the history of New England's Protestant progress, Chauncy was clearly seeking to encourage his hearers as they faced their own challenges. But he was also referring to a theme of civil resistance that, while less frequent in his works than in those of the more belligerent Mayhew, had been evident since at least the 1740s.[27]

An earlier sermon to feature similarly pro-Protestant sentiment while equally harking back to the history of the Glorious Revolution in Britain and New England was *Counsel of Two Confederate Kings* (1746). Chauncy devoted about half of this discourse on Isaiah 7:5–7, which he directly applied to "the Present REBELLION in Favour of the Pretender," to political issues surrounding the 1745–6 uprising led by Charles Edward Stuart, popularly known as Bonnie Prince Charlie. He argued that the accession of Charles's father James to the British throne would lead to the destruction of both English civil and religious liberties under a despotic Catholic king who could only be expected to rule "with a Rod of Iron." The obvious historical parallel was the reign of the "Pretender's" father, James II, in the previous century, when "he took such large Steps, under the Influence of popish and despotic Principles, that, in a few years, he went a great way" towards establishing Catholic tyranny. The "ill Effects" of that king's policies had clearly been seen in New England, where "our Fathers . . . groaned under the oppressive Burden of his popish and tyrannical Power." "By his insupportable Tyranny," Governor Edmund Andros had, in fact, "occasion'd" nothing less than "a REVOLUTION here; not altogether unlike that which was effected, some Months before, by the glorious King WILLIAM." And Chauncy was as lavish as Mayhew in praise of William and Mary and the Protestant succession that had now led to the reign of "his present Majesty King GEORGE the Second," who was "the only support and Hope, under God, of our happy Constitution, and the invaluable Advantages accruing to us from it, both as Englishmen and Protestants."[28]

Just over a year later, in his election sermon, *Civil Magistrates* (1747), Chauncy presented his fairly conventional political theory (see pages 177–8). But he again found occasion, when addressing the duty of rulers to "take

---

27. Chauncy, *Trust in God*, 35, 32–33, 24, 15–19.

28. Chauncy, *Counsel of Two Confederate Kings*, title page, 23–24, esp. 24, 26–27, 28, 35–6.

all proper care to preserve entire the civil rights of a people," to highlight the "arbitrary reign of king JAMES the second" as an example of "danger" from "those in the highest station." When faced with his despotism, Chauncy observed that "those entrusted with the guardianship of the nation's rights were spirited to take such measures, as issued in that revolution, and establishment of the succession, on which his present majesty's claim to the British throne is dependent." He also expressed the ardent wish that "the same spirit, which settled it there, prevail in the rulers of the English nation, so long as the sun and moon shall endure!" As in earlier sermons, Chauncy clearly, if sometimes only implicitly, supported the right of resistance against unjust rulers. He did not explore the theoretical foundations for that view until events surrounding the Stamp Act and its repeal prompted him to do so. But when he finally came to reflect on such issues in *Discourse on "The Good News"* (1766), he showed more caution, both in tone and content, than Mayhew.[29]

The celebratory, Anglophile, and royalist tenor of this discourse has already been noted. Chauncy was keen to stress that "the REPEAL, of which we have had authentic accounts, has opened the channels for a full flow of our former affection towards our brethren in Great-Britain," and he expressed that generously. But he also acknowledged the earlier damage done by the Stamp Act, which had given rise to "a general suspicion" of British authorities, and to a "jealousie" that "might have gradually brought on an alienation of heart, that would have been greatly detrimental to them, as it would also have been to ourselves." Chauncy openly deplored "mobish actions" like "the outrage at Lieut. Governor HUTCHINSON's house," but he had mixed feelings about the prospect of open resistance raised by the Stamp Act. On the one hand, he clearly recognized the principle, exemplified in the Glorious Revolution, that "there may be such exercise of power, and in instances of such a nature, as to render non-submission warrantable upon the foot of reason and righteousness." He also conceded that "the Colonists generally and really thought . . . it [the Stamp Act] might be opposed without their incurring the guilt of disloyalty or rebellion." On the other hand, he refused to pass judgment on the morality or legality of such opposition and he obviously deemed the ultimate criteria for justifiable resistance, even against British authority, to be defined by English constitutional standards. So he contended that "none, I believe, who are the friends of liberty, will deny, that it [resistance] would have been justifiable, should it be first supposed, that THIS ACT essentially broke in upon our CONSTITUTIONAL RIGHTS as Englishmen." Although Chauncy claimed that the colonists had no desire to

29. Chauncy, *Civil Magistrates*, 33–34.

be "an independant people," it was "a sentiment they had imbibed, that they should be wanting neither in loyalty to their King, or a due regard to the British-Parliament, if they should defend those rights which they imagined were unalienable, upon the foot of justice, by any power on earth." They were thus "led into this way of thinking upon what they imagined were the principles which, in their operation, gave KING WILLIAM, and QUEEN MARY, of blessed memory, the Crown of England."[30]

Chauncy's concern to be guided by British constitutional standards, even when faced with perceived injustices perpetrated by metropolitan authorities, is one of the most remarkable and consistent themes in his attitudes to the question of civil resistance. His basic rationale for "non-submission" was clear and inherently pragmatic. It had to be "warrantable" in certain circumstances. "Otherwise it will be difficult, if possible," he observed, "to justifie the REVOLUTION, and that ESTABLISHMENT in consequence of it, upon which his present Majesty sits upon the British throne." After all, it was the Glorious Revolution, Chauncy reminded Bostonians in *Trust in God* (1770), which had guaranteed "the religious and civil liberties and privileges, both of the mother-country and the American colonies." And it was the same "constitution, laws, priveleges, and interests of this people," which those elected were entrusted to defend. Such ambivalent expressions of disappointment, even sometimes outrage at British excesses, combined with loyalty, however strained, to British constitutional authorities were to continue in Chauncy's correspondence of the immediate pre-revolutionary period.[31]

By 1772, it is clear from an October 5 letter to the British Unitarian minister Richard Price that he still viewed the state of New England as deteriorating. "The situation of political affairs in this Province, particularly, is very unhappy," he informed Price, and he had strong complaints about the bias of judges. The British authorities were "endeavouring to fasten on us the chains of slavery," he thought, and the Governor was "an absolute despot." The colonists faced either "a submission to slavery, or an exertion of our selves to be delivered from it," and Chauncy was unsure of the outcome. But what aggravated local "unhappiness" was "a situation in which taxes were "unconstitutionally taken out of our pockets and wickedly made use of to annihalate [sic] our privileges by charter and rights as Englishmen." Chauncy continued to judge government officers by the same British standards that he thought them pledged to uphold, which gave New Englanders legal protection. In three letters to Price two years later, Chauncy chronicled

---

30. Chauncy, *Discourse on "The Good News,"* 17, 25, 21n, 20–21.
31. Ibid., 21n; *Trust in God*, 20, 33.

increased tensions as a result of British measures which he consistently described as tyrannous. But he was yet to endorse open rebellion of any kind.[32]

On May 30, 1774, Chauncy described the Boston Port Act as "so palpably cruel, barbarous, and inhumane, that even those who are called the friends of Government complain bitterly of it; nor do I know of any whose eyes are not opened to see plainly that despotism, which must end in slavery, is the plan to be carried into execution." Yet while he warned that "we have more virtue and resolution than to sit still and suffer chains to be fastened on us," he looked to the effectiveness of non-importation agreements to secure "the enjoyment of our constitutional rights and privileges." On July 18, 1774, Chauncy noted that oppressive British measures had brought "the whole Continent" to a state of "readiness to exert themselves to the utmost in all reasonable ways to bring forward our deliverance" and he looked forward to the Philadelphia Continental Congress in September. Yet he assured Price that it was not "the intention of the Deputies going to the abovementioned Congress, or of any of the people in this, or the other Colonies, to contend with Great Britain." In fact, he thought that it would be "highly grievous, and the last thing the Colonies would wish, to be obliged to stand upon their own defence against military force should it be used with them." All that the colonists sought was

> the full enjoyment of their rights and priveleges; and should this be granted to them, Great Britain would hear of no commotions or disturbances, but that we were all united in love to the mother Country, and in a concern to promote the honor and welfare of the English nation: nor would his Majesty have, in any part of his extended dominions, any subjects who would more readily venture their fortunes and lives in defence of his crown and the support of his government.

In a letter of introduction for Josiah Quincy of September 13, 1774, Chauncy bluntly described Massachusetts as "the first, in the view of administration, to be reduced to a state of slavery." He later offered a much lengthier portrayal of the situation in Boston after the imposition of the Boston Port Act in *Letter to a Friend* (1774).[33]

This public letter provided graphic and moving detail of resulting "hardships and sufferings." "Vast numbers," Chauncy wrote, "not less . . .

---

32. Chauncy to Price, October 5, 1772, in Price et al., "The Price Letters," 265–56, esp. 265.

33. Chauncy to Price, May 30, 1774, ibid., 266–68, esp. 267; Chauncy to Price, July 18, 1774, in ibid., 268–70, esp. 269–70; Chauncy to Price, September 13, 1774, in ibid., 270–71, esp. 270.

than fifteen thousand at the lowest computation, are reduced to a starving condition." As a result of the act, "the wharfs and landing-places in the town of Boston, which are the property of numerous individuals . . . are . . . wrested out of their hands, and put into the King's, to be disposed of at his pleasure." But his main focus was on the political abuses that Boston had suffered at British hands. The town was "considered as chargeable with this destruction [of tea during the Boston Tea Party]," he reported, "and punished for it in an awfully severe manner; and this too, without giving them notice of their crime, or opportunity of saying a word in defence of themselves. If this is not unconstitutional, arbitrary conduct, mankind in common will, I am sure, call it rigorously hard and cruel." Despite the agreement of "all the American colonies . . . in thinking it unconstitutional to be taxed by the parliament, as they are not represented there," the British government seemed set on reducing "America, by the iron hand of power, to submit to sovereign pleasure." There was no other conclusion, Chauncy argued, than that "the plan to be carried into execution, and by forcible measures, is, intire obedience to the demands of despotism, instead of those constitutional laws we are perfectly willing to be governed by."[34]

The Whiggish tone of Chauncy's comments in his 1774 *Letter to a Friend* and other writings of the revolutionary period has often been highlighted. But equally striking here, as elsewhere, is his appeal to the "constitutional" entitlements of Englishmen that he had been making for more than thirty years. Although Chauncy still did not advocate open rebellion, he acknowledged that "knowing that forcing from us our rights and privileges as English subjects, is the grand point in view, we shall naturally be urged on to contrive expedients to prevent, if possible, our being in this way, brought into bondage." He found it unimaginable that "a decree thus mixed with contrived severity, and thus big with distress and ruin to thousands of poor innocents, could have had existence given it by an English Parliament," especially since "the inhabitants of Boston are English subjects, as well as the citizens of London and may with equal justice utter their cries against that arbitrary exercise of power, which indiscriminately makes the use of their rightful property." Yet like other Bostonians, who had "always been as much disposed to honor and support constitutional government as any of the people in England," Chauncy continued to affirm loyalty to the Crown. He even expressed the hope that the colonists' counter-measures, like non-importation agreements, might prove "expedients reasonable in themselves, and wisely adapted to secure the enjoyments of their rights and privileges,

---

34. Chauncy, *Letter to a Friend*, title-page, 6, 12, 18–19, 20, 24–25.

and to promote, at the same time, harmony and love between Great-Britain and America . . . for the common interest of all."[35]

On January 10, 1775, Chauncy described an ever more militarized situation. "You can't easily imagine the greatness of our embarissment . . . ," he wrote to Price, "if it be remembered that the town, while filled with troops, is at the same time encompassed with ships of war, and the harbour so blocked up as that an intire stop is put to trade, only as it is carried on at the amazing charge of transporting every thing from Salem, not less than 28 miles by land." His tone was also more militaristic. "Can it in reason be thot [sic] that Americans, who were freeborn, will submit to such cruel tyranny?" Chauncy reported favourably on the economic boycott resulting from the 1774 Continental Congress which had been summoned in response to the British Coercive Acts of that year. He also warned of "a spirit for martial skill" that had been "strangely catched from one to another throughout at least the New-England colonies" and predicted that by spring there would be "at least one hundred thousand men well qualified to come forth for the defence of our liberties and rights, should there be a call for it." But while those in "North America" chose "death rather [than] to live in slavery, as they must do, if they submit to that despotic government which has been contrived for them," their rationale was a very traditional one. According to Chauncy, they were "united in their resolution to defend themselves against any force which may be used with them to deprive them of the rights they have a just claim to, not only as men made of one blood with the rest of the human species, but as Englishmen, and Englishmen born heirs to a royal grant of Charter rights and privileges."[36]

By July 18, 1775, once armed hostilities had begun, Chauncy's tone from exile in Medfield was understandably more defiant. He offered Price an account of "facts as they have happened, previous to the present civil war and since it began to this day," including the Battles of Lexington and Concord on April 19 and Bunker Hill on June 17. Chauncy claimed that the former was "wholly occasioned by those who are seeking our ruin" and that in the latter, "not more than 15 hundred [Americans] fought with three thousand, and killed and wounded one half of the whole." Above all, he stressed American unity in opposition to British leaders, like Governor Gage or Lieutenant Governor Oliver, who were no longer regarded as "constitutional officers":

---

35. Chauncy, *Letter to a Friend*, 25, 9, 12, 16, 27. On Chauncy's "Whiggish tone," see, for example, most recently, Noll, *America's God*, 140–41.

36. Chauncy to Price, January 10, 1775, in Price et al., "The Price Letters," 275–78.

> Our spirits continually rise in warmth, our union is daily growing in strength and vigor, and such care is taken throughout the Colonies to bring into event the commercial plan, that, humanely speaking, there is not the least probability of a failure ... Our people in all the Colonies are firmly united and resolutely fixt to defend their rights, whatever opposition they meet with ... I have never heard one who was not a Tory, so much as lispe, —Let us submit to the Parliamentary acts.

Four days later, Chauncy wrote again to express his astonishment that

> the people in England are so blind as not to see that every thing that is done against us is done against them. They may be ruined; but this will not be our case, tho we may suffer greatly ... the Colonies are all united and courageously resolute to suffer death, rather than submit to arbitrary, despotic government.

But even in this early state of open warfare, Chauncy made it clear that the acid test for the legitimacy of colonial rebellion remained the British constitutional standards that he had vigorously upheld for decades. The war was being pursued by the colonies "in defence of [their] rights and privileges" and the general view, he reported on July 18, was that they might "constitutionally act" in taking hostile action against those who had forfeited their right to rule.[37]

In view of such evidence, Lippy's contention that Chauncy's support for "active resistance to British policy" before 1775 included "the armed conflict which might ensue" goes beyond what can justifiably be inferred. Although Chauncy clearly was recognized "by the people of Boston as a pugnacious champion of political liberty," so does Griffin's argument that the First Church minister was a militant early revolutionary, who "probably worked with the Whig Club and other patriotic societies to nullify the Stamp Act" and became "politically radicalized" in the 1770s. Chauncy certainly supported opposition to British measures well before 1775, and Akers has demonstrated his involvement in various political machinations behind the scenes. He was publicly identified as one of Boston's leading ministers with Whig sympathies. He initiated a resolution passed at a meeting of Boston ministers in November 1774 to cease reading official government proclamations in their churches. But Chauncy did not fully endorse revolutionary action publicly until hostilities had already begun and his everyday ministry continued to focus on other, more mundane themes. Despite the obvious challenges of the times, for example, his Thursday Lecture sermon

---

37. Chauncy to Price, July 18, 1775, in ibid., 294–300, esp. 295, 296, 298, 299; Chauncy to Price, July 22, 1775, in ibid., 300–301, esp. 301.

Christian Love (1773) was a fairly unremarkable exposition of Acts 4:32, in which he sought to show that while Christians had a duty to help the poor, the common ownership of property was not a biblical commandment. He also voiced continuing complaints about the moral decline of the church and "the lamentably bad state of religion among us."[38]

All that can reliably be deduced about the full flowering of Chauncy's revolutionary commitment is that he had clearly, and quite enthusiastically, joined the patriot cause by the year the American Revolution began. In a letter of August 14, 1776, Abigail Adams was thus able to inform her husband, the future second president of the United States, John Adams, that when she had attended Boston's First Church the previous Sunday, "the Declaration of Independence was read from the pulpit by order of Counsel." "Dr. Chauncys address pleasd [sic] me," reported Adams. "The Dr. concluded with asking a Blessing 'upon the united States of America even untill the final restitution of all things.'" Yet despite this clear endorsement of the Revolution in 1776, Chauncy's last published sermon of the revolutionary period, *Accursed Thing* (1778), was hardly a ringing call to arms. It provided further evidence that Chauncy largely came over to the cause of independence to defend and conserve the traditional New England "rights and privileges" that he saw under threat by Britain. Its underlying analysis of the conflict also highlighted the providentialist terms in which he, like Mayhew, ultimately construed all human affairs. Warfare was a means of divine chastisement and potential moral improvement. "The parties in the war may both of them have sinned against the Lord . . . ," Chauncy observed, "in which case, they are both made use of in the providence of God to chastise one another; and to which of them God will give the advantage is known only to himself; unless that party in the war, whose cause is just, should put away the accursed thing." [39]

---

38. Lippy, *Seasonable Revolutionary*, 98–99; Griffin, *Old Brick*, 144, 141; Akers, *Divine Politician*, e.g., 139, 143, 150, 191–92; Chauncy, *Christian Love*, 8. On other evidence of Chauncy's sympathies between 1774 and 1776, see Griffin, *Old Brick*, 154–64. On Chauncy's public identifification as "one of Boston's leading ministers with Whig sympathies," see, for example, "Boston Ministers, A Ballad—First and Second Parts" and "Boston Ministers: A Ballad." Chauncy's support of the clergy resolution to cease reading official government proclamations in churches was clearly an act of civil disobedience, if not revolutionary resistance to British rule. See, further, Lippy, *Seasonable Revolutionary*, 99. Citing *SHG*, 6:439–67, esp. 453, and Anon, "To the Officers and Soldiers," Griffin questioned the origins of an advertisement in that newspaper including Chauncy in a list of fifteen "authors" of "rebellion." He also noted Shipton's suspicion that "the Whigs planted this notice as propagandistic nose-thumbing" (*Old Brick*, 156, citing *SHG*, 6:453). The document has been reprinted as "Copy of a Royalist Handbill."

39. Abigail Adams, letter to John Adams, August 14, 1776, in John Adams et al. *Adams Family Correspondence*, 2:92–93; Chauncy, *Accursed Thing*, 15

Chauncy saw a direct correlation between progress or setbacks in battle and the spiritual and moral health of the combatants:

> By remarkable interpositions, in the government of Providence, we have been marvellously succeeded, at one time and another, in our attempts against the enemy; but, as the accursed thing has been retained among us, they, by like interpositions of heaven, have been succeeded in their attempts against us.

The "accursed thing," as he defined it, based on an exposition of Joshua 7:13, was, predictably, human sin, not "in its nature only, but in its effects and consequences also." Moreover, while Chauncy generally questioned whether New England had ever been "in a more corrupt and degenerate state" or "in a more unhappy situation, morally speaking, to engage in war," he perceived a central, moral problem at the heart of current military unreadiness. "As oppression of the poor, the fatherless, and the widow, is eminently the accursed thing in the midst of us," he contended, "it ought to be taken away, so far as may be, by the powers ordained of God to be his ministers for good." As a result of currency depreciation, some of the weakest members of society were unjustly suffering. Three years into the Revolutionary War, Chauncy viewed divine providence and Christian morality, conceived in very traditional terms, as the keys to colonial victory. And two years later, in his final extant letter to Price, Chauncy continued to bemoan the economic challenges and the sin that lay creeping at American doors while he admired the people's resolve and commitment, with Congress, "to the liberties and independence of America." "One great fault they are justly chargeable w[i]th," he wrote of the states, was that "they have almost universally been too attentive to the getting of gain, as there have been peculiar temptations hereto since the commencement of the present contest."[40]

Defending a right of resistance against unjust rulers may have become commonplace in Massachusetts election sermons by 1776, but for Chauncy, as for Mayhew ten years earlier, it was clearly one thing to uphold it in principle and another to support active rebellion against British imperial authority in practice. Rather than providing evidence of revolutionary ardor before that date, Chauncy's writings in the immediate pre-revolutionary period actually demonstrate a continuing commitment to traditional British values and ideals, which extended beyond the Declaration of Independence. They reveal an inherent social and sociopolitical traditionalism which he shared with his late West Church colleague, but which scholars have often neglected. Like many of his contemporaries, Chauncy hesitated to endorse

---

40. Chauncy, *Accursed Thing*, 24, 8, 13, 16. See, further, 25–26, 10; Chauncy to Price, May 20, 1779, in Price et al., "The Price Letters," 319–21, esp. 321, 320.

the American Revolution fully before it became a matter of fact. His political views were clearly influenced by similar currents of Whig opinion as those of his West Church colleague, although not to such an extent, and he never preached the kind of incendiary sermon that Mayhew did on August 25, 1765. At the same time, his worldview remained profoundly religious in orientation and, like Mayhew, he interpreted events theologically and providentially, including those of the Revolutionary War itself. There is little trace of jingoistic militarism in Chauncy's works, and his concern for civil and righteous order remained such that he regretted violent or sinful excess from any quarter, including Patriot forces. In that sense, like Mayhew after the Stamp Act riot, he sometimes retreated from the material and/or sociopolitical consequences of his own views.[41]

In the final analysis, whatever their rhetoric, neither Chauncy nor Mayhew rushed to urge rebellious or revolutionary action against British authorities; nor did they justify it except in terms of metropolitan constitutional values and the "Protestant interest" which they purportedly upheld. Even when the two Boston ministers advocated active resistance to or change of the status quo, they saw themselves acting to conserve a valued inheritance, rather than to replace it with something radically new. Their influence on their contemporaries, which was considerable at times, may also have been greater precisely because they framed their arguments in such terms.

---

41. Counts, "Political Views," esp. 123–27.

— 8 —

Mayhew, Chauncy, and Revolutionary Change

ON MARCH 4, 1815, the second President of the United States, John Adams, wrote from retirement in Quincy, Massachusetts, to the pioneer American geographer, Connecticut minister and historian, Jedidiah Morse. Morse had approached Adams with a request for assistance with an intended supplement to Benjamin Trumbull's *General History of the United States of America* (1810), which eventually became *Annals of the American Revolution* (1824). Despite Adams's initial skepticism about the project, and indeed about history in general—"I read it as I do Romance, believing what is probable & rejecting what I must . . . Our American history for the last fifty years is already as much corrupted as any half century of Ecclesiastical history"— he was to prove a faithful and fascinating correspondent. Adams did not promise Morse any new archival resources, and predicted that any personal memories and judgments would be found deceptive, even villainous by "a hundred [other] writers." But he also raised the alluring and ultimately fruitful prospect that he might send "two or three samples of such a history as I should write. Anecdotes of no kind of consequence now; unless they should serve to shew how many thousand facts, are wholly concealed, & unknown to the world, and how many more, will be finally unknown to posterity; Facts, which mark characters, & might materially influence great events."[1]

---

1. Trumbull, *General History;* Morse, *Annals of the American Revolution*: John Adams to Morse, March 4, 1815, in Adams, *Works,* 10:133-34. Citations from Adams, *Works,* have been checked against and sometimes edited in light of John Adams et al., *Microfilms of The Adams Papers,* and/or Founders Online [Early Access], wherever possible. Morse's biographical sketch of Adams in *American Geography,* 270–71n, was reprinted in a preface to the third edition of Adams's *Defence of the Constitutions,* 1:3–6. For strong, recent biographies of Adams, see Ferling, *A Life;* Grant, *Party of One.* For a helpful overview of the development of Adams's religious views, see Fea, "John Adams and Religion."

In his vigorous opening to a letter of November 29, 1815, Adams informed Morse that his understanding of the American Revolution went much deeper than "an History of military Operations from April 19th. 1775, to the 3d of September 1783." He preferred to focus on "the Revolution . . . in the Minds and Hearts of the People, and in the Union of the Colonies, both of which were Substantially effected before Hostilities commenced." He first located "this great intellectual moral and political Change . . . in the Towns of Boston and Salem," and singled out the early leadership of James Otis. Otis's influence was especially significant from 1761 in his fight against British writs of assistance (general search warrants) to counter colonial smuggling in contravention of the Molasses Act of 1733, and it extended for the next decade. More generally, growing resistance to British trade regulations marked the beginning, Adams thought, of "the Revolution in the Principles Views Opinions, and Feelings of the American People." Once their "Eyes were opened to a clear Sight of the danger that threatened them and their Posterity and the Liberties of both, in all future generations," a "general Aspiration for a Union of the Colonies soon followed." Otis, whose insurrectionary role Adams likened to that of Luther in the European Reformation, served to encapsulate mounting colonial opposition in his *Rights of the British Colonies Asserted* (1764), but he was just part of a burgeoning movement against British fiscal and governmental impositions, especially following the Stamp Act.[2]

Another significant factor in the rise of American revolutionary sentiment and conviction was the "apprehension of Episcopacy." This "contributed 50 years ago, as much as any other cause," Adams wrote on December 2, 1815, "to arouse the attention not only of the enquiring mind but of the common people . . . And urge them to close thinking on the Constitutional Authority of Parliament over the Colonies." The colonists' chief concern was less over the ecclesiastical appointment of a Church of England bishop based in America than over the exercise of parliamentary authority that it would require. The fear was that such governmental intervention might also result in the introduction of a wide range of accompanying powers and privileges, including the collection of tithes, the outlawing of dissent, and the construal of "Schism [as] Heresy." To strengthen his historical argument, Adams cited examples of the expansion, presumtions, and prerogatives of the English church in various colonies, culminating in his native Massachusetts, where he found the activities and publications of East Apthorp particularly threatening.[3]

2. John Adams to Morse, November 29, 1815, in Adams, *Works*, 10:182–85, esp. 182–84; Adams to Morse, December 5, 1815, in ibid., 188–91, esp. 189, citing Otis, *Rights of the British Colonies*.

3. John Adams to Morse, December 2, 1815, in ibid., 185–88, esp. 185.

Since Jonathan Mayhew had been Apthorp's chief protagonist in the 1760s publication war over an American bishop, especially in *Observations* (1763)—his "comparison, between the charter, and conduct" of the SPG, "shewing their non conformity with each other"—it is not surprising that Adams viewed the West Church minister as a key leader in the pre-revolutionary period. But it is also clear from Adams's correspondence with Morse and others that he saw Mayhew as a major opinion leader and consciousness-raiser in the fight against British imperialism generally. Naming Massachusetts Treasurer Harrison Gray, one of Mayhew's most devoted parishioners, among early defectors to the loyalist cause, Adams suggested on December 22, 1815, for example, that if Gray's "oracle" and "Mentor" had lived beyond 1766, he "would never have been a Refugee." Speculating to Morse seventeen days earlier whether "the People of the Colonies would . . . have resisted" a British military expedition in support of the Stamp Act, Adams deferred to the opinions of Chauncy as well as Mayhew in post-repeal sermons that "the Colonies," to quote the former, "would [more than probably] not have submitted, unless they had been obliged to it by superior power." In two later letters to two other correspondents, Adams helped explain his high estimation of Mayhew's wider influence.[4]

The first, sent July 18, 1818, to Adams's long-time colleague and rival, former President Thomas Jefferson, amounted to little more than a brief note accompanying the gift of Mayhew's *Discourse Concerning Unlimited Submission* (1750). Yet Adams chose to describe this work as much more than "a curious Piece of New England Antiquity." It was nothing less than "a tolerable Chatechism for The Education of a Boy of 14 Years of Age [like him], who was destined in the future Course of his Life to dabble in so many Revolutions in America, in Holland and in France." The second, written February 13, 1818, to journalist and historical documentarian, Hezekiah Niles, represents a longer disquisition on the meaning of the American Revolution as a change in popular sentiment "effected before the War commenced," as well as on some of "the Characters, the most conspicuous, the most ardent and influential" in the attendant "AWAKENING and . . . REVIVAL of American Principles and Feelings." For Niles as for Morse, Adams especially focused on the period specifically between 1760 and 1766 when this "revival," which

---

4. Ibid., 188; John Adams to Morse, December 22, 1815, in ibid., 192–97, esp. 193; Adams to Morse, December 5, 1815, in ibid., 188–91, esp. 191; Chauncy, *Discourse on "The Good News,"* 19–20. Mayhew argued that "the greater part . . . tho' I may be mistaken in this, were firmly united in a consistent, however imprudent or desperate a plan, to run all risques, to tempt all hazards, to go all lengths, if things were driven to extremity, rather than to submit; preferring death itself to what they esteemed so wretched and inglorious a servitude" (*Snare Broken*, 18).

subsequently "went on increasing till in 1775 it burst out in open Violence, Hostility and Fury," was most apparent. While he ostensibly eschewed any "Glorioroles [sic] of Individual Gentlemen" as "of little Consequence," contending that "THE MEANS AND THE MEASURES" were "the proper Objects of Investigation," Adams also named eight leaders as particularly influential. Among them, the former president ranked Mayhew fifth after Otis, Oxenbridge Thacher, Samuel Adams, and John Hancock, and above Samuel Cooper and his brother William; Mayhew was one of just three, with Thacher and Thomas Cushing, whom Adams wrote about in any detail.[5]

Adams, who began his letter to Niles by defining a "Change" in the colonists' "Religious Sentiments of their Duties and Obligations," especially toward the monarchy and other British constitutional authorities, as a key element in the "Revolution . . . in the Minds and the Hearts of the People," predictably thought Mayhew's *Discourse Concerning Unlimited Submission* (1750) an important work. With this publication and others, he argued, including *Seven Sermons* (1749), "Mayhew Seemed to be raised up to revive all their [Americans'] Animosity against Tyranny, in Church and State, and at the Same time to destroy their Bigotry, Fanaticism and Inconsistency." But Adams also saw Mayhew as a much bigger figure, to draw whose "Character . . . would be to transcribe a dozen Volumes," and he once more signaled the significance of the West Church minister's role in the American Episcopate controversy, especially its wider political dimensions. Adams's concluding paragraph on that dispute, while undoubtedly tending somewhat to hyberbole, went to the heart of colonial fears, particularly in New England, as he understood them fifty-five years later:

> If any Gentleman Supposes this Controversy to be nothing to the present purpose, he is grossly mistaken. It Spread an Universal Alarm against the Authority of Parliament. It excited a general and just Apprehension that Bishops and Dioceses [sic]

---

5. John Adams to Jefferson, July 18, 1818, in Abigail Adams et al, *Adams-Jefferson Letters*, 2:527; John Adams to Niles, February 13, 1818, in Adams, *Works*, 10:282–89, esp. 282–84, 287–88. Adams did not name Mayhew's *Discourse Concerning Unlimited Submission* in his letter to Jefferson, and his comment that the work that he was sending "made a Noise in Great Britain where it was reprinted and procured the Author a Diploma of Doctor in Divinity" might seem more applicable to *Seven Sermons*, which was published in 1749, the year Adams became fourteen. However, Adams also described the unnamed publication as a "discourse" and *Discourse Concerning Unlimited Submission* is a much more political work. Adams explicitly named "Dr Mayhews Thirtieth of January Sermon," which he again termed "a Curiosity," in a similar letter to James Madison a week later, where he referred to the reprinting of *Discourse Concerning Unlimited Submission* in Baron, *Pillars of Priestcraft*, 2:259–337. See Adams to Madison, July 25, 1818, in Founders Online [Early Access].

and Churches, and Priests and Tythes, were to be imposed upon Us by Parliament. It was known that neither King nor Ministry nor Archbishops could appoint Bishops in America without an Act of Parliament; and if Parliament could Tax Us they could establish the Church of England with all its Creeds, Articles, Tests, Ceremonies and Tythes, and prohibit all other Churches as Conventicles and S[chi]sm Shops.[6]

Exemplars of Enlightenment?

However significant the source, Adams's view of Mayhew's pre- or proto-revolutionary political importance remains just one among several explored here. But such a line of interpretation has clearly been influential through the work of historians from Alice Baldwin through Bailyn to Mullins and *Conservative Revolutionaries* has shown how Chauncy has been similarly viewed. It has also documented how scholars have judged both Boston ministers as the kind of forward-thinking theologians to whom revolutionaries like Adams and other free spirits of his and later generations could turn, and find in Mayhew's *Seven Sermons* (1749), or in some of Chauncy's later works, good grounds for breaking with religious as well as political orthodoxy. Henry May's placement of the two men at the heart of a transformation of traditional New England theology accompanying a "moderate" phase of *The Enlightenment in America* (1976) between 1688 and 1787 has found a significant, if not definitive, place in more specialized scholarship, especially in the work of Corrigan and Mullins.[7]

---

6. John Adams to Niles, February 13, 1818, in Adams, *Works*, 10:282–89, esp. 282, 288.

7. Adams mentioned Chauncy much less frequently in his correspondence, but apparently saw him in similar terms to Mayhew. See, for example, John Adams to Morse, December 5, 1815, in Adams, *Works*, 10:188–91, esp. 191; Adams to William Wirt, January 5, 1818, in ibid., 271–72, esp. 271. See also May, *Enlightenment in America*, 42, 55–59, esp. 57, 56, 58; Corrigan, *Hidden Balance*; Mullins, "Father of Liberty." May, whose "Moderate Enlightenment" was especially characterized by concerns for "order, balance, reason, and moderation," understandably focused on Chauncy's and Mayhew's Arminian ideas and on their emphases on free will, divine benevolence, and Christianity as a rational "system of morality." With like-minded clergy of eastern Massachusetts, their sources, he argued, were "the respectable mainstays of the Moderate Enlightenment: Locke, Clarke, Tillotson and those Dissenters who tended toward rationalism." May thus saw the two Boston ministers' "moralistic and individualistic" religion, with its tendencies toward universalism and Unitarianism, as "moderate English rationalism adapted to a Calvinist audience."

The major problem with an unduly narrow understanding of Chauncy and Mayhew as Enlightenment pioneers and/or political revolutionaries remains the simple reality that they were also much more traditionalist figures than they have often been portrayed. As historians have developed a more complex and nuanced picture of the Enlightenment's religious dimensions and influences on eighteenth-century leaders on both sides of the Atlantic, recent advances in scholarship have lent greater credibility to that recognition. A deeper exploration of the diversity of eighteenth-century American responses to enlightened ideas, including a significant re-interpretation of connections between evangelicalism and the Enlightenment have been of particular relevance to this study.[8]

Fiering's work (1981) on the "first American Enlightenment," which persuasively showed the influence of Tillotson and other "philosophical Anglicans" on Harvard's leadership and curriculum at a time when Chauncy and Mayhew were students there, has already been noted. So has Corrigan's monograph on the similar sources and "catholic" mentality of a significant group of Harvard-educated clergy, who were "influenced by [English] latitudinarian thought," including Foxcroft, Colman, and three other ministers. Alongside Robert Ferguson's comprehensive, but more politically focused, overview of the literature of the American Enlightenment in the seventy

---

8. May was already more accommodating of religion than other scholars, not least Peter Gay, who in his seminal work, *Enlightenment*, often portrayed the Enlightenment in what Brekus described as "skeptical and anti-Christian" terms (*Sarah Osborn's World*, 8). That accommodation has continued among other historians, notably Roy Porter. Porter devoted a whole chapter in his seminal work to "Reforming Religion by Reason" and placed religious change front and center, especially in "the main Protestant regions," where "advanced thinkers" were "concerned to achieve a purified, refined expression of faith . . . commensurable with reason and science" (*Enlightenment*, 3, 36, 32–41). He later contended that "Enlightenment in Britain took place within, rather than against, Protestantism" and offered an overview of the development of "rational" religion (*Creation of the Modern World*, 99, 96–129). More recent studies have echoed that judgment, both in Europe and North America. Religion has thus consistently featured in a growing number of more localized, as well as general, histories, with historians chronicling its different roles in what has increasingly been seen as a multiplicity of national "Enlightenments." On this see esp. Porter and Teich, *Enlightenment in National Context*. Porter argued there, for example, that "all the shibboleths of Enlightenment were familiar to English lips: reason and experience; law, liberty and justice; happiness, humanity and nature; knowledge is power is progress; *sapere aude* ["dare to know"], and the rest—as I have argued, the baby Enlightenment's first words were spoken in an English nursery" (ibid., 7). Pocock meanwhile posited "a family of Enlightenments, displaying both family resemblances and family quarrels" (*Barbarism and Religion*, 1:9). Black suggested, in a British context, that "Reason led very few . . . to attack Christianity . . . Far from seeing reason and religion as incompatible, most intellectuals and churchmen shared John Locke's view that a rational appreciation of man's situation would lead people to be Christians" (*Eighteenth-Century Britain*, 148),

years after 1750, such studies have generally supported familiar interpretations of leaders like Chauncy and Mayhew—partly captured by May's emphasis on their theological rationalism and moralism—as progressive theologians and militant activists for political change. Yet recent scholarship has also recognized the role of more orthodox thinkers who sought to engage and sometimes embrace Enlightenment ideas and influences, while maintaining allegiance to more traditional religious and political doctrines of the kind highlighted here in the works of Chauncy and Mayhew. Studies of eighteenth-century evangelicalism have been especially fruitful in suggesting fresh ways of understanding such a process of critical engagement.[9]

An important point of connection has been David Bebbington's seminal work, *Evangelicalism in Modern Britain* (1989). With its empiricist, voluntarist, religiously tolerant, and socially activist preoccupations, Bebbington interpreted "the early phase of Evangelicalism," including Wesleyan Methodism, as "an adaptation of the Protestant tradition through contact with the Enlightenment," not as a reaction against it. He defined four key "characteristics" or "qualities" as "the special marks of Evangelical religion": "conversionism," "biblicism," "crucicentrism," and "activism." Describing present as well as past adherents, David Hempton helpfully summarized Bebbington's "scheme" as follows:

> evangelicals have been those who have emphasized a conscious religious conversion over inherited beliefs, the Bible as an authoritative sacred text in determining all matters of faith and conduct, Christ's death on the cross as the centerpiece of evangelical theologies of atonement and redemption, and disciplined action as a way of redeeming people and their cultures.

Bebbington laid particular emphasis on evangelical "devotion to science, experiment and investigation" as evidence of Enlightenment influences, and on an appreciation of a "law-governed universe," with a natural "order" that could rightly be explored in terms of "natural theology." Through such

---

9. Fiering, "First American Enlightenment"; Corrigan, *Prism of Piety*, 31; Ferguson, "American Enlightenment," esp. 393–94, 400–401, 407 (on Chauncy), and 353–54, 390–91, 402, 407–8 (on Mayhew). Colin Kidd argued that "for the majority of its supporters, certainly in the Protestant world, the Enlightenment was a further wave of Reformation. It was not about the wholesale rejection of Christianity, but rather a tidying exercise which might well see untenable superstitions or inessential but problematic beliefs cast out of the churches, but only in order to conserve and bolster a purer and stronger Christianity" (*Forging of Races*, 83). Alongside the "religious radicalism of a sceptical, deistic Enlightenment," Kidd further pointed to "a moderate, clerical Enlightenment" that "yoked reason and sophistication to the cause of religion." Guyatt has similarly written of "a 'conservative Enlightenment' within Anglicanism" (*Providentialism*, 56n), See, further, Pocock, "Clergy and Commerce."

means, he argued, "Evangelicals were integrating their faith with the rising philosophy" and so "in harmony with the spirit of the age." They also shared an "optimistic temper," believing that "humanity enjoyed great potential for improvement." Bebbington saw this especially reflected in "the Arminianism of the Methodists," which was an "'optimism of grace,' a theology that [did] not limit the possibility of Christian renewal to the narrow company of the elect." Evangelicals were even "convinced that God wished human beings to be happy." "Identification of happiness as the grand goal of humanity" was thus "shared by Calvinists as well as Methodists," as were other evangelical perspectives, including a more "flexible, tolerant, utilitarian" approach to the practice of ministry.[10]

But Bebbington's views on connections between evangelicalism and the Enlightenment have not gone unchallenged. In a fascinating brief examination of the themes of "Enlightenment and Enthusiasm," Hempton offered the more complex argument that "Methodism operated in a dialectical tension between enthusiasm and enlightenment that had enormous consequences for the sort of movement it became." In the case of John Wesley, he saw clear evidence of enlightened influences in the Methodist leader's "indebtedness to Lockean empiricism and sensationalist psychology, his endorsement, within limits, of the scientific method," as well as his "defense of religious toleration, advocacy of slavery abolition, concern for bodily and mental health, and dislike of all persecution and violence." A significant scholar to have focused on broader links between evangelicalism and Enlightenment in a colonial American context has likewise described the "relationship" between the two as "fraught with tensions." Yet Catherine Brekus, in her perceptive study of *Sarah Osborn's World* (2013), clearly highlighted the empiricism, "faith in human progress," "humanitarian ideals," "emphasis on the affections," and "individualism" of eighteenth-century evangelicals among "aspects of Enlightenment thought" absorbed by them.[11]

Chauncy's and Mayhew's identification with moderate American Enlightenment thought has generally militated against their ideas being

---

10. Bebbington, *Evangelicalism in Modern Britain*, 2–3, 50–69, esp. 53, 58–60, 65; Hempton, *Evangelical Disenchantment*, 5. Hempton, 5–6, also paraphrased two other definitions of evangelicalism. For Ward, evangelicals were "broadly united in their embrace of a hexagon of religious ideas: experiential conversion, mysticism, small-group religion, vitalist conceptions of nature, a deferred eschatology, and opposition to theological systems" (*Early Evangelicalism*, 4). For Marsden, evangelicals were "those who believe in the final authority of Scripture, the historical reality of God's saving work as recorded in Scripture, salvation to eternal life based on the redemptive work of Christ, the centrality of evangelism and missions, and the importance of a spiritually transformed life" (*Understanding Fundamentalism*, 1).

11. Hempton, *Methodism*, 52, 41; Brekus, *Sarah Osborn's World*, 10.

linked with evangelicalism at all. Because they both became strong opponents of the Great Awakening as early as the 1740s, such a connection seems factually implausible, as well as theoretically counter-intuitive. Yet simply by demonstrating traditionalist aspects of their religious and political thought, which reflect similar positions to those held by evangelicals long after the eighteenth century, *Conservative Revolutionaries* has signaled significant points of congruity. In terms of their theological development, it has presented strong grounds for viewing the two Boston ministers as religious leaders who did not simply reject key aspects of their Calvinist, New England, heritage in light of the moderating and expansive influences of Enlightenment and other sources. Instead, like many eighteenth-century evangelical counterparts, although more inclusively, they redefined and adapted some of their more conventional positions, while retaining others largely intact.[12]

Men of Their Times

Both ministers started out with a fairly orthodox Calvinist faith, and Chauncy long retained it. Mayhew, although he later came to reject the excesses of the Great Awakening, was at first an early convert. Chauncy's primary criticisms of revivalism were of some of its methods and the resulting social unrest; he actually supported the major goal and much of the theology of the revival movement. Both, of course, eventually deserted Calvinism for Arminianism. Yet their embrace of an Arminian soteriology ultimately represented no more of a departure from previous orthodoxy than that of Wesley and his Methodist followers; nor did their tendencies, such as they were, toward moralism and rationalism, their optimistic views of divine benevolence and human capabilities, or their firm, though in Chauncy's case somewhat conflicted, emphasis on human free will. Mayhew's subordinationist Christology and Chauncy's late universalism eventually led them well beyond the pale of what more conventional contemporaries found theologically acceptable, and Mayhew faced significant opposition for such transgressions. But one of the most striking indicators of the two ministers' continuing traditionalism is that, despite such innovations, both could arguably still merit the label "evangelical" in Bebbington's terms, if not necessarily according to more stringent criteria.[13]

---

12. An implicit assumption in this paragraph is that the immediate origins of later American evangelicalism have often been traced back to the Great Awakening. See, for example, Noll, *Rise of Evangelicalism*, 18.

13. It is worth noting that both Ward's and Marsden's definitions of evangelicalism,

While they valued New England's doctrinal inheritance, for example, Chauncy and Mayhew remained strong advocates of the need for decisive Christian conversion, and the First Church minister retained that conviction even after he came to the conclusion that God would ultimately save the whole of humankind. Chauncy and Mayhew differed somewhat in their understandings of the person and work of Christ, and the former's positions remained more orthodox. Yet despite the West Church minister's adoption of a Christology in which Christ was deemed subordinate to God the Father, both remained decidedly crucicentric in seeing his sacrificial and mediatorial death on the cross as vital to human redemption from sin and evil and to reconciliation with God. The two ministers' activism was also indisputable. They personally undertook an exhausting round of activity, combining extensive writing and scholarship with their pastoral ministries. They vigorously engaged in a wide variety of societal issues and participated in various voluntary organizations. They especially urged the need for good works, and, much like the early Methodists, their strong emphasis on righteous living as an essential part as well as a natural expression of saving faith served to intensify their calls for gospel obedience. Last but not least, in terms of Bebbington's evangelical *quadrilateral*, Chauncy's and Mayhew's biblicism has emerged as a striking feature of their works. Such was their devotion to the sacred text as the ultimate authority in matters of faith and morality that they were prepared to set it above and beyond any other source of doctrine—even the classical formulations of their theological heritage. In one sense, it was precisely their willingness to set such store by scripture that led them, with similar theological innovators of their day, to their occasional departures from orthodoxy. In another, that same commitment encouraged them to defend their heterodox, as well as more traditionalist, positions on the most reliable, biblical grounds deemed available to them.

While significant elements of Chauncy's and Mayhew's theology may thus qualify as "evangelical," this does not imply that the two ministers are best identified as such—especially at a time when evangelicalism was in its earliest stages as a recognizable movement which they largely opposed. What it does underline are the strong elements of traditionalism that they retained and adapted despite their obvious departures from New England orthodoxy. Enlightenment influences and sources are plainly evident in their moves towards Arminianism, Christological heterodoxy, and universalism, as well as in their emphases on the power of reason, ethical moralism, divine benevolence, and the goal of human happiness. But their overall positions

---

as cited by Hempton, *Evangelical Disenchantment*, 5–6, might also encompass the views of Chauncy and Mayhew.

were much more complex. The anachronistic categorization of Chauncy or Mayhew as "liberal" theologians becomes especially problematic once it is recognized that their Arminianism, whatever its origins, was itself characteristic of other much more traditionally minded figures, not least Wesleyan Methodists. A much more promising approach to understanding Chauncy and Mayhew lies in viewing them first and foremost as eighteenth-century Bostonian ministers whose views, however sophisticated, ultimately reflected their engagement with a wide range of influences, including inherited traditions, some of which they continued to cherish, as well as newer ideas, some of which they came to embrace.

Seen that way, it is not surprising to find Chauncy and Mayhew repeatedly urging a long-standing commitment to the primacy of scripture, for example, while feeling free to adopt relatively heterodox positions based on novel methods of biblical exegesis and a willingness to prioritize their conclusions over the tenets of traditional doctrinal formulations. Viewed in this light, their ongoing homiletic preoccupations with conventional themes of "sin-salvation-service" are as much to be expected as their readiness to reframe those themes to reflect changes in their soteriology and theological anthropology toward more synergistic, benevolent, and optimistic interpretations of divine and human relations. Although his journey was delayed by personal and professional constraints that did not hinder Mayhew, Chauncy traveled further from Calvinist orthodoxy, especially in his final embrace of universalism and of a thoroughly heterodox understanding of original sin. Yet appropriately contextualized, his continuing high Christology makes as much sense as Mayhew's subordinationist, if not Arian, view of Christ, which echoed that of other free-thinking theologians whose concerns for rationality were offended and confounded by the mysteries of Nicene Trinitarianism. Making similar allowance for the immediate settings in which they lived and worked, the two ministers' rigorous adherence to established Congregationalist polity and their vigorous anti-Catholicism are as much to be expected as their more enlightened, though still somewhat restrictive, views on religious toleration and Chauncy's willingness to speak out against the injustices of slavery or the enforced cultural assimilation of indigenous peoples.

Attempting to understand Chauncy and Mayhew as men of their time and place, including their peculiar professional, social, educational, and intellectual backgrounds, also results in a more historically authentic engagement with their political positions. Heimert was right to stress their commitment to the traditional, hierarchical, sociopolitical structures in which they were born and bred, their inherent aversion and resistance to forces threatening them, their high valuation of their own positions in society, and their resulting tendencies toward elitism. Yet the two ministers lived in turbulent times. Just as they were receptive to some of the main philosophical and theological emphases of the Enlightenment, their worldviews were shaped by the Whig political ideas that influenced many contemporaries. Their Whiggery admittedly took different forms. In Mayhew's case, the strong influence of more radical, Real Whig ideology is undeniable, while Chauncy's views are best described in more mainstream terms. Yet both maintained key commitments—to British constitutionalism, monarchism, and religious toleration, for example—that were common among Whigs in the eighteenth-century Atlantic world.

Chauncy's and Mayhew's political worldviews also reflected older traditions. They allowed for justifiable acts of rebellion *in extremis*, but both held a high view of civil authorities and of the duties owed to them. Both embraced a typically Puritan, providentialist understanding of colonial and international history and politics, in which Britain and New England were divinely ordained forces for good. Both were not only deeply loyal to the British mixed constitution and to the monarchy that remained central to it, they saw themselves as defenders of New England's "Protestant interest" and they believed that the traditional liberties which it upheld were crucial to the progress of Christian civilization and so to the welfare of all humankind. Moreover, just as this "interest" embraced both political and religious concerns, their discourse often defies the imposition of modern distinctions between "sacred" and "secular." Their understandings of the key eighteenth-century concept of liberty are a classic case in point.

Based on a key series of definitions drafted by Mayhew, it is possible to trace up to six senses in which Chauncy and Mayhew used the term "liberty," ranging from philosophical through civil to religious liberty. The evidence of Locke's influence on their usage is decisive in at least two of them, but two are solely scriptural in origin and orientation. In addition to their ample biblical content, Mayhew's and Chauncy's political writings are also saturated with a libertarian discourse directly grounded in a traditional understanding of spiritual liberty. Even when advocating overtly political notions of freedom, the two ministers primarily conceived it in scriptural terms. In that sense, their discourse of liberty displays strong intellectual continuity with that of their Puritan forebears, for whom spiritual freedom to serve God and neighbor was primary.

Such issues inevitably come to the fore when discussing how much either minister was fully prepared to endorse rebellious or revolutionary action against civil authorities. Because he died ten years before the American Revolution, it is harder to make a definitive case for Mayhew. But his historical links with violent opposition to the Stamp Act in 1765, together with the persistent significance of his sermons advocating civil resistance as attested by Adams, have arguably made him a more important figure in the historiography of revolutionary ideology than Chauncy, even though the latter not only lived through the War of Independence, but remained a major community leader for the duration. As with the ministers' general political positions, evidence for their revolutionary commitment remains conflicting.

Both clearly prized a right of resistance philosophically, theologically, and historically. But confronted by the practical consequences of its exercise, they were deeply ambivalent. When an allegedly incendiary sermon led to public disorder in 1765, Mayhew soon retreated from his rhetoric and ended his brief career in paeans of praise for the British government following the repeal of the Stamp Act. Chauncy clearly supported the Patriot cause by 1776 and he was politically engaged before then. But, like many of his contemporaries, he only endorsed the American Revolution after it became a matter of fact. Even during the Revolutionary War itself, Chauncy's works show little evidence of jingoism. Instead, he viewed the conflict in largely theological and providential terms, regretting undue violence on both sides. The issue that he and Mayhew found most difficult to resolve was simple. Their commitment to British constitutional liberties was so integral to their political and religious values that they struggled to justify any act of rebellion against metropolitan authorities deemed to have secured them.

Such complexities also highlight another key question concerning Chauncy's and Mayhew's political thought, which is the extent to which either can truly be described as making any major departure from previous ways of thinking. This becomes especially pressing in light of earlier scholarship that has stressed their alleged radicalism. Yet, as in the case of their theological development, the available evidence suggests a greater need for historical nuance than dogmatic certainty. In addition to the Puritanism of their New England heritage and their differing degrees of Whiggery, key areas of thematic continuity also indicate the influence of other intellectual traditions on their political and theological discourse, which have much in common with those generally linked with early dissenting Protestantism and its various denominational expressions.

Rejecting almost completely (and somewhat unfairly) the influence of Real Whig ideology, Jonathan Clark described "the public ideologies widespread in the Anglophone world by the late eighteenth century" in the following terms:

[They] warned against "slavery," denounced "tyranny," pointed out the ways in which men could be defrauded of their ancient liberties, recorded the threat posed by standing armies, and lamented the enervating effects of vice and luxury. All these themes were prominent in the rhetoric of American revolutionaries, but it was rare that they were greatly owed to a reading of authors like Henry Neville, Walter Moyle or Robert, Viscount Charlesworth. Most were standard themes of the folk memories of Protestant denominations; they formed part of their myths or histories of their origins, of the reason for dissent from the Church of England, and of their principled resistance to episcopacy or "Popery."

Clark noted that "all parties to many different disputes claimed the 'rights of Englishmen' or appealed to the libertarian inheritance of the Reformation; but they interpreted these in different ways" and "the American colonies seemed to triumph in the success of the Glorious Revolution." He stressed the consistent concern of Congregationalists, with members of other dissenting denominations, to protect their "ancient principles of ecclesiastical polity." Clark also described New England's "frenzied anti-Catholicism" as "the most consistent theme both of popular sentiment and of ideological exegesis" through "all the vicissitudes of English politics from the 1530s to the 1830s and beyond."[14]

The significance of such themes has clearly emerged in *Conservative Revolutionaries*. Taken together, the two ministers' staunch anti-Catholicism (and, by extension, anti-Episcopalianism), their vigorous apologetics for Congregationalist structures, their regular denunciations of "arbitrary" government, either in church or state, and their fear of "slavery" at the hands of despotic powers offer cumulative evidence of the influence of precisely the kind of dissenting Protestant intellectual traditions that Clark identified as of crucial importance in the eighteenth-century, Anglo-American world generally. Equally corroborative are their high valuation of English constitutional traditions, especially following the Glorious Revolution, their frequent appeals to the rights and liberties guaranteed by such authorities, and their ardent admiration for England's Protestant monarchy. This is not to deny the significance of Whig, Enlightenment, and other influences, not least the biblicist and Puritan theological traditions in which they were educated. But it is to suggest that, rather than reading Chauncy's and Mayhew's writings through a single interpretative lens, they are better understood in terms of what Alan Gibson has helpfully described in the context of

14. Clark, *Language of Liberty*, 24–25, 219, 364, 250, 238.

late-eighteenth century American political thought as "multiple traditions." Approaching their works from that perspective enables the reader to see how they, like many others of their time, "drew on numerous intellectual traditions to address... concrete problems." More specifically, much as their Enlightenment sources supplemented but did not supplant more traditional theological ones, Chauncy's and Mayhew's Whiggery was not as definitive in the development of their political thought as has often been suggested. For it arguably supported and extended ideas and preoccupations that ultimately stemmed from older traditions. Such contextualization also helps explain why the religious and political ideas of the two Boston ministers were sometimes more traditionalist, even reactionary, than scholars have suggested, especially when arguing from an inherently proleptic conception of eighteenth-century theological and philosophical development culminating in Enlightenment, revolution, and religious liberalism.[15]

Given the evidence, it becomes problematic to label either Chauncy or Mayhew as an outright "revolutionary," theologically or politically. The heterodoxy of their religious views, while clearly significant, has often been exaggerated and more conventional themes in their theology have frequently been neglected. While both periodically wrote in favor of a right to civil rebellion, and Chauncy eventually participated in insurrectionary action, the general traditionalism of their political views is just as remarkable as their oft-alleged radicalism. If these men were revolutionaries at all, they were, as Heimert suggested fifty years ago, decidedly "conservative" ones. Not surprisingly in view of their diverse interests and influences, the two ministers defy simplistic attempts to define them according to anachronistic labels or categories. They were, in different times and places, both traditional Calvinists and heterodox theologians; sociopolitical reactionaries and proponents of civil and even military resistance; faithful pastors and outspoken controversialists; scrupulous scholars and wily political operators; and diplomatic defenders and vigorous critics of the status quo.

Questions of Influence

Throughout the various vicissitudes of their lives, Chauncy and Mayhew successfully retained the ministerial positions at two of Boston's most prominent churches which helped ensure their influence during a crucial period of change in colonial and revolutionary American history. The full force of their impact is impossible to measure well over two centuries later. For precisely that reason, this study has not focused on major historical

15. Gibson, *Understanding the Founding*, 163. See, further, 136–37.

debates about connections between religion and the American Revolution or the rise of Unitarian Universalism. Yet their changing positions continue to raise important issues which have not always received the scholarly attention that they deserve.

The political and religious transformations in eighteenth-century New England defy simple explanation, if only because of their sheer scale. Yet historians, in their quest to explain how relatively insignificant colonial outposts of the British Empire could become leading states in a burgeoning new nation, have understandably looked to significant actors, as well as to key intellectual, political, and socioeconomic factors. How could a largely uniform, Calvinist, Congregationalist establishment give way to multiple Christian denominations embracing differing theologies? In pursuit of the sources and originators of this complex process, as of "the intellectual, moral, and political change" preceding revolutionary conflict, scholars have likewise, and predictably, gravitated toward leaders who advocated and/or enacted significant departures from the status quo. They have also tended to see those like Mayhew and Chauncy, who were willing to present fresh ways of thinking, as transitional as well as creative figures, and have prioritized their more innovative ideas and actions over others.[16]

The broader conceptual problems inherent in such a "Whig" interpretation of history were adumbrated in the preface and will not be repeated here. Some of the resulting problems have also been observed—especially in the work of historians who have primarily viewed Chauncy's universalist or Mayhew's political writings, for example, as key staging posts en route to Unitarian Universalism or the American Revolution. What have also emerged repeatedly are the interpretative dangers and distorted conclusions that can arise from highlighting the Boston ministers' departures from traditional doctrines without paying sufficient attention to their more conventional positions. Yet in the context of eighteenth-century colonial America, which literally claimed the right of self-determination and where so many broke new ground theologically, the potentially wider significance of Chauncy's and Mayhew's changing positions can scarcely be ignored.

The practical consequences of any shift in worldview to which they may have contributed may not readily yield to meaningful measurement; nor may the extent of that contribution. But when a significant number of people depart, as they did in New England, from a traditional understanding of their place in the world as depraved individuals lacking freedom of choice without the supernatural intervention of an all-powerful deity, the

---

16. John Adams to Morse, November 29, 1815, in Adams, *Works*, 10:182–84, esp. 182.

impact must surely be considerable. When they also replace an inherently deterministic self-understanding with one that makes greater allowance for the innate good, as well as evil, of humankind, for the exercise of authentic free will, and for a common ability to improve the human condition, the implications must be significant. And when a more optimistic view of humanity is combined with a fresh understanding of God as an essentially benevolent being who actively fosters the happiness of humanity and predetermines no set limits on salvation, such effects would seem magnified.

Societal changes potentially resulting from such radical transformations in self-identity are, of course, even more immeasurable. But should those imbued with this new-found sense of human capability also come to a deep conviction that they have a divinely permissible right to resist civil or imperial authorities when they act unjustly, the results could ultimately prove revolutionary. Moreover, in a highly religious culture like that of eighteenth-century New England, which remained steeped in biblicist discourse, any call to resistance would surely have proven more effective when couched in such rhetoric and directly appealing to powerfully ambiguous concepts like "liberty." In the absence of conclusive supporting evidence, such ideas must inevitably remain hypothetical. Since they are partly intended to provoke further thought and discussion, they are deliberately expressed in such terms. But they are not totally without empirical grounding in the context of this study.[17]

Both Chauncy and Mayhew clearly sensed the wider implications of their ideas on free will, divine benevolence, and a more inclusive doctrine of salvation, and they actively urged their hearers to make the most of them, individually and collectively. But they carefully and quite deliberately presented their most radical departures from orthodoxy with as much support from traditional sources, especially the Bible, as they could muster, and they couched them in as traditional terms as possible. Except in Chauncy's last decade, by which time he freely admitted the heterodoxy of his universalism, both Boston ministers also fought hard to preserve their reputation as mainstream thinkers, especially when challenged publicly, as Mayhew was, by those who viewed them otherwise. Finally, following Mayhew's provocative sermon of August 1765, neither could be unaware of the potential power of their biblicist rhetoric, particularly when deployed to urge Christian freedom not only to serve God and others, but to resist the perceived injustice of local and metropolitan officials.

---

17. A key assumption here is that revolutionary ideas may more likely be received with favor when presented within a plausible intellectual framework and viewed as a natural progression from tradition, rather than a disruptive break with it.

Beyond some immediate responses, largely from ministerial colleagues and a few other members of the elite social circles of which Chauncy and Mayhew were part, exactly how their words and actions were received often remains unclear, especially among those in less exalted stations. That is one of the shortcomings of this study. Yet the example of the 1765 Stamp Act rioters remains telling. So, from a rather different position in society, does that of John Adams. Adams was only in his teens when, as a new Harvard student, he first came across Mayhew's writings. But we know from sources as early as 1756 that they made a profound impression on him—so profound that he was still writing about Mayhew sixty-two years later. And which two works had the greatest impact? In addition to the overtly political *Discourse Concerning Unlimited Submission* (1750), the other cited by Adams was a strictly theological work, Mayhew's earliest and most boldly Arminian publication, *Seven Sermons* (1749).[18]

To readers of today, *Seven Sermons* is not the most stirring publication. Its discourses on such titles as "The Difference betwixt Truth and Falshood, Right and Wrong," "The natural Abilities of Men for discerning these Differences," "The Right and Duty of private Judgment," "The Love of God," and "The Love of our Neighbour" may ostensibly offer little more than an ample dose of moralism. Yet it provoked significant controversy on publication. Moreover, just as Mayhew's *Discourse* offered free rein to resist oppressive doctrines of the divine right of kings and "unlimited submission" to civil authorities, it seems reasonable to assume that *Seven Sermons* may have inspired the young Adams with a fresh vision of human free will, of the value of a properly exercised moral conscience, and of the "right and duty" to judge for himself. Together with his Harvard education and the Arminian teaching of Lemuel Briant, who was minister of the Quincy Congregationalist Church, where Adams's father served as a deacon, from 1745 to 1753, Mayhew's work could well have helped ease the future president's transition from his Calvinist heritage to Arminianism and, perhaps, ultimately even to Unitarianism. To the extent that it offered Adams permission to think for himself and to have confidence in his conclusions, *Seven Sermons* may certainly have encouraged a more critical and activist mindset, ready to question established authority and where necessary, to reject and resist it.[19]

---

18. John Adams, *Diary and Autobiography*, 1:14–15, March 17, 1756.

19. John Adams to Jefferson, July 18, 1818, in Abigail Adams et al., *Adams-Jefferson Letters*, 2:527; Worthley, *Inventory of Records*, 503. Fea described Adams as a "devout Unitarian" ("John Adams and Religion," 197), Evidence from Adams's papers clearly shows that he was personally affected by a dispute at Quincy church which led to Briant's resignation. In his autobiography, Adams wrote, "Between the Years 1751 when I entered, and 1754 [i.e., 1755] when I left Colledge a Controversy was carried on between

Because of what he eventually became, Adams's testimony to the power of Mayhew's writings is uniquely significant, though obviously it cannot be applied more generally. But it remains an impressive indicator of Chauncy's and Mayhew's influence on their fellow citizens, not only through their many writings, but over the course of nearly eighty years of combined ministry at two of Boston's leading churches. Adams's comments also provide a useful reminder that simply by virtue of their willingness to espouse and teach novel and sometimes heterodox ideas, Chauncy and Mayhew were both, in the broadest sense, progressive figures. But they remained deeply rooted in the traditional, theological, and sociopolitical cultures in which they were educated, lived, and worked. Indeed, that very grounding may help explain their success as agents of transformation as well as upholders of tradition in eighteenth-century Boston and beyond.

Mr. Bryant the Minister of our Parish and some of his People, partly on Account of his Principles which were called Arminian and partly on Account of his Conduct, which was too gay and light if not immoral. Ecclesiastical Councils were called and sat at my Fathers House. Parties and their Accrimonies arose in the Church and Congregation, and Controversies from the Press between Mr. Bryant, Mr. Niles, Mr. Porter, Mr. Bass, concerning the five Points. I read all these Pamphlets and many other Writings on the same Subject and found myself involved in difficulties beyond my Powers of decision. . . Very strong doubts arose in my mind, whether I was made for a Pulpit in such times, and I began to think of other Professions" (*Diary and Autobiography*, 3:262). In 1756, Adams shared with a friend that "the frightful Engines of Ecclesiastical Co[u]ncils, of diabolical Malice and Calvinistical good nature never failed to terrify me exceedingly whenever I thought of Preaching" (John Adams to Richard Cranch, August 29, 1756, in *Papers of John Adams*, 1:15–17, esp. 17). As already noted, Adams much later, albeit proleptically, listed Briant, his "own Minister" of "Sixty five years Ago," with four others, including Mayhew and Gay, as "Unitarians" (John Adams to Morse, May 15, 1815, in Founders Online [Early Access]). On Briant, see pages 50–1.

Bibliography

Short titles are also listed for works by Charles Chauncy and Jonathan Mayhew.

Abbreviations

ANB Online   *American National Biography*. New York: Oxford University Press, 2000. Copyright © 2000 American Council of Learned Societies. Online: http://www.anb.org.

CMHS   *Collections of the Massachusetts Historical Society*. Boston, MA: Massachusetts Historical Society, 1792–.

FP   Foxcroft, Thomas, et al. Foxcroft Papers. Bortman, Mark and Llora and Foxcroft and Mayhew Family Papers. Howard Gotlieb Archival Research Center. Boston University Library, Boston, MA.

MP   Mayhew Family Papers. Bortman, Mark and Llora and Foxcroft and Mayhew Family Papers, Howard Gotlieb Archival Research Center, Boston University Library, Boston, MA.

ODNB Online   *Oxford Dictionary of National Biography*. Oxford: Oxford University Press, 2004; online ed., 2004–15. Online: http://www.oxforddnb.com.

OED Online   *Oxford English Dictionary*. Oxford: Oxford University Press, 1989; online ed., 2015. Online: http://www.oed.com.

PMHS   *Proceedings of the Massachusetts Historical Society*. Boston, MA: Massachusetts Historical Society, 1897–1998.

SHG	Sibley, John, Clifford K. Shipton, et al. *Biographical Sketches of those who Attended Harvard College* . . . Boston, MA: Massachusetts Historical Society, 1873–1999.
WJE	*The Works of Jonathan Edwards.* 26 vols, ed. Perry Miller, et al. New Haven, CT: Yale University Press, 1957–2008.
WJE Online	*Works of Jonathan Edwards Online.* Jonathan Edwards Center, Yale University, 2008–. Online: http://edwards.yale.edu/archive.

Primary Sources

Chauncy, Charles

Chauncy, Charles. *The Accursed Thing Must Be Taken Away from among a People, if They Would Reasonably Hope to Stand before Their Enemies. A Sermon Preached at the Thursday-Lecture in Boston, September 3, 1778. And Printed at the Desire of the Hearers.* Boston: Thomas and John Fleet, 1778. [*Accursed Thing*]

———. *All Nations of the Earth Blessed in Christ, the Seed of Abraham. A Sermon Preached at Boston, at the Ordination of the Rev. Mr. Joseph Bowman, to the Work of the Gospel-Ministry, More Especially among the Mohawk-Indians, on the Western Borders of New-England. August 31. 1762.* Boston: John Draper, 1762. [*All Nations*]

———. *The Appeal to the Public Answered, in behalf of the Non-Episcopal Churches in America; Containing Remarks on What Dr. Thomas Bradbury Chandler Has Advanced, on the Four Following Points. The Original and Nature of the Episcopal Office; Reasons for Sending Bishops to America. The Plan on Which It Is Proposed to Send Them. And the Objections against Sending Them Obviated and Refuted. Wherein the Reasons for an American Episcopate are Shewn to Be Insufficient, and the Objections against It in Full Force.* Boston: Kneeland and Adams for Thomas Leverett, 1768. [*Appeal to the Public Answered*]

———. *The Benevolence of the Deity, Fairly and Impartially Considered. In Three Parts. The First Explains the Sense, in Which We Are to Understand Benevolence, as Applicable to God. The Second Asserts, and Proves, that This Perfection, in the Sense Explained, is One of His Essential Attributes. The Third Endeavours to Answer Objections. Under One or Other of These Heads, Occasion Will Be Taken to View Man as an Intelligent Moral Agent; Having within Himself an Ability and Freedom to Will, as well as to Do, in Opposition to Necessity from Any Extraneous Cause Whatever:- To Point Out the Origin of Evil, both Natural and Moral:- And to Offer What May Be Thought Sufficient to Shew, that There Is No Inconsistency between Infinite Benevolence in the Deity, Which Is Always Guided by Infinite Wisdom, and Any Appearances of Evil in the Creation.* Boston: Powars & Willis, 1784. [*Benevolence of the Deity*]

———. *The Blessedness of the Dead Who Die in the Lord. A Sermon Preached the Lord's Day after the Funeral of Mrs. Anna Foxcroft, the Amiable and Pious Consort of the Reverend Mr. Thomas Foxcroft, Who Died October 9th 1749, in the 53d Year of Her Age.* Boston: Rogers and Fowle, 1749. [*Blessedness of the Dead*]

———. "Breaking of Bread," in Remembrance of the Dying Love of Christ, a Gospel Institution. Five Sermons. In Which the Institution Is Explained; a General Observance of It Recommended and Enforced; Objections Answered; and Such Difficulties, Doubts, and Fears, Relative to It, Particularly Mentioned, and Removed, Which Have too Commonly Discouraged Some from an Attendance at It, and Proved to Others a Source of Discomfort, in the Regard They Have Endeavoured to Pay to It. Boston: D. Kneeland for Thomas Leverett, 1772. ["Breaking of Bread"]

———. Character and Overthrow of Laish Considered and Applied. A Sermon Preached at the Desire of the Honourable Artillery-Company, In Boston, June 3. 1734. Being the Anniversary Day for Their Election of Officers. Boston: S. Kneeland and T. Green for D. Henchman, 1734. [Character and Overthrow]

———. "The Charge," reprinted in John Hunt, A Sermon Preached September 25, 1771. At His Ordination, and at the Instalment of the Rev. John Bacon. to the Joint Pastoral Charge of the South-Church in Boston. To Which is Added, the Charge by the Rev. Dr. Chauncy, and the Right Hand of Fellowship by the Rev. Dr. Elliot, 29–32. Boston: Kneeland and Adams, 1772. ["The Charge"]

———. Charity to the Distressed Members of Christ Accepted as Done to Himself, and Rewarded, at the Judgment-day, with Blessedness in God's Everlasting Kingdom. A Sermon, Preached the Lord's-Day after the Death of Mr. Edward Gray. Who Departed This Life July 2nd, 1757, in the 84th Year of His Age. Boston: Green & Russell, 1757. [Charity]

———. Christian Love, as Exemplified by the First Christian Church in Their Having All Things in Common, Placed in Its True and Just Point of Light. In a Sermon, Preached at the Thursday-Lecture, in Boston, August 3d. 1773. From Acts 4.31. Wherein It Is Shown, that Christian Churches, in Their Character as Such, Are Strongly Obliged to Evidence the Reality of Their Christian Love, though not by Having All Things in Common, yet by Making Such Provision, According to Their Ability, for Their Members in a State of Penury, as that None of Them May Suffer through Want of the Things Needful for the Body; and that Deacons Are Officers Appointed by Christ to Take Care of His Poor Saints, Making All Proper Distributions to Them in His Name, and as Enabled Hereto by the Churches to Which They Respectively Belong. Boston: Kneeland & Davis for Thomas Leverett, 1773. [Christian Love]

———. Civil Magistrates Must Be Just, Ruling in the Fear of God. A Sermon Preached before His Excellency William Shirley, Esq; The Honourable His Majesty's Council, and House of Representatives, of the Province of the Massachusetts Bay in N. England; May 27, 1747. Being the Anniversary for the Election of His Majesty's Council for Said Province. Boston: House of Representatives, 1747. [Civil Magistrates]

———. A Compleat View of Episcopacy, as Exhibited from the Fathers of the Christian Church, until the Close of the Second Century: Containing an Impartial Account of Them, of Their Writings, and of What They Say Concerning Bishops and Presbyters; with Observations, and Remarks, Tending to Shew, that They Esteemed These One and the Same Order of Ecclesiastical Officers. In Answer to Those, Who Have Represented It as a Certain Fact, Universally Handed Down, even from the Apostles Days, that Governing and Ordaining Authority Was Exercised by Such Bishops Only, as Were of an Order Superior to Presbyters. Boston: Daniel Kneeland for Thomas Leverett, 1771. [Compleat View of Episcopacy]

———. *Cornelius's Character. A Sermon Preach'd the Lord's-Day after the Funeral of Mr. Cornelius Thayer, One of the Deacons of the First Church of Christ in Boston; Who Died, April 10, 1745. Aetat 60.* Boston: D. Gookin, 1745. [*Cornelius's Character*]

———. *The Counsel of Two Confederate Kings to Set the Son of Tabeal on the Throne, Represented as Evil, in It's Natural Tendency and Moral Aspect. A Sermon Occasion'd by the Present Rebellion in Favour of the Pretender. Preach'd in Boston, at the Thursday-Lecture, February 6th. 1745,6.* Boston: D. Gookin, 1746. [*Counsel of Two Confederate Kings*]

———. *A Discourse on "the Good News from a Far Country." Deliver'd July 24th. A Day of Thanks-giving to Almighty God, throughout the Province of the Massachusetts-Bay in New-England, on Occasion of the Repeal of the Stamp-Act; Appointed by His Excellency, the Governor of Said Province, at the Desire of It's House of Representatives, with the Advice of His Majesty's Council.* Boston: Kneeland and Adams for Thomas Leverett, 1766. [*Discourse on "The Good News"*]

———. *A Discourse Occasioned by the Death of the Reverend Dr. Joseph Sewall, Late Colleague Pastor of the South-Church in Boston: Who Departed This Life, On the Evening of June 27. 1769. In the 81st. Year of His Age. Delivered the Lord's-Day after His Decease.* Boston: Kneeland and Adams, 1769. [*Discourse Occasioned by the Death of the Reverend Dr. Joseph Sewall*]

———. *A Discourse Occasioned by the Death of the Reverend Jonathan Mayhew, D. D. Late Pastor of the West-Church in Boston: Who Departed This Life on Wednesday Morning, July 9, 1766, Aetatis 46. Delivered the Lord's-Day after His Decease.* Boston: R. and S. Draper, Edes and Gill; and T. and J. Fleet, 1766. [*Discourse Occasioned by the Death of the Reverend Jonathan Mayhew*]

———. *A Discourse Occasioned by the Death of the Reverend Thomas Foxcroft, M. A. Late Colleague-Pastor of the First Church of Christ in Boston: Who Departed This Life on Lord's-Day Forenoon, June 18, 1769. In the 73d Year of His Age. Delivered the Lord's-Day after His Decease.* Boston: Daniel Kneeland for Thomas Leverett, 1769. [*Discourse Occasioned by the Death of the Reverend Thomas Foxcroft*]

———. *Divine Glory Brought to View in the Final Salvation of All Men. A Letter to the Friend to Truth. By One Who Wishes Well to All Mankind.* Boston: T. and J. Fleet, 1783. [*Divine Glory*]

———. *The Duty of Ministers to "Make Known the Mystery of the Gospel"; and the Duty of People to "Pray for Them," that They May Do It "with Boldness," or Fortitude. A Sermon Preached at the Ordination of the Reverend Mr. Penuel Bowen, a Colleague-Pastor of the New-South-Church in Boston, April 30, 1766.* Boston: Edes and Gill, 1766. [*Duty of Ministers*]

———. *Early Piety Recommended and Exemplify'd. A Sermon Occasioned by the Death of Elisabeth Price, an Eminently Pious Young Woman, Who Departed This Life, February 22, 1731/2. In the Seventeenth Year of Her Age.* Boston: S. Kneeland & T. Green for B. Gray, 1732. [*Early Piety*]

———. *The Earth Delivered from the Curse to Which It Is, at Present, Subjected. A Sermon Occasioned by the Late Earthquakes in Spain and Portugal, as well as New-England; and Preached at the Boston-Thursday-Lecture, January 22, 1756. Published by the General Desire of the Hearers.* Boston: Edes and Gill, 1756. [*Earth Delivered*]

———. *Earthquakes a Token of the Righteous Anger of God. A Sermon Preached at the Old-Brick-Meeting-House in Boston, the Lord's-Day after the Terrible Earthquake,*

Which Suddenly Awoke Us out of Our Sleep in the Morning of the 18th of November, 1755. Boston: Edes and Gill, 1755. [*Earthquakes a Token*]

———. *Enthusiasm Described and Caution'd Against. A Sermon Preach'd at the Old Brick Meeting-House in Boston, the Lord's Day after the Commencement, 1742. With a Letter to the Reverend Mr. James Davenport.* Boston: J. Draper for S. Eliot and J. Blanchard, 1742. [*Enthusiasm Described*]

———. *Five Dissertations on the Scripture Account of the Fall; and Its Consequences.* London: C. Dilly, 1785. [*Five Dissertations*]

———. *The Gifts of the Spirit to Ministers Consider'd in Their Diversity; with the Wise Ends of Their Various Distribution, and the Good Purposes It Is Adapted to Serve. A Sermon Preach'd at the Boston Thursday-Lecture, Decemb. 17, 1741. And Made Publick at the Desire of the Hearers.* Boston: Rogers and Fowle for S. Eliot, 1742. [*Gifts of the Spirit*]

———. *The Horrid Nature, and Enormous Guilt of Murder. A Sermon Preached at the Thursday-Lecture in Boston, November 19th. 1754. The Day of the Execution of William Wicer, for the Murder of William Chism.* Boston: Thomas Fleet, 1754. [*Horrid Nature*]

———. *The Idle-Poor Secluded from the Bread of Charity by the Christian Law. A Sermon Preached in Boston, before the Society for Encouraging Industry and Employing the Poor. Aug. 12, 1752.* Boston: Thomas Fleet, 1752. [*Idle-Poor Secluded*]

———. *Joy, the Duty of Survivors, on the Death of Pious Friends and Relatives. A Funeral Discourse on the Death of Mrs. Lucy Waldo, the Amiable Consort of Mr. Samuel Waldo, Merchant in Boston: Who Departed This Life August 7th 1741, in the 38th Year of Her Age.* Boston: S. Kneeland and T. Green, 1741. [*Joy*]

———. *A Letter to a Friend, Containing Remarks on Certain Passages in a Sermon Preached, by the Right Reverend Father in God, John Lord Bishop of Landaff, before the Incorporated Society for the Propagation of the Gospel in Foreign Parts, at Their Anniversary Meeting in the Parish Church of St. Mary Le-Bow, February 20, 1767. In Which the Highest Reproach Is Undeservedly Cast Upon the American Colonies.* Boston: Kneeland and Adams for Thomas Leverett, 1767. [*Letter to a Friend, Containing Remarks*]

———. *A Letter to a Friend; Giving a Concise, but Just, Account, according to the Advices hitherto Received, of the Ohio-Defeat; and Pointing out also the Many Good Ends, This Inglorious Event Is Naturally Adapted to Promote: or, Shewing Wherein It Is Fitted to Advance the Interest of All the American British Colonies. To Which Is Added, Some General Account of the New-England Forces, with What They Have already Done, Counter-ballancing the above Loss.* Boston: Edes and Gill, 1755. [*Letter To a Friend (Ohio-Defeat)*]

———. *A Letter to a Friend. Giving a Concise, but Just, Representation of the Hardships and Sufferings the Town of Boston Is Exposed to, and Must Undergo in Consequence of the Late Act of the British-Parliament; Which, by Shutting Up It's Port, Has Put a Fatal Bar in the Way of That Commercial Business on Which It Depended for It's Support, Shewing, at the Same Time, Wherein This Edict, however Unintended, Is Powerfully Adapted to Promote the Interest of All the American Colonies, and even of Boston Itself in the End.* Boston: Greenleaf, 1774. [*Letter to a Friend*]

———. *A Letter from a Gentleman in Boston, to Mr. George Wishart, One of the Ministers of Edinburgh, Concerning the State of Religion in New-England.* Edinburgh,

1742. Reprint, *Clarendon Historical Society Reprints*, March 1883. [*Letter from a Gentleman in Boston*]

———. *A Letter to the Reverend Mr. George Whitefield, Vindicating Certain Passages He Has Excepted Against, in a Late Book Entitled, Seasonable Thoughts on the State of Religion in New-England; and Shewing that He Has neither Sufficiently Defended Himself, nor Retracted His Past Misconduct*. Boston: Rogers and Fowle for S. Eliot, 1745. [*Letter to the Reverend Mr. George Whitefield*]

———. "Life of the Rev. President Chauncy, Written At the Request of Dr. Stiles." *CMHS*, 1:10 (1809), 171–80. ["Life of the Rev. President Chauncy"]

———. *Man's Life Considered under the Similitude of a Vapour, that Appeareth for a Little Time, and then Vanisheth Away. A Sermon on the Death of That Honorable & Vertuous Gentlewoman Mrs. Sarah Byfield, the Amiable Consort of The Honorable Nathanael Byfield, Esq; Who Died Decemb. 21st, 1730. In the 58th Year of Her Age*. Boston: B. Green, 1731. [*Man's Life Considered*]

———. *Marvellous Things Done by the Right Hand and Holy Arm of God in Getting Him the Victory. A Sermon Preached the 18th of July, 1745. Being a Day Set Apart for Solemn Thanksgiving to Almighty God, for the Reduction of Cape-Breton by His Majesty's New England Forces, under the Command of The Honourable William Pepperrell, Esq; Lieutenant-General and Commander in Chief, and Covered by a Squadron of His Majesty's Ships from Great Britain, Commanded by Peter Warren, Esq*. Boston: T. Fleet, 1745. [*Marvellous Things Done*]

———. *Ministers Cautioned against the Occasions of Contempt. A Sermon Preached before the Ministers of the Province of the Massachusetts-Bay, in New-England, at Their Annual Convention, In Boston; May 31, 1744*. Boston: Rogers and Fowle for Samuel Eliot, 1744. [*Ministers Cautioned*]

———. *Ministers Exhorted and Encouraged to Take Heed to Themselves, and to Their Doctrine. A Sermon Preached the 7th of November, at the Instalment of the Rev. Mr. Thomas Frink to the Pastoral Care of the Third Church in Plymouth*. Boston: Rogers and Fowle for S. Eliot, 1744. [*Ministers Exhorted and Encouraged*]

———. *The Mystery Hid from Ages and Generations, Made Manifest by the Gospel Revelation; or, the Salvation of All Men the Grand Thing Aimed at in the Scheme of God, as Opened in the New-Testament Writings, and Entrusted with Jesus Christ to Bring into Effect*. London: Charles Dilly, 1784. [*Mystery Hid*]

———. *Nathanael's Character Display'd. A Sermon, Preach'd The Lord's Day after the Funeral of The Honourable Nathanael Byfield, Esq; Late Judge of the Vice Admiralty, and One of His Majesty's Council for This Province. Who Died at His House in Boston, on the 6th of June, 1733. In the 80th Year of His Age*. Boston: n.p., 1733. [*Nathanael's Character*]

———. *The New Creature Describ'd, and Consider'd as the Sure Characteristick of a Man's Being in Christ: together with Some Seasonable Advice to Those Who Are New Creatures. A Sermon Preach'd at the Boston Thursday-Lecture, June 4, 1741. And Made Public at the General Desire of the Hearers*. Boston: G. Rogers for J. Edwards and S. Eliot, 1741. [*New Creature Describ'd*]

———. *The Only Compulsion Proper to be Made Use of, in the Affairs of Conscience and Religion. A Sermon Preach'd at the Old Brick Meeting-House in Boston, September 2d 1739. And Printed at the Desire of Many Who Heard It*. Boston: J. Draper for J. Edwards, 1739. [*Only Compulsion Proper*]

———. *The Opinion of One That Has Perused the Summer Morning's Conversation, Concerning Original Sin, Wrote by the Rev. Mr. Peter Clark, in Two Things Principally: First, that He Has Offered That, Which Has Rendered It Impossible the Doctrine of the Imputation of Adam's Guilt to His Posterity, Should Be True in the Sense It Is Held by Calvinists. Secondly, that tho' He Pretends to Be a Friend to the Calvinistical Doctrine of Imputed Guilt, yet He Has Deserted This Doctrine and Given It Up into the Hands of Its Enemies, as It Teaches the Liableness of All Mankind, without Exception, to the Torments of Hell, on Account of the First Sin. To Which Is Added, a Few Remarks on the Recommendatory Preface by Five Reverend Clergymen. In a Letter to a Friend.* Boston: Green & Russell, 1758. [*Opinion of One*]

———. *The Out-pouring of the Holy-Ghost. A Sermon Preach'd in Boston, May 13. 1742. On a Day of Prayer Observed by the First Church there, to Ask of God the Effusion of His Spirit.* Boston: T. Fleet for D. Henchman and S. Eliot, 1742. [*Out-pouring of the Holy-Ghost*]

———. *Prayer for Help a Seasonable Duty upon the Ceasing of Godly and Faithful Men. A Sermon Occasion'd by the Death of Several Worthy Members of the First Church in Boston: Preach'd the Lord's-day following the Anniversary Fast, Being the Sabbath after the Funeral of Mr. Jonathan Williams, One of the Deacons of Said Church; Who Departed This Life, March 27th. 1737. Aetat 63.* Boston: T. Fleet, 1737. [*Prayer for Help*]

———. *A Reply to Dr. Chandler's "Appeal Defended": Wherein His Mistakes Are Rectified, His False Arguing Refuted, and the Objections against the Planned American Episcopate Shewn to Remain in Full Force, notwithstanding All He Has Offered to Render Them Invalid.* Boston: Daniel Kneeland for Thomas Leverett, 1770. [*Reply to Dr. Chandler's "Appeal Defended"*]

———. "The Right Hand of Fellowship," in Naphtali Daggett, *The Testimony of Conscience a Most Solid Foundation of Rejoicing. A Sermon Preached at the Ordination of The Rev. Mr. Joseph Howe, to the Pastoral Care of the New-South Church in Boston, May 19th, 1773. By the Rev. Naphtali Daggett, A.M. President of Yale College in New-Haven, and Professor of Divinity in the Same. To Which Is Added, the Charge by the Rev. Aaron Brown, and the Right Hand of Fellowship by the Rev. Dr. Chauncy. Printed at the Desire of the Church.* Boston: Mills and Hicks, 1773. ["Right Hand of Fellowship"]

———, and John Clarke. *Salvation for All Men, Illustrated and Vindicated as a Scripture Doctrine, in Numerous Extracts from a Variety of Pious and Learned Men, Who Have Purposely Writ upon the Subject. Together with Their Answer to the Objections Urged against It. By One Who Wishes Well to All Mankind.* Boston: T. and J. Fleet, 1782. [*Salvation for All Men*]

———. *Seasonable Thoughts on the State of Religion in New-England, a Treatise in Five Parts. I. Faithfully Pointing out the Things of a Bad and Dangerous Tendency, in the Late, and Present, Religious Appearance, in the Land. II. Representing the Obligations Which Lie Upon the Pastors of these Churches in Particular, and upon All in General, to Use Their Endeavours to Suppress Prevailing Disorders; with the Great Danger of a Neglect in so Important a Matter. III. Opening, in Many Instances, Wherein the Discouragers of Irregularities Have Been Injuriously Treated. IV. Shewing What Ought to Be Corrected, or Avoided, in Testifying Against the Evil Things of the Present Day. V. Directing Our Thot's [sic], More Positively, to*

What May Be Judged the Best Expedients, to Promote Pure and Undefiled Religion in These Times. With a Preface Giving an Account of the Antinomians, Familists and Libertines, Who Infected These Churches, above an Hundred Years Ago: Very Needful for These Days; the Like Spirit, and Errors, Prevailing now as Did then. The Whole Being Intended, and Calculated, to Serve the Interest of Christ's Kingdom. Boston: Rogers and Fowle for Samuel Eliot, 1743. [*Seasonable Thoughts*]

———. *A Second Letter To a Friend; Giving a More Particular Narrative of the Defeat of the French Army at Lake-George, by the New-England Troops, than Has yet Been Published: Representing also the Vast Importance of This Conquest to the American-British-Colonies. To Which is Added, Such an Account of What the New-England Governments Have Done to Carry Into Effect Their Design against Crown-Point, as Will Shew the Necessity of Their Being Helped by Great-Britain, in Point of Money.* Boston: Edes and Gill, 1755. [*Second Letter to a Friend*]

———. *A Sermon, Delivered at the First Church in Boston, March 13th, 1785: Occasioned by the Return of the Society to Their House of Worship, after Long Absence, to Make Way for the Repairs That Were Necessary.* Boston: Greenleaf and Freeman, 1785. [*Sermon, Delivered at the First Church*]

———. *A Sermon Preached May 6, 1767. At the Ordination of The Reverend Simeon Howard, M.A. to the Pastoral Care of the West-Church in Boston. To Which the Charge, and Right-Hand of Fellowship, Delivered upon the Same Occasion, Are Added.* Boston: R. Draper, Edes & Gill, and T. & J. Fleet, 1767. [*Sermon Preached May 6, 1767*]

———. "A Sketch of Eminent Men in New-England. In a Letter from the Rev. Dr. Chauncy to Dr. Stiles." *CMHS*, 1:10 (1809), 154–65. ["Sketch of Eminent Men in New-England"]

———. *Trust in God, the Duty of a People in a Day of Trouble. A Sermon Preached, May 30th. 1770. At the Request of a Great Number of Gentlemen, Friends to the Liberties of North-America, Who Were Desirous, notwithstanding the Removal of the Massachusetts General-Court (Unconstitutionally as They Judged) to Cambridge, that God Might Be Acknowledged in That House of Worship at Boston, in Which Our Tribes, from the Days of Our Fathers, Have Annually Sought to Him for Direction, Previous to the Choice of His Majesty's Council.* Boston: Daniel Kneeland for Thomas Leverett, 1770. [*Trust in God*]

———. *Twelve Sermons on the Following Seasonable and Important Subjects. Justification Impossible by the Works of the Law. The Question Answered, "Wherefore then Serveth the Law"? The Nature of Faith, as Justifying, Largely Explained, and Remarked on. The Place, and Use, of Faith, in the Affair of Justification. Human Endeavours, in the Use of Means, the Way in Which Faith is Obtained. The Method of the Spirit in Communicating the "Faith, by Which the Just Do Live": The Inquiry of the Young Man in the Gospel, "What Shall I Do that I May Have Eternal Life"? With Interspersed Notes, in Defence of the Truth; Especially in the Points Treated On, in the above Discourses.* Boston: D. and J. Kneeland for Thomas Leverett, 1765. [*Twelve Sermons*]

———. *An Unbridled Tongue a Sure Evidence, that Our Religion Is Hypocritical and Vain. A Sermon Preach'd at the Boston Thursday-Lecture, September 10th. 1741. And Publish'd at the Desire of the Hearers.* Boston: Rogers and Fowle, 1741. [*Unbridled Tongue*]

———. *The Validity of Presbyterian Ordination Asserted and Maintained. A Discourse Delivered at the Anniversary Dudleian-Lecture, at Harvard-College in Cambridge New-England, May 12. 1762. With an Appendix, Giving a Brief Historical Account of the Epistles Ascribed to Ignatius; and Exhibiting Some of the Many Reasons, Why They Ought not to Be Depended on as His Uncorrupted Works*. Boston: Richard Draper, 1762. [*Validity of Presbyterian Ordination*]

———, and Thomas Foxcroft. "To the Reader." Preface to Samuel Whittelsey, *The Woful Condition of Impenitent Souls in Their Separate State. A Sermon Preach'd to the Old or First Gather'd Church in Boston, on the Lord's-Day, April 4, 1731*. Boston: S. Kneeland and T. Green for S. Gerrish, 1731. ["To the Reader"]

Mayhew, Jonathan

Mayhew, Jonathan. *Christian Sobriety: Being Eight Sermons on Titus II.6. Preached with a Special View to the Benefit of the Young Men Usually Attending the Public Worship at the West Church in Boston. Published More Particularly at Their Desire, and Dedicated to Them*. Boston: Richard and Samuel Draper, 1763. [*Christian Sobriety*]

———. *Collection of Sermons by Jonathan Mayhew, 1749–1764*. San Marino, CA: Huntington Library, microfilm HM 8046-8053. [*Collection of Sermons*]

———. *A Defence of the Observations on the Charter and Conduct of the Society for the Propagation of the Gospel in Foreign Parts, against an Anonymous Pamphlet Falsly Intitled,* A Candid Examination of Dr. Mayhew's Observations, &c. *and also against the Letter to a Friend Annexed thereto, Said to Contain a Short Vindication of Said Society. By One of Its Members*. Boston: R. & S. Draper, Edes & Gill, T. & J. Fleet, 1763. [*Defence of the Observations*]

———. *Discourse Concerning Unlimited Submission and Non-Resistance to the Higher Powers: with Some Reflections on the Resistance Made to King Charles I. And on the Anniversary of His Death: in Which the Mysterious Doctrine of That Prince's Saintship and Martyrdom Is Unriddled: the Substance of Which Was Delivered in a Sermon Preached in the West Meeting-House in Boston the Lord's-Day after the 30th of January, 1749–50. Published at the Request of the Hearers*. Boston: D. Fowle and D. Gookin, 1750. [*Discourse Concerning Unlimited Submission*]

———. *A Discourse Occasioned by the Death of King George II. And the Happy Accession of His Majesty King George III, to the Imperial Throne of Great-Britain; Delivered Jan. 4th 1761. And Published at the Desire of the West Church and Congregation in Boston, New-England*. Boston, MA: Edes & Gill, 1761. [*Discourse Occasioned by the Death of King George II*]

———. *A Discourse Occasioned by the Death of The Honourable Stephen Sewall, Esq; Chief-Justice of the Superiour Court of Judicature, Court of Assize, and General Goal-Delivery; as also a Member of His Majesty's Council for the Province of the Massachusetts-Bay in New England: Who Departed this Life on Wednesday-Night, September 10, 1760. Aetatis 58. Delivered the Lord's-Day after His Decease*. Boston, MA: Richard Draper, et al., 1760. [*Discourse Occasioned by the Death of The Honourable Stephen Sewall*]

———. *A Discourse on Rev. XV. 3d, 4th. Occasioned by the Earthquakes* in November 1755. *Delivered in the West-Meeting-House, Boston, Thursday December 18, Following. In Five Parts, with an Introduction. Part I. Of the Greatness of God's*

Works. Part II. Of Their Marvellous and Unsearchable Nature. Part III. Of the Moral Perfection and Government of God. Part IV. Of Our Obligation to Fear, Glorify and Worship Him. Part V. Practical Reflections upon the Subject, Relative to the Occasion. Boston: Edes & Gill and R. Draper, l755. [*Discourse on Rev. XV. 3d, 4th*]

———. *The Expected Dissolution of All Things, a Motive to Universal Holiness. Two Sermons Preached in Boston, N.E. on the Lords-Day, Nov. 23, 1755; Occasioned by the Earthquakes Which Happen'd on the Tuesday Morning, and Saturday Evening Preceeding.* Boston, MA: 1755. [*Expected Dissolution*]

———. *God's Hand and Providence to be Religiously Acknowledged in Public Calamities. A Sermon Occasioned by the Great Fire in Boston, New-England, Thursday March 20, 1760. And Preached on the Lord's-Day Following.* Boston: Richard Draper, Edes and Gill and Thomas Fleet, 1760. [*God's Hand and Providence*]

———. *A Letter of Reproof to Mr. John Cleaveland of Ipswich, Occasioned by a Defamatory Libel Published under His Name, Intitled, An Essay to Defend Some of the Most Important Principles of the Reformed System of Christianity, &c. against the Injurious Aspersions Cast on the Same by Jonathan Mayhew, D.D. in His Late Thanksgiving Sermons on Psalms CXLV,9. In Which, &c.* Boston: Edes and Gill; T. and J. Fleet, 1764. [*Letter of Reproof*]

———. "Letter of Rev. Jonathan Mayhew to Richard Clarke, 1765," edited by Daniel Denison Slade, *New England Historical and Genealogical Register*, 46 (January 1892), 15–20.

———. "Appendix A: Jonathan Mayhew's Memorandum." In Bernard Bailyn, "Religion and Revolution: Three Biographical Studies," *Perspectives in American History*, 4 (1970), 140–3. ["Memorandum"]

———. *Observations on the Charter and Conduct of the Society for the Propagation of the Gospel in Foreign Parts; Designed to Shew Their Non-Conformity to Each Other. With Remarks on the Mistakes of East Apthorp, M.A. Missionary at Cambridge, in Quoting, and Representing the Sense of Said Charter, &c. as also Various Incidental Reflections Relative to the Church of England, and the State of Religion in North-America, Particularly in New-England.* Boston: Richard and Samuel Draper, Edes and Gill, Thomas and John Fleet, 1763. [*Observations*]

———. *Popish Idolatry: A Discourse Delivered in the Chapel of Harvard-College in Cambridge, New-England, May 8. 1765. At the Lecture Founded by The Honorable Paul Dudley, Esquire.* Boston: R. and S. Draper, Edes & Gill, and T. & J. Fleet, 1765. [*Popish Idolatry*]

———. *Practical Discourses Delivered on Occasion of the Earthquakes in November, 1755. Wherein is Particularly Shown, by a Variety of Arguments, the Great Importance of Turning Our Feet unto God's Testimonies, and of Making Haste to Keep His Commandments; Together with the Reasonableness, the Necessity, and Great Advantage, of a Serious Consideration of Our Ways.* Boston: Richard Draper, 1760. [*Practical Discourses*]

———. *Remarks on an Anonymous Tract, Entitled An Answer to Dr. Mayhew's Observations on the Charter and Conduct of the Society for the Propagation of the Gospel in Foreign Parts. Being a Second Defence of the Said Observations.* Boston: R. and S. Draper, Edes and Gill, T. & J. Fleet, 1764. [*Remarks on an Anonymous Tract*]

———. *A Sermon Preached at Boston in New-England, May 26. 1751. Occasioned by the Much-lamented Death of His Royal Highness Frederick, Prince of Wales.* Boston: Richard Draper and Daniel Gookin, 1751. [*Sermon Preached at Boston*]

———. *A Sermon Preach'd in the Audience of His Excellency William Shirley, Esq; Captain General, Governour and Commander in Chief, The Honourable His Majesty's Council, and The Honourable House of Representatives, of the Province of the Massachusetts-Bay, in New-England. May 29th 1754. Being the Anniversary for the Election of His Majesty's Council for the Province. N.B. The Parts of Some Paragraphs Passed Over in the Preaching of This Discourse, Are now Inserted in the Publication.* Boston: Samuel Kneeland, 1754. [*Sermon Preach'd*].

———. *Sermons upon the Following Subjects, Viz. On Hearing the Word: on Receiving It with Meekness: on Renouncing Gross Immoralities: on the Necessity of Obeying the Gospel: on Being Found in Christ: on Justification by Faith: on the Nature, Principles and Extent of Evangelical Obedience. On the Deceitfulness of the Heart, and God's Knowledge Thereof. On the Shortness and Vanity of Human Life: and on the True Value, Use and End of Life; together with the Conduciveness of Religion to Prolong, and Make It Happy.* Boston: Richard Draper, 1755. [*On Hearing the Word*]

———. *Seven Sermons upon the Following Subjects, Viz. The Difference betwixt Truth and Falshood, Right and Wrong. The Natural Abilities of Men for Discerning These Differences. The Right and Duty of Private Judgment. Objections Considered. The Love of God. The Love of Our Neighbour. The First and Great Commandment, &c. Preached at a Lecture in the West Meeting-House in Boston, Begun the First Thursday in June, and Ended the Last Thursday in August, 1748.* Boston: Rogers and Fowle, 1749. [*Seven Sermons*]

———. *The Snare Broken. A Thanksgiving-Discourse Preached at the Desire of the West Church in Boston, N.E. Friday May 23, 1766. Occasioned by the Repeal of the Stamp Act.* Boston: R. & S. Draper, Edes & Gill, T. & J. Fleet, 1766. [*Snare Broken*]

———. *Striving to Enter In at the Strait Gate Explain'd and Inculcated; and the Connexion of Salvation Therewith, Proved from the Holy Scriptures. In Two Sermons on Luke XIII.24.* Boston, MA: 1761. [*Striving to Enter*]

———. *Two Discourses Delivered November 23d. 1758. Being the Day Appointed by Authority to be Observed as a Day of Public Thanksgiving: Relating, More Especially, to the Success of His Majesty's Arms, and Those of the King of Prussia, the Last Year.* Boston: R. Draper, Edes & Gill, Green & Russell, [1758]. [*Two Discourses Delivered November 23d. 1758*]

———. *Two Discourses Delivered October 25th. 1759. Being the Day Appointed by Authority to be Observed as a Day of Public Thanksgiving, for the Success of His Majesty's Arms, More Particularly in the Reduction of Quebec, the Capital of Canada. With an Appendix, Containing a Brief Account of Two Former Expeditions against That City and Country, Which Proved Unsuccessful.* Boston: R. Draper et al., 1759. [*Two Discourses Delivered October 25th. 1759*]

———. *Two Discourses Delivered October 9th, 1760. Being the Day Appointed to be Observed as a Day of Public Thanksgiving for the Success of His Majesty's Arms, More Especially in the Intire Reduction of Canada.* Boston: R. & S. Draper, Edes & Gill, T. & J. Fleet, 1760. [*Two Discourses Delivered October 9th. 1760*]

———. *Two Sermons on the Nature, Extent and Perfection of the Divine Goodness. Delivered December 9. 1762. Being the Annual Thanksgiving of the Province, &c.*

On Psalm 145.9. Published with Some Enlargements. Boston: D. and J. Kneeland, 1763. [*Divine Goodness*]

———, and East Apthorp. *Observations on the Charter and Conduct of the Society for the Propagation of the Gospel in Foreign Parts; Designed to Shew Their Non-Conformity to Each Other. With Remarks on the Mistakes of East Apthorp, M.A. Missionary at Cambridge, in Quoting and Representing the Sense of Said Charter, &c. As also Various Incidental Reflections Relative to the Church of England, and the State of Religion in North-America, Particularly in New-England. By Jonathan Mayhew, D. D. Pastor of the West-Church in Boston. To Which Is Subjoined Apthorp's Considerations.* London: W. Nicoll, 1763. [*Observations*]

———, and Thomas Hollis. "Thomas Hollis and Jonathan Mayhew: Their Correspondence, 1759–1766," ed. Bernard Knollenberg, *Proceedings of the Massachusetts Historical Society*, 69 (1956), 102–93.

Other

Anon. "Advertisement. A Certain Jonathan Mayhew . . . ." Boston: 1769(?).

———. "Advertisements." *The Boston Weekly News-Letter*, 1582 (May 23–30, 1734) 2.

———. *At a Council of Ten Churches . . . .* Boston: 1734.

———. "The Boston Ministers: A Ballad." *The New-England Historical and Genealogical Register* 13/2 (April 1859) 131.

———. "The Boston Ministers, A Ballad—First and Second Parts." *The New-England Historical and Genealogical Register* 14/4 (October 1860) 369.

———. *Brief Notes on the Creed of St. Athanasius.* London (?), 1694.

———. "Copy of a Royalist Handbill Distributed among the British Soldiers at Boston, September 1774." *New England Historical and Genealogical Register* 21/1 (1867) 60.

———. *A Narrative of the Proceedings of Those Ministers of the County of Hampshire . . . .* Boston: 1736.

———. *The New-England Primer Enlarged. For the More Easy Attaining the True Reading of English. To Which Is Added, Milk for Babes.* Boston: S. Kneeland & T. Green, 1727.

———. *A Philosophical Survey of Nature: in Which the Long Agitated Question Concerning Human Liberty and Necessity, Is Endeavoured to Be Fully Determined from Incontestable Phaenomena.* London: 1763.

———. *The Report of a Committee of the First Church in Braintree . . . .* Boston: 1753.

———. *The Result of a Late Ecclesiastical Council.* Boston: 1753.

———. "To the Officers and Soldiers of His Majesty's Troops in Boston." Advertisement in *The Boston Evening-Post*, September 19, 1774, 4.

———. *The Wonderful Narrative . . . .* Boston: Rogers and Fowle, 1742.

Adams, Abigail, et al. *The Adams–Jefferson Letters: The Complete Correspondence between Thomas Jefferson and Abigail and John Adams.* Edited by Lester J. Cappon. 2 vols. Chapel Hill: University of North Carolina Press, 1959.

Adams, John. *A Defence of the Constitutions of Government of the United States of America, against the Attack of M. Turgot in His Letter to Dr. Price, Dated the Twenty-second Day of March, 1778, . . .* 3rd ed. 3 vols. Philadelphia, PA: Budd and Bartram, for William Cobbett, 1797/1787.

———. *Diary and Autobiography of John Adams*. Edited by L. H. Butterfield et al. 4 vols. Cambridge, MA: Belknap, 1961.

———. "From John Adams to James Madison, 25 July 1818." Founders Online [Early Access], National Archives. Online: http://founders.archives.gov/documents/Adams/99-02-02-6941.

———. "From John Adams to Jedidiah Morse, 15 May, 1815." Founders Online [Early Access], National Archives. Online: http://founders.archives.gov/documents/Adams/99-02-02-6468.

———. *Papers of John Adams*. Edited by Robert J. Taylor et al. 17 vols. Cambridge, MA: Belknap, 1977–.

———. *The Works of John Adams, Second President of the United States: with a Life of the Author, Notes and Illustrations, by His Grandson Charles Francis Adams*. 10 vols. Boston: Little, Brown & Co., 1856.

Adams, John, and Abigail Adams. *Familiar Letters of John Adams and Abigail Adams during the Revolution*. Edited by Charles Francis Adams. New York: Hurd & Houghton, 1876.

Adams, John, et al. *Adams Family Correspondence*. Edited by L. H. Butterfield et al. 11 vols. Cambridge, MA: Harvard University Press, 1963–2013.

———. *Microfilms of The Adams Papers Owned by the Adams Manuscript Trust and Deposited in the Massachusetts Historical Society*, 608 Reels. Boston: Massachusetts Historical Society, 1954–1959.

Aplin, John. *Verses on Doctor Mayhew's Book of Observations* . . . . Providence, RI: William Goddard, 1763.

[Appleton, Nathaniel?]. *A Letter to the Reverend Mr. George Whitefield, Publickly Calling upon Him to Vindicate His Conduct or Confess His Faults* . . . . Boston: Thomas Fleet, 1744.

Apthorp, East. *Considerations on the Institution and Conduct*. . . . Boston: W. Nicoll, 1763.

———. *A Review of Dr. Mayhew's Remarks on the Answer to His Observations*. . . . London: John Rivington, 1764.

Balch, William. *The Apostles St. Paul and St. James Reconciled*. . . . Boston: J. Edwards, 1743.

———. *False Confidences Exposed*. . . . Boston: J. Edwards, 1743.

———. *A Vindication of Some Points of Doctrine*. . . . Boston: J. Edwards, 1746.

———. *The Vindication of the Second Church in Bradford*. . . . Boston: J. Edwards, 1746.

———, et al. *Letters from the First Church in Glocester*. . . . Boston: J. Edwards, 1744.

Ballou, Hosea, II. "Dogmatic and Religious History of Universalism in America." *Universalist Quarterly and General Review* 5 (January 1848) 79–104.

Baron, Richard. *The Pillars of Priestcraft and Orthodoxy Shaken* . . . . 2nd ed. 4 vols. London: Cadell et al., 1768.

Bayly, James, et al. *A Brief Narrative of Some of the Brethren of the Second Church in Bradford* . . . . Boston: J. Edwards, 1746.

Belknap, Jeremy, et al. "The Belknap Papers." *CMHS* 5/2–3 (1877).

———, et al. "The Belknap Papers." *CMHS* 6/4 (1891).

Bellamy, Joseph. *The Law, Our Schoolmaster* . . . . New Haven, CT: James Parker, 1756.

———. *Sermons upon the Following Subjects* . . . . Boston: Edes and Gill and S. Kneeland, 1758.

———. *True Religion Delineated* . . . . Boston: S. Kneeland, 1750.

Bolingbroke, Henry St. John. *The Works of The Late Right Honourable Henry St. John, Lord Viscount Bolingbroke*, 5 vols. London: D. Mallet, 1754.

Bolton, Robert. *Some Generall Directions for a Comfortable Walking with God Delivered in the Lecture at Kettering in Northhamptonshire, with Enlargement*. 2nd ed. London: Edmund Weaver, 1626.

The Book of Common Prayer . . . According to the Use of the Church of England. Oxford: Oxford University Press, 1965.

The Boston Gazette. Boston, MA: 1719–98.

The Boston Evening-Post. Boston, MA: 1735–75.

The Boston Weekly News-Letter. Boston, MA: 1730–57.

Brattle, William. "To the Author of the Vindications of Mr. Whitefield's Journal, Touching His Remarks upon the College in Cambridge." *Boston Gazette*, June 15–22, 1741, 1–2, and June 22–29, 1–2.

Robert Breck, "Confession of Faith." In William Cooper, *The Work of Ministers Represented . . . .* Boston: J. Draper, 1736.

Briant, Lemuel. *The Absurdity and Blasphemy of Depretiating Moral Virtue . . . .* Boston: D. Gookin, 1749.

———. *Some Friendly Remarks . . . .* Boston: D. Gookin, 1750.

———. *Some More Friendly Remarks . . . .* Boston: D. Gookin, 1751.

Browne, Arthur. *Remarks on Dr. Mayhew's Incidental Reflections . . . .* Portsmouth, NH: D. Fowle, 1763.

Burnet, Thomas. *Telluris Theoria Sacra . . . .* London: Gualt. Kettilby, 1681. Translated as *The Theory of the Earth*. London: W. Kettilby, 1690, and *The Sacred Theory of the Earth*. 4th ed. London: John Hooke, 1719.

Burr, Aaron. *The Supreme Deity of Our Lord Jesus Christ . . . .* Boston: J. Draper, 1757.

Butler, Joseph. *Fifteen Sermons Preached at the Rolls Chapel . . . .* London: W. Botham for James and John Knapton, 1726.

Calvin, John. *Institutes of the Christian Religion*. Edited by John T. McNeill. Library of Christian Classics 20. Philadelphia: Westminster, 1960.

Caner, Henry. *A Candid Examination of Dr. Mayhew's Observations . . . .* Boston: Thomas and John Fleet et al., 1763.

Caner, Henry, and Kenneth Cameron. *Letter-book of the Rev. Henry Caner, S.P.G. Missionary in Colonial Connecticut and Massachusetts until the Revolution; a Review of His Correspondence from 1728 through 1778*. Hartford: Transcendental, 1972.

Chandler, Thomas. *An Appeal to the Public . . . .* New York: James Parker, 1767.

———. *The Appeal Defended . . . .* New York: Hugh Gaine, 1769.

———. *The Appeal Farther Defended . . . .* New York: Hugh Gaine, 1771.

Checkley, John. *Choice Dialogues . . . .* Boston: Thomas Fleet, 1720.

———. *A Modest Proof of the Order and Government Settled by Christ and His Apostles . . . .* Boston: Benjamin Eliot, 1723.

Clark, Peter. *The Scripture-Doctrine of Original Sin, Stated and Defended . . . .* Boston: S. Kneeland, 1758.

Clarke, Samuel. *A Discourse Concerning the Unchangeable Obligations of Natural Religion, and the Truth and Certainty of the Christian Revelation . . . .* 2nd ed. London: Will. Botham for James Knapton, 1708.

———. *The Scripture-Doctrine of the Trinity . . . .* London: James Knapton, 1712.

———. *Sermons on the Following Subjects....* 10 vols. London: W. Botham, for James and John Knapton, [1730]–31.

———. *The Works*, 4 vols. London: J. and P. Knapton, 1738. Reprint, New York: Garland, 1978.

Cleaveland, John. *An Essay, to Defend Some of the Most Important Principles in the Protestant Reformed System of Christianity....* Boston: D. and J. Kneeland, 1763.

———. *A Reply to Dr. Mayhew's Letter of Reproof....* Boston: W. McAlpine and D. Fleming, 1765.

Coade, George. *A Letter to a Clergyman, Relating to His Sermon on the Thirtieth of January....* London: J. Robinson, 1746.

Colman, Benjamin. *Benjamin Colman Papers, 1641–1806*. Boston: Massachusetts Historical Society Microform Edition, 1978.

———. "Extract of a Letter from the Rev. Dr. Colman of Boston, to the Rev. Mr. George Whitefield." *PMHS* 53 (October 1919–June 1920) 197–98.

———. "Letter to George Whitefield [?], June 8, 1741." *PMHS* 53 (October 1919–June 1920) 202–3.

Cooke, Samuel. *A Sermon Preached at Cambridge....* Boston: Edes and Gill, 1770.

Cooper, William. *The Work of Ministers Represented....* Boston: J. Draper, 1736.

Cotton, John. *Spiritual Milk for Boston Babes in Either England....* Cambridge, MA: Samuel Green for Hezekiah Usher, 1656.

D'Anvers, Caleb. *The Country Journal: or, The Craftsman*. Edited by Henry St. John, Viscount Bolingbroke et al. London: Richard Francklin, 1727–50.

Davis, Isaac. *What Love Jesus Christ Has for Sinners*. Somers, CT: n.d.

Dickinson, Jonathan. *The True Scripture-Doctrine....* Boston: S. Eliot, 1741.

Eckley, Joseph. *Divine Glory Brought to View in the Condemnation of the Ungodly....* Boston: Robert Hodge, 1782.

Edwards, John. *Veritas Redux. Evangelical Truths Restored....* 2 vols. London: Jonathan Robinson, et al., 1707.

Edwards, Jonathan. *A Careful and Strict Enquiry into the Modern Prevailing Notions of That Freedom of Will....* Boston: S. Kneeland, 1754.

———. *A Faithful Narrative of the Surprising Work of God....* Boston: S. Kneeland and T. Green, 1738.

———. *God Glorified in the Work of Redemption....* Boston: D. Henchman, 1731.

———. *The Great Christian Doctrine of Original Sin Defended....* Boston: S. Kneeland, 1758.

———. *Sinners in the Hands of an Angry God....* Boston: S. Kneeland and T. Green, 1741.

———. *Some Thoughts Concerning the Present Revival of Religion in New-England....* Boston: S. Kneeland and T. Green, 1742.

———. *A Treatise Concerning Religious Affections....* Boston: S. Kneeland and T. Green, 1746.

Edwards, Jonathan, Jr. *Brief Observations on the Doctrine of Universal Salvation....* New Haven, CT: Meigs, Bowen and Dana, 1784.

Eliot, Andrew. "Letters from Andrew Eliot to Thomas Hollis." *CMHS* 4/4 (1858) 398–461.

———. "Remarks on the Bishop of Oxford's Sermon Preached before the Incorporated Society for the Propagation of the Gospel in Foreign Parts, 1740." *CMHS* 2/2 (1814) 190–216.

———. *A Sermon Preached before His Excellency Francis Bernard.* . . . Boston: Green and Russell, 1765.
Ellys, Anthony. *A Sermon Preached before the Incorporated Society for the Propagation of the Gospel in Foreign Parts.* . . . London: E. Owen and T. Harrison, 1759.
Emerson, Joseph. *Mr. Emerson's Exhortation to his People with Respect to Variety of Ministers.* Boston: S. Kneeland and T. Green, 1742.
Emlyn, Thomas. *An Humble Inquiry into the Scripture-Account of Jesus Christ.* . . . London [?], 1702. 5th ed. Boston: Edes & Gill, 1756.
———. "Memoirs of the Life and Sentiments of the Reverend Dr. Samuel Clarke." In *Historical Memoirs of the Life and Writings of Dr. Samuel Clarke* . . . , edited by William Whiston, "Appendix" 14–32. 3rd ed. London: John Whiston, 1748.
———. *The Works.* . . . 3 vols. 4th ed. London: John Noon and John Whiston, 1746.
Evans, Charles, et al. *Early American Imprints, Series I: Evans, 1639–1800.* New Canaan, CT: Readex; Worcester, MA: American Antiquarian Society, 2002–. Online: http://www.readex.com/content/early-american-imprints.
Ewer, John. *A Sermon Preached before the Incorporated Society for the Propagation of the Gospel in Foreign Parts* . . . . London: E. Owen and T. Harrison, 1767.
Filmer, Robert. *Patriarcha: or, The Natural Power of Kings.* London: Walter Davis, 1680.
Flavel, John. *The Whole Works of the Reverend Mr. John Flavel, Late Minister at Dartmouth in Devon. In Two Volumes* . . . . 2nd ed. 2 vols. London: John Nicholson, J. and B. Sprint et al., 1716.
Fleming, Caleb. *The Palladium of Great Britain and Ireland. Or Historical Strictures of Liberty, from before the Reformation down to the Present Times. Which Prove, to Whom and to What It Has Chiefly Owed Its Origin and Preservation, in These Islands.* London: C. Henderson, T. Becket and P. A. de Hondt, 1762.
Flynt, Henry. Diary of Henry Flynt, 1723–1747. December and January 1740, Archives, Harvard University, Cambridge, MA.
Foster, James. *Discourses on All the Principal Branches of Natural Religion and Social Virtue* . . . . 2 vols. London: Mr. Noon, J. and P. Knapton et al., 1749–52.
Foxcroft, Thomas. *An Apology in behalf of the Revd Mr. Whitefield* . . . . Boston: Rogers and Fowle, 1745.
———. *Humilis Confessio* . . . . Boston: S. Kneeland and T. Green, 1750.
———. *Like Precious Faith Obtained* . . . . Boston: Green & Russell, 1756.
———. *Some Seasonable Thoughts on Evangelic Preaching* . . . . Boston: S. Eliot, 1740.
Freeman, James. *Sermons on Particular Occasions.* 3rd ed. Boston: Sewell Phelps, 1821.
Gay, Ebenezer. *The Alienation of Affections from Ministers* . . . . Boston: Rogers and Fowle, 1747.
———. *The True Spirit of a Gospel-Minister Represented, and Urged* . . . . Boston: D. Gookin, 1746.
Gordon, Thomas. *An Examination of the Facts and Reasonings in the Lord Bishop of Chichester's Sermon* . . . . 4th ed. London: J. Peele, 1732.
Gordon, William. *The Doctrine of Final Universal Salvation Examined* . . . . Boston: T. and J. Fleet, 1783.
Gray, Harrison. "Memoir of Dr. Jonathan Mayhew, by Harrison Gray." Edited by Louis Leonard Tucker. *Proceedings of the Bostonian Society* (January 17, 1961) 26–48.
Hanley. *That Jesus Christ Is God by Nature* . . . . Boston: Green & Russell, 1756.
———. *Two Letters to a Very Eminent and Learned Gentleman* . . . . London: J. Peele, 1726.

Hartley, David. *Observations on Man* . . . . 2 vols. London: S. Richardson et al., 1749.
Hoadly, Benjamin. *The Measures of Submission to the Civil Magistrate Consider'd* . . . . . London: Tim. Childe, 1706.
———. *The Original and Institution of Civil Government, Discuss'd* . . . . London: James Knapton, 1710.
———. *The Reasonableness of Conformity to The Church of England* . . . . 4th ed. London: James Knapton, 1720.
———. *Sixteen Sermons Formerly Printed, now Collected into One Volume*. London: John and Paul Knapton, 1754.
Holyoke, Edward, et al. *The Testimony of the President, Professors, Tutors and Hebrew Instructor of Harvard College* . . . . Boston: T. Fleet, 1744.
Homes, William. "Diary of Rev. William Homes of Chilmark, Martha's Vineyard, 1689–1746." *New-England Historical and Genealogical Register* 50 (April 1896) 155–66.
Homologistes (pseud.). "To the Printer of The S: J. chronicle." *The St. James's Chronicle*, 824 (June 12–14, 1766) 1.
Hooper, William. *The Apostles neither Impostors nor Enthusiasts* . . . . Boston: Rogers and Fowle, 1742.
Hopkins, Samuel. *An Inquiry Concerning the Future State of Those Who Die in Their Sins* . . . . Newport, RI: 1783.
Hutchinson, Thomas. *The History of the Colony of Massachusets-Bay, from the First Settlement Thereof In 1628. Until Its Incorporation with the Colony of Plimouth, Province of Main, &cc. By the Charter of King William and Queen Mary, in 1691*. Boston: Thomas & John Fleet, 1764. [*History of the Colony of Massachusets-Bay*]
———. *The History of the Province of Massachusetts Bay, from 1749 to 1774* . . . . Edited by John Hutchinson. London: J. Murray, 1828. [*History of the Province of Massachusetts Bay*]
"J.B." "To the Printers, &c." February 18, 1763. *Boston Gazette* 412 (February 21, 1763) 3.
Johnson, Samuel. *A Letter from a Minister of the Church of England to His Dissenting Parishioners* . . . . New York: John Peter Zenger, 1733.
———. *A Second Letter from a Minister of the Church of England* . . . . Boston: 1734.
Jones, Jeremiah. *A New and Full Method of Settling the Canonical Authority of the New Testament* . . . . 3 vols. London: J. Clark and R. Hett, 1727. Reprint, Oxford: Clarendon, 1798.
Kent, Benjamin. *A Sermon Preached at a Lecture in Marlborough* . . . . Boston: 1734.
Locke, John. *Two Treatises of Government: in the Former, the False Principles, and Foundation of Sir Robert Filmer and His Followers Are Detected and Overthrown. The Latter Is an Essay Concerning the True Original, Extent, and End of Civil Government*. London: Printed for Awnsham Churchill, 1690.
———. *Two Treatises of Government by John Locke*. 6th ed. London: A. Millar, H. Woodfall, et al., 1764.
———. *Two Treatises of Government: A Critical Edition with an Introduction and Apparatus Criticus*. Edited by Peter Laslett. 2nd ed. Cambridge: Cambridge University Press, 1967.
———. *Two Treatises of Government: A Critical Edition with an Introduction and Apparatus Criticus*. Edited by Peter Laslett. Student ed. Cambridge: Cambridge University Press, 1988.

———. *The Works of John Locke Esq.* . . . . 4th ed. 3 vols. London: Edmund Parker, Edward Symon, et al., 1740.
Mather, Cotton. *A Christian Conversing with the Great Mystery of Christianity. The Mystery of the Trinity* . . . . Boston: T. Green, 1709.
———. *The Minister. A Sermon* . . . . Boston: 1722.
———. *Ratio Disciplinae Fratrum Nov-Anglorum* . . . . Boston: S. Gerrish, 1726.
———. "The Sentiments of Several Ministers in Boston . . . ." *CMHS* 2/2 (1814) 133–36.
———. *Theopolis Americana. An Essay on the Golden Street of the Holy City* . . . . Boston: B. Green for Samuel Gerrish, 1710.
Mather, Samuel. *All Men Will not Be Saved Forever* . . . . Boston: Benjamin Edes & Sons, 1782.
Mayhew, Experience. *All Mankind, by Nature, Equally under Sin* . . . . Boston: Samuel Gerrish, 1725.
———. *A Discourse Shewing* . . . . Boston: Samuel Gerrish, 1720.
———. *Grace Defended* . . . . Boston: D. Henchman, 1744.
———. *Indian Converts* . . . . London, 1727.
———. *Experience Mayhew's Indian Converts: A Cultural Edition.* Edited by Laura Arnold Liebman. Amherst: University of Massachusetts Press, 2008.
———. *A Letter to a Gentleman* . . . . Boston: S. Kneeland and T. Green, 1747.
———. *A Right to the Lord's Supper Considered* . . . . Boston: D. Henchman, 1741.
Molesworth, Robert. *An Account of Denmark as It Was in the Year 1692.* London, 1694.
Morse, Jedidiah, *The American Geography; or, a View of the Present Situation of the United States of America* . . . New ed. London: John Stockdale, 1794/1789.
Murray, John. *Letters and Sketches of Sermons.* 3 vols. Boston: Joshua Belcher, 1812.
———. *Records of the Life of The Rev. John Murray* . . . . Boston: Munroe and Francis, 1816.
———. *Some Hints Relative to the Forming of a Christian Church.* Boston: Joseph Bumstead for Benjamin Larkin, 1791.
———. *Universalism Vindicated* . . . . Charlestown, MA: J. Lamson, 1798.
Nicolai, Georg-Klein [pseud. Siegvolck, Paul]. *The Everlasting Gospel* . . . . Germantown, PA: Christopher Sower, 1753.
Niles, Samuel. *A Vindication of Divers Important Gospel-Doctrines* . . . . Boston: S. Kneeland, 1752.
Oliver, Peter. *Peter Oliver's Origin and Progress of the American Rebellion: A Tory View.* Edited by Douglass Adair and John A. Schutz. San Marino, CA: The Huntington Library, 1961.
Osborn, Samuel. *The Case and Complaint of Mr. Samuel Osborn* . . . . Boston: 1743.
Otis, James. *The Rights of the British Colonies Asserted and Proved.* Boston: Edes and Gill, 1764.
Pascal, Blaise. *Thoughts on Religion, and Other Subjects* . . . . Translated by Basil Kennet. London: A. and J. Churchil, 1704.
Pemberton, Ebenezer. *All Power in Heaven, and in Earth Given unto Jesus Christ* . . . . Boston: D. Fowle and Z. Fowle, 1756.
"Philanthropos" [pseud.]. "To the Reverend Mr. J——n M——w," *Boston Evening-Post* 714, April 17, 1749, 1.
Porter, John. *The Absurdity and Blasphemy of Substituting the Personal Righteousness of Men* . . . . Boston: Samuel Kneeland and Timothy Green, 1750.

Porter, John, and John Cotton. *A Vindication of a Sermon Preached at Braintree* . . . . Boston: S. Kneeland, 1751.

Price, Richard, et al., "The Price Letters." *PMHS* 17 (May 1903) 263–378.

Relly, James. *Union: or a Treatise on the Consanguinity and Affinity between Christ and His Church*. London, 1759.

Rich, Caleb. "A Narrative of Elder Caleb Rich." *The Candid Examiner* 2/23–26 (April 30, May 14, May 28, and June 18, 1827) 179–81, 185–89, 193–97, 200–202.

Sandeman, Robert. *Letters on Theron and Aspasio* . . . . Edinburgh: Sands, Donaldson, Murray, and Cochran, 1757.

Scott, Joseph Nicol. *Sermons, Preached in Defence of All Religion* . . . 2 vols. London: John Noon, 1743.

Secker, Thomas. *An Answer to Dr. Mayhew's Observations* . . . London, 1764.

———. *The Works of Thomas Secker* . . . . 3rd ed. 6 vols. Dublin: J. Williams, 1775.

Sewall, Samuel. "Extracts from Interleaved Almanacs, for the Years 1724 and 1732, in the Handwriting of Samuel Sewall, Jr." *New-England Historical and Genealogical Register* 16/1 (January 1862) 63–71.

Sharp, John. *The Works of the Most Reverend Dr. John Sharp*. . . . 3rd ed. 7 vols. London: J. and P. Knapton et al., 1754.

Shepard, Thomas. *A Short Catechism Familiarly Teaching the Knowledge of God, and of Our Selves* . . . . Cambridge, MA: Samuel Green, 1654.

Sherlock, Thomas. *Several Discourses Preached at the Temple Church.* . . . Dublin: G. Ewing et al., 1754.

Sidney, Algernon. *Discourses Concerning Government*. London, 1698.

———. *Discourses Concerning Government by Algernon Sydney, with His Letters, Trial, Apology and Some Memoirs of His Life*. London: A. Millar, 1763.

Stamp Act Congress (1765). *Proceedings of the Congress at New-York*. Annapolis, MD: Jonas Green, 1766.

Stiles, Ezra. *Extracts from the Itineraries and Other Miscellanies of Ezra Stiles, D.D., LL.D. 1755–1794 with a Selection from His Correspondence*. Edited by Franklin Dexter. New Haven, CT: Yale University Press, 1916.

———. *The Literary Diary of Ezra Stiles*. 2 vols. Edited by Franklin Bowditch Dexter. New York: Scribner's, 1901.

Stillingfleet, Edward. *A Discourse Concerning the Idolatry Practised in the Church of Rome* . . . . London: Robert White for Henry Mortlock, 1671.

Stonhouse, James. *Universal Restitution a Scripture Doctrine* . . . . London: R. Dodsley, 1761.

Taylor, John. *A Paraphrase with Notes on the Epistle to the Romans* . . . . London: J. Waugh, 1747.

———. *The Scripture-Doctrine of Original Sin* . . . . London: J. Wilson, 1740.

Thacher, Peter. *That the Punishment of the Finally Impenitent Shall Be Eternal* . . . . Salem, MA: Samuel Hall, 1783.

Trenchard, John. *A Discourse of Standing Armies; Shewing the Folly, Uselesness, and Danger of Standing Armies in Great Britain. By Cato*. London: T. Warner, 1722.

———. *The Independent Whig*. London: J. Peele, 1721.

———. *A Short History of Standing Armies in England* . . . . London, 1698.

———. *Standing Armies Standing Evils* . . . . London: T. Free, 1749.

Trenchard, John, and Thomas Gordon. *Cato's Letters*. London: W. Wilkins et al., 1723–24.

Tucker, John. *A Sermon Preached at Cambridge*.... Boston: Richard Draper, 1771.
Turner, Charles. *A Sermon Preached before His Excellency Thomas Hutchinson*.... Boston: Richard Draper, 1773.
Twisse, William. *Vindiciae Gratiae Potestatis ac Providentiae Dei*. Amsterdam: Johannes Jansonnius, 1632.
Tyrrell, James. *Patriarcha Non Monarcha*.... London: Richard Janeway, 1681.
Wadsworth, Benjamin. *Mutual Love and Peace among Christians*.... Boston: B. Green, & J. Allen, for Benjamin Eliot, 1701.
Warburton, William. *The Alliance between Church and State*.... London: Fletcher Gyles, 1736.
Watts, Isaac, et al. *Faith and Practice Represented in Fifty-four Sermons on the Principal Heads of the Christian Religion*.... 2 vols. London: R. Hett and J. Oswald, 1735.
Webster, Samuel. *A Winter Evening's Conversation upon the Doctrine of Original Sin*. Boston: Green and Russell, 1757.
West, Samuel. *A Sermon Preached before the Honorable Council*.... Boston: John Gill, 1776.
West Church, Boston. Record Book; Boston, 1736–1854. Rare Books and Manuscripts Department, Boston Public Library.
Westminster Assembly. *The Grounds and Principles of Religion, Contained in a Shorter Catechism*.... London: Lords and Commons, 1647.
———. *The Humble Advice of the Assembly of Divines, now by Authority of Parliament Sitting at Westminster, Concerning a Confession of Faith*. London: Company of Stationers, 1646.
———. *The Humble Advice of the Assembly of Divines, Sitting at Westminster, Concerning a Larger and a Shorter Catechisme*. Edinburgh: Evan Tyler, 1647.
White, Jeremiah. *The Restoration of All Things*.... London: N. Cliff and D. Jackson, 1712.
White, John. *New England's Lamentations*.... Boston: T. Fleet, 1734.
Whitefield, George. *A Brief and General Account of the Life of the Reverend Mr. Geo. Whitefield*.... Philadelphia: B. Franklin, 1740.
———. *A Continuation of the Reverend Mr. Whitefield's Journal from Savannah*.... Boston: Fowle for Kneeland & Green, 1741.
Wigglesworth, Edward. *A Letter to the Reverend Mr. George Whitefield*.... Boston: T. Fleet, 1745.
———. *Sober Remarks*.... Boston: Samuel Gerrish, 1724.
Wigglesworth, Samuel, and John Chipman, *Remarks on Some Points of Doctrine*.... Boston: S. Kneeland and T. Green, 1746.
Winchester, Elhanan. *An Attempt to Collect the Scripture Passages in Favour of the Universal Restoration*.... Providence, RI: Bennett Wheeler, 1786.
———. *The Holy Conversation, and High Expectation, of True Christians*.... London: R. Hawes et al., 1799.
———. *The Outcasts Comforted*.... Philadelphia, 1782.
———. *The Seed of the Woman Bruising the Serpent's Head*.... Philadelphia, 1781.
———. *The Universal Restoration*.... Philadelphia: T. Dobson, 1792.
Winthrop, John. "Speech to the General Court, July 3, 1645." In *The Puritans*, edited by Perry Miller and Thomas H. Johnson, 1:204–7. 2 vols. New York: Harper Torch, 1963.
Wise, John. *The Churches' Quarrel Espoused*.... New York: William Bradford, 1713.

―――. *A Vindication of the Government of New-England Churches* . . . . Boston: J. Allen for N. Boone, 1717.
Wollaston, William. *The Religion of Nature Delineated* . . . . London, 1722.

Secondary Sources

Akers, Charles. *Called unto Liberty: A Life of Jonathan Mayhew, 1720-1766*. Cambridge, MA: Harvard University Press, 1964.
―――. *The Divine Politician: Samuel Cooper and the American Revolution in Boston*. Boston: Northeastern University Press, 1982.
―――. Review of John Corrigan, *Hidden Balance*. *American Historical Review* 94/3 (1989) 846-47.
Allen, Joseph, and Richard Eddy, *A History of the Unitarians and Universalists in America*. New York: Christian Literature, 1894.
Appleby, Joyce. *Capitalism and a New Social Order: the Republican Vision of the 1790s*. New York: New York University Press, 1984.
Avery, Gillian. "Origins and English Predecessors of the New England Primer." *Proceedings of the American Antiquarian Society* 108/1 (1999) 33-61.
Bailyn, Bernard. "The Central Themes of the American Revolution: An Interpretation." In *Essays on the American Revolution*, edited by Stephen G. Kurtz and James H. Hutson, 3-31. Chapel Hill: University of North Carolina Press, 1973.
―――. *The Ideological Origins of the American Revolution*. Cambridge, MA: Belknap, 1992.
―――. *Pamphlets of the American Revolution, 1750-1776*. Vol. 1. Cambridge, MA: Belknap, 1965-.
―――. "Religion and Revolution: Three Biographical Studies." *Perspectives in American History* 4 (1970) 85-169.
Baldwin, Alice M. *The New England Clergy and the American Revolution*. New York: F. Ungar, 1958.
Bebbington, David. *Evangelicalism in Modern Britain: A History from the 1730s to the 1980s*. London: Unwin Hyman, 1989.
Beneke, Christopher. "The Critical Turn: Jonathan Mayhew, the British Empire, and the Idea of Resistance in Mid-Eighteenth-Century Boston." *Massachusetts Historical Review* 10 (2008) 23-56.
Bercovitch, Sacvan. *The American Jeremiad*. 2nd ed. Madison: University of Wisconsin Press, 2012.
Bergman, Marvin. Review of Barry Shain, *Myth of American Individualism*. *Church History* 66/4 (1997) 847-49.
Berry, Amanda. "Stonhouse, Sir James, Seventh and Tenth Baronet (1716-1795)." *ODNB Online*: http://www.oxforddnb.com/view/article/26582.
Black, Jeremy. *Eighteenth-Century Britain, 1688-1783*. 2nd ed. Houndmills, UK: Palgrave, 2008.
Bonomi, Patricia. Review of Barry Shain, *Myth of American Individualism*. *American Historical Review* 101/3 (1996) 905-6.
Bozemann, Theodore Dwight. *To Live Ancient Lives: the Primitivist Dimension in Puritanism*. Chapel Hill: University of North Carolina Press, 1988.

Bradford, Alden. *Memoir of the Life and Writings of Rev. Jonathan Mayhew* . . . . Boston: C. C. Little & Co., 1838.

Brekus, Catherine A. *Sarah Osborn's World: the Rise of Evangelical Christianity in Early America*. New Haven, CT: Yale University Press, 2013.

Bressler, Ann Lee. *The Universalist Movement in America, 1770-1880*. New York: Oxford University Press, 2000.

Bridenbaugh, Carl. *Mitre and Sceptre: Transatlantic Faiths, Ideas, Personalities, and Politics, 1689-1775*. New York: Oxford University Press, 1962.

Browne Anne S., and David D. Hall. "Family Strategies and Religious Practice: Baptism and the Lord's Supper in Early New England." In *Lived Religion in America: Toward a History of Practice*, edited by David D. Hall, 41-68. Princeton: Princeton University Press, 1997.

Burgess, Glenn. "Filmer, Sir Robert (1588?-1653)." In *ODNB Online*: http://www.oxforddnb.com /view/article/9424.

Butler, Jon. "Enthusiasm Described and Decried: the Great Awakening as Interpretive Fiction." *Journal of American History* 69 (1982-83) 305-25.

Butterfield, Herbert. *The Whig Interpretation of History*. New York: AMS, 1978.

Byrd, James P. *Sacred Scripture, Sacred War: The Bible and the American Revolution*. Oxford: Oxford University Press, 2013.

Cassara, Ernest. *Universalism in America: A Documentary History*. Boston: Beacon, 1971.

Christianson, Paul. *Reformers and Babylon: English Apocalyptic Visions from the Reformation to the Eve of the Civil War*. Toronto: University of Toronto Press, 1978.

Clark, Jonathan C. D. *English Society, 1660-1832: Religion, Ideology and Politics during the Ancien Regime*. Cambridge: Cambridge University Press, 2000.

―――. *The Language of Liberty, 1660-1832: Political Discourse and Social Dynamics in the Anglo-American World*. Cambridge: Cambridge University Press, 1994.

Clark, Joseph Sylvester. *A Historical Sketch of the Congregational Churches in Massachusetts, from 1620 to 1858* . . . . Boston: Congregational Board of Publication, 1858.

Clymer, Wayne K. "The Life and Thought of James Relly." *Church History* 11/3 (September 1942) 193-216.

―――. "Union with Christ: The Calvinist Universalism of James Relly (1722-1778)." In *"All Shall Be Well": Explorations in Universalism and Christian Theology from Origen to Moltmann*, edited by Gregory MacDonald, 116-40. Eugene, OR: Cascade, 2011.

Collins, Leo W. *This Is Our Church: The Seven Societies of the First Church in Boston, 1630-2005*. Boston: The Society of the First Church in Boston, 2005.

Condren, Conal. *The Language of Politics in Seventeenth Century England*. New York: St. Martin's, 1994.

Cooke, George Willis. *Unitarianism In America; A History of Its Origin and Development*. St. Clair Shores, MI: Scholarly, 1902.

Corrigan, John. *The Hidden Balance: Religion and the Social Theories of Charles Chauncy and Jonathan Mayhew*. Cambridge: Cambridge University Press, 1987.

―――. *The Prism of Piety: Catholick Congregational Clergy at the Beginning of the Enlightenment*. New York: Oxford University Press, 1991.

―――. "Religion and the Social Theories of Charles Chauncy and Jonathan Mayhew." PhD diss., University of Chicago, 1982.

Counts, Martha. "The Political Views of the Eighteenth Century New England Clergy as Expressed in Their Election Sermons." PhD diss., Columbia University, 1956.
Cronon, William. "Two Cheers for the Whig Interpretation of History." *Perspectives on History*, September 2012. Washington, DC: American Historical Association. https://www.historians.org/publications-and-directories/perspectives-on-history/september-2012/two-cheers-for-the-whig-interpretation-of-history.
Cross, Arthur Lyon. *The Anglican Episcopate and the American Colonies*. Hamden, CT: Archon, 1964.
Daggy, Robert E. "Education, Church, and State: Timothy Cutler and the Yale Apostasy of 1722." *Journal of Church and State* 43 (1971) 43–68.
Dexter, Franklin Bowdich. *Documentary History of Yale University: Under the Original Charter of the Collegiate School of Connecticut, 1701–1745*. New Haven, CT: Yale University Press, 1916.
Dunn, Richard S. "The Glorious Revolution and America." In *The Origins of Empire: British Overseas Enterprise to the Close of the Seventeenth Century*, edited by Nicholas Canny, 1:445–66. Oxford: Oxford University Press, 1998.
Eddy, Richard. *Universalism in America: A History*. 2 vols. Boston: Universalist Publishing House, 1891–94.
Ellis, Arthur B. *History of the First Church in Boston, 1630–1880*. Boston: Hall and Whiting, 1881.
Ellis, Joseph. *The New England Mind in Transition: Samuel Johnson of Connecticut, 1696–1772*. New Haven, CT: Yale University Press, 1973.
Fea, John. "John Adams and Religion." In *A Companion to John Adams and John Quincy Adams*, edited by David Waldstreicher, 184–98. Hoboken, NJ: John Wiley & Sons, 2013.
Ferguson, J. P. *An Eighteenth Century Heretic: Dr. Samuel Clarke*. Kineton, UK: Roundwood, 1976.
Ferguson, Robert A. "The American Enlightenment, 1750–1820." In *The Cambridge History of American Literature*, edited by Sacvan Bercovitch et al., 1:470–95. Cambridge: Cambridge University Press, 1994.
———. "The Dialectic of Liberty: Law and Religion in Revolutionary America." In *Liberty and the American Experience in the Eighteenth Century*, edited by David Womersley, 103 52. Indianapolis: Liberty Fund, 2006.
———. "The Literature of Public Documents." In *The Cambridge History of American Literature*, edited by Sacvan Bercovitch et al., 1:345–538. Cambridge: Cambridge University Press, 1994.
Ferling, John. *John Adams: A Life*. Knoxville: University of Tennessee Press, 1992.
Ferm, Robert L. *Readings in the History of Christian Thought*. New York: Holt, Rinehart, and Winston, 1964.
Fiering, Norman. "The First American Enlightenment: Tillotson, Leverett, and Philosophical Anglicanism." *The New England Quarterly* 54/3 (September 1981) 307–44.
———. *Jonathan Edwards's Moral Thought and Its British Context*. Chapel Hill: University of North Carolina Press, 1981.
———. *Moral Philosophy at Seventeenth-Century Harvard: A Discipline in Transition*. Chapel Hill: University of North Carolina Press, 1981.
Fischer, David Hackett. *Albion's Seed: Four British Folkways in America*. Oxford: Oxford University Press, 1989.

Fixler, Michael. *Milton and the Kingdoms of God*. Evanston, IL: Northwestern University Press, 1964.

Foote, Henry Wilder, et al. *Annals of King's Chapel from the Puritan Age of New England to the Present Day*. 2 vols. Boston: Little, Brown, 1900.

Fowler, William Chauncey. "President Charles Chauncy, His Ancestors and Descendants." *New England Historical and Genealogical Register* 10/4 (1856) 323–36.

Gaustad, Edwin. "Charles Chauncy and the Great Awakening: A Survey and Bibliography." *Papers of the Bibliographical Society of America* 45 (1951) 125–35.

Gay, Peter. *The Enlightenment, An Interpretation: The Rise of Modern Paganism*. New York: Vintage, 1966.

Geertz, Clifford. "Ideology as a Cultural System." In *The Interpretation of Cultures*, 193–233. New York: Basic, 1973.

Gerardi, Donald F. M. "The Episcopate Controversy Reconsidered: Religious Vocation and Anglican Perceptions of Authority in Mid-18th Century America." *Perspectives in American History* 3 (1986) 81–114.

Gewehr, Wesley Marsh. *The Great Awakening in Virginia, 1740–1790*. Gloucester, MA: P. Smith, 1965.

Gibbs, Norman. "The Problem of Revelation and Reason in the Thought of Charles Chauncy." PhD diss., Duke University, 1953.

Gibbs, Norman B., and Lee W. Gibbs. "Charles Chauncy: A Theology In Two Portraits." *Harvard Theological Review* 83/3 (1990) 259–70.

———. "'In Our Nature': The Kenotic Christology of Charles Chauncy." *Harvard Theological Review* 85/2 (1992) 217–33.

Gibson, Alan. *Understanding the Founding: The Crucial Questions*. 2nd ed. Lawrence: University Press of Kansas Press, 2010.

Gibson, William. "The Persecution of Thomas Emlyn." *Journal of Church and State* 48/3 (2006) 525–39.

Goen, Clarence C. *Revivalism and Separatism in New England, 1740–1800*. New Haven, CT: Yale University Press, 1962.

Goff, Philip. "Revivals and Revolution: Historiographic Turns since Alan Heimert's Religion and the American Mind." *Church History* 67/4 (1998) 696–721.

Gonzales, Justo L. *Essential Theological Terms*. Louisville: Westminster John Knox, 2005.

Grant, James. *John Adams: Party of One*. New York: Farrar, Straus and Giroux, 2005.

Greenstone, J. David. *The Lincoln Persuasion: Remaking American Liberalism*. Princeton: Princeton University Press, 1993.

Griffin, Edward M. "A Biography of Charles Chauncy (1705–1787)." PhD diss., Stanford University, 1966.

———. *Old Brick: Charles Chauncy of Boston, 1705–1787*. Minneapolis: University of Minnesota Press, 1980.

Guyatt, Nicholas. *Providence and the Invention of the United States, 1607–1876*. New York: Cambridge University Press, 2007.

Hall, David. "Editor's Introduction." In *Works of Jonathan Edwards: The Ecclesiastical Writings*, 12:1–90, New Haven, CT: Yale University Press, 1994.

———. "Learned Culture in the Eighteenth Century." In *A History of the Book in America*, edited by Hugh Amory and David Hall, 1:411–33. Chapel Hill: University of North Carolina Press, 2007.

———. *A Reforming People: Puritanism and the Transformation of Public Life in New England*. New York: Knopf, 2011.
Haroutunian, Joseph. *Piety Versus Moralism: The Passing of the New England Theology*. Hamden, CT: Archon, 1964.
Harvard University. *Historical Register of Harvard University, 1636–1936*. Cambridge, MA: Harvard University Press, 1937.
Hatch, Nathan O. *The Democratization of American Christianity*. New Haven, CT: Yale University Press, 1989.
———. *The Sacred Cause of Liberty: Republican Thought and the Millennium in Revolutionary New England*. New Haven, CT: Yale University Press, 1977.
———. "Sola Scriptura and Novus Ordo Seclorum." In *The Bible in America: Essays in Cultural History*, edited by Nathan Hatch and Mark Noll, 59–78. New York: Oxford University Press, 1982.
Haydon, Colin. *Anti-Catholicism in Eighteenth-Century England c. 1714–80*. Manchester: Manchester University Press, 1993.
Heimert, Alan. *Religion and the American Mind from the Great Awakening to the Revolution*. Cambridge, MA: Harvard University Press, 1966.
Hempton, David. *Evangelical Disenchantment: Nine Portraits of Faith and Doubt*. New Haven, CT: Yale University Press, 2008.
———. *Methodism: Empire of the Spirit*. New Haven, CT: Yale University Press, 2005.
Hibbard, Carolyn. *Charles I and the Popish Plot*. Chapel Hill: University of North Carolina Press, 1983.
Hill, Andrew M. "Relly, James (1721/2–1778)." *ODNB Online*: http://www.oxforddnb.com/view/article/23359.
Holifield, E. Brooks. *Theology in America: Christian Thought from the Age of the Puritans to the Civil War*. New Haven, CT: Yale University Press, 2003.
Hoogenboom, Olive. "Murray, John." *ANB Online*. American Council of Learned Societies. Oxford University Press, 2000. http://www.anb.org./articles/08/08-01062.html.
Howe, Charles A. "How Human an Enterprise: The Story of the First Universalist Society in Boston during John Murray's Ministry." *Proceedings of the Unitarian Universalist Historical Society* 22 (1990–1991) 19–34.
Howe, Daniel Walker. *Making the American Self: Jonathan Edwards to Abraham Lincoln*. Cambridge, MA: Harvard University Press, 1997.
Hoyt, Albert Harrison. *Sketch of the Life of the Rev. Thomas Bradbury Chandler* . . . . Boston: New-England Historical and Genealogical Register, reprint 1873.
Hughes, Peter. "The Davis Family of Oxford, Massachusetts," "Caleb Rich," and "Adams Streeter." *Dictionary of Unitarian and Universalist Biography*, Unitarian Universalist History and Heritage Society, 1999–2013. Online: http://uudb.org/index.html.
Hurstfield, Hoel. *Freedom, Corruption and Government in Elizabethan England*. London: Jonathan Cape, 1973.
Hutton, Sarah. "Thomas Jackson, Oxford Platonist, and William Twisse, Aristotelian." *Journal of the History of Ideas* 39/4 (1978) 635–52.
Johnson, Allen, and Dumas Malone. *Dictionary of American Biography*. New York: Scribner's, 1928.
Jones, Barney Lee. "Charles Chauncy and the Great Awakening in New England." PhD diss., Duke University, 1958.

Jones, James W. *The Shattered Synthesis: New England Puritanism before the Great Awakening*. New Haven, CT: Yale University Press, 1973.

Kammen, Michael G. *Spheres of Liberty: Changing Perceptions of Liberty in American Culture*. Madison: University of Wisconsin Press, 1986.

Kidd, Colin. *The Forging of Races: Race and Scripture in the Protestant Atlantic World, 1600–2000*. Cambridge: Cambridge University Press, 2006.

Kidd, Thomas S. *George Whitefield: America's Spiritual Founding Father*. New Haven, CT: Yale University Press, 2014.

———. *The Great Awakening: The Roots of Evangelical Christianity in Colonial America*. New Haven, CT: Yale University Press, 2009.

———. *Protestant Interest: New England after Puritanism*. New Haven, CT: Yale University Press, 2004.

Lake, Peter. *Moderate Puritans and the Elizabethan Church*. Cambridge: Cambridge University Press, 1982.

Lambert, Frank. *Pedlar in Divinity: George Whitefield and the Transatlantic Revivals, 1737–1770*. Princeton: Princeton University Press, 1994.

Lippy, Charles. "Restoring a Lost Ideal: Charles Chauncy and the American Revolution." *Religion in Life* 44/4 (1975) 491–502.

———. "Seasonable Revolutionary: Charles Chauncy and the Ideology of Liberty." PhD diss., Princeton University, 1972.

———. *Seasonable Revolutionary: The Mind of Charles Chauncy*. Chicago: Nelson-Hall, 1981.

———. "Trans-Atlantic Dissent and the Revolution: Richard Price and Charles Chauncy." *Eighteenth-Century Life* 4/2 (1977) 31–37.

Lovejoy, David S. *The Glorious Revolution in America*. Middletown, CT: Wesleyan University Press, 1972.

Lowell, Charles. "A Discourse on William Hooper." In *The West Church and Its Ministers*, edited by Cyrus Augustus Bartol and Charles Lowell, 61–78. Boston: Crosby, Nichols, 1856.

Lubert, Howard L. "Jonathan Mayhew: Conservative Revolutionary." *History of Political Thought* 32/4 (2011) 589–616

Maier, Pauline. *From Resistance to Revolution: Colonial Radicals and the Development of American Opposition to Britain, 1765–1776*. London, Routledge & Kegan Paul, 1973.

Marini, Stephen A. *Radical Sects of Revolutionary New England*. Cambridge, MA: Harvard University Press, 1982.

Marsden, George. *Jonathan Edwards: A Life*. New Haven, CT: Yale University Press, 2003.

———. *Understanding Fundamentalism and Evangelicalism*. Grand Rapids: Eerdmans, 1991.

May, Henry. *The Enlightenment in America*. New York: Oxford University Press, 1976.

Mayer, David N. "The English Radical Whig Origins of American Constitutionalism." *Washington University Law Quarterly* 70/1 (1992) 131–208.

McGrath, Alister E. *Christian Theology: An Introduction*. 5th ed. Oxford: Wiley-Blackwell, 2011.

———. *Reformation Thought: An Introduction*. 4th ed. Oxford: Oxford University Press, 2012.

McKillop, Alan. "The Background of Thomson's *Liberty*." *The Rice Institute Pamphlet* 38/2 (July 1951).
McLoughlin, William G. "The American Revolution as a Religious Revival: 'The Millennium in One Country.'" *New England Quarterly* 40 (1967) 99–110.
McNeill, John T. *The History and Character of Calvinism*. New York: Oxford University Press, 1954.
Mead, Sidney. "Through and Beyond the Lines." *Journal of Religion* 48/3 (1968) 274–88.
Miller, John C. "Religion, Finance, and Democracy in Massachusetts." *New England Quarterly* 6/1 (1933) 29–58.
Miller, Perry. *Jonathan Edwards*. New York: William Sloane, 1949.
———. *The New England Mind from Colony to Province*. Boston: Beacon, 1961.
———. *The New England Mind: The Seventeenth Century*. Cambridge, MA: Harvard University Press, 1954.
Miller, Perry, and Thomas H. Johnson. *The Puritans*. 2 vols. New York: Harper Torch, 1963.
Miller, Russell E. *The Larger Hope: The First Century of the Universalist Church in America, 1770–1870*. Boston: Unitarian Universalist Association, 1979.
Moore, Frank, *The Patriot Preachers of the American Revolution*. New York, 1862.
Morais, Herbert M. *Deism in Eighteenth Century America*. New York: Archon, 1964.
Morgan, Edmund S. *The Gentle Puritan: A Life of Ezra Stiles, 1727–1795*. New Haven, CT: Yale University Press, 1962.
———. *Visible Saints: The History of a Puritan Idea*. New York: New York University Press, 1963.
Morgan, Edmund S., and Helen M. Morgan. *The Stamp Act Crisis: Prologue to Revolution*. 3rd ed. Chapel Hill: University of North Carolina Press, 1995.
Morison, Samuel Eliot. *Harvard College in the Seventeenth Century*. Cambridge, MA: Harvard University Press, 1936.
———. *Three Centuries of Harvard, 1636–1936*. Cambridge, MA: Harvard University Press, 1936.
Mullins, J. Patrick. "Father of Liberty: Jonathan Mayhew and the Intellectual Origins of the American Revolution." PhD diss., University of Kentucky, 2005.
———. "'A Kind of War, Tho' Hitherto an Un-Bloody One': Jonathan Mayhew, Francis Bernard and the Indian Affair." *Massachusetts Historical Review* 11 (2009) 27–56.
———. "Research." J. Patrick Mullins, Department of History, Marymount University. http://jpatrickmullins.wix.com/jpatrickmullins#!research/c1bnb.
———. "The Sermon That Didn't Start the Revolution: Jonathan Mayhew's Role in the Boston Stamp Act Riots." In *Community without Consent: New Perspectives on the Stamp Act Crisis*, edited by Zachary McLeod Hutchins, 3–35. Lebanon, NH: Dartmouth College Press, 2016.
Murray, J. A. H., et al. *A New English Dictionary on Historical Principles: Founded Mainly on the Materials Collected by the Philological Society*. 13 vols. Oxford: Clarendon, 1888–1933.
Nash, Gary B. *The Unknown American Revolution: The Unruly Birth of Democracy and the Struggle to Create America*. New York: Viking, 2005.
Noll, Mark. *America's God, from Jonathan Edwards to Abraham Lincoln*. Oxford: Oxford University Press, 2002.
———. *Christians in the American Revolution*. Grand Rapids: Christian Universities Press, 1977.

———. *The Rise of Evangelicalism: The Age of Edwards, Whitefield and the Wesleys.* Downers Grove, IL: InterVarsity, 2010.

Oakes, John S. "Beyond the 'Democrat' and 'Conservative' Dichotomy: John Wise Reconsidered." *New England Quarterly* 88/3 (September 2015) 483–508.

———. "'Conservative Revolutionaries'—A Study of the Religious and Political Thought of John Wise, Jonathan Mayhew, Andrew Eliot, and Charles Chauncy." PhD diss., Simon Fraser University, 2008.

Parry, Robin. "Between Calvinism and Arminianism: The Evangelical Universalism of Elhanan Winchester (1751–1797)." In *"All Shall Be Well": Explorations in Universalism and Christian Theology from Origen to Moltmann*, edited by Gregory MacDonald, 141–70. Eugene, OR: Cascade, 2011.

Pettit, Norman. *The Heart Prepared: Grace and Conversion in Puritan Spiritual Life.* New Haven, CT: Yale University Press, 1966.

Pierce, Frederick. *History of Grafton, Worcester County, Massachusetts.* Worcester, MA: Chas. Hamilton, 1879.

Pierce, Richard. "The Records of the First Church in Boston, 1630–1868." *Proceedings of the Colonial Society of Massachusetts* (1961) 39–41.

Plumstead, A. W. *The Wall and the Garden: Selected Massachusetts Election Sermons, 1670–1775.* Minneapolis: University of Minnesota Press, 1968.

Pocock, J. G. A. *Barbarism and Religion.* 5 vols. Cambridge: Cambridge University Press, 1999–2010.

———. "Clergy and Commerce. The Conservative Enlightenment in England." In *L'Età dei Lumi. Studi Storici sul Settemento Europeo in Onore di Franco Venturi*, edited by Raffaele Ajello et al., 523–62. Naples, Italy: Jiovene Editore, 1985.

———. "Machiavelli, Harrington, and English Political Ideologies in the Eighteenth Century." In *Politics, Language and Time: Essays On Political Thought and History*, 104–47. New York: Atheneum, 1971.

———. *The Machiavellian Moment: Florentine Political Thought and the Atlantic Republican Tradition.* Princeton: Princeton University Press, 1975.

Porter, Roy. *The Creation of the Modern World: The Untold Story of the British Enlightenment.* New York: Norton, 2000.

———. *The Enlightenment.* Houndmills, UK: Macmillan Education, 1990.

———, and Mikulás Teich. *The Enlightenment in National Context.* Cambridge: Cambridge University Press, 1981.

Reid, John Phillip. *The Concept of Liberty in the Age of the American Revolution.* Chicago: University of Chicago Press, 1988.

Robbins, Caroline. *The 18th Century Commonwealthman: Studies in the Transmission, Development, and Circumstance of English Liberal Thought from the Restoration of Charles II until the War with the Thirteen Colonies.* Cambridge, MA: Harvard University Press, 1959.

———. "The Strenuous Whig: Thomas Hollis of Lincoln's Inn." *William and Mary Quarterly* 7/3 (July 1950) 406–53.

Robbins, Chandler. *A History of the Second Church, or Old North, in Boston.* Boston: A Committee of the Society, 1852.

Robinson, David. *The Unitarians and the Universalists.* Westport, CT: Greenwood, 1985.

Rodgers, Daniel T. "Republicanism: the Career of a Concept." *Journal of American History* 79/1 (1992) 11–38.

Rossiter, Clinton. "The Life and Mind of Jonathan Mayhew." *William and Mary Quarterly* 7/4 (1950) 531–58.

———. *Seedtime of the Republic: The Origin of the American Tradition of Political Liberty.* New York: Harcourt, Brace, 1953.

Rozbicki, Michal Jan. "Between Private and Public Spheres: Liberty as Cultural Property in Eighteenth-Century British America." In *Cultures and Identities in British Colonial America*, edited by Robert Olwell and Alan Tully, 293–318. Baltimore: Johns Hopkins University Press, 2006.

———. *Culture and Liberty in the Age of the American Revolution.* Charlottesville: University of Virginia Press, 2011.

Sandoz, Ellis. *Political Sermons of the American Founding Era, 1730–1805.* 2 vols. Indianapolis: Liberty, 1991.

Savelle, Max. *Seeds of Liberty: The Genesis of the American Mind.* New York: Knopf, 1948.

Shagan, Ethan. *The Rule of Moderation: Violence, Religion, and the Politics of Restraint in Early Modern England.* Cambridge: Cambridge University Press, 2011.

Shain, Barry Alan. *The Myth of American Individualism: The Protestant Origins of American Political Thought.* Princeton: Princeton University Press, 1994.

Shipton, Clifford. *New England Life in the 18th Century: Representative Biographies from Sibley's Harvard Graduates.* Cambridge, MA: Harvard University Press, 1963.

Smith, H. Shelton. *Changing Conceptions of Original Sin: A Study in American Theology since 1750.* New York: Scribner's, 1955.

Sprague, William B. *Annals of the American Pulpit; Or, Commemorative Notices of Distinguished American Clergymen of Various Demominations from the Early Settlement of the Country to the Close of the Year Eighteen Hundred and Fifty-five.* 9 vols. New York: Robert Carter and Brothers, 1857–69.

Stanwood, Owen. *The Empire Reformed: English America in the Age of the Glorious Revolution.* Philadelphia: University of Pennsylvania Press, 2011.

Stebbins, Rufus P. *Centennial Discourse Delivered to the First Congregational Church and Society in Leominster, September 24, 1843 . . . .* Boston: Freeman and Bolles, 1843.

Stout, Harry S. *The Divine Dramatist: George Whitefield and the Rise of Modern Evangelicalism.* Grand Rapids: Eerdmans, 1991.

———. *The New England Soul: Preaching and Religious Culture in Colonial New England.* New York: Oxford University Press, 1986.

Sweeney, Joseph R. "Elhanan Winchester and the Universal Baptists." PhD diss., University of Pennsylvania, 1969.

"Test act." *Encyclopedia Britannica*, 2015. http://www.britannica.com/topic/test-act.

Thomas, D. D. Lloyd. *Locke on Government.* London: Routledge, 1995.

Thornton, John Wingate. *The Pulpit of the American Revolution: Or, the Political Sermons of the Period of 1776.* New York: Da Capo, 1970.

Tracy, Joseph. *The Great Awakening: A History of the Revival of Religion in the Time of Edwards and Whitefield.* Boston: C. Tappan, 1845.

Trueman, Carl R. *John Owen: Reformed Catholic, Renaissance Man.* Aldershot: Ashgate 2007.

Van Tyne, Claude H. "Influence of the Clergy, and of Religious Sectarian Forces, on the American Revolution." *American Historical Review* 19 (1913) 44–64.

Waldstreicher, David. *A Companion to John Adams and John Quincy Adams*. Hoboken, NJ: Wiley, 2013.

Walker, Williston. "The Sandemanians of New England." In *Annual Report of the American Historical Association for the Year 1901*, 133–62. Washington, DC: American Historical Society, 1902.

———. *Ten New England Leaders*. New York: Silver, Burdett, 1901.

Warch, Richard. *School of the Prophets: Yale College, 1701–1740*. New Haven, CT: Yale University Press, 1973.

Ward, Lee. *The Politics of Liberty in England and Revolutionary America*. Cambridge: Cambridge University Press, 2004.

Ward, W. R. *Early Evangelicalism: A Global Intellectual History, 1670–1789*. Cambridge: Cambridge University Press, 2006.

Weis, Frederick Lewis. *The Colonial Clergy and the Colonial Churches of New England*. Baltimore: Clearfield, 2010.

Wilder, David. *The History of Leominster, or the Northern Half of the Lancaster New or Additional Grant* . . . . Fitchburg, MA: The Reveille Office, 1853.

Wilson, Robert J. *The Benevolent Deity: Ebenezer Gay and the Rise of Rational Religion in Colonial New England, 1696–1787*. Philadelphia: University of Pennsylvania Press, 1984.

———. Review of John Corrigan, *Hidden Balance*. *William and Mary Quarterly* 45/4 (1988) 805–7.

Wood, Gordon S. *Creation of the American Republic, 1776–1787*. New York: Norton, 1972.

———. "Religion and the American Revolution." In *New Directions in American Religious History*, edited by Harry Stout and D. G. Hart, 173–205. New York: Oxford University Press, 1997.

Worthley, Harold Field. *An Inventory of the Records of the Particular (Congregational) Churches of Massachusetts Gathered 1620–1805*. Cambridge, MA: Harvard University Press, 1970.

Wright, Conrad. *The Beginnings of Unitarianism in America*. Boston: Starr King, 1955.

Yenter, Timothy, and Ezio Vailati. "Samuel Clarke (Revised)." In *The Stanford Encyclopedia of Philosophy*, edited by Edward N. Zalta and Uri Nodelman. Stanford, CA: Metaphysics Research Lab Center for the Study of Language and Information, 2009. Online: http://plato.stanford.edu/entries/clarke/.

York, Neil L. *The Boston Massacre: A History with Documents*. New York: Routledge, 2010.

Youngs, William T. *God's Messengers: Religious Leadership in Colonial New England, 1700–1750*. Baltimore: Johns Hopkins University Press, 1976.

Zuckert, Michael P. *Natural Rights Republic: Studies in the Foundation of the American Political Tradition*. Notre Dame: University of Notre Dame Press, 1996.

———. Review of Barry Shain, *The Myth of American Individualism*. *William and Mary Quarterly* 53/3 (1996) 670–72.

Index

Absurdity and Blasphemy of Depretiating Moral Virtue (Briant), 50
Accursed Thing (Chauncy), 69–70, 115, 235
Acts 4:32, 235
Adams, Abigail, 235
Adams, John
   on distrust of historical memory, 238
   letter to Jefferson, 240, 241n5
   letter to Niles, 240
   on Mayhew's influence, 90n26, 240–41, 241n5, 255–56
   on Mayhew as a Unitarian, 90n26, 256n19
   references to Chauncy, 242n7
   on the ideologies underlying the Revolutionary War, 239–42, 241n5
Akers, Charles
   on Chauncy, 234
   on curriculum at Harvard, 51–52
   on Mayhew, 3–4, 16, 18n4, 20, 23–24, 51, 52n20, 53n22, 83–84n16, 89–90, 111n1, 145n1, 147, 147n3, 211n2, 227n26, 234
All Power in Heaven (Pemberton), 88
"Alphabetical List of Books," (Mayhew), 20
American Enlightenment, 6, 10–11, 243–45, 243n8
American Episcopate controversy. *See also* anti-Catholicism
   Adams's understanding, 239–42

   and American-British tensions, 180, 239–40
   and Catholic notions of episcopacy, 136
   Chauncy's involvement in, 38–39, 38n1, 122–25, 129–32, 149, 180–81, 193–94
   Mayhew's involvement in, 82, 126–29, 147, 148–49n6, 156, 159
   and New England Congregationalism, 122–23, 164
American Revolution. *See also* rebellion, "justifiable"; revolution, violent
   Adams on ideological precursors to, 239–41
   Chauncy's commitment to, 174–75, 232–37, 235n38
   Mayhew's and Chauncy's ideological contributions, 4
   rhetoric of, 2
   suffering caused by, 236
America's God (Noll), 3n3, 150–51n7, 208n38, 233n35
Andros, Edmund, 176, 228
Anglican church. *See* Church of England, Anglicans
Answer to Dr. Mayhew's Observations (Secker), 126–27n26, 129, 160
anti-Catholicism. *See also* American Episcopate controversy
   Calvinist critiques, 135
   and the Catholic church as an abomination, 134–35, 137

INDEX

anti-Catholicism *(continued)*
  Chauncy's expressions of, 109, 13–6, 176–77, 177n46, 181–83
  in eighteenth-century New England, 133–34, 251
  Mayhew's expressions of, 86–87, 133, 136–40, 159–61, 166, 169–73, 215–17
  and providential views of current events, 176
  and Real Whig rhetoric, 155–56
Apology in Behalf of The Revd Mr. Whitefield (Chauncy), 92
Apostles Neither Impostors Nor Enthusiasts (Hooper), 53
The Apostles St. Paul and St. James Reconciled (Balch), 48–49, 48–49n15
Appeal Defended (Chandler), 130–31, 130n31
Appeal to the Public Answered (Chauncy), 38n1, 123, 130–31, 134n38, 180, 193–94, 201–2
Appleby, Joyce, 207
Appleton Nathaniel, 35n30, 53
Apthorp, East, 82, 126–28, 155, 159–60, 218n13, 239–40
Arianism. *See also* subordinationist views on the Trinity; Trinitarianism
  Christology of, 7n9
  Mayhew's and Chauncy's alleged shift towards, 83–90, 83–84n16, 115–17, 117–18n12
  orthodox responses to, 87–90, 90n26
Arminianism. *See also* Balch, William; Gay, Ebenezer
  and Chauncy's theology, 10–11, 65–70, 109n55, 248
  eighteenth century meanings, 16–17n3, 40, 40–41n4, 242n7
  and the evangelical revival movement, 47–48
  growth of in New England, 41–46, 63
  Johnson on, 41–42n5

  and Mayhew's theology, 10–11, 16–17, 37, 51–62
  orthodox Calvinist responses to, 41–51, 92
  Taylor's writings on, 62–63
  teachings associated with, 16, 40, 61, 99, 99n41, 202
"Articles of Charge" against Samuel Osborn, 45–46
Artillery Election sermon (Chauncy), 112
Athanasian Creed, 83n16, 86, 101, 120
atonement, redemption. *See also* salvation; universalism, universalist theology
  Chauncy's understanding, 70–71, 101–3, 115–17
  and Christ's self-sacrifice, 86, 96, 102–3
  Dickinson's understanding, 58–59
  limited atonement, 30
  Mayhew's understanding, 58–59, 58–59n29, 59n30
  Murray's teachings, 72–73
  universal, Winchester's views on, 99–100
"To the Author of the Vindications" (Brattle), 82n14

Bailyn, Bernard
  critiques of analysis, 150, 151n8, 155
  Ideological Origins, 152–54, 15 54n11
  on Mayhew's Whiggery, 155, 166–67
  on Real Whigs, 152–54, 225
  response to Heimert, 148
Balch, William, 47–49, 48–49n15, 62
Baldwin, Alice M., 150–51n7, 242
Baptists, 96, 98
Bebbington, David, 244–45
Beissel, Conrad, 95
Belknap, Jeremy, 72, 73
Bellamy, Joseph, 88–90
Beneke, Christopher, 148–49n6
Benevolence of the Deity (Chauncy), 39, 73, 97, 101, 104–6, 108, 117, 141, 189–90
Berkeley, George, 43

Bernard, Francis, 145–48, 147n3, 148–49n6, 159
the Bible, acceptance of primacy of, 63, 101–2, 101n44, 108–9, 118–22, 148, 196–200, 203–6, 213, 221–22, 247–48. *See also* providentialism
Book of Common Prayer, 79
"Book of Extracts" (Mayhew), 20, 82, 82n14
Boston Evening-Post, "Philanthropos" letter mocking Mayhew, 16
Boston Tea Party/Massacre/British occupation and Port Act, 173–74, 226–28, 230–33
Boston Public Latin School, 24
Boston Weekly News-Letter, 89, 123, 123–24n22, 213–14n6
Bowen, Penuel, Chauncy's ordination sermon, 115
Bowman, Joseph, Chauncy's ordination sermon, 179, 201
Bradford, Alden (*Memoir*), 4n5, 52–53, 52n20, 81–82, 82–83n16, 145n1, 188n6
Bradford, Massachusetts, Second Church controversy, 47–49
Brattle, William, 19, 20n8, 82n14
"*Breaking of Bread*" (Chauncy), 67–68, 206
Breck, Robert, 44–45, 45n10, 77, 79
Brekus, Catherine, 245
Briant, Lemuel
   Arminian leanings, 45
   charges against and vindication, 51n19
   critique of Calvinist orthodoxy, 50–51
   influence on Adams, 90n26, 255, 255–56n19
   response to Porter's and Cotton's criticisms, 50–51n18
Brief Notes on the Creed of St. Athanasius, 82
Britain, loyalty to. *See* citizenship rights, British; liberty, British; parliamentary monarchical government, British

Burnet, Thomas, 20
Burr, Aaron, 89
Butterfield, Herbert, 8n10
Byfield, Nathanael, 27

Called unto Liberty (Akers), 3–4, 18n4, 20–21n9, 51–52, 52n20, 53n22, 83–84n16, 111n1, 145n1, 147n3, 234
Calvin, John, 57n27
Calvinism, Calvinists. *See also* atonement; Congregationalism, New England Puritanism; Synod of Dort; Trinitarianism
   and biblical authority, 101, 108, 118–19, 118n13
   Briant's critique, 50, 62
   Christocentric theology, 32, 58–59, 108, 140
   and divine grace and atonement, 33, 58–59
   and election, the elect, 28–30, 55, 57, 58n28, 103, 104–5n48
   eternal reprobation, 41, 58, 105–6
   Foxcroft's commitment to, 91–92
   and justification by faith, 18–19, 30–32, 60n31, 65–66, 66n39, 68
   Mayhew's father's allegiance to, 19
   original sin, 27, 56, 69–70, 111–15
   total depravity doctrine, 18n5, 54–55, 70
   and unconditional election, 28–29, 55, 57–58, 103, 104–5n48
   Westminster Confession of Faith, 42–44, 75, 118n13, 209n39
   Westminster Shorter Catechism/ Westminster Larger Catechism, 19, 75, 78
Cambridge Church, and Mayhew's ordination, 53
Caner, Henry (*Candid Examination of Dr. Mayhew's Observations*), 126–27n26, 140, 211n2
Cape Breton reduction, 176–77, 177n46, 181–82
Catholic church. *See* anti-Catholicism
ceremonial law, freedom from, 54, 187, 187n5, 202

Chandler, Thomas
  Appeal Defended, 130n31
  Appeal to the Public, 130–31,
    180n51, 201
  Chauncy's criticisms, 38, 130–33,
    131n33, 180–81, 201
Charity (Chauncy), 33, 135, 183n55
Charles I, execution, arguments
  justifying, 167–68, 214, 217
Charles II, Mayhew's views on, 216
charter-grants, British, 193
Chauncy, Charles
  birth and early education, 24–25
  caution and traditionalism of,
    10–11, 35, 37, 40, 97, 109, 124,
    140–41, 174–75, 175n44, 181,
    183, 234–35
  comparisons with Mayhew, value,
    6–8, 7n9
  defense of slaves and indigenous
    people, 182–83, 201–2
  and delayed publication of writings,
    39–40, 40n3, 72–74, 73–74n3,
    90–94
  as evangelical, 117–18n12, 246
  evolution/revelation of theological
    and political thinking, 47,
    62–73, 66n39, 101–2, 107–8,
    109n55, 115–18, 117–18n12,
    120–22, 230–31, 246–48,
    251–52
  exile in Medfield, 233
  role as transitional figure, 11–12,
    247–49, 252–56
  marriages, 25–26, 26n16
  ordination and early ministry, 25–26
  relationship with Mayhew, 7, 10–11
  scholarly perspectives on, 2–10, 3n3,
    7n9, 149–50, 150–51n7, 234,
    242–48
  theology and politics, 10–11, 26–37,
    64–65, 67–71, 73–74, 97, 98n39,
    100–109, 106n51, 140–41, 190,
    247, 249
Chauncy, Charles (father), 24
Chauncy, Charles (great-grandfather), 1
Chauncy, Nathaniel, Chauncy letter to,
  62–63

Checkley, John, 25, 41
Chilmark, Martha's Vineyard, Mayhew's
  birth, 17
Chipman, John, 49
Choice Dialogues (Checkley), 41
Christ, co-equal divinity of. *See*
  God, as supreme authority;
  Trinitarianism
Christ, as mediator, 81, 84–86,
  101–3, 103–4n47, 247. *See also*
  Arminianism; subordinist views;
  unitarianism
Christian Love (Chauncy), 235
Christian rationalism, 4n6
Christian Sobriety (Mayhew), 59, 85–86,
  165, 204
Church of England, Anglicans. *See
  also* American Episcopate
  controversy; Latitudinarianism
  Bernard as member of, 147
  conversion of Davenports to, 123,
    123–24n22
  establishment of, fears associated
    with, 126–29, 132–33, 161
  as political threat, 41, 82, 128–29,
    131–33, 132n34, 159–60, 194
  and right to episcopal worship, 192
  tolerance for Catholicism, 137
"A Circumstantial Narrative" (Mayhew),
  146–47
citizenship rights, British. *See also*
  civil rights/civil disobedience;
  rebellion, "justiable"
  Chauncy's appreciation for, 232–34
  and lack of colonial representation
    in parliament, 184–86
  Mayhew's appreciation for, 222–23
civil liberty/civil disobedience. *See also*
  rebellion, "justifiable"; Stamp
  Act
  Chauncy's views, 200–202, 233
  divine right monarchy and non-
    resistance doctrine, 151–52, 168,
    214, 255
  and just *vs.* unjust rulers, 8, 178,
    193, 212–14, 215n8, 216, 223,
    225, 229, 236
  Locke's views, 195–96, 221

Mayhew's views, 187, 195–200, 211–14, 218–25
and Real Whig ideology, 161–62, 225
and responses to British taxation laws, 173–74, 181n52, 185–86, 226–33
Civil Magistrates Must Be Just (Chauncy), 121, 177–78, 193, 228–29
Clap, Thomas, 44–45, 77, 79
Clark, Jonathan, 9, 10n12, 83, 133, 208, 250–51
Clark, Peter, 63–64, 65n37
Clarke, John, 73, 94, 96–97, 116
Clarke, Richard, Mayhew's letter to, 186, 200, 211, 221–23
Clarke, Samuel, 79–80, 82, 83–84n16, 87, 101
Cleaveland, John, 110–11, 111n1-2, 165
Coercive Acts, Chauncy's response, 181n52, 233
Colman, Benjamin
  as "catholick Congregationalist," 93n33, 243
  concerns about Arminianism, 43
  on the Great Awakening at Harvard, 21, 81
  Hooper letter to, 52n21
  and Mayhew's ordination, 53
  vote against Mather's dismissal from the Second Church, 47
Colossians 1:12, 55n25
Communion, Chauncy's views on, 67–68
Compleat View of Episcopacy (Chauncy), 39, 121, 123, 125, 136
"Confession of Faith" (Breck), 44–45, 77
Congregationalism, New England Puritanism. *See also* anti-Catholicism; Calvinism, Calvinist orthodoxy
  "catholick Congregationalism," 93, 93n33
  and Chauncy's Christology, 115–17
  and concepts of liberty, 208–9, 209n39
  E. Mayhew's connections with, 17

eighteenth century transformation of, 30, 41, 88–90, 90n26, 242–44, 242n7, 243n8, 249
enduring primacy of *Sola Scriptura*, 118n13
polity and traditions, Mayhew's and Chauncy's allegiance to, 10, 109, 111, 111n2, 122–33, 136, 141, 147, 164, 172–73, 196, 215, 236–37
and spiritual liberty, 174, 204, 209n39
Considerations (Apthorp), 126, 159–60
constitutional monarchical government, British. *See also* civil liberty/civil disobedience
  Chauncy's faith in, 174, 179–80, 229–34
  Mayhew's ambivalence about, 146, 164, 166–73, 192
  and Mayhew's and Chauncy's political worldviews, 183, 249, 250–51
Continental Congress, Chauncy on, 233, 236
Cooper, Chauncy and Samuel, 16, 150–51n7, 226
Cooper, William, 42–43, 44, 78n8
1 Corinthians
  4:1, 122n20
  8:4, 85
  8:4–6, 86
  15:22, 203n31
2 Corinthians
  3:17, 197, 203, 204n32
  5:15, 86n20
  6:15, 197n20, 224n22
Corrigan, John
  "catholick Congregationalism," 93, 93n33
  comparative study of Chauncy and Mayhew, 3, 3n3, 5–7, 148, 150–51n7, 242
  interpretative paradigms for understanding life and work of Chauncy and Mayhew, 2
  on latitudinarian influences at Harvard, 243

Corrigan, John *(continued)*
  on social standing of First and West Church members, 52n21
Cotton, John
  catechism, 75
  leadership of First Church, 91
At a Council of Ten Churches, 44, 77
Counsel of Two Confederate Kings (Chauncy), 177–78, 193, 228
Counts, Martha, 168n31, 214–15
Cronon, William, 8n10
crucifixion, Christ's sacrifice, 32, 58–59
Cutler, Timothy, 41
Cutter, Ammi Ruhammah, 44

Daniel 7:19, 134
Davenport, Addington, 39n2, 123, 123–24n22
Davenport, James, 34
Davenport, Jane Hirst, 39n2, 123, 123–24n22
Davis, Isaac, 96, 97n38, 98
de Benneville, George, 95, 98–99n40
"Declarations of the Rights and Grievances of the Colonists," 185, 185n2
Defence of the Observations (Mayhew), 87n22, 111n2, 123n21, 126–28, 128–29n29, 140, 164–65n27, 192–93
Dickinson, Jonathan, 18, 56–59, 60n31, 61, 91–93
Discourse Concerning Unlimited Submission (Mayhew), 146, 148–49n6, 155, 164–65n27, 166–69, 192, 199–200, 212–14, 240–41, 241n5, 255
Discourse Occasioned by the Death of the Reverend Dr. Joseph Sewall (Chauncy), 68
Discourse on "The Good News" (Chauncy), 179–80, 182, 184–85, 186, 193, 229–30, 240n4
Divine Glory (Chauncy), 73, 97, 102, 104, 106, 108, 115, 117, 140–41
Divine Glory Brought to View in the Condemnation of the Ungodly (Eckley), 97, 117n11

Divine Goodness (Mayhew), 54, 58, 59, 82–83n15, 110, 203
divine right episcopacy, 124, 132
divine right kingship, 152, 168, 214, 255
"The Divinity of Christ" (Bellamy), 89–90
Duty of Ministers (Chauncy), 69, 121, 122, 134–35n38

Early Piety Recommended (Chauncy), 26n16, 27, 35, 120
earthquakes, providential perspective, 27, 27n18, 136–37
Earthquakes a Token (Chauncy), 27, 27n18, 28
Ecclesiastes
  1:9, 224n22
  7:20, 27n18
Eckley, Joseph, 97, 102, 104–5n48
Edwards, Jonathan
  as Calvinist, 47, 64n36
  defense of the Great Awakening, 34–35
  Foxcroft's strong support of, 93, 93n32
  God Glorified in the Work of Redemption, 42
  Great Christian Doctrine of Original Sin Defended, 63
  on "natural morality," 55–56n25
  Religious Affections and *Faithful Narrative*, 34–35n29
  Sinners, 28n19
  Some Thoughts, 34
  upholding of Calvinist orthodoxy, 42, 87–88
election, the elect, 28–29, 55, 57, 58n28, 103, 104–5n48
election sermons
  Chauncy's, 173–74, 177–78, 227, 228–29
  Cooke's, 227
  Mayhew's, 166, 68
  theme of civil disobedience/resistance in 214, 236
Eliot, Andrew, 16, 72, 129, 209n40, 215n8
Eliot, John, 72–73, 73–74n3

Emerson, Joseph, 206
Emlyn, Thomas, 79–82, 84, 88–89
English Test Act, 132n34
The Enlightenment in America (May), 11, 242, 242n7, 243n8, 244
Enlightenment writers, influence, 20, 113, 148–49n6, 249. *See also* American Enlightenment
Enthusiasm Described (Chauncy), 27, 34, 176
An Essay, to Defend Some of the Most Important Principles in the Protestant Reformed System of Christianity (Cleaveland), 110
evangelicalism
   in Mayhew's and Chauncy's theologies, 4–5n6, 247
   scholarly perspectives, 244–46, 245n10
Evangelicalism in Modern Britain (Bebbington), 244–45
evangelical revival movement. *See also* Great Awakening
   and Chauncy's views, 33–36, 246
   confusion with Arminianism, 47
   Edward's promotion of, 34–35n29
Everett, Oliver, 74n3
Everlasting Gospel (Nicolai), 99
Ewer, John, 129–30
"Exclusion Crisis," 151
Expected Dissolution (Mayhew), 119

faith, justification by. *See* justification
Faithful Narrative (Edwards), 34–35n29
False Confidences Exposed (Balch), 48
Ferguson, Robert, 243
Fiering, Norman, 19–20, 20–21n9, 243
Filmer, Robert, 152, 152n9
Five Dissertations (Chauncy), 39, 65, 70, 73, 97, 102, 104, 109n55, 112, 117, 121–22, 140, 206
Fleming, Caleb (*Palladium . . . Or Historical Strictures of Liberty*), 157
Flynt, Henry, 20–21
Foxcroft, Thomas
   "catholick Congregationalism," 93, 243
   Chauncy as assistant minister to, 25, 91–94
   Chauncy's funeral sermon for, 67, 94
   commitment to orthodox Calvinism, 26, 40, 43, 91–92
   criticism of Mayhew, 56
   death, 91
   death of wife, 135
   defense of the Great Awakening, 26n17, 93, 93n32
   Edwards's letters to, 87–88
   Humilis Confessio, 92
   and Mayhew's ordination, 53
   stroke and incapacitation, 26
Frederick, Prince of Wales, Mayhew's sermon following death of, 166, 169, 215
freedom of expression, importance to Mayhew, 148, 148n5
free will, freedom of choice
   Chauncy's emphasis on, 104–7, 104–5n48
   Mayhew's emphasis on, 54, 57, 61–62
   and personal freedom as a concept, 207
   and personal responsibility, 61–62, 189
   role in salvation, 29, 57, 106–7, 116, 190
Frink, Thomas, Chauncy's sermon at installation of, 31
funeral sermon for Cornelius Thayer (Chauncy), 31
funeral sermon for Foxcroft (Chauncy), 67, 94
funeral sermon for Sewall (Mayhew), 68, 146, 164
Galatians
   4:12–16, 54
   5:1, 54–55n24, 191, 197, 203, 204n32, 205–6, 205n34
   5:6, 92
   5:12–13, 186, 186n3, 187, 195, 200, 203n31, 210
   5:13, 203, 203n31, 204n32, 210
   5:19, 57n27
Gardner, Francis, 78–79

Gay, Ebenezer
    Arminian views, 40, 46, 49–50
    as "Unitarian," 90n26, 256n19
    influence on Mayhew, 52, 52n20
    judgment on Kent, 78n8
    and Mayhew's ordination, 53–54
    Natural Religion, 63
Gee, Joshua, 46–47
George I, 152, 194–95
George II, 169, 177, 214, 216, 228
George III, 159n18, 174, 180, 184
Gibson, Alan, 154, 251–52
Glorious Revolution of 1688
    Chauncy's views, 176, 193, 228, 230, 251
    and the emergence of Whiggism, 151, 152
    impact on American political structures, 164, 173
    Mayhew's views, 147, 215, 251
Gloucester, Massachusetts
    Murray's universalist ministry, 95, 97n38
    White's Congregationalist ministry, 43, 48
God, as supreme authority. *See also* the Bible; Calvinism; Trinitarianism; unitarianism
    as basis for philosophical liberty, 189n7
    and Chauncy's soteriology, 29–30, 30n21, 65, 70–71, 116
    and divine goodness, 57, 203
    Mayhew's views on, 58, 84–87
    and philosophical liberty, 188–90
    and religious liberty, 193
God Glorified in the Work of Redemption (Edwards), 42
Good Luck, New Jersey, Murray's congregation in, 94–95
good works, doing good. *See also* Arminianism
    in Chauncy's and Mayhew's theologies, 55, 60, 68, 103, 247
    and moral behavior, 54, 113–14, 114n6, 190, 202
    and salvation, Catholic doctrine related to, 135
    and spiritual liberty, 203–4
Gorton, Samuel, 95
gospel-obedience, 66, 66n39, 247
Grace Defended (Experience Mayhew), 18–19
gracious liberty, Mayhew's definition, 187, 187n5, 200, 202–4
Grafton, Massachusetts, dismissal of Prentice, 78
Gray, Harrison, 15–16, 52n20, 146, 240
"Great Apostasy" controversy, Yale University, 41, 42–43n6
Great Awakening
    Chauncy's views, 27–28, 30, 33–37, 36n31, 92–93, 135
    confusion with Arminianism, 47
    Edwards's defense of, 34
    enthusiasm/excesses associated with, 23–24, 35–36
    Foxcroft's defense of, 26n17, 91–93, 93n32
    impact on Congregationalist practice, 4–5n6, 33
    and later American evangelicalism, 246n12
    Mayhew's response, 21–23
    and need for spiritual awakening, 19, 35
Great Christian Doctrine of Original Sin Defended (Edwards), 63
Griffin, Edward
    assessment of Chauncy, 4, 149, 234, 235n38
    on fears about British religious and imperial rule, 181n52
    on Taylor's views on sin, 63n35
Guyatt, Nicholas, 179n49, 244n9

"Half-Way Covenant," 91
Hartley, David, 73, 97, 100
Harvard University
    and Arminianism, 44
    Chauncy's great-grandfather's presidency, 1
    Chauncy's studies at, 24–25
    Great Awakening at, 21
    Holyoke's presidency, 19–20

liberalizing influences, 19–20, 23–25, 81, 243
Mayhew's studies at, 18, 81–82
Nathan Mayhew at, 17–18
removal of the colonial government to, 226
Wigglesworth's role at, 25
Hatch, Nathan, 101, 109, 118, 208
Haven, Jason, 88–89
On Hearing the Word (Mayhew), 54, 56–62, 83–84n16, 84–87, 90, 113, 119–20, 188, 202–4
Hebrews
   2:14, 86n20
   10:38, 68n42
Heimert, Alan
   evangelical/liberal distinction, 36, 36–37n32
   on Mayhew and Chauncy as social reactionaries, 2, 36–37n32, 148, 165, 252
Hempton, David, 244–45, 245n10, 246–47n13
Hidden Balance (Corrigan), 5–6, 52n21, 150–51n7
Hingham Church. *See* Gay, Ebenezer
"Hints and References Alphabetically Disposed" (Mayhew), 137–38
Hirst, Elizabeth, marriage to Charles Chauncy, 25–26
History of the Massachusetts-Bay (Hutchinson), 157
History of the Province of Massachusetts Bay (Hutchinson), 210
Holifield, E. Brooks, 40, 95, 99n41
Hollis, Thomas, 129, 156–63, 217–18
Holyoke, Edward, 19–20, 156–57
Hooper, William, 52–53, 52n21
Humble Inquiry into the Scripture-Account of Jesus Christ (Emlyn), 79–81, 88–89
Humilis Confessio (Foxcroft), 26n17, 92
Hutchinson, Aaron, 78
Hutchinson, Thomas
   Chauncy's response to vandalism at home of, 229
   gratuity controversy, 146

History of the Massachusetts Bay, 157
Mayhew's letter to regarding vandalism, 186, 200, 210–11, 220–21
relocation of colonial government to Cambridge, 226–27
response to Mayhew's sermon on the Stamp Act, 218n13
vandalism at home of, 186, 210, 217–18

Ideological Origins (Bailyn), 2n2, 152–54, 153–54n11–12, 181, 207
Idle-Poor Secluded (Chauncy), 183n55
idolatry, Mayhew's definition, 138
Ignatius of Antioch, 124–25
imputed righteousness doctrine, 26n17, 40, 40–41n4, 50, 59, 104, 104–5n48. *See also* Calvinism, Calvinist orthodoxy
Indian Converts (E. Mayhew), 18n5
indigenous peoples' rights, Chauncy's views, 182–83, 201
individualism, 36n32
infant salvation, Chauncy's views, 64–65, 65n37
insurrection, revolt. *See* revolution, violent
irresistible grace, 28–30, 33, 61–62, 103–4. *See also* Calvinism, Calvinist orthodoxy
Isaiah
   7:5–7, 228
   33:14, 28n19
   42:8, 85n18
   48:11, 85n18
   57:15, 113n4
   57:29, 113n4
   61:1, 205n34
   64:6, 92

Jacobite Rebellion, 176–77, 193, 215
James, book of
   1:25, 203, 204n32, 206, 207n36
   2:12, 203, 204n32
James II, 151, 216, 218, 228–29

Jefferson, Thomas, Adams's letter to, 240, 241n5
"jeremiad" sermons, 43n7, 112, 115, 178
John
  5:8, 197
  8:36, 197–98, 198n22, 203, 204n32
  17, 85
  17:12, 134n38
  20:17, 86n20
1 John
  5:7, 77, 79, 79n11
Johnson, Samuel, 41, 41–42n5
Jones, Barney, 35
Jones, James W., 3n3, 59n30, 60–61, 114n6
Jones, Jeremiah, 79, 79n11
Joshua 7:13, 236
Judges, references to, 112, 181
Judges 18:27–28, 175
justification. *See also* good works
  definition, 30n22
  and faith, 18–19, 30–32, 60n31, 65–66, 66n39, 68, 92
  and good works, 55, 59–60, 60n31, 100, 103, 135, 247
  and spiritual liberty, 203–4
  universalist teachings, 96, 100
just *vs.* unjust rulers, 8, 178, 193, 212–16, 215n8, 223, 225–26, 229, 236

Kent, Benjamin, 44, 51, 77, 78n8, 81
Kidd, Thomas, 11n13, 134, 173
Kneeland, Samuel, 88
Knowles Riot, 148–49n6

Language of Liberty (Clark), 83n16, 208
Latitudinarianism, 4n6, 10, 20, 21n9, 80–82, 93n33, 152, 243. *See also* Church of England
Leominster, Mass., Rogers's ministry at, 64n36, 78–79, 79n10
Letter to a Friend, Containing Remarks (Chauncy), 123, 130, 131, 193
"Letter to a Minister of the Gospel" (E. Mayhew), 23
Letter of Reproof (Mayhew), 59n30, 110–11

Letters on Theron and Aspasio (Sandeman), 65
Leverett, John, 19–20, 20n8
Liberalism, 36
liberty. *See also* citizenship rights, British; rebellion, "justifiable"
  colonial concepts, 207–9, 207–8n37
  prescriptive, 191, 191n10, 205–6, 208
  as right, 172
liberty, Chauncy's views
  and appreciation for British citizenship, 227
  complexity of, 249–50
  Congregationalist traditions and, 207, 209
  natural and civil liberty, 200–202
  philosophical liberty, 189–90
  religious liberty, 177–78, 193–95
  spiritual liberty, 205–6
  summary, 184–85
liberty, Mayhew's views
  biblicist definitions, 187, 187n5
  and the combining of religious and political language, 207
  complexity of, 148, 148n5, 164, 191, 249–50
  Congregationalist traditions and, 148n5, 207, 209
  moral liberty, 202
  natural and civil liberty, 195–200
  philosophical liberty, 188–89, 189n7
  religious liberty, 128–29n29, 191–93
  spiritual liberty, 202–5
  summary, 186–87
limited atonement, 26, 26–27n17, 30, 58, 100
Lippy, Charles, 3, 5, 6, 62, 91, 98n39, 108, 108n54, 150, 150–1n7, 234
Locke, John
  concepts of natural and civil liberty, 195–96
  general influence, 20, 80, 157, 243n8, 245
  grounds for "justifiable rebellion," 199–200, 215

influence on Mayhew, 81–82, 155–
    56, 195–96, 196n19, 200, 213,
    221–22, 249
  liberalism espoused by, 20, 151–52
  Wesley's debt to, 245
Lowell, Charles, 52n21, 53
Lubert, Howard, 3n3, 148, 148–49n6,
    199
Luke
  4:18, 205n34, 206, 206–7n36
  6:31, 202n29
  13:24, 114
  14:23, 134
Luther, Martin, 41n4, 60, 101, 239

Marini, Stephen, 98, 98–99n40
Mark 2:9, 197
Marlborough, Mass., dismissal of Kent
    at, 44, 77
Marsden, George, 43–44, 245n10,
    246–47n13
Mary II, 151, 228
Mather, Cotton
  Foxcroft's citing of, 92, 92n30
  letter to J. Edwards, 42n6
  upholding of Calvinist orthodoxy,
    20, 26, 42
Mather, Samuel, 33, 45–47
Matthew
  3:8–9, 23–24
  22:21, 200, 222n19
  25, 135
May, Henry, 10, 242, 242n7, 243n8
Mayhew, Experience, 15, 17–20, 18n5,
    23, 41, 53
Mayhew, Jonathan, 6–7. *See also*
    Arianism; Arminianism; West
    Church
  biographies, 3, 4n5
  Chauncy's description, 201
  complexity and evolution of
    political/religious thinking,
    2–3, 54, 140–41, 147, 164–65,
    197–99, 241–43, 246–52
  criticisms of, 15, 56, 87–90, 90n26,
    110–11, 140n47, 165
  early life, 17–20, 22–23
  as evangelical, 245–46
  Harvard career, 19–20, 20–21n9,
    81–82
  influence as a transitional figure,
    3n4, 11, 247–49, 252–56
  influences on, books read, 19–20,
    21n9, 81–82, 82–84n16, 156–57,
    195–96
  lecture series at West Church, 15–16
  limited archival record for, 2
  ordination, 53–54, 53n22, 54n23
  scholarly perspectives on, 2–10,
    3n3–4, 7n9, 147–48, 148–49n6,
    150–51n7, 242–46
  theology and politics, 15–16, 51–62,
    55–56n25, 111–14, 140–41,
    147, 148–49n6, 164–66, 197–99,
    242–43, 246–49, 251–52
  traditionalist, elitist views, 10, 17,
    109, 111, 111n1, 165–66, 183
  willingness to take risks, 11, 140,
    211
Mayhew, Nathan, 17–18
Mayhew, Thomas, 17
Mayhew, Zachariah, 21–22, 146
McIntosh, Ebenezer, 210
"Memoir of Dr. Jonathan Mayhew"
    (Gray), 15–16, 53n22
"Memorandum" (Mayhew), 155,
    186–87, 195–96, 211, 218–20,
    218n13
Methodists, Methodism, 244–45
Miller, Perry, 35, 40–41n4, 43n7, 150–
    51n7, 208
Milton, John, 153n11, 156–57, 157n16,
    196, 213n6
missionary work. *See also* SPG (Society
    for the Propagation of the
    Gospel in Foreign Parts)
  among indigenous people, 201
  E. Mayhew's, 17
  as providential, 179
Molasses Act, 239
moral behavior, relationship with faith,
    54, 112–14, 114n6, 190, 202. *See
    also* good works
Morgan, Edmund and Helen, 38, 91n29,
    185, 210
Morison, Samuel Eliot, 19–20

Morse, Jedidiah, 90, 238–40
Mullins, J. Patrick, 2, 3n3–4, 147, 148–49n6, 211n3, 242
Murray, John
　background and teachings, 94–96
　Chauncy's criticisms of, 73, 96–97
　Christological theology, 98–99n40
　Eliot's concerns about, 74n3
　influence on Chauncy, 94–95, 94n35
　universalist precepts, 72–73, 95–98, 98–99n40
Mystery Hid (Chauncy), 39–40, 64n36, 73, 97, 101–9, 101n44, 103–4n47, 104–5n48, 117, 121, 141, 190, 205

Nathanael's Character (Chauncy), 26n16, 27–28, 181n53
nationalism, American, 36n32
natural liberty, Mayhew's views on, 195–200
Natural Religion (Gay), 63
natural sciences, 20
natural theology, 244
"Of the Nature and Principle of Evangelical Obedience" (Mayhew), 84–85, 188
New Creature Describ'd (Chauncy), 28, 33–34, 35, 36n31
New England Primer, 75, 76n6
New-England's Lamentations (White), 43
"New Lights," 47
Newton, Isaac, 20, 82
New York Stamp Act Congress, 185
Nicene Creed, 75, 75n4
Nicolai, Georg-Klein, 99
Niles, Hezekiah, 240–42
Noll, Mark, 3n3, 148, 150, 150–51n7, 181–82, 208, 208n38, 233n35, 246n12
Norton, John, 91
Nova Scotia, British control over, 182
Observations (Mayhew), 87, 126–28, 159, 164–65n27, 192–93, 240
Old Brick (Griffin), 2n2, 4, 25, 34n28, 63n35, 94n35, 181n52, 234, 235n38

"Old Lights," 47
Oliver, Andrew, 145–46, 186, 217–18, 233
Oliver, Peter, 150–51n7
Olson, Judah, 145
Only Compulsion Proper (Chauncy), 26n16, 31, 134, 175, 206
Opinion of One that Has Perused the Summer Morning's Conversation (Chauncy), 63–65
ordination, Congregationalist, Chauncy's rationale for, 124–25
original sin
　Chauncy's views, 70, 104
　Calvinist definitions, 56, 57n27, 62–63
　and the debate over Taylorism, 63–64, 63n35
　Mayhew's views, 56–57
Osborn, Samuel, 33, 34n28, 45–46, 46n12, 51
Otis, James (*Rights of the British Colonies Asserted*), 157, 239
Out-pouring of the Holy-Ghost (Chauncy), 32, 33–34, 66n39

Palladium . . . Or Historical Strictures of Liberty (Fleming), 157
parliamentary government, British. See citizenship rights, British; civil liberty/civil disobedience; constitutional monarchal government
Pascal, Blaise, 20
Patriarcha Non Monarcha (Filmer), 152, 152n9
Paul, apostle, Mayhew's citing of, 84–85, 203n31. See also specific epistles
Pemberton, Ebenezer, 88–89, 90n26, 93n33
Pensées (Pascal), 20
1 Peter
　2:16, 148, 148n5, 200, 204, 204n32
　2:17, 199, 205, 224
　3:15, 34n29
2 Peter 2:19, 204n32
Philadelphia Continental Congress, 231

Philippians
  2, 84
  2:12, 114n6
  3:8–9, 92
philosophical liberty
  Chauncy's references to, 189–90
  Mayhew's references to, 187–89
Pitt, William, 158, 162–63, 171, 197
the poor, Chauncy's support for the rights of, 183n55
Popish Idolatry (Mayhew), 133, 137–40, 160–61, 172
Porter, John, 50, 50–51n18
Porter, Roy, 243n8
Potter, Thomas, 94–95
Practical Discourses (Mayhew), 61–62, 113–14, 202
Prayer for Help (Chauncy), 26n16, 31
predestination, doctrine of, 41, 93, 106
Prentice, Solomon, 78
prescriptive liberties, 191n10
Price, Richard, 230–31, 233–34, 236
Prince, Thomas, 42–43, 89, 90n26
Proverbs 25:25, 184
providentialism
  Chauncy's perspective, 177n46, 181–82, 193–95, 212, 227–28, 236, 249
  definition, 179n49
  Mayhew's perspective, 197–98, 212, 216–17, 222–25, 249
  and the success of British Protestantism, 166–73, 176–82, 180n50, 217
Psalms
  118:9, 169
  124:2–8, 197
  124:7–8, 172n38, 197
  126, 197
"pudding," Chauncy's meaning, 74n3
purgatory, Catholic doctrine of, 135, 138
Puritans. *See* anti-Catholicism; Calvinism, Calvinist orthodoxy; Congregationalism, New England Puritanism

Quincy, Josiah, 231

Quincy, Mass, First Church, Briant controversy, 255–56n19

"rational biblicism," Chauncy's and Mayhew's, 101, 109, 118–22
rational religion, American, 2, 54, 188
Real Whig ideology. *See also* Whig ideology
  anti-Catholicism, 155–56
  and civil disobedience, 161–62, 225
  demands for political reform, 153–56, 153–54n11, 161–62
  influence on American revolutionaries, 10, 154
  Mayhew's adherence to, 148, 148–49n6, 154–55, 249
rebellion, "justifiable." *See also* revolution, violent; Stamp Act
  complexity of views on, 199–200, 210–15, 225–26, 236–37, 249–50
  as a limited right, 183, 210–16
  Locke's grounds for, 199–200
  and providential perspectives, 209, 212, 227–28
  and responses to British taxation efforts and coercion, 173–74, 181n52, 185–86, 240n4, 226–35
redemption, salvation. *See also* Calvinism; universalism
  Chauncy's views, 69, 91, 114–15
  Mayhew's views, 58–59, 58–59n29
Religion and the American Mind (Heimert), 2n2, 36, 36–37n32, 148, 165, 212
Religious Affections (Edwards), 34–35n29
religious excess, Chauncy's criticisms of, 205. *See also* the Great Awakening
religious liberty. *See also* American Episcopate controversy
  Chauncy's views, 182–83, 193–95
  Gay's views, 54
  Mayhew's views, 54, 128–29n29, 166, 187, 191–93
  and providentialism, 177–79

Relly, James, 72–73, 94–95, 95n36, 96n37, 98
Remarks on an Anonymous Tract (Mayhew), 123n21, 126–27, 137
repentance
   in Calvinist theology, 18–19
   Chauncy's views, 28–29, 66, 68
   Mayhew's views, 23, 60, 220
Reply to Dr. Chandler's "Appeal Defended" (Chauncy), 38n1, 123, 130, 132–33, 193, 206
reprobation, eternal, doctrine of, 41, 58, 105
Revelation
   2:9, 134n38
   17:5–6, 134, 140n46
   17 & 18, 137
   21:8, 28n19
revolution, violent
   and ideology vs. practice, 254n17
   Chauncy's views, 212, 233–37
   evolving historiography concerning, 154
   influence of Real Whigs on, 152, 154
   Mayhew's views, 211n3, 237, 240n4
Revolutionary War. *See* American Revolution
Rich, Caleb, 96, 97n38, 98
Rights of the British Colonies Asserted (Otis), 157, 239
Robbins, Caroline, 152, 153–54n11, 156n15
Robinson, David, 95n36, 98–99n40, 99n41
Rogers, John, 64n36, 78–79, 79n10, 81
Rogers, John (Rogerenes), 95
Romans
   3:24, 32n24
   4:25, 116n10
   5:11, 59n30
   5:13, 205n34
   5:20, 203n31
   5:21, 117n11
   6:23, 119n15
   8:1–8, 167
   8:21, 197, 199n24, 203, 203n31, 204n32, 205, 205n34
   8:32, 31n23
   13:1–2, 222n19
   13:1–8, 199–200, 212–13
   13:4–5, 222n19
   13:5, 200
Rossiter, Clinton, 4n6, 18, 52–53, 83, 83n16, 126
Rozbicki, Michal Jan, 207–8n37

Sacred Theory of the Earth (Burnet), 20
salvation, eternal
   Catholic views, 135
   Chauncy's views, 30–32, 65, 67–68, 70–71, 115–17
   Puritan perspective, 32, 114–15
salvation, universal, 95–103. *See also* free will, freedom of choice; spiritual liberty; unversalism
Salvation for All Men (Chauncy and Clarke), 73, 73–74n3, 94, 96–97, 98n39, 116
Sandeman, Robert, 65–66
Sarah Osborn's World (Brekus), 243n8, 245
Scott, Joseph Nicoll, 73, 97, 100
Scripture-Doctrine of Original Sin (Clark), 63
Scripture-Doctrine of Original Sin (Taylor), 62–63
Scripture-Doctrine of the Trinity (Clarke), 79
Seasonable Thoughts (Chauncy), 27, 30n21, 32, 33n27, 34–35, 36n31, 206, 206–7n36
Secker, Thomas (*Answer to Dr. Mayhew's Observations*), 126–27n26, 129, 137, 156, 160, 211n2
second coming, Chauncy's views, 103–4n47
Second Treatise (Locke), 199
Sermon Preach'd (Mayhew), 168, 192, 215
Sermon Preached (Kent), 77
Sermon Preached at Boston (Mayhew), 11n13, 166, 169, 215–16
Sermons on Particular Occasions (Morse), 90
Sermons upon the Following Subjects (Bellamy), 89–90

INDEX

Seven Sermons (Mayhew), 16, 16n2, 24, 37, 51, 54–55, 57, 82, 113, 166, 188, 191, 241–42, 255
Seven Years' War, providential view of, 170, 178–79, 182, 215–16
Sewall, Stephen, Mayhew's funeral sermon for, 146, 147n3, 164
Sewall, Samuel, 25, 123–24n22
Shain, Barry, 154n12, 191n10, 208–9, 209n39–40
Shattered Synthesis (Jones), 3n3, 114n6
Shipton, Clifford, 25, 45–46, 49, 51n19, 123–24n22, 235n38
"On the Shortness and Vanity of Human Life Occasioned by the Death of a Young Person" (Mayhew), 202
Sidney, Algernon, 151–52, 152n9, 156–57, 196
sin, sinfulness, 27, 27n18, 56, 69–70, 111–13, 236. *See also* Calvinism; total depravity doctrine
slavery, Chauncy's condemnation of, 182, 201–2
Snare Broken (Mayhew), 155, 155n13, 163, 171–73, 196–99, 200, 211 223–25, 240n4
social injustice, Chauncy's condemnations of, 201–2
social order, religious heterodoxy as threat to, 96–97, 150–51n7, 164, 175–78, 225. *See also* civil liberty/civil disobedience; rebellion, "justifiable"
Society for the Propagation of the Gospel in Foreign Parts. *See* SPG
Some Thoughts Concerning the Present Revival of Religion in New-England (Edwards), 34
"Sons of Liberty," 186
Sophia, Princess of Hanover, 228
SPG (Society for the Propagation of the Gospel in Foreign Parts), 159. *See also* the American Episcopate controversy
  Addington's work in, 123
  Bernard's membership, Mayhew's mention of, 147
  Mayhew's arguments against, 82, 87, 122–23, 126–31, 155, 240

tolerance of Catholicism, 137
spiritual liberty, 202–9, 209n39. *See also* religious liberty
Spiritual Milk for Boston Babes (Cotton), 75–76
spiritual renewal, rebirth, 35, 36n31. *See also* evangelical revival movement; Great Awakening
Sprague, William, 83–84n16, 90–91
Stamp Act crisis. *See also* rebellion, "justifiable"
  Chauncy's responses, 4n6, 149, 150–51n7, 184–85, 229–30, 240
  and civil unrest, 185–86, 186n3, 210
  and concerns about arbitrary exercise of British power, 161–63
  Mayhew's responses, 148–49n6, 162–63, 171–72, 197–99, 217–18, 222–26, 249–50
  provisions, 185
  repeal, providentialist interpretations, 179–80, 193
Stamp Act Congress, 162
Stiles, Ezra
  biographical sketch, 1n1
  Chauncy's correspondence with, 1–2, 24, 35, 38–39, 39n2, 123
  intended ecclesiastical history, 38n1
St. James's Chronicle, on the "Episcopizing of the Colonies," 156
Stoddard, Mary, 26n16
Stonhouse, James, 99
Story, William, 145–46
Stout, Harry, 35, 36–37n32, 109n56, 111, 112n3, 118n13, 208
St. Paul and St. James Reconciled (Balch), 48
  Chipman's critique, 49
Streeter, Adams, 96, 97n38
Striving to Enter (Mayhew), 55–56n25, 61
Stuart, Charles Edward, 228
Stuart, James, 176–77
Stuart monarchs, Mayhew's denunciations of, 146, 215

subordinationist views on the Trinity, 10–11, 79–81, 80n12, 84–87, 119, 247. *See also* Arianism
Sugar Act, 185
Supreme Deity of Our Lord Jesus Christ (Burr), 89
Synod of Dort
    Arminian rejection of, 40
    definition of "faith," 61n32
    doctrine of limited atonement, 58–59n29
    doctrine of the perseverance of the saints, 62n34
    precepts on election, 58n28
    and reformed orthodoxy, 26, 26–27n17

Tallman, James, petition to General Court and gratuity incident, 145–46
Taylor, John, 62–64, 63n35, 64n36, 79, 101, 101n44, 109n55
Tennent, Gilbert, 21, 23
The Testimony of the President, Professors, Tutors and Hebrew Instructor of Harvard College in Cambridge, against the Reverend Mr. George Whitefield, and his Conduct, 24
That Jesus Christ is God by Nature, 89
Thayer, Cornelius, 31
theological rationalism, 244
2 Thessalonians
    2:3–4, 134n38
    2:7, 134n38

Thomas, D. A. Lloyd, 199
Tillotson, John, 20, 20–21n9, 81–82, 243
1 Timothy
    2:4, 106n51
    2:5, 85
    2:6, 58n29
total depravity doctrine, 18n5, 54–55, 70. *See also* sin, sinfulness
Townsend, Elizabeth Phillips, marriage to Charles Chauncy, 26
Treaty of Paris, 158

Trinitarianism. *See also* Arminianism; Calvinism, Calvinist orthodoxy; unitarianism
    and Chauncy's Christology, 115
    early anti-Trinitarian views, 76–79, 82
    Mayhew's problems with and response, 84–90
    rationalist and subordinationist approaches, 79–81, 80n12
    theological assumptions, 75–76, 76n6
True Scripture-Doctrine (Dickinson), 18, 56–59, 60n31, 61, 91–92
Trumbull, Benjamin, 238
Trust in God (Chauncy), 173–74, 194–95, 227–28, 230
Twelve Sermons (Chauncy), 26, 65–67, 66n38, 104, 112–13, 115, 121, 135–36, 205–6
Twisse, William, 111n2
Two Discourses Delivered October 25th 1759 (Mayhew), 170–71
Two Discourses Delivered October 9th 1760, 204
tyranny, rebellion against. *See also* civil liberty/civil disobedience; rebellion, "justifiable"
    Chauncy's views, 228–29
    Mayhew's views, 146, 167–68, 172, 199–200, 217
Tyrrell, James, 151–52

Unbridled Tongue (Chauncy), 28, 28n19, 34, 34n28
unconditional election. *See* Calvinism, Calvinist orthodoxy; election, the elect
Union (Relly), 96n37
Unitarians, Unitarian Universalists, Mayhew as "forerunner" of, 10, 87, 90, 90n26, 255–56n19
unitarianism. *See* Arianism; Trinitarianism
universalism, universalist theology
    Chauncy's slowness to reveal, 39–40, 74, 91, 94, 96–97, 140–41
    Chauncy's views, 73–74, 100–3, 107–8, 248

eighteenth century American perspectives, 96–100, 98–99n40–41
Murray's approach, 72–73, 94–96
teachings associated with, 91, 94–103
Universal Restitution: A Scripture Doctrine (Stonhouse), 99
University of Aberdeen, Mayhew's honorary degree from, 16, 16n2
unlimited submission, Mayhew's views on, 212–26

Vailati, Ezio, 7n9, 80, 80n12
Validity of Presbyterian Ordination (Chauncy), 123–25, 206
Vindication (Porter and Cotton), 56
Vindication of Some Points (Balch), 49

Wadsworth, Benjamin, 93n33
Wainwright, Elizabeth, 90
Waldo, Lucy, 29
Walley, John and Sarah, 24
Walpole, Robert, 153, 153–54n11
Ward, Lee, 152, 152n9, 154n12
Ward, W. R., 245n10, 246–47n13
Watts, Isaac, 93
Webb, John, 43, 78n8
Webster, Samuel, 63
West Church, Boston. *See also* Mayhew, Jonathan
 Arminian tradition, 11
 Briant's sermon at, 50–51
 founding, founding principles, 52–53
 letter from Hooper to Colman, 52n21
 and Mayhew's ordination, 53–54, 53n22, 54n23
 pre-ordination and ordination council for Mayhew, 53
Westminster Confession of Faith, 42–44, 75, 118n13, 209n39. *See also* Calvinism, orthodox Calvinists; Congregationalism, New England Puritanism

Westminster Shorter Catechism/Larger Catechism, 19, 75, 78
Whig ideology. *See also* Real Whig ideology
 anti-Catholicism and, 152
 Chauncy's espousal of, 174–75, 182, 232, 235n38, 249
 in eighteenth century Britain, 152, 158–59, 166–67
 and government as a contract, 152
 growing American support for, 152–53, 227
 historical interpretations, critiques, 8–9, 8n10
 integration of politics and religion, 151–52, 151n8
 Mayhew's espousal of, 163–64, 212–14, 225–26, 249
 moderate *vs.* Real Whigs, 151–53, 153–54n11
 origins, 151–52
 Ward definition, 152, 152n9
Whitby, Daniel, 80, 109n55
White, Jeremiah, 73, 97, 100, 116
White, John, 43, 48
Whitefield, George, 5n6, 21, 23, 26n17, 81, 93, 94
Wigglesworth, Edward, 25, 25n15, 77, 79, 87–89
Wigglesworth, Samuel, 49
William III/William of Orange, 82, 151, 176, 216, 228, 230
Wilson, Robert, 41, 45, 50, 52, 52n20, 53, 54, 63
Winchester, Elhanan, 96, 97n38, 98–99n40, 99–101, 99n41, 103
Winter Evening's Conversation (Webster), 63–64
Winthrop, John, 204, 209n39
Wise, John, 122, 123n21
Wollaston, William, 20, 21n9
Works (Edwards), 93n32
Wright, Conrad, 41, 63, 76, 79–80

Yale University, 1n1, 41–43
Yenter, Timothy, 7n9, 80, 80n12
Youngs, William, 40

www.ingramcontent.com/pod-product-compliance
Lightning Source LLC
Chambersburg PA
CBHW070059020526
44112CB00034B/1630